the

revolution

wasn't

televised

302.
23
REV

the

revolution

wasn't

televised

sixties

television

and

social conflict

edited by

lynn spigel

and

michael curtin

routledge
new york and london

Published in 1997 by

Routledge
29 West 35th Street
New York, NY 10001

Published in Great Britain in 1997 by

Routledge
11 New Fetter Lane
London EC4P 4EE

Printed in the United States of America
Typography: Jack Donner

Library of Congress Cataloging-in-Publication Data

The revolution wasn't televised: sixties television and social
    conflict / edited by Lynn Spigel and Michael Curtin.
        p.   cm.
    ISBN 0−415−91121−4 (hc).—ISBN 0−415−91122−2 (pbk.)
        1. Television broadcasting—Social Aspects—United States.
    I. Spigel, Lynn.   II. Curtin, Michael.
    PN 1992.6.R47   1996
    302.23'45'097309046—dc20   96−28782
                                                                  CIP

contents

part three: nation and citizenship

introduction

lynn spigel and michael curtin

In the late 1960s, Gil Scott Heron's "The Revolution Will Not Be Televised" blasted its way to a number one hit on the AM charts, assuring the nation that television was a medium of hopeless consensus, aimed at the white majority and suited only to reproducing the lackluster shop-a-day world of happy homebodies. Proclaiming that one day "*Green Acres*, [the] *Beverly Hillbillies*, and *Hooterville Junction* will no longer be so damn relevant," Heron sang of a better world, better in part because, as he said in his famous last line, rather than being on TV, the "revolution will be live."

Of course, television has always promised to be even bigger than life, and its penchant for producing an illusion of liveness has convinced many that its pictures are "real" and capable of capturing events, even revolutionary events, as they unfold. Still, Heron did have a point, because even though numerous revolutions were televised in the 1960s (think of the coverage of Watts, the Democratic Party Convention in Chicago, or the 1968 uprising in

Paris), television preferred to label such rebellions as senseless "riots" staged by unruly mobs who reveled in self-destructive violence (and, obviously, the coverage of the 1992 "Los Angeles Riots" adheres to this tradition). So too, the networks presented the social movements of the 1960s less as a break with television's general entertainment logic than as part of the flow of its "something for everyone" programming philosophy, from the "zany" military comedy of *Gomer Pyle USMC* to the Vietnam protest music of Joan Baez that played, after considerable doses of network censorship, on *The Smothers Brothers Comedy Hour* at the end of the decade.

As Heron's hit single suggests, the 1960s is most notable for its culture vs. counter-culture, "us vs. them" logic, and within this set of oppositions, mass media—especially television—was almost always *them*. This opposition not only structured the logic of popular culture in that period, but it also runs through the more recent popular nostalgia for the decade. Given the fact that many historians of the 1960s lived through the time, it is perhaps no coincidence that these oppositions often permeate scholarly studies of the decade. Although nostalgia and history can never be clearly distinguished or separately defined, it does seem important to revisit the decade with some critical distance from the "us vs. them" paradigm, and to investigate how culture might be conceptualized in a less cartoonish way. This book, which is devoted to looking at television programs in the context of larger social, political, and cultural forces, attempts to understand the struggles that took place over representation on the nation's most popular communications medium.

So popular was this medium that by 1960, just twelve years after the networks began to offer complete prime-time schedules, roughly 89 percent of the population had at least one television set. Over the course of the decade many households were busy exchanging their worn-out consoles for newer, groovier models like the Westinghouse "Jet Set" advertised in a 1966 issue of *TV Guide* as one of the fashionable "tote-alongs" designed to give each family member a portable receiver, custom-made for their own moveable viewing feast. But despite the emphasis on motion, by all estimations the average American was actually going fewer places because they were sitting in front of the set for about five hours a day. Indeed, by 1960 television was the country's dominant form of entertainment and information. The speculations regarding its centrality in American households and public life—speculations that had been so much part of the popular culture of the 1950s—were now less and less the stuff of science fiction and more and more a practical reality of everyday experience.

By the latter half of the 1950s and throughout the 1960s, television—as a media institution—was in a period that might be called "classical," a period in which production, distribution, and exhibition practices were standardized (albeit with some variation) and remained intact at least until the early 1970s. By the mid 1950s, the previous production center of New York (famous for "live," theatrically-based TV) gave way to Hollywood, where major film studios, independent telefilm companies, and talent agencies like MCA grew to become the central forces behind prime-time production. Programs were produced by these Hollywood companies; distributed nationally and often owned or co-owned by the networks; sponsored by major corporate advertisers and their Madison Avenue representatives; regulated by the Federal Communications Commission (FCC); and received in the private homes of citizens across the country. The television industry furthermore established clearly standardized patterns of exchange, using the nationwide audience measurements of one company, the A.C. Nielsen Corporation, for "box office" data that it traded with sponsors who in effect financed the system. And, on the audience side, *TV Guide*, which became a national magazine in 1952, served as a source of scheduling information, and, perhaps more importantly, as a site of critical and fan discourse that bound individuals together—at least in their imaginations—as a "national audience" of TV watchers.

In short, the 1960s saw the consolidation of what documentarian Michael Moore has more recently called a "TV Nation." However, as numerous essays in this volume suggest—from Victoria Johnson's exploration of the long-standing cultural denigration of Lawrence Welk's "middle-American" do-gooder image to Roberta Pearson's investigation of the Native American response to the short-lived western *Custer*—nationalism was not a simple matter. Instead, numerous struggles took place in defense of specific group identities. Even as the networks attempted to standardize their affiliate markets and transform regional and ethnic differences into the common denominator of a "national audience," they were often met by resistance at the local level.

Despite these instances, however, the television industry maintained a buoyant optimism about the medium's ability to bring together huge audiences across the nation and, as ABC Vice President Donald Coyle put it, fulfill "its natural function as a giant pump fueling the machine of consumer demand, stepping up the flow of goods and services to keep living standards high and the economy expanding." Even more, Coyle asserted that television could do for the rest of the world what it was doing for the United States. His enthusiasm was encouraged, no doubt, by the fervent internationalism of the Kennedy administration's "New Frontier," which, in the spirit of the economic and cultural colonialism of Cold War policy, presented America's will to conquer foreign markets as the benign growth of the "Free World." With the 1962 launching of Telstar, the United States became the first nation to orbit a commercial communications satellite; that same year, foreign syndication sales for off-network programming exceeded domestic sales for the very first time. As the purchase of television sets around the world grew at a feverish pace, industry executives had reason to anticipate an even more lucrative future.

Given its attempts to homogenize consumption habits and address different audiences with a unified appeal, it is no surprise that television standardized its product into program types such as the sitcom, the western, and the variety show. These genres, which developed their televisual forms over the course of the 1950s, had clear narrative patterns that creative staff knew how to generate and that audiences could seek out, depending on what they wanted to watch (and with whom) on a given night. They also had relatively clear production costs and standards, although the profit margin for any single television series was never quite reliable. Why, for example, was *Mr. Ed*, which featured a man and his talking horse, a hit while *My Mother the Car*, which showcased a man and his talking auto, a relative failure? In the long run, who is to say why a wisecracking horse who watches TV is more profitable than a chatty car radio inhabited by the ghostly voice of someone's dead mother? Pondering these questions of taste and popular pleasure—as networks and producers always do—means accepting the fact that entertainment is not a predictable industry. For this reason, a major producer like Screen Gems, with the economies of scale that allowed for a margin of risk, saw fit to produce series in a variety of genres from sitcoms such as *The Donna Reed Show* to police dramas such as *Naked City*, knowing that some would flop and some would prevail. More generally, even within the formulaic codes of genre production, there was always a certain amount of innovation, for as Mark Alvey points out, any industry needs to vary its output, if only for purposes of product differentiation. Yet as many other essays in this book demonstrate, changes in television programming over the course of the decade were also attributable to forces outside of these production economies.

The purpose of these essays is to show just how important those outside forces were in shaping program content, form, and audience interpretations. Some of these forces existed within the institutional framework of broadcasting itself, but as the authors demonstrate, the broadcast institution was in turn affected by—and had affects on—the politics and rhetoric of other social institutions, including the institutional mechanisms by which audiences made their voices heard.

Indeed, in the land of the New Frontier, numerous pressures came to bear on television that were not immediately in the purview of the industry leaders themselves. While, for example, the industry pumped up its export market in ways that often coincided with the government's goals of economic expansion overseas, sometimes their efforts actually conflicted with the government's cultural struggles to gain ideological (and not just economic) supremacy as the arbiter of a "Free World." As William Boddy shows in his article on Senator Thomas Dodd's violence hearings, political leaders worried about the way excessive violence in shows like *The Untouchables* would portray Americans overseas, and they chided the industry for its portrayal of U.S. values and attitudes.

More generally, as Steven Classen, Aniko Bodroghkozy, Roberta Pearson, and Lynn Spigel demonstrate, African American, New Left, and Native American movements all made their voices heard, both behind the scenes and on the screen. Sometimes this generated reactionary responses from conservative broadcasters, network executives, or even local governments. Television was often a site of struggle between contending social factions, but it also served as a barometer of changing social mores. As Julie D'Acci shows in her chapter on TV's first action heroine, Honey West, social movements were often incorporated into entertainment programming even when there was no direct media activism involved. In this case, notions of sexual liberation and even nascent feminism were crucial to the construction of Honey's character, as ABC sought ways to keep pace with the sexual revolution.

Above all, then, while the industry no doubt had a good deal of power over the course that television would take, it is also clear that, like all technological systems, this "giant pump" was fueled by larger social, political, and cultural forces. Television was subject to intense debates and struggles—over "taste," over its national and international purpose, and over its social role in addressing the concerns of increasingly fragmented audience segments composed of radical youth, "new" women, politicized civil rights groups, and resistant conservatives who challenged what they saw as television's moral decline.

By the end of the decade, these struggles did not die down—but the broadcast institution did find new ways to manage them. On the one hand, as numerous critics have demonstrated, the networks found ways to make conflict seem "tasteful" and even morally valuable in "quality" programs like *The Mary Tyler Moore Show* (which engaged certain aspects of the feminist movement) and *All in the Family* (which dealt with a litany of "too hot to handle" issues including such topics as racism, homosexuality, and Vietnam). On the other hand, however, many of the conflicts of the 1960s—especially the disappointments about television's insipid commercialism and its failure in its role as public servant—resurfaced in the policy debates concerning the emerging cable industry, a point Thomas Streeter demonstrates in his article on the "blue sky" scenarios through which people imagined new and better possibilities for cable. But as Streeter also points out, in the end cable eventually came to look more and more like commercial TV.

At a time when we are witnessing the "Disneyfication" of broadcasting and the "Turnerization" of cable, it does seem wise to acknowledge that although social and cultural struggles like the ones considered here are certainly important in transforming their local historical contexts, they do not often succeed in the grand historical sense of "revolution." In this regard, it is worth considering in some more detail how we might account for relationships among media, culture, and society. What types of theories and methods do we have at our disposal to understand these relationships as well as the ways they change over time? And why should we write and read this kind of media history in the first place?

looking backward: thinking about theory and method

It seems appropriate that a book on 1960s television should appear at this moment, if only because the 1960s saw the rise of television criticism as a distinct "professionalized" and increasingly academic field. A new breed of intellectual found inspiration in the work of literary critic-turned-media guru Marshall McLuhan, who made serious contemplation about TV attractive — or even, as he might say, "cool." By mid-decade, the Canadian scholar had become the darling of the New York glitterati and was portrayed as the prince of pop criticism in mainstream media. Meanwhile, on the opposite coast, from his San Diego beach house, Herbert Marcuse was launching savage barbs at the consciousness industry. Allied to radical political figures like Angela Davis, Marcuse came to represent the opposite end of the spectrum in 1960s media criticism. Nevertheless, he too would become something of a pop icon—an irony no doubt attributable to the regime of repressive tolerance. Meanwhile, from a more humanist tradition, literary and art critics such as Leslie Fielder and Susan Sontag began to demand that the popular arts be examined with the same "seriousness" as the so-called "high arts." As the aesthetic distinctions between high and low were increasingly relativised and challenged over the decade (especially with such movements as POPism and Minimalism, and with the advent of critical terms like "anti-art" and "non-art" being bandied around), it became increasingly possible to apply literary and art criticism to television. It was during the 1960s that the National Academy of Television Arts and Sciences began to publish *Television Quarterly*, which often included literary critics' interpretations of television programs. Television criticism multiplied throughout the decade as the medium became the centerpiece for wide-ranging debates over art, education, taste, and the meaning of culture.

Over the course of the 1970s and through the present, as television studies grew into a field (or more accurately a "plot") of academia, the questions of taste, art, nationalism, and culture that fascinated reformers and critics of the 1960s have been connected to issues of family life and domesticity—the very topics that first engaged the social scientists and market researchers in the 1950s. Just as these topics have become intertwined, so too have methodological approaches—a development that is no doubt due in large part to the interdisciplinary focus and neo-Marxist underpinnings of Cultural Studies. In addition, the glaring absence of women TV critics in the 1960s was met over the course of the 1970s by a new feminist-inspired critique of television, largely drawn from activist groups and later from film theory. Looked at from a feminist and Marxist-informed perspective, the issues that fascinated critics in the first two decades seem more and more connected to one another. So now we typically speak of the need to consider the micro-processes of everyday life in relation to macro-structures such as nationalism, globalism, and public art. Moreover, as the technologies themselves have changed, and as television becomes more and more global, critics like Hamid Naficy, Marie Gillespie, Ien Ang, David Morley, and Kevin Robins have argued that we need to study the local contexts, or "spaces of identity" (of family, region, ethnicity, etc.) in relation to the global environment.

As with this new work on globalism that moves back and forth between spatial contexts, the authors in this volume, who are more concerned with time, suggest the importance of moving back and forth between past and present. Even while we often challenge the New Frontier's "enlightenment" notions of history as a road to progress, the acts of writing and reading history still have a social purpose. At the risk of recycling the often cited but consistently compelling ideas of Walter Benjamin, it seems more useful to insist that remembering the past can serve to "shock" us out of the present. For even if the revolution wasn't televised, and even if it never will be, looking back at '60s television can serve to shake up our present day conceptions of communications technologies, conceptions which all too often give technology the power to revolutionize the world while the whole world sits back on its collective easy chair and watches for change, as if change were the same as a station break.

Today, as in the decade under study, U.S. power at home and around the globe manifests itself in many forms, media being one of the most important. At a time when communication is increasingly privitized and commercialized by global conglomerates, it seems especially important to reflect on the mechanisms of power and struggle through which people have and might still speak to one another in a more democratic fashion. As Raymond Williams suggested in the early 1970s, we need to imagine new and better uses for telecommunications and to find ways of making these aspirations a practical reality.

For their part, historians and critics, such as the ones in this book, need to write about those people in the past who did imagine better ways to use technology and who did partake in activist movements that tried to change the face of broadcasting. Historians ought to think about these "micro" struggles just as much as they ought to critique the "macro" power of the television industry. One the prime lessons of this book—and a central paradox at the heart of '60s TV—is that television was often used as a tool for silencing vocal minorities while purporting to give voice to the ever elusive "silent majority."

Of course, despite the uneven power relations between media elites and their detractors, and despite the oligopoly power exerted by the networks and their numerous institutional supports, there are always moments of opportunity that escape the "logic" of the system itself. What, for example, made it possible for Gil Scott Heron to sing his political, anti-broadcasting, black power anthem in a nation led by a conservative administration and in a broadcast system that—despite all the charges of media liberalism—was primarily conservative as well? In fact, one of the prime reasons this song did flourish was because of the media competition between radio and television at the time. Radio—even the AM stations on which the tune soared to popularity—was finding a new liberal youth audience after losing the mass audience to television. So, ironically, even if the revolution would not be televised, it seemed possible to broadcast it through other channels, and even make it into a hit single. This is not to say that Heron's tune was understood as "revolutionary" by all AM listeners, nor is it to argue that we should just be happy and not worry because laissez-faire capitalism, the "marketplace of ideas," and good old media competition will correct all ideological and political evils. Instead, this example suggests that there are ways in which power must accommodate dissent, if only to remain powerful.

Furthermore, Heron's music shows us how the rapidly shifting sands of culture and politics can transform the marginal into the mainstream. Only a few years later, in the midst of Watergate, Heron would be harmonizing with newspaper and television headlines when he sang, "Haldeman, Ehrlichman, Mitchell, and Dean; it follows a pattern if you dig what I mean." In 1974, the opposition suddenly seemed popular and powerful. It was a moment inextricably connected to years of organizing and struggle in the streets, but it was also a moment at which those working within the culture industries who sympathized with oppositional movements saw the opportunity to promote the politics of change and to justify their work to superiors by touting its popular appeal.

As this case demonstrates, media institutions can sustain their power only by constantly courting innovation and popularity. As George Lipsitz has suggested about popular music, even while mass media serve to homogenize the local traditions and values of various racialized and ethnicized groups, the mass media often also circulate these same traditions and values so that they reach the ears of people who would not normally hear them. In short, it seems more productive to understand the ways in which powerful media institutions must transmit certain types of popular knowledge that ultimately disrupt the logic of their own functional requirements for economic stability.

This cultural dynamic, which is generally theorized through Antonio Gramsci's concept of hegemony, is used consistently throughout this book. The concept of hegemony shows us how powerful institutions like media are involved in a perpetual struggle (never fully won, always ongoing) to incorporate social conflict and reach popular consensus. Such notions have moved media historians and critics away from the "conspiratorial" view that mass media are simply opium for the masses—which in more contemporary television lingo translates into "the plug in drug" argument. Instead, the concept of hegemony emphasizes the social conflicts involved in cultural processes, and as such, serves as a mode of explaining the way television responded to and perpetuated these conflicts in the 1960s. As Todd Gitlin first applied the concept to American media, hegemony becomes a way to understand how the networks negotiated between the will for social change and the opposing urge for stasis by incorporating revolutionary ideas into the more consensual fictions of television.

How we interpret this process is of course up for grabs. While some critics might insist that hegemonic processes of incorporation simply rob revolutionary movements of their political meaning, others, like Lipsitz, are more interested in how revolutionary impulses seem to stubbornly resist total incorporation and re-emerge in new ways in a continual pursuit to be heard. There are, of course, limits. For as Gramsci argued, when cultural hegemony doesn't work, when dissent cannot be incorporated into the logics of ruling elites, the state calls in the overtly repressive forces at its disposal. For television, as Aniko Bodroghkozy points out, this means censorship, or, in the case of the *Smothers Brothers*, cancellation. Still, as Bodroghkozy also claims, the cancellation itself provoked an outpouring of public debate voiced in both the underground and the popular press. In retrospect, then, while it seems evident that the revolution (if we can call it that) wasn't televised, it is also true that there is still much to be learned about television's role in mediating— and even at times promoting—social change.

That said, the ways in which media historians make connections between media, society, and culture, and the ways they explain change over time, remain difficult and generally under-theorized problems. While almost everybody seems to assume that television affects and reflects social change, it is clear that we really don't know how to explain the relationships among media texts and social contexts in ways that are very convincing. As Horace Newcomb suggests with regard to the Western, even the most thoughtful work on this issue often relies on tautological reasoning that reduces complex social events to a set of narrow meanings and structures that the critic then matches and fits with meanings and structures he or she claims the television program contains. This book does not provide an answer for this ultimately philosophical question, but it does present some tools for thinking through these problems in relation to the case at hand. And, we hope, it generates some possibilities for future work on this and other cases.

All of the essays share a conviction that television cannot be understood in isolation from its various contexts, even while in a media culture those contexts are not always grounded by shared traditions or even physical locations. Often instead, contexts are what Benedict Anderson, in his work on nationalism, calls "imagined communities." Here, these imagined communities are not only ones of nation, but also generation, taste, region, and other "demographic" communities that television's institutional processes (such as ratings) and symbolic practices (such as programs, ads, even TV set design) help to construct. Through this notion of context, the authors stress the importance of looking at culture as a deeply social, productive force. In this regard, they continue with traditions in Cultural Studies that move away from thinking about texts as mere "reflections" on the social order, and instead think about texts as sites where meaning is made in their interaction with their various publics.

Another way to put this is to say that these essays move away from the either/or logic of the "structuralist" vs. "culturalist" debates in media sociology. The structuralists have generally assumed that a society and its cultural products change only when institutional structures (such as housing policies or media ownership) change. Conversely, the culturalists would argue that the structure of social institutions and society itself changes only when the ruling ideas of that society (its ideology as generated by media like television) change. This either/or logic puts all its weight in one camp and fundamentally turns into the chicken and the egg question, "which comes first, structural change or cultural change?"

However, as much of the work in Cultural Studies has taught us, culture and structure need to be seen in more holistic ways. From this perspective, while it may be true, for example, that media ownership does influence the types of products made, it is also the case that cultural perspectives about "ownership" in turn influence the structural form that social institutions take. (For example, culturally-based ideas of exclusive possessiveness in western capitalism generate institutional practices like zoning laws that give way to racist housing policies or copyright laws, which in turn generate legal disputes over sampling in rap and hip-hop). So rather than ask the chicken or egg question—"which comes first, structure or culture?"—these essays assume that the two are always in dialectical tension with one another. That said, it still is the case that some authors in this volume stress structure while others emphasize culture—a situation which probably has more to do with the discursive conventions of writing about media than with any necessary "truth." In other words, while these essays do not escape the logic of privileging one term over the other, they all do share a conviction that in the last analysis culture and structure cannot really be separated.

The authors in this volume also share the conviction that prime-time television affords us a distinctive opportunity to explore significant social issues at a time when representation was being increasingly defined as a key political issue that helped constitute group identities (such as hippies, new women, or Black Power) forged in opposition to "mainstream" culture. Valuable contributions have already been made regarding television's role in reporting some of the turbulent events of the decade, for example: Todd Gitlin's analysis of network news portrayals of the New Left, Daniel Hallin's re-assessment of Vietnam coverage during America's first "uncensored war," and Barbie Zelizer's critique of the struggles for cultural and professional authority among journalists who covered the Kennedy assassination. As opposed to this focus on actuality programming, this volume is one of the few to explore the cultural, social, and political implications of popular entertainment series during the period.

In choosing to speak of popular television series, this book assumes that prime-time programs were not mere escapism, but were centrally involved in sustaining, interrogating, and even transforming social relations and cultural affinities throughout the decade. In distinction to those people who might say, "hey, that's just entertainment," we see the concept of entertainment itself as a cultural construct which exists only because our society has formed certain conventional ways for thinking and speaking about what topics constitute "real knowledge," and in what forms this kind of knowledge should be distributed. In the discursive framework of television, entertainment has always existed as a concept only in relation to its opposite: information. Through this binary opposition, the media have naturalized the idea that entertainment is about fiction while news is about science, and audiences come to expect that entertainment is created and packaged in fictional genres while news is just reported through the objective, scientific lens of the camera. But, as the essays in this volume suggest, the lines between science and

11

fiction, news and entertainment, are never clear. For example, what makes the Vietnam war entertaining when it is discussed on *The Smothers Brothers Comedy Hour*, as opposed to "objective" scientific information when it appears on the *Huntley-Brinkley Report*? Both program types used certain *fictional conventions* to transmit knowledge about the war that audiences had come to expect. The *Smothers Brothers* used the convention of a vaudeville comedy team composed of a straight man and a buffoon to convey one perspective on the war. Although certainly not a variety show, *The Huntley-Brinkley Report* recalled many of the conventions of a vaudevillian duo, while filmed reports from distant locales invoked realist conventions of Hollywood cinema. Or, to approach this problem from another direction, as Roberta Pearson does, what made ABC's *Custer* series entertaining to some audiences, while for the Native American movement the series was an historical travesty filled with "mis-formation" about their Native American culture? While of course broadcast journalists have professional standards for telling the truth, and they usually do try to do so, our point here (and one that other scholars have made before us) is that the news is a genre just as much as comedies or westerns are. News uses certain conventionalized forms for mediating knowledge that relativize its status as truth. As such cases demonstrate, the categories of entertainment and information are themselves historical (as opposed to universally true) categories, and thus open to change.

At the time of this writing, television entertainment still has a kitsch status, and 1960s popular television is still largely conceptualized as "Wasteland," (or, in some circles, "Camp,"), fare. The following essays, however, build on a critical tradition that sees television—whether TV news or TV comedy—as centrally contributing to our sense of the historical past, the immediate present, and possible futures.

design

As a whole, then, this book contains a broad range of essays that accentuate various aspects of television's institutional structures and cultural forms, and which together articulate the interconnections between and among them. The first section, "Home Fronts and New Frontiers," emphasizes social change through scientific engineering. Here, authors consider how the "science"—or science fictions—of child-rearing, female sexuality, dating, domestic science, and even space science influenced (and sometimes was influenced by) the representation of family life. These essays also detail how television produced certain kinds of stories that drew on the larger media contexts (such as music, comic books, magazines, radio, advice books) of the times. This "intertextual" approach allows for an examination of the way popular texts reinforce, but also sometimes contradict, one another. It provides a fuller understanding of the "discursive fields" in which programs were developed by creative staff and interpreted by audiences.

The first two articles look at the relationship between public and private agendas in the New Frontier, particularly in terms of how the nation's goals in space science provided a new set of metaphors for representations of family life—and especially the family activity of watching TV. Jeffrey Sconce's analysis of the science fiction/horror anthology *The Outer Limits* situates the program in relation to the history of speculative fiction about electronic media and their link to the world beyond the grave. He shows how the program represented television as an alienating evil machine that caused the death of human consciousness, and he looks at how various episodes linked this grim view of television to such consciousness flatteners as nuclear war and suburban complacency. Next, Lynn Spigel examines the racism and sexism at the heart of the televised space race. She considers how both mainstream news coverage and fiction TV represented space as a "final frontier" to be colonized by the white suburban family. Conversely, critics in African American media usually spoke of the journey to outer space as one more example of "white flight" that left blacks back on earth to grapple with poverty in inner cities.

The next three articles analyze television programs in relation to the explosive debates about the new sexuality. All of these articles demonstrate that the so called "sexual revolution" did not simply amount to a period of freedom or enlightenment for all; rather, the sexual revolution was a "discourse" through which it became possible to generate a new set of statements about what were perceived to be "normal" or "deviant" modes of power and pleasure for men and women. Julie D'Acci's examination of *Honey West* shows how scientific studies of female sexuality (most notably the Kinsey Report) and popular discourses on "sex and the single girl" informed the stylization of TV's first "swinging" female detective. She argues that while ABC attempted to attract a younger and hipper audience with this sexy action heroine, the producers and network were nervous about Honey's explosive sexuality, and they tamed her down for a family medium. The result, D'Acci shows, was a contradictory program that, for a variety of reasons, was quickly canceled and had little immediate influence on TV's portrayal of women characters. Moya Luckett's analysis of *The Patty Duke Show* continues with the theme of "sex and the single girl," but explores it in relation to psychological and market research on teenage girls. She particularly shows how the program's narrative motif of doubling (its "gimmick" of having Duke play the twin roles of Patty, an out-of-control American teenager, and Cathy, her more lady-like British cousin) served both to foreground and resolve contradictions about femininity in '60s America. In particular, this doubling motif highlighted the contradiction between social demands for women to channel their sexual/ emotional needs into heterosexual marriage, and girls' preference to remain in a homosocial (all girl) culture where they had more sexual, emotional, and social autonomy. Finally, Henry Jenkins examines *Dennis the Menace* in the context of the new permissive child-rearing methods most typically associated with Dr. Benjamin Spock. He argues that Dennis's "bad boy" character (as well as the child-rearing literature itself) expressed misogynist ideas about masculine freedom from and contempt for the "feminine" sphere of domesticity. Furthermore, he argues, Dennis's willful male persona, and the freedom he symbolized, should be seen as popular entertainment's response to widespread anxieties about the perceived breakdown of men's authority at work and at home.

The second section focuses on "Institutions of Culture," showing how policy debates, industrial practices, and organized pressure groups all played a role in shaping the everyday experience of watching television. Mark Alvey establishes the industrial background, explaining the institutional practices that generated the possibilities and also delineated the boundaries for creative production during the period. He demonstrates how the networks, Hollywood studios, independent production companies, and talent agencies organized a highly profitable system, but one that was also dependent upon a certain amount of "regulated innovation" in order to sustain the popular appeal of its programming. William Boddy's discussion of Senate hearings on violence in television programming reveals some of the tension points within the Hollywood system, involving outside pressure groups and federal concerns over program violence. While these pressure groups and government officials typically presented themselves as guardians of children, Boddy shows how these advocates often used the violence issue for their own political purposes. Joseph Turow analyzes another dimension of these struggles over program content in his essay on the way the American Medical Association (AMA) teamed up with the producers of medical dramas to become script consultants for the shows. According to Turow, the AMA did so in order to shape a positive image of doctors and private health care at a time of growing national debate over the merits of private vs. socialized medicine. Turow additionally demonstrates that while the AMA used this liaison in an attempt to secure popular consent for its profession, the producers of medical dramas used the AMA "seal of approval" to legitimate their programs as a form of high "science" with pedagogical value.

Later in the decade, as the cracks in the traditional structures of authority began to manifest themselves in numerous institutions, new and different struggles emerged. Now comedy sketches and popular songs associated with the antiwar and civil rights movements would become the object of intense struggle, a point that Aniko Bodroghkozy demonstrates through her reading of corporate censorship memos regarding *The Smothers Brothers Comedy Hour* as well as her textual analysis of the program's increasingly political content over the course of its network run. Finally, Thomas Streeter shows how, at the end of the decade, numerous parties with different concerns participated in a series of policy debates concerning the emerging cable industry. Streeter argues that these groups were bound by a set of rules for speaking about cable that he calls "the discourse of the new technologies." This discourse, which drew on a history of utopian speculation about telecommunications, governed the very terms in which people could imagine and speak about cable, and in many ways it took on a kind of life of its own, quite apart from what the individual speakers meant when they engaged it.

The final section, "Nation and Citizenship," examines how notions of the TV nation were mobilized by network prime-time television. At the same time, it investigates how various citizens groups in local, regionally identified communities responded to these nationalized representations. In the land of the "New Frontier," where the myth of westward expansion was re-channeled to suit the "progressive" spirit of the space age, the American vernacular was being redefined. In turn, marginalized groups who did not share (or were not included) in the New Frontier's "expansive" spirit often resisted this nationalized, network consumer culture, attempting to retain their sense (however fantasized) of local place and group identity.

Michael Curtin's essay deals with the early part of the decade, showing how the dream of global satellite TV was promoted by the Kennedy administration in its efforts to consolidate its influence over the vast, variegated, and culturally diverse "community" of the Free World. Positioning itself as the symbol for a modern, cosmopolitan, worldly culture, the Kennedy circle explicitly contrasted itself with the supposedly provincial ways of middle America. The resentments engendered by this strategy would come home to roost later in the decade in the figure of the "silent majority," but Vicky Johnson shows how *The Lawrence Welk Show* operated throughout the 1960s to promote and sustain a midwestern-inspired sense of community identity that attempted to conserve traditions of the American "frontier myth" and, in complex ways, redefine these in relation to the progressive spirit of the New Frontier. Despite the image of good old community harmony that the bubbly band leader portrayed with his "Welk family" singalongs and square dance steps, the heartland, as all regions of the country, was sorely divided by the cultural revolutions of the 1960s, and the program often exhibited tensions between generations, regions, and races. Like Johnson, Horace Newcomb is interested in the redefinition of America's "frontier myth," as it was established in the television western. Newcomb shows how the Old West became a setting for the negotiation of contemporary social problems after the war, problems that especially revolved around changing styles of manhood and the meaning of heroism. Also dealing in part with the western, Steven Classen's work details one of the most innovative civil rights campaigns, mounted by college students in Jackson, Mississippi, who agitated against the "whites only" theaters in the town by asking stars of popular television shows like *Bonanza* not to show up for local promotional appearances scheduled for segregated theaters. The pressure they brought to bear on the racist town hierarchy hinged, unexpectedly, on the pleasures they were able to deny white television viewers disappointed by the perceived disloyalty of their favorite stars. This local agitation campaign also had important political implications for future struggles in Jackson, the home of the notoriously racist television station WLBT, whose license was eventually revoked in a precedent-setting case that had wide-reaching implications for the public's right to be heard at the FCC. As Roberta Pearson shows, the Native American movement—which positioned itself in contrast to white society but which also wished to distinguish itself from African American civil rights campaigns—organized their forces against television in somewhat different ways. One of the first major issues to become the subject of collective strategy debates among Indian tribes was ABC's curious decision in 1967 to develop the series *Custer*, a program that seemed starkly contrary to broader social trends regarding race, politics, and representation. Pearson combines an analysis of the movement's responses to ABC with a textual analysis of the programs themselves that shows how the series evolved in relation to prior conventions of the Custer mythology in comics and adventure books. Finally, Herman Gray reflects on the ways contemporary television programs like *I'll Fly Away* remember the civil rights movement. In the process he explores the intertextual nature of memory itself, showing how these recent nostalgia programs recycle images from 1960s television and other '60s media. Television's failure to portray African Americans outside the conventional image of what Gray calls the "civil rights subject" continues to limit our nation's ability to come to terms with issues of race and difference.

As the contemporary penchant for nostalgia reminds us, the 1960s is in many respects not over—at least in the cultural imagination. In this regard, like any other decade, the 1960s does not start or end in a neatly packaged ten–year time period. Obviously, the social, cultural, and political climate of one decade often persists into the next. Depending on their subject, then, for some authors the 1960s begins in the mid-1950s, while for others it blends into the present.

The impact of the past on the present is especially important in our case, since the 1960s set a climate of debate about television that still informs the way we imagine the medium and its overall value. Indeed, it seems likely that one of the reasons that 1960s entertainment genres are barely studied is the continued cultural biases against 1960s Hollywood TV that the "Vast Wasteland" speech made into a federal case. Public service intellectuals like Newton Minow—who in fact just published a book that extends his Wasteland critique and reform agenda to contemporary children's television—still hold the fort on the question of television's status in American culture, and still view culture with a capital "C." Meanwhile, conservative House Leader Newt Gingrich tries to pull the plug on public television and attacks its culture with a capital "C" ethos. So today, television continues to fare badly on either side of the fence. Either liberal cultural elites damn its over-commercialization, conservative tax payers cut its public functions out of the budget, or, in the case of former Vice President Quayle and now President Clinton, politicians use it as a scapegoat for all sorts of social dilemmas from welfare mothers to rampant violence.

Life magazine recently published an issue that presents a huge close-up of a child's innocent face with numerous words depicting social evils written across the margins—words such as "violence," "incest," "abuse," "alienation," and "television." That television is made equal to a list of social pathologies is so naturalized by this point in history that most readers probably won't even notice that television is not the same kind of thing as rape or violence. In a nation where millions grew up on *Sesame Street*, we would assume that the people at *Life* would know (as the famous *Sesame Street* ditty put it) "one of these things is not like the other." Then again, perhaps the people at *Life* have never watched *Sesame Street*—which is, after all, one of the most positive children's programs on television and which is, of course, a result of the more pro-social activist imagination that was spurred by the era of the Vast Wasteland.

Although Minow himself was calling for social change on television, the Wasteland critique was taken up in such a way that it universalized the utter "badness" of television, and turned that into the McLuhanite notion that television is a high-tech prosthesis evolving from the structures of the human psyche—what he called "an extension of man." Only now, mixed up with the tropes of the Wasteland, it becomes "an extension of man at his worst." In other words, even while Minow did not intend it this way, the Wasteland metaphor was transformed from his reformist agenda into an "essentialist" property of the medium, so that in the minds of many critics, television, a priori, was (and still is) simply a desolate, evil machine that replicates the lowest depths of the human spirit.

Indeed, the rhetoric of the Vast Wasteland typically manifests itself in a demonization of television that resonates in the political, intellectual, and popular culture of our times. This demonization has become a form of narcissism in the extreme, where all one has to do is scoff at television to appear more socially responsible and culturally "in the know" than the people who watch it. (To be sure, narcissism has also been known to manifest among those self-styled popular intellectuals like McLuhan who secure their own authority as media gurus by saying that everything is, so to speak, "cool," and toss out the project of strategic reform altogether by assuming that the technology generates change by itself).

For such reasons, an exploration of 1960s programming, its institutional foundations, its social contexts, and its reception by audiences, can help to denaturalize some of the reigning cultural and political myths by which television has become the whipping post for problems that people themselves perpetuate in government, at home, and in their local communities. This book, then, attempts to move past the Wasteland logic that keeps us from looking seriously at the ways our most popular communication medium engaged with the social conflicts of the 1960s. We do this not to retrieve some romantic version of the decade filled by counterculture rebels or artistically "golden" programs, but rather to provide a "shock of recognition" in the present.

This history reminds us that the revolution may never be televised, but this is not because television is in itself incapable of imagining constructive social change. Rather, the revolution will not be televised because our reigning belief systems about television make it impossible for us to imagine the medium as a tool for anything but social and cultural depravity. One of the central lessons to be learned from 1960s television, then, is that the debilitating rhetoric on the medium which flourished in that period still informs the way we speak and think about television, even in the so called high-tech age of the information superhighway. It is in the hopes of getting off this road to nowhere and onto something more engaging that we offer this collection of essays.

home fronts

and

new frontiers

part one

Elizabeth Montgomery in *Bewitched*

Promotional Illustration for "The Galaxy Being," *The Outer Limits*

the

"outer limits"

of

oblivion

jeffrey sconce

In a medium already renowned for its intrusive presence in the American home, few television shows have featured opening credit sequences as calculatedly invasive as that of *The Outer Limits*. A narrational entity known only as the "control voice" opened each week's episode with these unnerving words of assurance:

> There is nothing wrong with your television set.
> Do not attempt to adjust the picture.
> We are controlling transmission.
> We will control the horizontal.
> We will control the vertical.
> We can change the focus to a soft blur, or sharpen it to crystal clarity.

On screen, the control voice demonstrated its power by taking command of the picture tube to program a display of warbling sine waves, vertical rolls, and other forms of electronic choreography. Having now completely gained possession of the family console, the control voice issued its final command and warning:

> For the next hour, sit quietly, and we will control all that you see and hear. You are about to participate in a great adventure. You are about to experience the awe and mystery that reaches from the inner mind to *The Outer Limits.*

At this cue, the theme music would swell for the opening credits, after which the control voice would relinquish command, at least momentarily, to the "true" masters of the screen—the commercial advertisers. At the end of each week's episode, the control voice would make one last announcement, coming back to "return control" of the television to its temporarily dispossessed owner.

Debuting in the fall of 1963 on ABC's Monday night schedule, *The Outer Limits* was never a major commercial success. While the program rated as high as the top twenty shortly after its premiere, a scaled-down and less lavish version of the show continually faced the prospects of cancellation during its second season, a fate to which it finally fell victim when ABC replaced the series in January of 1965 with *The King Family.* During its brief run on Monday and then Saturday nights, *The Outer Limits* served first as ABC's lead-in to *Wagon Train* and then to *The Lawrence Welk Show.* During its second season, the program found itself the loser in head to head competition with such formidable cultural icons as Flipper, Jackie Gleason, and Mr. Magoo. Less than a triumph in terms of its network run, the series lasted only a season and a half to compile a meager total of forty-eight episodes. Like many other television science fiction series, *The Outer Limits* has subsequently grown in stature and legend to become somewhat of a cult classic, and is now often compared and conflated in popular memory with Rod Serling's *The Twilight Zone.* But when the individual episodes are sorted out, clear differences emerge between the two series. What perhaps most distinguishes *The Outer Limits* from Serling's more prolific and widely syndicated show is *The Outer Limits'* consistently bleak tone, both thematically and stylistically, as well as its emphasis on relentlessly pessimistic social commentary. Even in the midst of a tale of the apocalypse, *The Twilight Zone* would at least occasionally crack a sinister smile.[1] Not so *The Outer Limits.* Debuting in the months immediately preceding the assassination of President Kennedy and vanishing at the threshold of the nation's growing civil unrest at mid-decade, *The Outer Limits* presented a signature moment of unmitigated doom on American television, often suggesting that the sciences, technologies, and citizens of "the new frontier" were on a collision course with oblivion.

Significantly, the original title planned for the series had been *Please Stand By*, the familiar invocation of panicked broadcasters when confronting social or technological disaster. This interruption in the routinized flow of commercial broadcasting always makes viewers take pause as they consider the possibility of an impending catastrophe. Such alarm was especially pronounced during the Cold War years, when the intrusion of a network "special report" could signify imminent nuclear annihilation. Debuting in the still palpable wake of the Cuban Missile Crisis, *The Outer Limits'* invasive credit sequence exemplified the program's larger textual solution to a persistent challenge in adapting the horror genre to television. As the most "domestic" of entertainment media, television has always posed difficulties in accommodating horror, a genre objectionable not only to watchful parents but also to squeamish advertisers. From the beginning of network programming, science fiction and horror programs such as NBC's *Lights Out* and CBS's *Suspense* were consistently under attack for broadcasting material thought to be too disturbing for the family living room. *The Outer Limits* also became a target of such controversy, and on occasion provided ABC with headaches in standards and practices and affiliate clearance. But what made the series more threatening than a simple "monster show," and yet somewhat immune to standard forms of network censorship, was its unique strategy for maximizing television's intrinsic potential for horror. Ingeniously, *The Outer Limits* framed its tales of monsters, aliens, and mad scientists by casting television itself as a medium of the void, suggesting that its transmissions might expose the viewer to a horrifying oblivion. Exploiting a long-standing fascination in American culture with the potentially supernatural qualities of all electronic media, *The Outer Limits* transformed television's "window on the world" into a window on the "otherworldy," and threatened to exile the viewer to this vast "electronic nowhere" that seemed to lurk behind the otherwise celebrated technologies of "the new frontier."

This essay examines the rather obsessive centrality of cathode-ray "oblivions" in *The Outer Limits*, analyzing the series' visions of the void in relation to the decade's primary site for domestic and technological interaction—the television set. "Oblivion" was the only truly recurring monster in this anthology program, and it took a variety of forms over the forty-eight episode run of the series. Regardless of its shape or dimension, however, oblivion in *The Outer Limits* was almost always mediated by some form of paranormal electronic technology and centered most immediately on the American family, a scenario that offered repeated parables about the audience's own relationship to their TV set, and the set's relationship, in turn, to a vast electronic "nowhere." Whether faced with new beings, mysterious powers, or strange technologies, the characters in these stories (and the viewer at home) had to struggle against uncanny and frequently electronic forces that threatened not just to kill them, but to dissolve them into nothingness.

Of course, even as vast and seemingly boundless a concept as "oblivion" exists within some degree of historical specificity. Surveying the ubiquity of this trope across the run of the series, one is left with the question as to why this particular invocation of televisual nothingness should have such resonance within this historical period. Answers to such complex representational questions must remain imprecise, but three looming and often interrelated "oblivions" of the New Frontier era would seem to be key in producing these electronically mediated visions of the void—the infinite depths of outer space, the emotional "limbo" of suburban domesticity, and the specter of absolute nuclear annihilation. Both in the social reality of the audience and the science fictional "unreality" of the series, television figured as the crucial bridge between these realms as the pivotal technology in the New Frontier's melding of space, science, and suburbia. In this respect, *The Outer Limits* can be considered within the same cultural moment described by Lynn Spigel as informing the "fantastic family sitcom," a cycle of programs she identifies as engaging in a parody of the narrative and social conventions of domestic comedy. Spigel argues that the fantastic sitcom, like much of the popular culture of this era, developed in response to a series of disappointments in American life during the 1950s, chief among these being the homogenizing conformity demanded by suburban living and the seeming vulnerability of American technology in the wake of Sputnik. "[T]his historical conjuncture of disappointments provided the impetus for a new utopian future—one based on the rhetoric of Kennedy's New Frontier and fortified with the discourse of science and technology."[2] As with the supernatural science fiction sitcoms discussed by Spigel (*Bewitched, I Dream of Jeannie*, and *My Favorite Martian*), *The Outer Limits* also exploited the era's emerging fascination with space and science to interrogate the bland "ideology of domesticity" cultivated during the Eisenhower years. But while *The Outer Limits* shared the same cultural project of the fantastic sitcom in reexamining American family life, differences in terms of genre (horror rather than comedy) and format (anthology drama rather than episodic series) often pushed *The Outer Limits* into territory that was far more disturbing and apocalyptic. Unencumbered by the burden of continuing characters and a consistent "situation," *The Outer Limits* had the occasional license to destroy the centerpiece of both postwar life and episodic television, the nuclear family. From episode to episode, there was the persistent subtext that America's intense investment in space, science, and domesticity masked an immense abyss, an anomic nothingness lurking at the core of the nation's identity. While acknowledging the "awe and mystery" of new territories of scientific exploration, *The Outer Limits* also suggested that America might find the "New Frontier" itself to be a terrifying vacuum, an annihilating and discorporative void accessed through television.

The intersection of the series' highly self-reflexive commentary on television as a system beyond human control and its continuing narrative preoccupation with electronic technology as a gateway to oblivion suggests that television remained, even a decade after its introduction into the American home, a somewhat unsettling and alien technology. As a medium of powerful instantaneousness, television displayed a perilously immediate relationship to public danger and disaster, exerting an ambiguous and unknown "control" over the American family. Following a decade of both fascination and disillusionment with the new medium, *The Outer Limits* narrativized the increasingly endemic critiques leveled at television as a potentially threatening technological zone within domestic space. In this respect, the series elaborated the rhetoric of television's many detractors who already considered the medium to be its own form of "oblivion," one that in extreme cases could deliver families into an even more remote and terrifying "vast wasteland" than the one envisioned by FCC Chair Newton Minow. The format of the series implied that the viewer was also vulnerable to such assimilation simply by watching TV, thereby exploiting the medium's potential for terror to the fullest. A viewer who watches a horror film at a theater, after all, can return to the safety of their home and put the experience behind them. The very premise of the *The Outer Limits*, on the other hand, allowed that fear to linger with the viewer. The intervention and presence of the "control voice" suggested that even after the program was over and the receiver was turned off, the television set itself still loomed as a gateway to oblivion simply by sitting inert and watchful in the living room. And this, perhaps, is what made the show too unsettling for its own historical moment and yet such a success in the years following its cancellation. For the first generation to grow up with TV sets lurking in their living rooms, *The Outer Limits* combines the pleasures of horror and nostalgia. It remains the only show to evoke so explicitly the dual sense of fascination and fear that attended the early years of television, a time when the TV set became the most ubiquitous, obsequious, and yet imperious of technologies to occupy domestic space and childhood memory.

monsters in the static

Stories of "haunted" televisions had circulated throughout the decade preceding the premiere of *The Outer Limits,* and were already a stock part of American folklore. On December 11th of 1953, readers of *The New York Times* met a family from Long Island that had been forced to "punish" their decidedly paranormal TV set for scaring the children with visions of a soul lost in

25

the electronic nowhere. As Jerome E. Travers and his three children were watching "Ding Dong School," the face of an unknown woman mysteriously appeared on the screen and would not vanish, even when the set was turned-off and unplugged. "The balky set," which "previously had behaved itself," according to the *Times*, "had its face turned to the wall. . . for gross misbehavior in frightening little children."[3] The haunted television finally gave up the ghost, so to speak, a day later, but not before scores of newspapermen, magazine writers, and TV engineers had a chance to observe the phenomenon. Visitors to the Travers' home also included Francey Lane, a singer from the Morey Amsterdam show that had preceded "Ding Dong School" on the day of the initial haunting. Lane was thought to be the face behind the image frozen on the screen, and her agent apparently felt it would make for good publicity to have the singer meet her ghostly cathode double.[4]

Even before television, the theme of the electronic "nowhere" in telecommunications had a long history in pulp magazines, dimestore paperbacks, and B movies. Radio, telephony, and telegraphy had each inspired tales of uncanny, haunted, and otherwise alien media, ranging from stories of phone calls from the dead to aspirations of contacting other planets through the wonders of wireless. Such tales, in turn, had their roots in the Spiritualist movement of the nineteenth century. The Spiritualists had looked to the electromagnetic telegraph as both an inspiration and a model of explanation for their belief in the "spiritual telegraph," an otherworldly telecommunications device they believed to have been fashioned in the afterlife by such figures as Socrates and Benjamin Franklin. In this earliest cultural conflation of electrical science, telecommunications technology, and parapsychology, the vast "electronic nowhere" was thought to be a peaceful and benevolent haven that housed electrically charged souls.[5]

In *The Outer Limits* and other tales of television's "electronic nowhere," however, these beneficent images of an electronic heaven became instead visions of terrifying isolation, rendering the comforting notion of the afterlife into the more ominous realm of an electromagnetic void. Appropriately, the close association of broadcasting and oblivion in *The Outer Limits* began with the program's pilot. In "The Galaxy Being," which also served as the series premiere on September 16th of 1963, an inventor scans the airwaves with a powerful transceiving device that draws energy from a nearby radio station. He captures strange signals, "three-dimensional static," that transform on a viewscreen into the image of an alien. When the inventor leaves the radio station that evening, an accident teleports the alien to earth via the transmitted signal, where as a three-dimensional electronic being, he quickly becomes the prey of local authorities. Cornered by his attackers, the alien destroys the radio tower as a demonstration of his power, and then warns the encroaching mob. "There are powers in the universe beyond anything you know," he says. "There is much you have to learn....Go to your homes. Go and give thought to the mysteries of the universe." The crowd disperses while the inventor and the alien return in peace to the radio station. But the alien laments that he cannot return to his home planet because he has broken a law forbidding contact with other worlds. Exiled from home and only an electronic phantom on earth, the alien consigns himself to oblivion. "End of transmission," he says as he reduces the transmitter power that first brought him to earth, turning the dial until at last he completely vanishes.

This poignant tale was a fit debut for a series that would continue to explore the relationship among electronic transmission, physical discorporation, and social alienation. As a story of an alien being contacted and then teleported through the "three-dimensional static" of an intergalactic television set, "The Galaxy Being" dramatized decades of cultural speculation that wireless might be used to contact other planets, especially Venus and Mars.[6] Centered squarely in the rhetoric of the New Frontier, "The Galaxy Being" developed this familiar premise into a more disturbing tale of electronic existentialism. "You must explore. You must reach out," says the alien, echoing the words of NASA officials and its patron administration. But while advocating interstellar exploration, this episode also played on the suspense and fear encouraged by news broadcasts as NASA launched Alan Shepard, John Glenn, and other astronauts into the great void of outer space. By simultaneously maximizing the drama of these launches while mediating the home viewer's entry into outer space, television became not only the preferred medium for witnessing the space race, but also a seemingly privileged means of anxious access to space itself. With the Galaxy Being "tuning" himself out of existence, this debut episode cultivated such anxiety by portraying outer space and television's electronic space as a common limbo where one might be "transmitted" into nothingness.

Such themes continued in the second episode of The Outer Limits, "The Borderland." In this episode, experiments with high-powered electrical fields reveal the possibility of an alternate dimension. During an experiment to contact a wealthy man's dead son, a malfunction disrupts the equipment and blows the breakers, trapping a scientist in an eerie electrical netherworld that exists between the dimensions of life and death. Unable to navigate through this limbo realm, the man cries out helplessly to his wife as he describes the terrifying nothingness that engulfs him. The viewer sees him as a figure thrashing behind a wall of static, as if trapped within the viewer's own television set. In the end, the scientist is saved, but not before the wealthy patron of the experiment leaps through the wall of static in search of his son, only to be forever lost in the other electrical dimension.

With their mutual fixation on electronic transmission as a bridge between worlds, both "The Galaxy Being" and "The Borderland" exploited to the fullest *The Outer Limits'* simulation of an intercepted paranormal transmission, suggesting the possibility of alternate life forms and dimensions lurking in the familiar realm of televisual static. TV transmission in general, even in its more mundane forms, was a topic of much public interest in the early 1960s, as "ultra high frequency" radio signals and orbiting space capsules both tested "the outer limits" of the atmosphere. Beyond the usual articles advising husbands how to take to the rooftops to improve reception, the popular press also gave wide coverage to the decade's emerging forms of signal transmission, including UHF and color TV.[7] Most influential in associating television transmission with outer space was the 1962 launch of "Telstar," the American satellite that first made possible live television broadcasts across the ocean. As with a host of other international media that preceded it, Telstar inspired a series of utopian predictions concerning telecommunications and world peace that portrayed the space-traveling television signal as a world ambassador.[8] A symbol of the earth united through the heavens, the launching of Telstar strengthened an already strong cultural association between television and outer space, and reinvigorated television's status as an extraordinary and fantastic technology.

In the paranormal imagination, however, television transmission presented more a terrifying electronic "nothingness" than an avenue of political utopia, especially when these signals were imagined traveling through the lonely infinitude of outer space. Where does the Galaxy Being go when he turns off the transmitter? What exactly is this strange electromagnetic limbo between life and death represented in "The Borderlands"? In the paranormal broadcast signal encountered with television, the phenomenon of transmission is not so much a link to other worlds as an uncanny, alternate dimension in and of itself, a limbo realm not unlike the vast expanses of outer space that television so frequently depicted during the decade. This is the horror facing the Galaxy Being, the scientists in "The Borderlands," countless other characters on *The Outer Limits*, and even the viewer at home. Television does not threaten to transport them "elsewhere," but succeeds in assimilating them, at least temporarily, into its own "nowhere." Television thus threatened to consume its subjects, if not into the actual vacuum of outer space, then into its own logics and fictions that existed in an etherial space which, nevertheless, could often feel more real, more "live" than the everyday material environment of the viewer's home.

One of the more interesting antecedents of *The Outer Limits'* fascination with television, space, and oblivion comes from the otherwise mundane pages of *TV Guide*. In a piece dubbed "Television's Biggest Mystery," the magazine shared with its readers the enigma of KLEE, a station once based in Houston, Texas.

> At 3:30 pm, British Summer Time, September 14, 1953, Charles
> W. Brafley of London picked up the call letters KLEE-TV on his
> television set. Later that month and several times since, they
> have been seen by engineers at Atlantic Electronics, Ltd., Lan-
> caster, England.... The call letters KLEE-TV have not been
> transmitted since July, 1950, when the Houston station changed
> its letters to KPRC-TV.... A check of the world's television sta-
> tions confirms the fact that there is not now and never has been
> another KLEE-TV.[9]

In this fantastic scenario, KLEE's signal has somehow become "lost" in what should have been the nanosecond separating transmission and reception, an infinitesimal moment in time transformed into an apparently infinite limbo. Combining anxieties over agency with the mysteries of physics, the KLEE story posited an electrical form of consciousness at the center of this riddle, one not unlike the Galaxy Being or the interdimensional scientist of *The Outer Limits*. Temporarily forgotten, the KLEE enigma returned when the vagabond station was spotted once again, this time on the TV set of Mrs. Rosella Rose of Milwaukee, Wisconsin, sometime in February of 1962, a full twelve years after the Houston station had abandoned the KLEE station card.[10] In this updated version, KLEE's mysterious signal now carried more than just a station identi-fication, allowing a glimpse into an alternate universe on the other side of the television screen. Mrs. Rose reported briefly seeing the image of an unknown man and woman arguing on a balcony. "The picture faded out then and the KLEE flashed on again," reported Mrs. Rose, "and here's the really strange part—superimposed over the KLEE, which was still on, the word 'HELP' flashed on, off, and on again. The screen then went black."[11] This captive's cry for help suggests that television could serve, not only as a realm of oblivion, but also as a seemingly sentient gatekeeper or cruelly malevolent jailer. This installment in the KLEE story thus makes manifest an anxiety common to all other televisual tales of the electronic nowhere. It provokes the fear that viewers too might one day find themselves trapped within the television set, whisked away by this most domestic of technologies into an electronic netherworld.

The KLEE mystery and *The Outer Limits* stories that followed it, be they based on "true" incidents or long-standing legends, are unsettling for the same reasons that the telegraph of 1848 must have seemed so utterly fantastic. The fleeting and inexplicable transmissions of KLEE, the Galaxy Being, and the "borderlands" are eerie in that they are symptomatic of a general loss of "self-presence" felt socially in electronic communications as a whole. As readers thumbed through their weekly copies of *TV Guide*, the KLEE mystery reminded them that "live" messages and "living" messengers were no longer coterminous, and that consciousness itself could exist in seeming independence from either a sender or a receiver. Similarly, *The Outer Limits* alluded to the existence of an invisible and perhaps imperious empire in the ether. And while the Spiritualists found this dissolution and reconstitution of consciousness via electronic media to be a promising mode of spiritual contact, even a utopian key to solving all of the material world's problems, the wandering consciousness in these tales suggests that by the time of television, signals once under human command seemed either out of control, or even worse, under the control of increasingly sinister forces. By the early 1960s, the once wondrous "otherworld" of electronic telecommunications had become a vast reservoir of cultural anxiety, presenting a localized fear about television itself, certainly, but also a more general unease over the increasingly atomized world television had helped to create. The great electronic nowhere, in other words, no longer represented a gathering of souls, but presented instead their atomization and dispersal across infinity.[12]

But abduction and assimilation by television's electromagnetic nowhere was not the only anxiety expressed in these tales. As a story of television's "distant sight," KLEE also fascinates because it suggests a certain "vision on the air," positing an electrical omniscience associated with television broadcasting as an invisible blanket covering the earth. Even if the television cannot actually assimilate us, there remains the disturbing thought that, just as we can potentially peer into other worlds through the television, these other worlds may be peering into our own living room. Such anxieties must have been particularly acute in the early 1960s as both the United States and Soviet Union launched satellites into the stratosphere for the explicit purpose of surveying the world below to the smallest detail. In an age of growing satellite saturation in the sky and absolute set penetration in the home, the spatiotemporal enigmas of TV transmission provided a sinister variation on a cultural anxiety dating back to the earliest days of television. Spigel notes that early discourses on television often expressed "a larger obsession with privacy, an obsession that was typically expressed through the rhetorical figure of the window, the border between inside and outside worlds."[13] In its more benevolent form, the "window" of television activated the medium's marvelous "aesthetics of presence," showcasing the medium's ability to transport the viewer "live" to localities around the world. Within this growing complex of surveillance technologies and political tensions, however, television was also the most plausible agent to serve as a "window on the home." Period accounts of television often pondered the seemingly inevitable reversibility of the watcher and the watched presented by all telecommunications technology. Of Telstar, for example, Arthur C. Clarke waxed poetically that "no dictator can build a wall high enough to stop its citizens' listening to the voices from the stars." And yet he also conceded that the launching of such communications satellites would eventually make "absolute privacy impossible."[14] In the mad political and scientific race to colonize, communicate, and survey from the sky, who could know exactly what capacities Telstar, Comsat, and their Soviet counterparts actually had or to what uses these secret technologies might eventually be put?

Surveillance technology has long been a fixture of science fiction, of course, and *The Outer Limits* made frequent use of this device. One episode in particular, however, forged a most explicit relationship between advanced television technology, outer space, and seemingly paranormal forms of surveillance, again playing on public anxieties about television as an electronic eye in the home. "O.B.I.T." (1963) told the story of a highly advanced video monitoring system in use at an American military base, a device that allows its operator to monitor secretly the actions of any individual on or near the compound. An investigating senator sets out to learn more about the machine, the Outer Band Individuated Teletracer, or O.B.I.T. as it is known for short. He is told that each person generates his or her own distinct electronic signal, and that the O.B.I.T. machine has the ability to tune in these frequencies anywhere within a range of a few hundred miles. In a dramatic courtroom finale, a general appears on the stand to insist that a "monster" lurks the base and haunts the O.B.I.T. screen. Surveying the courtroom with O.B.I.T. reveals a sinister computer technician to be the monster, an alien from another world whose human disguise can only be uncloaked by this mysterious form of television. The creature boasts that it has brought the O.B.I.T. technology to earth in order to demoralize, divide, and conquer the planet by instilling fear and suspicion through the entire population. "The machines are everywhere," he says to the stunned humans, "and they'll demoralize you, break your spirit, create such rifts and tensions in your society that no one will be able to repair them!" A less than subtle reworking of Orwell with a touch of HUAC paranoia added for good measure, "O.B.I.T." nevertheless concretized a suspicion no doubt held by many during this period. If television can be seen anywhere and everywhere at once, then why could it not potentially "see" anywhere and everywhere as well? The device of the "Individuated Teletracer" expanded the fear of surveillance beyond the actual apparatus of the home television set by appealing to the existence of this larger electro-magnetic blanket enveloping the earth, a realm where each person unknowingly sent off electrical signals that could be intercepted and monitored on "alien" TV sets. The story of "O.B.I.T" may have seemed outlandish, but no more so than a *Life* magazine article from 1964 reporting on a device called T.E.S.T., or the "Tanner Electronic Survey Tabulator." *Life* described T.E.S.T. as a "spooky little truck" that patrolled suburban streets, "its innards. . .crammed full of fancy electronic equipment that can and does silently violate the sanctuary of those lighted living rooms to determine 1) whether the occupants are watching their television sets, and if so, 2) on what channel."[15] The inventor of T.E.S.T. predicted his device would revolutionize the imprecise science of "ratings" by covertly monitoring televisions and families in the home, whether they chose to be monitored or not. If a mere panel truck could accomplish such a feat, then it was reasonable to suppose that high-tech satellites could watch over entire nations, cities, and neighborhoods, perhaps even telecasting private images from the home to any number of sinister agencies, be they governmental or extra-terrestrial.

The "control voice's" closing narration to the "O.B.I.T." episode reminded viewers that Americans were their own worst enemies in terms of such suspicion. Exploiting the insatiable American desire to know the secrets of both outer space and the family next door, the aliens are confident that this nation of atomized, isolated, and alienated citizens can easily be brought to its knees. A fragmented and distrustful society connected only through the dull glow of its televisions screens is no match for this seductive technology of alien surveillance, one that allows these estranged citizens to spy on one another's personal traumas and family secrets. In these particularly paranoid transmissions from *The Outer Limits*, television threatened to expose another mammoth void structuring American consciousness in the early 1960s—the suffocating emotional oblivion to be found within the American home.

domestic asylum

As many social historians have noted, the nuclear family emerged as the primary social unit in American postwar society. In a coordinated effort to encourage commodity consumption, stimulate housing starts, and repopulate the nation, a variety of forces in postwar America coalesced to renew faith in family life and to reinvent its meanings in new mass-produced consumer suburbs. But this reorientation of American social life was not without profound consequences. In flight from the nation's urban centers and severed from a whole nexus of earlier community relations, the nuclear families of white suburbia suddenly stood in self-imposed isolation as their own primary network of personal identity and social support. Within the increasingly isolated family, the middle-class mother became the abandoned keeper of the household. This shift in social identity from the community to the family restructured many Americans' engagement with both the social world and the family circle, and provided each member of the family with a new social role to internalize and obey.[16]

Throughout the 1950s and into the 1960s, television developed a highly codified series of narrative conventions to represent this emerging suburban ideal, constructing a middle-class utopia of labor-saving appliances, manicured lawns, and spacious architecture, all designed to showcase the white suburban housewife as the ultimate symbol of material success and domestic bliss. Within this ordered space, postwar wives traded one form of "freedom" for another: exiled from the workplace and public life, they were "liberated" within the home through a series of consumer goods. As Mary Beth Haralovich notes, housewives were "promised psychic and social satisfaction for being contained within the private space of the home; and in exchange for being targeted, measured, and analyzed for the marketing and design of consumer products, [they were] promised leisure and freedom from housework."[17] Even with its newly purchased array of "emancipating" ovens, irons, and washing machines, however, the suburban home and the rigid social order it presupposed could be a prison at times, especially for women, but also for men who became caught up in the "rat race" of consuming for status. Yet, as Elaine Tyler May observes in her study of postwar families, there was little incentive to change the decade's often oppressive domestic regime. "Forging an independent life outside of marriage carried enormous risks of emotional and economic bankruptcy, along with social ostracism," observes May. "As these couples sealed the psychological boundaries around the family, they also sealed their fates within it."[18]

At times, however, this sealing of "psychological boundaries" around the family could produce not only a general sense of disaffection, but clinical diagnoses of psychosis and possible institutionalization. A study of schizophrenia in the early 1950s, for example, revealed that married women were far more likely to suffer schizophrenic episodes than married men, and noted that a common stage in the "breakdown" of schizophrenic housewives was "the increasing isolation of the wife from family and social relationships, her more-or-less progressive detachment from participation in social reality."[19] Discussing this study some twenty-five years later, Carol Warren notes that "the problems in everyday living experienced by these women—loneliness, isolation, and the stress of the housewife role—were reflections of the conventional structure of marriage and the family in the 1950s. But they were also psychiatric symptoms."[20] Warren goes so far as to argue that the individual "psychopathologies" of these women were in fact socially symbolic prisons, and she describes the "delusions and hallucinations" experienced by these schizophrenic women as "metaphors for their social place."[21] One woman, for example, "saw herself as having been hypnotized by her husband

and her doctors, as punished for her offenses by [electro-shock therapy], and as the victim of a master conspiracy to rob her of control of her own life."[22] Another subject in the study heard voices that accused her of not properly caring for her children, a condition that worsened to the point that she eventually set fire to her own home.[23]

Glorifying the virtues of the privatized family and bound more to narrative than social conventions, television's domestic sitcom had no language with which to engage the potential mental disintegration of Mayfield, Springfield, and the other well-scrubbed communities of televisionland. And though the fantastic sitcom often played on the temporary illusion of suburban schizophrenia (talking horses, Martian uncles, maternal automobiles, etc.), it was *The Outer Limits* that presented the most expansive textual space in which to expose and explore this suburban psychopathology. Often presented in tandem with the vacuum of space and the vast "electronic nowhere" of television was *The Outer Limits'* equally terrifying portrait of a more claustrophobic "emotional nowhere." In these domestic visions of oblivion, husbands and wives found themselves trapped, either metaphorically or quite literally, within the suffocating confines of the American home, often to the point of madness. *The Outer Limits* frequently portrayed the American home as a "domestic asylum," cultivating the ambiguity between the dominant conception of the household as a cozy "refuge" from the real world and a more critical view of the home as a place of the insane. As explored in *The Outer Limits*, the "domestic asylum" of the American suburbs was a zone of torpor and constraint, an emotional void every bit as alienating as the electronic oblivion to be found in television.

Frequently presenting an explicit critique of the idealized portrait of the American family, *The Outer Limits* often explored the "delusions and hallucinations" that might befall a June Cleaver, Margaret Anderson, or Donna Stone once the camera was turned off. In "The Bellaro Shield" (1964), for example, a "deviant" housewife is driven insane by a literalized metaphor of her domestic confinement. Passed over for promotion in his father's company, a scientist forgets to deactivate a new laser technology he has been developing. Its beam intercepts an alien who is transported, much like the Galaxy Being before him, into the scientist's home.[24] When the scientist's socially ambitious wife, Judith, discovers that her husband has "captured" an alien, she is sure this scientific triumph will convince her father-in-law to make her husband chairman. Even more enticing, the alien carries with him a small device in his hand that allows him to activate an impenetrable shield, one that can be expanded to any dimension. Judith realizes this technology would revolutionize the defense industry and make her husband's company the most powerful in the world, so she arranges for the father to return to see an amazing demonstration of his son's "new invention." She then steals the technology from the alien, striking the creature in the back of the head and prying the device from his hand. When the father arrives, Judith demonstrates the wondrous new technology that she credits her husband for pioneering. Clicking the device, she activates the "Bellaro Shield," which she has named after both her husband and father-in-law. After demonstrating that the shield can withstand bullets and even laser fire, however, she discovers that she cannot deactivate the force field. She is trapped within its glass-like walls and is quickly running out of air. In the end, the alien regains consciousness, returns to the lab, and deactivates the shield before he expires. But the experience of entrapment has been too much for Judith. She continues to flail away at the now phantom shield. She has gone completely mad and is convinced that she is still imprisoned within it and will be forever.

"The Bellaro Shield" is a rich and conflicted text in what it says about the relationship of marriage, gendered ambition, and domestic asylum in the early 1960s. On the one hand, Judith is clearly "punished" for having disrupted her prescribed role as the passive homemaker. She is depicted early in the text as a suburban Lady MacBeth, aggressively pursuing her husband's corporate career even when he will not. For this alone, she might be considered demented in the social context of postwar suburbia, where such ambition could easily be categorized as "crazy."[25] On the other hand, while portraying the harsh penalty of gender deviance, "The Bellaro Shield" also evokes the potential terror of domestic isolation through an exaggerated technological metaphor of the overly restrictive household. The Bellaro Shield, a device named (appropriately enough) after the patriarchal forces that contain her in the home on a daily basis, presents an intense and focused field of power that threatens to imprison Judith forever. In this respect, one can not help but be struck by how the shield itself, as a box-like, glass prison within the home, stands as a metaphor for television. After activating the shield, Judith finds herself at the center of domestic space trapped behind suffocating panes of glass. The others look on in horror. Closeups of the entombed housewife present the illusion that Judith is actually pressing against the glass of the viewer's home screen. This dynamic image of a woman flailing behind glass walls, at first real and then imaginary, is a dense and multivalent emblem that merges the period's visions of electronic and domestic oblivion. Women such as Judith were trapped by television in two ways, physically removed from the world and isolated within the home by this imperious domestic technology, while also trapped within its constricting conventions of representation. If the suburban home was truly a "domestic asylum," then television was the household's watchful warden, enforcing the housewife's solitary confinement while also instructing her in the desired behaviors for suburban assimilation. As a televised housewife, Judith is perched between these electronic and domestic voids, trapped within a prison of brick and mortar on the one hand and of light and electricity on the other.

"The Bellaro Shield" aligns *The Outer Limits* with a larger cycle of period science fiction centering on mass society critiques of television, women, and the home. Keith Laumer's short story, "The Walls," first published in *Amazing Stories* in 1963, tells a similar tale of a "domestic asylum" with a housewife in the not-too-distant future slowly driven to madness by her husband's desire for an ever more constricting television system in the home. The story begins with Harry replacing the couple's conventional TV set with a "full-wall," a system that features a screen taking up an entire wall of the living room. Soon, Harry proudly adds a second "full-wall" unit adjacent to the first, transforming half of the living room into a giant TV screen. At this point, Flora's fate becomes inevitable. A third full-wall unit is installed and then a fourth until finally the entire apartment is pervaded by an omnidirectional spectacle so strong that the room's doors and corners can no longer be perceived. The saturation of sound and image proves to be too much, causing Flora to panic one day while Harry is still away at work. Just before fainting, she deactivates the system. When she wakes up, she finds herself alone in the apartment surrounded, like Judith Bellaro, by four glass walls that now recede as mirrors into infinity. Also like Judith, she "misreads" her domestic situation through a video induced psychosis.

> But how strange. The walls of the cell block were transparent now; she could see all the other apartments, stretching away to every side. She nodded; it was as she thought. They were all as barren and featureless as her own.... They all had four Full-walls. And the other women—the other wives, shut up like her in these small, mean cells; they were all aging, and sick, and faded, starved for fresh air and sunshine. She nodded again, and the woman in the next apartment nodded in sympathy. All the women were nodding; they all agreed—poor things.... She stood in the center of the room, not screaming now, only sobbing silently. In the four glass walls that enclosed her, she stood alone. There was no point in calling any longer.[26]

With their common themes of a lost reality within the home, these tales merge the electronic oblivion of television and the emotional oblivion of the home, not by pulling the victimized spectator into the television apparatus itself, but by having the void of television expand, both materially and symbolically, to become a totalizing and wholly simulated realm of electronic incarceration, one that concretizes a lonely emotional void already silently in place in the home. In this respect, both the Bellaro Shield and the full-wall system are manifestations of the emotional walls that already separate husband and wife in these tales, and which no doubt divided many actual suburban homes of the decade.

As bleak as this vision of marriage and domesticity may be, it was eclipsed by a 1964 episode of *The Outer Limits* entitled "The Guests." In this particularly hallucinatory tale, a young drifter (prominently coded as an independent bachelor who drives a convertible, wears a leather jacket, and dons sporty sunglasses) promises an injured man that he will go to a nearby house for help. He makes his way to a gloomy, gothic-looking house at the top of the hill and soon finds himself surrounded by a most peculiar "family," one that consists of an elderly married couple, an aspiring movie actress, and a young woman named Tess. "The Drifter," as this family calls him for most of the episode, has been lured into this domestic trap by an alien creature in the attic. The alien uses those in the house as subjects of an experiment, probing their minds for information on human emotions. When the drifter tries to flee, he discovers that all the doors and windows are sealed. A romance slowly develops between the drifter and Tess, and after a time, she confesses finally that there is a way to escape the "prisonhouse." Each person has an individual "exit door" through which they may leave. The drifter begs Tess to escape with him, but she says she cannot leave the house. Vowing his undying love, the drifter says he will spend eternity with Tess in the house. But she will not allow this fate to befall him. She dashes out of her personal exit door and promptly dematerializes, leaving behind only a locket. "There is nothing for me out there either, Tess," says the drifter as he turns despairingly to go back into the house. But the alien is done with the experiment. The drifter has revealed to him the "missing emotion" in his study of earthlings—love. The alien lets the drifter go and then destroys the house with the other occupants still trapped inside.

Much like "The Bellaro Shield," "The Guests" conducts a rather conflicted examination of love, marriage, and domesticity. Though the episode presents romantic love as the key for resolving the entire narrative, it does this only after portraying marriage and domestic life as little better than a waking death. The elderly wife in the house refers to their existence as a "dreamy nothingness," and when asked why she stays in the home replies, "A wife's duty is to share her husband's life sentence." She implies too that the drifter might also decide to "plunk right down here and dream a life. And live a dream." In the end, the drifter is willing to "settle down" with Tess and continue their vigil in the suffocating, dark, gray, Victorian house, but Tess "frees" him by sacrificing herself. Usually the prized object of display within the home, the housewife in this case becomes a vortex of stasis that threatens to draw the young bachelor forever into the domestic void.

Expanding the static borders of the "domestic asylum" to include an entire suburban neighborhood, a final and in many ways summarily emblematic episode of *The Outer Limits* is worth examining for its complex vision of "oblivion" as a melding of space, suburbia, and the American family. In "A Feasibility Study," a 1964 episode written by series creator Joseph Stefano, an alien space craft removes and then "telecasts," atom by atom, a six-block suburban neighborhood from Beverly Hills to the planet Luminous ("It works very much like your television transmission," says an alien later in the episode when explaining the process to a bewildered human). In the morning, residents of this community wake and prepare for the day unaware that their homes are now light years away from earth, having been telecast across the galaxy by an alien transmitter. Eventually, the humans learn that they are part of a "feasibility study" to see if humans can survive on Luminous to work as slaves. The Luminoids, as this race is called, have become literally petrified by an airborne virus so that they can no longer move. Slowly aging into rock-like creatures, they need a mobile species to do the more menial chores of running the planet. The humans also discover that they too can become infected with the petrifying virus should they actually touch a Luminoid. In the episode's climax, the human community gathers at the church to discuss their fate. Having come into direct contact with the Luminoids, an infected husband and wife stumble into the church already bearing signs of their imminent petrifaction. After a passionate plea by one of their neighbors, the community decides to trick the Luminoids into thinking that humans are also vulnerable to the airborne form of the virus and are therefore unsuitable to work on the planet. In order to save the human race back on earth from the fate of intergalactic slavery, the entire suburban community lines up to infect themselves by touching the already diseased husband and wife.

Explicitly an allegory about the horrors of slavery (albeit an ironic racial reversal where white suburbanites find themselves dispossessed, segregated, and in eventual solidarity), "A Feasibility Study" is equally remarkable for what it implicitly suggests about the incarcerating dimensions of suburbia in the early 1960s. The story concludes with a heroic and uplifting sacrifice, but this resolution does little to address the depressing portrait of suburban isolation and domestic alienation depicted in the previous hour. At the opening of the story, for example, the narrative's central couple is on the verge of separating. After a year of marriage, the wife complains that she can no longer tolerate her husband's demands that she give up her career interests and remain in the house. As the alien plot unfolds, this couple gradually falls back in love and eventually leads the sacrifice made by the entire community. This is an uplifting ending, perhaps, both in terms of combating intergalactic slavery and rekindling romantic love. But there is still something rather sinister about a story that begins with an oppressed wife packing to leave her husband and then ends with the same wife acquiescing as she is turned into a rock. Similarly, the image of an entire suburban neighborhood marooned on a remote planet and hurtling forever through the void of space makes for an eerie yet apropos commentary on the state of suburbia in the 1960s. For this community of suburban exiles, lost in the stars, yet permanently confined to a six-block patch of land, the decision to become infected by the petrifying virus may represent a brave sacrifice, but there is also the more nihilistic subtext that this final act of community is more of a suicide pact than a collective form of resistance.

"the world is unstable and may collide and blow up"

As these episodes demonstrate, *The Outer Limits*, like the fantastic sitcom, frequently drew attention to the conventionality of domestic life. Also like the fantastic sitcom, the series even reaffirmed on occasion romantic love and heterosexual marriage as the ideal resolution to certain textual and social problems. But its reliance on a separate set of narrative conventions and a profoundly different sense of the "fantastic" often placed the family, not as a site of (temporarily) renegotiated social roles, but as a source of violent disruption and a target of imminent extinction. Spigel notes that the fantastic sitcom operated through a logic of "displacement and distortion," employing "safety valves" that "diffused the 'trouble' in the text."[27] Compared to these sitcoms, the "fantastic" elements of *The Outer Limits*—its weird aliens and strange technologies—worked not so much to displace and distort anxieties about American life, but instead to *intensify* these anxieties by presenting the family with a series of apocalyptic crises that challenged the solvency and legitimacy of this social institution.

Perhaps no oblivion of the early 1960s was as palpable as that of nuclear annihilation, another void continually rehearsed both by *The Outer Limits* and television in general. "The Premonition" (1965), airing a week before the show's final exile from network airwaves, opens with a testpilot pushing record speeds in an experimental aircraft high above the desert. Below, his wife drives their daughter to the military base's day school. After the jet descends out of control and makes a crash landing, the pilot emerges to find that the entire world is frozen in time. Out on the desert plains, a coyote chasing a rabbit stands as a still tableau, as do birds hanging in the air around him. Seeing his unconscious wife still behind the wheel of her car, he revives her, and she too quickly remarks that time seems to be standing still. Together, they return to the base and find everyone absolutely frozen in place. In their struggles, they meet the "limbo being," a man who long ago also entered this "black oblivion" of frozen time. "I am what you are," he says, "trapped in this limbo-world between the present and the future." In perhaps the series' most vivid account of oblivion, he describes the hell that awaits them should they not escape. "Time will pass you by, and leave you where I am now, in the forever now, black motionless void . . . no light . . . no sun . . . no stars . . . no time . . . eternal nothing . . . no hunger . . . no thirst . . . only endless existence. And the worst of it? You can't die." The pilot and his wife also discover that their daughter will be killed immediately once time is unfrozen, as her tricycle stands only feet away from a runaway truck. Working together, they finally devise a plan to both save their daughter and re-emerge from the realm of the "limbo being." Once this is accomplished, they remember nothing of their experience outside of normal time. Nevertheless, they rush to the airbase with a strange premonition that their daughter might be in trouble. But they find her happy and at play, no longer endangered by the truck.

With its images of figures locked in time, the episode's lingering shots of frozen coyotes, static birds, and motionless human figures in the desert recall the unnerving imagery of the government's atomic tests at Yucca Flats in the mid-1950s, and by implication, the frozen moment of horror preceding the nuclear obliteration of Hiroshima and Nagasaki. In the Yucca Flats detonation, as is well known, the government built an entire town on the desert plains of New Mexico. "Survival City," as this outpost was called, featured a population of department store mannequins who occupied a row of houses on "Doomsday Drive." The entire experiment was staged as a high profile media event, with CBS and NBC sharing the production costs in the hopes of capturing a vividly personal and highly rated encounter with the A-bomb. In a perverse attempt to "humanize" the story, reporters even went so far as to "interview" a family of these clothing-store dummies, the "Darlings," as they sat posed for destruction. "With the help of Kit Kinne, Foods Editor of the *Home* show," observed *Newsweek* in the midst of the bomb's pre-blast publicity blitz, "American housewives inspected the Darlings' cupboards and iceboxes and speculated on the effects of the blast on such items as baby food, dishwashers, and children's nightgowns."[28] Such "survival" coverage in the mid and late 1950s helped precipitate the national mania for fallout shelter construction in the early 1960s, a campaign that once again placed the American home most palpably at the center of an impending oblivion. Civil defense literature evoked images of the suburban neighborhood as a final and lonely frontier. Faced with the prospect of nuclear annihilation, block after block of suburban families would be trapped, not just in their homes, but in the even more tomb-like concrete shelters in their basements and backyards. In the midst of such nuclear oblivion, their only link to the outside world or to the neighbors next door would come through an even more remote and disembodied form of television: the Emergency Broadcasting System.

The Yucca Flat nuclear test experienced delays to the point that the networks abandoned their extensive, in-depth coverage of the event.[29] Nevertheless, cameras were there to record the devastation as the bomb decimated "Survival City," the Darlings, and its other mute and motionless residents. These eerie images of post-blast mannequins scattered across the desert were exhibited on a number of television programs and made it in still form to the pages of *Life,*where all of America could scrutinize at their own leisure their possible fate in the nuclear age.[30] With its images of the static desert, "The Premonition" rehearsed this sense of nervous anticipation experienced before any big blast, be it a desert test or an imminent enemy launch. Vulnerable and helpless, the young married protagonists struggle, like so many other Americans of the period, to save their child from the seemingly inevitable destruction that awaits her. Lost in this eternal moment of anticipatory dread, their only contact is with the "limbo being," a creature who himself is a specter of the atomic blast. Wearing shredded clothing and deathly afraid of fire, the "limbo being" is filmed throughout the episode as a reverse negative. A black-and-white inversion of the world around him, the "limbo being" wanders as a glowing, irradiated creature doomed to "the forever now, the black motionless void."

As with so many other episodes of *The Outer Limits*, however, "The Premonition" ultimately returned the viewer back to images of the reigning space age. Test pilots, of course, were major cultural heroes of the time, seen as braving death to lay the groundwork for the eventual colonization of space. Breaking through a "new frontier" of speed, the pilot and his wife, like Shepard, Glenn, and the families of all other astronauts to follow, stand at the precipice of the greatest oblivion of all—the timeless and depthless expanses of outer space. In this respect, the televised volley of rocket launches in the late 1950s and early 1960s not only made Americans more aware of their technological competition with the Soviets, but also produced a new understanding of the earth and its rather humble place in the vastness of the universe. Like the Copernican revolution centuries earlier, NASA's frenzied launching of monkeys and men into the black void of space could not help but tangibly remind an already nervous world that it was very insignificant, incredibly vulnerable, and ultimately quite alone in the galaxy. "The growing preoccupation with outer space is one of the features of our present civilization," observed a psychiatrist writing in 1960. "It is not surprising that it should enter into the manifestations of certain neurotic symptoms."[31] Presenting a number of case studies in such neurosis, this psychiatrist discusses the plight of a thirty-three-year-old man who would no doubt feel quite at home in the world of *The Outer Limits,* a subject who felt "unsafe" because, as he put it, "'the earth is a ball spinning round and I am on it.'" The psychiatrist comments:

> He became completely incapacitated and had to be admitted to [the] hospital with the fear "of going to disappear in outer space." He felt that his feet were on the ground and that the sky was above and he had to keep reminding himself that the force of gravity was keeping him down—"otherwise I would float into space." ... Phrases which commonly occurred included: "it's space that's getting me—the curvature of the globe makes everything insecure." "We are surrounded by a hostile environment—if I think about it I want to run for cover." ... His home was described as "a little small house on the globe and all the space above—and that is insecure."[32]

Another patient reported a more specific fear of satellites and space stations, while still another admitted both fear and fascination with space programs on television. Describing her attraction/repulsion for these shows, she complained, "It's a nuisance when you are interested in things and they frighten you."[33] Living in the age of humanity's first tentative journeys into outer space gave her a general sense of anxiety over "peculiar things happening in the universe."[34] Her biggest fear was that "the world is unstable and may collide and blow up." "She became worried," notes the psychiatrist, "'about all the collisions there might be up in outer space because of all of this indiscriminate sending up of satellites.' She felt, 'there is no planning and it might affect the natural order of things.'"[35]

The Outer Limits, of course, exacerbated such fears and did indeed suggest that earthling science could easily result in instability and disaster, as slow-witted humans ventured into a realm in which they had no business interfering. At the disembodied mercy of the "control voice," the audience could do nothing better but watch, powerless to intervene as any number of cosmic catastrophes befell the earth. Although viewers never actually see outer space in "The Premonition," it is space technology that opens this time rift, unlocking a hellish limbo that concretizes the terrifyingly abstract infinity of outer space by mapping it temporally onto the everyday world. Replicating the vast spatio-temporal rhythms of the heavens, the frozen air base becomes an expansive void where humans remain separated, like stars and planets, by unimaginable gulfs of time and space. From this realm of suspended animation, the "black oblivion" of the limbo being, the parents must watch helplessly as their daughter "speeds" at an uncannily slow pace toward her death in front of the runaway truck, her temporally and spatially dislocated tricycle as distant, imperiled, and helpless as the most remote Mercury capsule.

In a particularly vivid account of the impending oblivion of the early 1960s, this episode thus united two very different borders along the New Frontier: the infinitesimal yet potentially cataclysmic intricacies of the atom and the infinite expanses of outer space. Both the atom and outer space challenged Americans to imagine a fantastic terrain mapped by courageous scientists, powered by mysterious orbital mechanics, and somehow accessed through the equally mystifying workings of the television set. Between the spinning stars, planets, and galaxies of the universe existed a void beyond human imagination, a "final frontier" on a scale so vast as to be terrifying. Within the whirling protons and electrons of the atom, meanwhile, existed a power beyond human imagination, a destructive force so devastating that it was almost incomprehensible. In between these two perilous borders of "new frontier" science stood the American family, plagued by their own often unstable dynamics and woefully unprotected from these other forces by their feeble suburban homes. Vulnerable and withdrawn, they could nevertheless witness the continuing exploration of these often terrifying realms through their television sets.

All ends well in "The Premonition," as the encroachment of oblivion remains just that, a premonition. But even so, this episode demonstrates once again how frequently and often quite explicitly *The Outer Limits* disrupted the medium's characteristically self-congratulatory monologue on both the American family and the prospects of unlimited progress in American science and technology. *The Outer Limits* was remarkable, if for no other reason, by virtue of this consistent opposition to the new public celebration of the family, science, and technology that dominated the early 1960s. Playing on topical fears and anxieties that posed often tangible threats to the family during this period, *The Outer Limits* repeatedly sided with the alien's often cataclysmic critiques of the homogenizing inertia bred in American suburbia and the technological hubris bred in American laboratories. The series consistently implied that destruction and chaos lurked behind the gleaming facades of the new social and scientific order represented by television, and suggested that television itself, as a technology of cascading electrons, radioactive waves, invisible frequencies, distant transmissions, and other "strange" sciences was a direct conduit for the domestic and electronic oblivions occupying the public mind in the early part of the decade. Invading the home as a broadcast emanating from these more alienating encampments along the New Frontier, *The Outer Limits* confirmed that television was indeed an oblivion of sorts, or at the very least an eerie electronic presence hovering over a number of potential "vast wastelands" in 1960s America.

1. This humor is perhaps epitomized in the famous episode "Time Enough at Last," which featured Burgess Meredith as an overworked clerk and nervous bookworm who finds himself the sole survivor of a nuclear holocaust. He finds the library is still standing, and, with unlimited time to read, he sets out to enjoy the classics of literature, only to break his special prescription reading glasses.

2. Lynn Spigel, "From Domestic Space to Outer Space: The 1960s Fantastic Family Sit-Com," in *Close Encounters: Film, Feminism, and Science-Fiction*, ed. by Elizabeth Lyon, Constance Penley and Lynn Spigel (Minneapolis: University of Minnesota Press, 1991), 209.

3. "Haunted TV is Punished: Set with Face that Won't Go Away Must Stare at the Wall," *The New York Times*, 11 December 1953, 33.

4. "Face on TV Set Goes, Mystery Lingers On," *The New York Times*, 12 December 1953, 16. See also *Television Digest*, 12 December 1953, 11.

5. For a more complete account of this history, see Jeffrey Sconce, *Television Ghosts: A Cultural History of Electronic Presence in Telecommunications Technology* (Durham: Duke University Press, forthcoming).

6. During the 1910s and 1920s, serious debate took place within the scientific community over the prospects of contacting Mars and other worlds via wireless transmissions. Some scientists even explored the possibility of creating a "universal" code language with which to engage the Martians once the radio link was established. See H.W. and C. Wells Nieman, "What Shall We Say to Mars? A System for Opening Communication Despite the Absence of any Common Basis in Language," *Scientific American*, 20 March 1920, 312. For many years, intergalactic communication was seen to be a fantastic yet most logical application of radio technology (a legacy that continues today in NASA's SETI program). NASA's SETI program (Search for Extra-Terrestrial Intelligence) involves using radio telescopes to monitor the universe for intelligent radio transmissions.

7. The FCC's decision to require "click-stop" tuning in all American-made television sets combined with the industry's vigorous promotion of color TV made both UHF and color topics of public anticipation and discussion in the early sixties. In their own way, UHF and color presented new "dimensions" in broadcasting, an association encouraged by accounts of radio astronomers and commercial broadcasters battling for control over these bandwidths and frequencies. See D.S. Greenberg, "Radio Astronomy: TV's Rush for UHF Threatens Use of Channel," *Science*, 1 February 1963, 393; and D.S. Greenberg, "Radio Astronomy: FCC Proposes Compromise to Share Frequencies with UHF Broadcasters," *Science*, 12 April 1963, 164.

8. One commentator on Telstar wrote, "To get to know each other on a worldwide scale is the human race's most urgent need today; and this is where Telstar can help us." He continued, "It can make it possible for each section of the human race to become familiar with every other section's way of living; and, once this mutual familiarity is established, there is some hope that we may all become aware of the common humanity underlying the differences in our local manners and customs." See Arnold J. Toynbee, "A Message for Mankind from Telstar," *The New York Times Magazine*, 12 August 1962, 31. Also see Michael Curtin's essay in this volume.

9. "TV's Biggest Mystery," *TV Guide*, 30 April 1964, 23.

10. Curtis Fuller, "KLEE ... Still Calling," *Fate*, April 1964, 39.

11. Fuller, 40.

12. *The Outer Limits* was undoubtedly the medium's most vocal commentator on its own powers of discorporation and alienation. But so dominant was this theme that even within the narrative universe of *Star Trek*, the most utopian of all television's explorations into space, one episode featured a disembodied Captain Kirk dissolved and abandoned in the translucent energy stream of the transporter. Having been transformed into an other-dimensional ghost by this now most

the "outer limits" of oblivion

familiar technology for the discorporation and "telecasting" of human beings, Kirk's electronic body floats eerily across the mirrors, halls, and viewscreens of the Enterprise until his eventual rescue and reconstitution, a cogent reminder that even in the twenty-fourth century, television transmission would remain the most immediate gateway to the terrifying voids of the universe. See "The Tholian Web" episode, *Star Trek* (NBC). The discorporation, teleportation, and telecasting of matter were also central devices in science-fiction cinema of the 1950s and 1960s, most notably in *The Fly* (20th Century-Fox, 1958).

13. Lynn Spigel, *Make Room for TV* (Chicago: University of Chicago Press, 1992), 117.

14. Telstar, Telstar—Burning Bright," *Life*, 3 August 1962, 4.

15. "A Watch Truck is Watching You," *Life*, 25 September 1964.

16. Within the period, many psychologists explicitly defined the family in such disciplinary terms as "a process of reciprocal roles perceived, expected, and performed by family members." According to this model, the "happiness" of any given family was "assumed to be reflected in the extent to which roles are accepted and shared among its members." See A. R. Mangus, "Family Impacts on Mental Health," *Marriage and Family Living* (August 1957): 261.

17. Mary Beth Haralovich, "Sit-coms and Suburbs: Positioning the 1950s Homemaker," in *Private Screenings: Television and the Female Consumer*, ed. by Lynn Spigel and Denise Mann (Minneapolis: University of Minnesota Press, 1992), 111.

18. Elaine Tyler May, *Homeward Bound: American Families in the Cold War Era* (New York: Basic Books, 1988), 36.

19. Harold Sampson, Sheldon L. Messinger, and Robert Towne, *Schizophrenic Women: Studies in Marital Crisis* (New York: Atherton Press, 1964), 21, 128.

20. Carol A. B. Warren, *Madwives: Schizophrenic Women in the 1950s* (New Brunswick: Rutgers University Press, 1991), 58.

21. Warren, 58.

22. Warren, 58.

23. Sampson, et. al., 158.

24. Preceding this broadcast, an article entitled "TV Transmission on Laser Beam Demonstrated by North American" appeared in *Aviation Weekly*, 18 March 1963, 83.

25. Psychological studies of the period argued that a married woman's sense of self-worth was most often bound to their "feminine" role of housekeeper and care-provider. See Robert S. Weiss and Nancy Morse Samelson, "Social Roles of American Women: Their Contribution to a Sense of Usefulness and Importance," *Marriage and Family Living* (November 1958): 358–366,

26. Keith Laumer, "The Walls," in *Nine by Laumer* (New York: Doubleday, 1967), 67-69.

27. Spigel, "From Domestic Space to Outer Space," 214.

28. "It Better Be Good," *Newsweek*, 9 May 1955, 84.

29. "Mouse at Yucca Flat: Televising Atomic Bomb Test," *Newsweek*, 16 May 1955, 63.

30. See "Victims at Yucca Flats: Mannequins," *Life*, 16 May 1955, 58; and "Close-up to the Blast," *Life*, 30 May 1955, 39–42.

31. R. J. Kerry, "Phobia of Outer Space," *Journal of Mental Science*, Vol. 106. (1960): 1386.

32. Kerry, *Phobia of Outer Space*, 1386.

33. Kerry, *Phobia of Outer Space*, 1386.

34. Kerry, *Phobia of Outer Space*, 1386.

35. Kerry, *Phobia of Outer Space*, 1386.

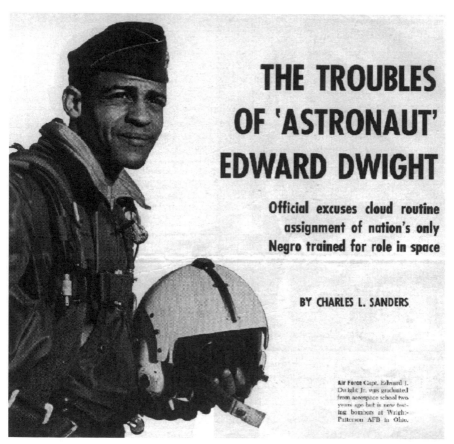

THE TROUBLES OF 'ASTRONAUT' EDWARD DWIGHT

Official excuses cloud routine assignment of nation's only Negro trained for role in space

BY CHARLES L. SANDERS

Air Force Capt. Edward J. Dwight Jr. was graduated from aerospace school two years ago but is now testing bombers at Wright-Patterson AFB in Ohio.

Ebony, June 1965

white flight

lynn spigel

In 1962, as a companion piece to its cave-toon family comedy *The Flintstones*, ABC aired Hanna-Barbera's *The Jetsons*. George, his son Elroy, daughter Judy, and Jane his wife were shown in the bouncy credit sequence riding their family rocket-sedan around an intergalactic freeway system. The Jetsons were not the only suburban TV family to live in—or be lost in—space, but they did give new meaning to the '50s migrations known as "white flight" in which white people moved from the problems and expense of urban America to create all white communities in the mass-produced suburbs. Now in the 1960s, as Civil Rights pressed for integration in suburban towns, whites found another "crabgrass frontier"—a place where no man or woman of any color had gone before and, if NASA could help it, ever would.

Indeed, like the red-line zoning laws and patriarchal family life experienced in the mass-produced suburbs, the space race was predicated on racist and sexist barriers that effectively grounded "racially" marked Americans and women in general. This is especially paradoxical given the fact that space exploration was conducted in the name of democracy and a 1960s version of multiculturalism best encapsulated by Gene Roddenberry's *Star Trek*. After the Soviet launching of Sputnik in 1957, and the subsequent establishment of the National Aeronautics and Space Administration (NASA) in 1958, U.S. energies in space were fueled by the language of freedom and the famous "peaceful uses of space" ethos, even while the development of space technology was always rooted in the colonialist will toward sovereign power —not only over nations—but symbolically over space itself (as the American flag planted on the moon reminds us).

Paradoxically too, like radio and television before it, space technologies (both rockets and communication satellites) were developed for the ambiguous purpose of military domination and international communication, both of which were often rhetorically positioned in terms of humanist understanding among the people of the world. But as Michael Curtin demonstrates, the utopian rhetoric of the Free World and the global free flow of information was by all accounts a means by which the U.S. government asserted its dominance as a superpower over other nations, attempting to win worldwide consent for the American (as opposed to Communist) way abroad.[1] In other words, as Donna Haraway has argued, in the postwar world of global capitalism, communication—in addition to and even more typically than the threat of overt military aggression— has served as a tool for domination.[2] Power over the hardware (the satellites) and the software (the technical, verbal, and visual language used to depict outer space) promised to make America a world center. For the Kennedy administration, which typically positioned the U.S. investment in space in ideological rather than scientific/military terms, television coverage of the space race provided a central tool for communicating ideas about "peace" and "democracy" that were often strategically linked to America's global supremacy.

Kennedy, for example, demonstrated his keen interest in the TV medium in his May 8, 1961 address to the National Association of Broadcasters (NAB), which took place one week after America's first space flight. At a time when Kennedy faced Congressional resistance to the enormous amount of tax dollars he had poured into space, this speech was clearly meant to convince people of the symbolic importance of space travel for beating the Russians in the Cold War. The written script contains the following comments:

> Last week millions of men and women throughout the free world felt first relief, and then elation, as Alan Shepard successfully completed America's first flight into space. This flight was not as spectacular as that which the Soviet Union conducted a few weeks ago. Our astronaut did not go as far, or as high. We

did not put a man into orbit and we did not "catch up with the Russians." But nevertheless this flight was a great achievement and, in a very real sense, the manner of the flight was a tribute to the strength of a free society.

For no secrecy surrounded the launching of our first astronaut. We did not conceal the anxious hours of waiting, the dangers of uncertain adventure, the possibilities of failure. On the contrary, the members of your association and the members of the press carried the news of each moment of tension and triumph to an anxious world.[3]

While probably intending to flatter his audience of broadcasters, Kennedy also knew that his speech was being filmed by television news cameras, and thus would be heard by a nationwide audience. Here as elsewhere, he spoke less about space technology and its projection of Americans into orbit than he did about communication technology—especially television—and its projection of America's national image. Indicative of Kennedy's TV-savvy is the fact that he improvised on the written speech cited above, adding the following introductory comments when he delivered it at the NAB meeting: "Ladies and Gentleman, we have with us today the nation's number 1 television performer who, I think, last Friday morning secured the largest rating of any morning show in recent history."[4] Kennedy thus immediately understood that television was a key tool for selling the country on space exploration, and importantly too, for selling the world on America.

What interests me in the following pages is the cultural colonialism at the heart of the space race, especially as it was communicated through television and other popular media. This colonialist fantasy—which I call "white flight"— existed on two levels. On the one hand, the fantasy of white flight was exhibited by the federal government's Cold War strategies to "contain" communism abroad. On the other hand, this fantasy can be seen at the level of everyday life in white America with its attempts to preserve racial segregation and female subordination at home. At its racist extreme, and according to NASA's Associate Administrator Robert C. Seamans, Jr., this colonialist fantasy was expressed by some overzealous "space cadets" as a plan for "settling our surplus populations on the planets."[5] (And note that the idea that space could be used as a place for relocating African Americans was voiced in popular culture at least since the late nineteenth century.)[6] More typically, however, by the postwar era the racism of the space race took the form of *The Jetsons'* dream for expanding white suburbia and its middle-class, consumer-oriented family life into the reaches of outer space.

However, I am concerned not only with the sexism, racism, and xenophobic nationalism that was exhibited on television's coverage of outer space, but also with the enormous amount of social criticism that the space race and televised images of it generated. I am especially interested in the way that groups who were excluded from space travel—especially African Americans and women of all colors—challenged the racist and sexist logic of the "giant leap for mankind." And finally, I am concerned with the way this colonialist fantasy, as well as the critical perspectives on it, were voiced on television and in other popular media.

from wasteland to new frontier

In Cold War America, the ideology of separate but mutually supportive public and private spheres served as a central foundational myth for the nation.[7] The state won the consent of the people by suggesting that government intervention and policy-making would protect the democratic freedoms of American citizens, especially their private homes and families. All sorts of government policies—from the anticommunist blacklisting tactics of the House UnAmerican Activities Committee to the segregationist zoning laws crafted by the Federal Housing Administration—were conducted in the name of democracy and the citizen's rights. However, these policies did not protect the rights of all Americans. Instead, they were based on a politics of suspicion in which the "citizen" was most typically figured as the white middle-class family in need of protection from threatening forces of communist foreigners and domestic "others."

As a medium that promised to bring the world inside the home, television played a key role in mediating the relationship between public and private spheres. As I have detailed elsewhere, after WWII, television was marketed as a new domestic technology that would strengthen family ties among its target consumers—the white middle class—and create demand for other consumer durables through national advertising. In another sense, however, television technology was also a tool used for world domination—not only through its representational regime of news and entertainment images that supported the American way and spread the fear of communism—but also through the research and development arms of companies like RCA that were busy building satellites that could survey populations across the globe. In these terms, it is not surprising that numerous television executives from RCA president David Sarnoff to NBC executive Sylvester Pat Weaver argued that the new medium was a key instrument through which the world might be kept safe for democracy—both at home and abroad.[8] Again, however, democracy in such statements typically meant the preservation of a narrowly defined and exclusive form of social life—the white nuclear family.

Over the course of the 1950s, however, citizen groups, critics and government officials began to worry that television might actually threaten the family, and thus the nation. Fears that the new medium might destroy family values by, for example, ushering in "blue" humor or promoting racial intermixing, were voiced at Congressional hearings in the early 1950s.[9] By the end of the decade, disappointment with commercial television culminated in the public hearings around the quiz show scandals in which producers and sponsors were charged with giving answers to contestants before the shows. Responding in part to critics who blamed regulators for allowing the airwaves to be controlled by sponsors, Federal Communications Commissioner Newton Minow called television a "vast wasteland" in his 1961 address to the National Association of Broadcasters. Despite the fact that commercial television remained vastly popular with the American public, the "vast wasteland," and its dismissal of popular television as the end of civilization, became the official terms for speaking about the medium among critics, regulators, educators, artists, and citizen groups.

During the same years, the international and militaristic developlement of satellite technology also resulted in public shame. In 1957, Americans witnessed the most stunning technological embarrassment of the times when the Russians beat the U.S. into space with Sputnik. Cold War logic was predicated upon America's ability to prevail in all technological endeavors, especially those associated with national security. Thus, the advent of a Russian rocket soaring into orbit sharply contrasted with previous conventions for representing American relations with the Soviets. Sputnik quickly became a media panic, and two months later when America's own rocket, Vanguard I, fell to the ground, the media called it such derisive names as "Flopnik," "Kaputnik," and "Stayputnik."[10]

These disappointments with the nation's technological agenda dovetailed with growing anxieties about suburbia and middle-class ideals. In 1957, the same year as Sputnik, the stock market underwent its first major slide of the decade. Over the course of the 1950s, private debt increased from $73 billion to $196 billion. Anxieties over a sagging economy and consumer debt mingled with related anxieties about mass-produced suburbs. Sociologists, activists, and journalists criticized suburbia's ethos of overconsumption, its rigid gender roles for men and women, its penchant for conformism and homogeneity.[11] Such concerns were also voiced in popular fiction. Even television sitcoms noted for their idealized portrayals of family life included episodes that revolved around the bitter anxieties of characters who could not cope with roles they were expected to assume in their domestic life. For example, an episode of *Father Knows Best* entitled "Margaret's Vacation" features housewife Maragret fed up with her family and bent on becoming a beatnik.

At the dawn of the 1960s, President Kennedy's "New Frontier" addressed

51

such anxieties by presenting a sense of a better future. While the New Frontier was not a total ideological break with the 1950s, it negotiated '50s ideals of consumerism and suburban family life with a new image of citizenship. Rather than the happy homebody of Eisenhower America, this New Frontiersman was an active hero who took an interest in the traditionally "masculine" world of science, physical fitness, and international intrigue. In turn, he would preserve traditional values by protecting his home (both his family and his nation) against threatening outside forces.

The reigning symbolism of the New Frontier was, of course, space travel and its presentation of heroic, physically fit young men bound for interplanetary glory. NASA packaged the Mercury and Apollo astronauts as Hollywood packaged stars, with public relations campaigns in all regions of the country and national media coverage.

It is, of course, difficult to say how much this cultural symbolism actually resonated with people back on earth. For example, a 1960 nationwide survey in *Look* suggested that for some Americans the space race hardly mattered at all. As one Milwaukee woman confided, "We are pretty far removed from space here on 71st Street." And "The chief worry of a lumber dealer in South Dakota," *Look* reported, "was 'having only one channel to watch on TV.'" Above all, *Look* suggested, the central concerns of most Americans were the home and family. Still, here as elsewhere, space remained a popular way to transform the doldrums of national complacency and sell the public on a sense of the future. *Look* called the issue "Soaring into the Sixties," and on its cover it displayed a rocket blasting off into the sky.[12] Indeed, the space race seems most important for its ability to provide a new symbolic future—different from Eisenhower's future (which he called the "New Look") and yet capable of retaining its most sentimentalized feature, the white nuclear family.

At a time when television was condemned as a "vast wasteland," this forward thrusting journey into space had a special meaning for network executives who wanted to prove that despite their commerical bottom line, they too had a public, civic-minded, even heroic purpose.[13] In the early 1960s, all three networks expanded their news shows from fifteen minutes to a half hour and also added documentary series to their line-ups. This increased attention to news and documentary provided a generic climate in which the dramatic adventures in outer space could take off. Even after Kennedy's assassination, and the Johnson administration's more pro-business approach to broadcast regulation, live news coverage of space travel continued up through the end of the decade, capped off by the most watched program to date in TV history, the Moon Landing.

Indeed, from the outset, TV executives found that space travel was not only good for the American future, but more importantly from their point of view, it was a commercial success. In 1962, the A.C. Nielsen rating service estimated that the average home was tuned-in for 5 hours and 15 minutes of the 10 hour coverage of John Glenn's orbital flight on February 20, 1962. This was, according to A.C. Nielsen, "by far the largest audience ever tuned to daytime TV"; even at its "low" moments the program reached "5 million more homes than typically tuned to the highest-rated network [prime-time] program, WAGON TRAIN."[14] Presumably, the public's fascination with the new frontier had far surpassed its passion for the old.

from suburb to space-burb

As the huge daytime ratings for outer space suggest, television and other popular media especially tried to make space appealing to a family audience. In this regard, the "documentary" coverage of the space race gave way to an intensive exploration of spectacularized family life with astronaut stars and their wives appearing on the airwaves, in newspapers, and on the covers of national consumer magazines. In these media spectacles, ideals of suburban domesticity and the fantastic voyage to outer space were intricately bound together.

Television news coverage of the launchings often merged family and national values. Perhaps because the coverage used the relatively tedious "talking head" format and presented hours of live footage that tracked uneventful technical preparations, newscasters often spiced up the shows by interviewing astronaut families. And insofar as these newscasts disrupted the daytime line-up of soaps and other "women's genres," the use of family iconography must have seemed a natural choice.

In addition to astronaut profiles, newscasters interviewed ordinary American families. For example, during the launching of Apollo 11, NBC newscasters interviewed families camped out on the freeway waiting to see the take off. When asked by a newscaster if he had ever experienced anything so exciting, one man likened this day to his wedding. A CBS news documentary entitled "A Day in the Life of the United States" and produced on the occasion of the Moon Landing was even more explicit in its use of the family as a narrative vehicle through which to communicate ideas about space travel. Here, newscaster Charles Kuralt (famous for his "on the road" news segments) travelled across the country in a quest to discover what Americans were doing on this historic day. At the outset Kuralt told the audience, "Family life is the most common thing Americans did on July 20th 1969," and the documentary went on to show the multitude of family lifestyles across the fifty states. The program in fact becomes quite self-reflexive about the fact that most of these families aren't terribly interested in the news coverage of Apollo 11. One man's comments even imply that he finds the coverage disappointing because he reads the news through the genre expectations of action/adventure. Commenting on how boring the Moon Landing was, he says, "You got a lot of suspense going for you when they get there . . . and then it's a big nothing." Presumably, the producers of this CBS News special thought something could be made of this "big nothing" by turning the public event of the Moon Landing into a document of family life. As this case illustrates, the nation's public agenda was intimately connected to and communicated through the private world of family life.

The discursive merger of family life and outer space that television news promoted was reinforced by other media, especially the popular weeklies. Much as Wendy Kozel suggests in her study of *Life* magazine in Cold War America, sentimental images of the family served to legitimate reigning public policies, while stories about public policies served to naturalize the idea that the white middle-class nuclear family was the only legitimate, and certainly most desirable, form of family relations.[15] *Life* 's portraits of astronauts follow this logic; the goals of NASA are sentimentalized through images of astronaut families, while the nuclear family is portrayed as a progressive ideal for all Americans who (presumably) want to live as the astronauts do.

In these profiles, *Life* presented technical information about space science alongside multi-page spreads depicting family portraits of the astronauts. The May 18, 1962 issue pictures Scott Carpenter with his wife Rene on the cover, while the inside photos showed them as the ideal American family: playing at home, enjoying a family vacation, and finally in the last pages of the essay, saying their farewells just before the space flight. In this way, the photographic narrative sequence suggested that Scott Carpenter's flight to the moon was one more in a series of "everyday" family activities.[16]

In a practical sense, this essay format allowed the magazines to appeal to diverse audiences because it conveyed technical, scientific information in the popular format of family drama. Discussions of domesticity made space familiar, offering a down-to-earth context for the often abstract reasoning behind space flights. When astronaut John Young went to space in 1965, this merger of science and domesticity was taken to its logical extreme. *Life* reported his flight by telling the story of his wife and children, who witnessed the event on television while sitting in their suburban home:

> In John Young's home outside Houston, the astronaut's family sits at the TV set as the seconds crawl toward launch time. Barbara Young fidgets, Sandy fiddles with a bit of string and Johnny,

still getting over chicken pox, stares unsmiling at the screen. At
lift off Mrs. Young hugs Sandy. "Fantastic," she crows ... as ship
soars skyward.[17]

The accompanying photographs show the Young family sitting before their
television set, much as other Americans would have done that day. Here as
elsewhere, the "fantastic" is communicated through the domestic, and space
technology is itself mediated through the more familial technology of
television.

Space scientists often used this same rhetorical strategy when trying to
explain their work to the public. In 1958, the same year that NASA was
formed, America's premiere space scientist Dr. Wernher von Braun described
the hardware of space rocketry through metaphors of domesticity. Von
Braun told *Life* that "missile building is much like interior decorating. Once
you put it all together you may see in a flash it's a mistake—the draperies
don't go with the slip covers. The same is true of missiles." The following
year, an episode of *CBS Reports* entitled "The Space Lag: Can Democracy Compete?" interviewed the Chief of the ICBM Atlas missile project, Dr. Simon
Rimeau, who boasted about his missile saying, "Every mother brags about his
own child." (Presumably, according to this odd use of pronouns, the mother
of invention was male). The scientist's use of domestic metaphors persisted
into the next decade. In 1969, just before Apollo 11's famous voyage, NASA
engineer John C. Houbolt told *Life* that a "rendezvous around the moon was
like being in a living room."[18]

To be sure, this fantasy of domesticated space travel was not all that new. It
can be seen as an outgrowth of what cultural theorist Raymond Williams
called "mobile privatization"—or the fantasy of going somewhere while
remaining in the safe locale of the home.[19] This fantasy, Williams tells us, was
the product of a particular historical conjuncture in the late nineteenth century which saw the rise of the private family home in the first suburban areas
and the simultaneous growth of communications technologies that linked
the private home to urban/industrial centers. Communication technologies
have long provided this sense of mobile privatization, and in the postwar
years television materialized these fantasies.

Since the 1920s, modernist designs for living—including housing, furniture, and appliance design—were fashioned on the related idea of what
might be called "privatized mobility." Streamlined and aerodynamic styles
presented a sense of the cruise ship or airplane in the context of domesticity.
In the postwar period, however, such designs became available at a mass market level and they were associated foremost with space travel. Moreover, they
took on a postmodern dimension as they were integrated firmly, and even in

a cartoonish way, into the material culture of everyday life in suburbia rather than simply exhibited in museums, movies, or uppercrust homes. Outer-space facades turned family restaurants and suburban car washes into fantastic adventures. To borrow Mike Featherstone's phrase, these space-age make-overs added up to an "aesthetization of everyday life," in this case predicated on the fantastic possibility of space travel as a new form of family and community relations, exclusively available to the white middle class.[20]

Indeed, in the postwar period, space travel served to redesign the suburban family ideal in significant ways. Advertisers turned to space imagery in attempts to create new consumer demand. The Ford corporation, for example, showed a little boy dressed in a space suit, exploring his brand new Fairlane family sedan and telling consumers that "Ford interiors are ... out of this world." Once the car was purchased, families could expect to take exciting vacations with space age themes.[21] This was suggested most emphatically in 1955 at Disneyland in a section of the theme park known as Tomorrowland. A 1958 article in *Look* showed a more low-tech variation on the space age theme vacation; it depicted a family relaxing on Florida's Cocoa Beach and watching for "imminent missile launchings" as they "take in the sun and sights at the same time."[22]

Domestic space and chores were also refashioned. Women's home magazines included recipes for "blast-off" space cakes, promoted "space-age homes," and suggested building "space platforms" instead of porches.[23] Furniture companies offered space-age-inspired kitchen dinettes that played with earlier modernist furniture designs. For example, a 1969 ad for Style Setter dinettes shows a couple on the moon dressed in NASA space suits, embracing each other as they sit at the table in their space-ship inspired bucket seat chairs (the NASA landing capsule was in the background). The caption read, "At Home in Any Atmosphere."[24]

Television sets were also advertised through appeals to outer space. In 1966, RCA offered its "Color TV custom-engineered the Space Age way." [25] The metaphor of space travel was even more intricately connected to the new mode of spectatorship offered by mini-portables that hit the market in 1966. Ads for these sets promised consumers a new mobile relation to television in the home, one that spoke to a general cultural fascination with travel, not only to outer space but in and out of domestic space as well. A 1966 issue of *TV Guide*, advertising mini-portables like the Westinghouse "Jet Set," played with the linguistic pun between aero-space science and new "swinger" lifestyles for women. The cover shows a woman literally running towards the reader as if she is on a runway. Dressed in orange mini-suit, white shoes, white gloves, and British Bobby hat (which ambiguously looks like a space helmet), she is holding a mini-portable in her outstretched hand, as if it were a purse. This woman and her TV purse signal a new look for female spectators in the space age, one that presents them not as homebodies in family scenes as most 1950s TV ads had done, but rather as people on the go. Still, despite all the space age imagery that surrounds her, this female spectator, with her TV purse, seems more likely to be going to the mall than to the moon. [26]

defamiliarizing family tv

Although the space age is probably more notable for changes in cultural style than it is for transitions in social practice, it did usher in some new possiblities for speaking about social unrest. For example, despite their continued representation as space age consumers, women did imagine themselves in more productive roles as scientists. Women wrote repeatedly to President Kennedy, asking why they were not part of the Mercury crew. The woman question also made itself felt in the same popular weeklies that promoted NASA's male agenda. In 1960, *Look*'s cover story asked, "Should A Girl Be First In Space?" The article went on to inform readers that while "some 2,000 American women, mostly teenagers, have volunteered for space flight," they were subject to sexism at NASA. "Women," the article went on, "have more brains and stamina per pound than men." As this article suggests, while popular culture typically privileged dominant views, it was not univocal. It did at times serve as a venue for a series of challenges to the status-quo. However, it should be noted that these challenges were typically muted. For example, in the case of this article, the writer concludes the first woman in space would be "married," possibly even the "scientist-wife of a pilot engineer."[27]

While explicit (if muted) critiques of space science were voiced in popular media, the space race also gave way to more implicit expressions of social unrest that emerged symptomatically in material culture and entertainment media. At this implicit symptomatic level, space iconography often disrupted the sentimentalized iconography of family life that had been so integral to twentieth-century visual culture. As in the case of *The Jetsons*, the space age family was often represented in ways that made the traditional rules of family life seem oddly out of step with the times.

57

This "time out of joint" sensibility is an effect of the merger of science fiction with genres (from portraiture to melodrama to situation comedy) that take the family as a central topic. As Fredric Jameson has argued, science fiction tends less to imagine the future than to "defamiliarize and restructure our experience of our own present."[28] While Jameson is speaking about literature and film, we can apply the same rule to other forms of material culture, including the community and domestic spaces of the suburbs. The redecoration of suburbia with outer-space architecture and space age dinettes suggests a profound reorganization of the familiar through the strange.

On television's fiction formats, representations of the space race often evoked this kind of defamiliarization. A perfect example is an episode from the syndicated series *Men Into Space*, which was produced from 1959 to 1960 and funded in part by the Defense Department. The episode entitled "First Woman on the Moon" tells the story of Renza Hale and her astronaut husband Joe who, upon the orders of his space department bosses, invites her to travel to the moon. Once Renza is on the moon, however, problems ensue. Renza is bored because the men won't let her leave the rocket, and her culinary talents go to waste since she can't get the hang of anti-gravity cooking. One night, after her Yorkshire pudding is too tough, Renza breaks down. The next morning, she ventures out onto the lunar landscape without informing the crew. After a panicked search, Joe is furious and in a scolding tone tells his wife, "Your place is on earth at home where I know you're safe." In this episode, tropes of science fiction fantasy allow for an exposition of anxieties that women faced in more everyday circumstances. This program turns out to be a thinly veiled exploration of domesticity and the gendered division of spheres that so pervaded ideas about women's place in the 1950s.

Like Captain and Renza Hale, numerous TV families were renegotiating their roles through the fantastic possibilities of space science. Programs such as *My Favorite Martian*, *It's About Time* , and *I Dream of Jeannie* belonged to a genre cycle that merged the 1950s suburban family sitcom with science fiction fantasy (or sometimes, as in the case of *The Munsters*, horror).[29] These fantastic family sitcoms used the conventional form of the domestic comedy—its gender conflicts, its middle-class suburban settings, its basic plot structure— but filled the form with inappropriate content so that, for example, witches and robots took the place of the dutiful wife. Increasingly over the 1960s, these programs (along with broken family sitcoms like *My Three Sons*) accounted for the mainstay of the genre while the classic nuclear family suburban sitcoms had virtually disappeared by 1966.

On the one hand, it might be argued that fantastic sitcoms like *Bewitched* or *I Dream of Jeannie* were simply more land-fill in the wasteland. Even worse, they often seemed to celebrate the sexism of suburbia by respectively featuring a witch and a genie who traded in their powers to live the life of dutiful wives and lovers. On the other hand, however, the collision of two unlikely forms also presented viewers with the possibility of thinking about the social constraints of suburban life. Indeed, these programs can be seen to give rise to the moment of "hesitation" which Tzvetan Todorov identifies as the "fantastic."[30] According to Todorov's account, the fantastic makes the reader uncertain about the status of the text. The story calls its own conventions of representation into question and makes the reader wonder whether the narrative situation is possible at all. In the fantastic family sitcom, the elements called into question are not the supernatural elements of the story (we are never made to question whether genies or Martians exist). Rather, the moment of hesitation takes place in the realm of the natural. We are, in other words, made to question the "naturalness" of middle-class suburban ideals, especially as those ideals had previously been communicated through the genre conventions of classic suburban sitcoms such as *The Adventures of Ozzie and Harriet* or *The Donna Reed Show*.

My Favorite Martian, for example, was premised on the idea of a Martian who landed in the yard of a young man's suburban home. The Martian took on the double identity of earthling Uncle Martin, moved in with the young man, and hid his true Martian self from suspicious folks around the neighborhood. This premise allowed not only for a comedic exploration of the social conformity demanded in suburban neighborhoods, it more specifically can be seen as a program that worked through nagging anxieties about bachelors, especially bachelors who lived with other men. Uncle Martin was constantly thwarting the advances of his overzealous land-lady, who could not understand why he preferred bachelorhood to her womanly ways.

As a companion piece for *My Favorite Martian's* homophobic nervousness about single men in suburbia, *I Dream of Jeannie* presented anxieties about sex and the single girl. Based on the exploits of astronaut Tony Nelson, who finds a beautiful genie (named Jeannie) after crashing his rocket on a beach, this program also dealt with the closeted sexuality that suburban social conventions demanded. When Tony brings Jeannie back to his suburban home, he has to hide his live-in supernatural girlfriend from the boys at NASA. But while he tries to literally bottle up Jeannie's powers, she typically escapes the rational logics of masculine science by using her feminine supernatural power to wreak havoc at home and at the space lab. And unlike NASA, which spends billions to get men up to the moon, Jeannie is able to wish her way there in a matter of seconds. The program thus functions as a contradictory mix of contemporary discourses on swinging singles (with Jeannie as the ultimate playmate) and the emerging discourses of women's liberation (with Jeannie as a superpowerful woman).

Although, of course, my analysis of these shows is rooted in the critical perspectives of the 1990s, its seems likely that audiences at the time were primed to interpret these sitcoms in similar ways, especially when considered in terms of the "intertext" surrounding them. This intertext included a growing climate of popular and academic television criticism that displayed a penchant for reading television parodically and allegorically.

On the popular front, magazines and comic strips aimed at kids—especially *MAD*—made fun of television programming on a regular basis, encouraging the young generation to interpret television in a tongue in cheek way. In 1966, *MAD* presented a cartoon saga of the perfect American TV family, Oozie, Harried, Divot and Rickety Nilsen, who "lived completely and hermetically sealed off from reality." The story's opening panel showed Oozie comfortably reading his newspaper, which Harried had doctored up in order to soothe the tensions of the day. Harried stands grinning in the foreground of the panel, where she tells her housewife friend, "I cut out all the articles that might disturb him"; as proof of her deed we see large cut-out areas under headlines that read "Vietnam," "Laos," and "race riots." Nevertheless, Oozie complains to Harried of his action-packed day. "First," he drones, "I pulled the wrong cord on the Venetian blind.... Then Art Linkletter's House Party was preempted by a Space Shot.... It's been one thing after another."[31] As *MAD* so humorously suggested, the middle-class suburban sitcom was vastly out of sync with the problems of the nation. Indeed, its codes of realism (the bumbling but lovable dads, the perfect loving wives, the mundane storylines) were, by this time, codes of satire and parody.

While popular magazines like *MAD* encouraged audiences to read television programs through parody, intellectual and academic writers were keen on allegorical interpretations. In the 1960s, when critics like Leslie Fielder were first applying modes of literary criticism to popular culture, *Television Quarterly*, the journal of the National Academy of Television Arts and Sciences, was filled with allegorical readings of popular television series. Indeed, TV critics became increasingly intent on the kind of "double readings" through which the fantastic is often resolved; that is, the critics resolved the moment of hesitation caused by implausible narrative events by interpreting the entire story as a morality tale that spoke in symbolic ways of social reality.

Such parodic and allegorical readings were encouraged by television programming itself. The use of outer space as an allegory for racism and sexism in the suburbs was most explicit in a new breed of filmed anthology dramas that began appearing on the networks in the late 1950s. Using science fiction and horror, anthologies such as *The Twilight Zone* (1959–1965), *The Outer Limits* (1963–1965), and *Science Fiction Theater* (1955–1957) inverted the rules of their own genre by turning away from the anthology's roots in New York theater and towards the new intellectual science fiction literary scene populated by people like Frederick Pohl, Ray Bradbury, Harlan Ellison, and cyberpunk's much celebrated "father," Philip K. Dick.

Through thinly veiled allegories, these anthology series presented cautionary tales about racism and xenophobia in suburbia, played out (as in much science fiction of the times) through the figure of the alien.[32] *Science*

Fiction Theater's "The People From Planet Pecos" (1957) presented a space engineer whose suburban home was located next door to a family suspected of being from another planet. When his children ostracize the little girl, the engineer realizes the evils of his earthling prejudice. At a time when foreigners were often feared as potential communist threats, *The Twilight Zone's* "The Monsters on Maple Street" (1960) presented an unflattering picture of a suburban town where belligerent citizens suspected that there was a space alien in their midst and conducted a ruthless witch hunt. Three years later, *The Outer Limits* premier episode "The Gallaxy Being" (1963) showed how suburbanites demonized a kindly extraterrestrial whose only wish was to communicate peacefully with them. Such liberal cautionary tales about interplanetary race relations often included didactic narration that asked audiences to question the more familiar acts of racism and xenophobia (as well as other types of social exclusion) in their own everyday suburban towns. Moreover, this narration was sometimes literally embodied by a narrative figure—the host—who encouraged audiences to read the tale allegorically at the beginning of the show (Rod Serling of *The Twilight Zone* is the paradigmatic example here).[33]

In all of these ways, the space race provided for a dialectical process in which the familiar and the strange existed in tension. While documentary and news formats on television and in popular magazines often presented space as a new outpost for the suburban dream, other elements of popular culture actually spoke in critical ways of this colonial process, questioning (albeit through displaced forms of parody, allegory, and fantastic representations) the central ideologies at work in the middle-class suburban ideal.

outer space and inner cities

Although television spoke allegorically of racism, the white-bias of that medium during the period mitigated against a more direct discussion of the issues. Still, explicit concerns about racism in the space project did find expression in other venues, especially in media that catered to racialized groups. The most publically vocal of these groups were African Americans who often spoke out against the racist logics of the space race—and the country more generally—in their premier picture magazine, *Ebony*. Targeted at the black middle class, *Ebony* addressed the space race through the genre of "social problem" criticism rather than the adventure/quest narratives found in media aimed at whites. Its critique of outer space was often explicitly tied to a critique of suburban segregation and the plight of blacks in the inner cities. Indeed, African American critics often saw these issues to be directly related as they spoke out against government policies that poured tax dollars into space while refusing to adequately finance housing starts in inner cities.

Given NASA's notorious exclusion of racial minorities, it is not surprising that *Ebony* featured proud profiles of the few black men who were able to find positions in the aerospace industry. So too, the magazine often presented space travel as a compelling metaphor for racial progress, race pride, and liberation from the problems back on earth.

As in the white magazines (although much less often), outer space was portrayed as a new cultural style for black consumers. A 1965 cover story, "Fashions in Orbit," showed glamorous black models in space wear, proclaiming that "the era of the space hero is ushered into fashion . . . by . . . lightweight space helmets and white pants with lacing [that] capture packaged 'astronautical' look."[34] Advertisers also connnected space travel to family life. For example, Aetna life insurance advertised its family-oriented service by showing a close-up of a boy wearing a space helmet, implicitly promising that the insurance would provide a better future not only for the family but also for the race.[35]

While in many ways this use of space iconography was similar to its use in white middle-class magazines, *Ebony* was not simply mimicking white culture or just assimilating its values. Instead, its articulations between space travel and everyday life had some important differences from those found on network television or in the pages of *Life*.

As bell hooks has suggested, travel has always meant something different in the black community than it has in the white because black migrations and even everyday modes of transportation have typically been accompanied by acts of white terrorism.[36] In the period of the Civil Rights movement, the black community would most certainly have connected travel to the terrorism encountered by Rosa Parks and others on the bus system in the South.[37] When seen in terms of this legacy of racialized travel, it is no surprise that space travel meant different things in *Ebony* than it did in the venues of white popular culture. Those differences were especially registered in terms of the meaning of family life and the politics of housing in black and white America.

At a time when the Moynihan Report revitalized concerns about the broken family in the black community, the representation of space travel was often presented in the context of divorce and/or the racist notion that black men were irresponsible providers. Such notions ran through *Ebony*'s documentary coverage of the rise and fall of astronaut-candidate Edward J. Dwight. Much like the astronaut essays in *Life*, when *Ebony* first presented Col. Dwight, it used metaphors of suburban family life, showing him at home reading books to his children and wife. But when NASA dropped Dwight from the space program, *Ebony* reported this by focusing on the fact that Col. Dwight was also in the middle of a divorce. In this way, the African American broken family was ultimately connected to the black man's inability to serve as a symbol of heroic space travel. But unlike much of the white majority that would have blamed the black male for the whole incident, *Ebony* connected Dwight's divorce both to the "'anti-Negro' attitude and social ostracism the Dwights faced at [the] California base" and to the housing discrimination they experienced in the suburbs:

> In an effort to make a home for his wife and family, he tried to rent a good-sized house near Wright-Patterson AFB, instead of settling on one of the barrack-type housing projects set aside for military personnel. Despite his Air Force uniform and silver captain's bars, he faced the same problems as other Negroes seeking homes in white neighborhoods.
>
> Finally, a Catholic layman who had seen Dwight's picture on the cover of a Church publication offered to rent him a house in Huber Heights, a Dayton suburb. Soon after the Dwights moved in, the harassment began.... Shouts 'niggers go home!' met the family almost every day.... Not long thereafter, Dwight's marriage went on the rocks.[38]

This story, then, inverts the myth of the ideal, white, suburban space age family by presenting instead a failed black family whose demise is caused by discrimination both in the space program and in the white suburbs.

More generally, *Ebony* connected the space race to substandard housing in inner cities and rural towns as well as the various forms of housing discrimination blacks faced. African American critics often drew a direct relation between racism at NASA and racist government housing policies. They criticized Congress for pouring tax dollars into space while at the same time refusing to finance housing starts in inner cities and rural towns. In the March 1965 issue, when the magazine reported on the test blasts for the manned moon rocket that were taking place in northern Alabama, it told the story of the nearby town of Triana. The article explained:

> Just five miles from the George C. Marshall Space Flight Center at Hunstville, Triana belongs more to the ante-bellum South than the era of astronauts. It is far from space-age—a collection of ramshackle farmhouses scattered randomly around two churches and a restaurant. City hall is a renovated shack heated by a coal stove, and about the closest thing to recreation in Triana is the chance of sharing a few catfish from the sluggish Tennessee River. Ten minutes away scientists are plotting ways to conquer the universe. Triana does not even have its own water system.[39]

While *Ebony* often linked housing discrimination and poverty to the nation's misconceived goals in space, for some people of color space travel nevertheless did provide a source of inspiration from which to imagine a better life. For example, in 1962 a young girl named Rose Viega wrote to President Kennedy, telling him that she wanted to volunteer to be an astronaut so that her penniless father could "have something to brag about." She connected her wish for space travel to the problems her family suffered from housing discrimination back on earth:

> You see we can't find a place to live because of our complexion. We are hunched up in a two room apartment with an old lady friend of ours. There are six of us, my parents and my brother sleep on the floor, while my sister, the old lady, and myself sleep in the bed. I don't like to sleep comfortable while my parents are suffering on the hard floor. We call the number for the apartment and they say to come and look at it. But when we go, and they see us they have an excuse of saying it's all ready [sic] rented, or things like that. I think it's a pity for people to treat other people like this.[40]

For Rose Viega, the desire to travel to outer space was quite literally connected to her racially determined plight in the town of Plymouth, Massachusetts and her lack of decent housing there. If the suburban dream had passed her by, there was still hope in the newer utopian dream of space travel.[41] Despite the fact that NASA was fundamentally rooted in white male colonialism, the space race did provide a discursive context in which people like Rose Viega could speak out against the politics of housing in America.

"one small step for 'the man'"

The strains of racism and sexism that ran through the popular discourse on outer space in the early 1960s, as well as the challenges to it, culminated in television's hugest TV spectacle of the decade, the Moon Landing. Again, the opposition between outer space and inner cities was a running theme for critics in the black press who pointed out that while the space project was busy sending white men to the moon, housing projects were undermining the nature of African American life. *Ebony*, for example, reminded its readers that

> Especially to the nation's black poor, watching on unpaid-for television sets in shacks and slums, the countdowns, the blastoffs, the orbitings and landings had the other-worldly alieness—though not the drama—of a science fiction movie.

From Harlem to Watts, the first moon landing in July of last year
was viewed cynically as one small step for "The Man," and probably a giant step in the wrong direction for mankind.[42]

Such criticism was turned into an alternative form of black poetry by
singer-songwriter Gil Scott Heron. Most famous for his popular hit "The
Revolution Will Not Be Televised," Heron composed a song he called "Whitey
On the Moon," which detailed the urban poverty experienced by his "sister
Nel" who, according to the lyrics, was bitten by a rat in the ghetto and unable
to pay doctor bills. Thus, in the tradition of black protest for the space project, Heron points out the injustice of spending tax dollars on the moon
while people on earth can't afford proper housing or medical care.

This relationship between space travel and the racially determined "politics of dwelling" back on earth was nowhere better drawn than in the CBS
news special "A Day in the Life of the United States." As I noted earlier, this
special featured reporter Charles Kuralt who took to the road in a quest to
understand what Americans were doing and thinking on the day that the
Apollo crew landed on the moon. His cross-country voyage provided a
special glimpse into the geography of American everyday life, displaying the
way "families" were rooted and uprooted as NASA staked its flag on an alien
landscape.

Claiming that family life is the prime concern of most Americans, the
documentary begins with the birth of a little boy, and then shows families
boating, a mother serving breakfast, a family eating dinner while watching
the Apollo coverage, and another at a barbecue. Among his travels, Kuralt
visits a family in a small Montana town; he watches a Vietnam pilot and his
wife reunite at an air force base in San Francisco; he follows a family of
Yugoslavian immigrants arriving in New York, awestruck by the city; he goes
to Hawaii where he chats with "natives"; he visits a commune and points out
with irony that no one there can operate technology; and he goes to New
York City where he remarks, "A city is a machine and the city machine is
breaking down." The proposed reason for the urban break down was clarified
when he traveled to the inner reaches of a "slum's slum" in Chicago. There,
the cameras penetrated a barroom on Langly and 43rd street, gaping at
African Americans dancing and drinking "cheap wine" in a world unim-
pressed by the white man's greatest colonialist venture to date. Significantly,
in the era of the Moynihan Report, which perpetuated the notion that the
black man's lack of paternal responsibility was to blame for the welfare state,
this Chicago barroom was a decidedly impoverished and non-familial space, a
space quite unlike those seen in previous segments.

This segment was also the only one in which the white Charles Kuralt was substituted with George Foster, an "insider" black reporter who explained:

> We've been here since Jamestown. But we haven't cleared customs yet. Four hundred years of traveling, and it's been economy class all the way.... Some of my brothers live another culture, talk another language, and you gotta subtitle them like you'd translate the astronauts.... I can tell you this about July 1969 at 43rd and Langly in Chicago, Illinois. I can tell you that nobody there understood or even listened to the language of the moon shot. That man on the right with the rolled up *Chicago Times*, with the headlines about Apollo 11, he told me he bought that paper to look at the want ads....

Here, the discussion about race, urban poverty, and outer space was self-consciously expressed in terms of a break down of communication, a use of different language systems in black and white America (and the switch from white to black narrators drove this point home). Among these different languages were the separate and racialized metaphors used to describe national geography. In this documentary as elsewhere, the metaphorical links between outer space and white suburban family life were consistently set in opposition to the racialized inner city and its degraded "slum" housing that opened onto an equally degraded public sphere (or what this segment actually referred to as a "nigger bar").

This strange exploration of everyday life on the day of the Moon Landing presented a nation divided between rich and poor, citizen and cast-off, black and white, and these divisions all overdetermined the schisms between cities, suburbs, and rural towns. In this documentary as elsewhere, the metaphor of travel—whether interplanetary, international, or cross country—served as a vehicle for an investigation of American family life—or the lack thereof—in different types of communities. Indeed, despite the attempt to conquer an alien landscape, the trip to moon turned out to be a voyage home.

from outer space to cyberspace

By the end of the 1960s, American critics in the mainstream media had become more cynical about the trip to the moon. Some skeptics even suggested (and do to this day) that the Moon Landing never happened, but instead was a cheap TV trick, staged by cameras for an easily duped public. Although this conspiracy theory represented the extreme view, even the popular weeklies that had once presented astronauts as American heroes were taking the hard line. As an editorial in *Life* stated, "The first requirement for a sensible post-Apollo 11 program is that President Nixon decline to sign the sort of blank check for an all-out manned Mars landing that vocal space agency partisans are urging on him."[43]

Critics particularly lamented the decidedly unpoetic sentiments that resulted from the exploration of the final frontier. *Saturday Review* complained about an "overly colloquial" reporter who, "when the lunar module successfully fired the engine that lifted it from the moon's surface, cried out 'Oh boy! Hot diggity dog! Yes Sir!'" Even the astronauts had to admit their disappointment. Reflecting on their journeys in Apollo 8, astronauts Frank Borman, Jim Lovell, and Bill Anders clearly were at a loss for the kind of poetic language upon which high culture thrived. Borman admitted that while the moon was beautiful it was also "so desolate, so completely devoid of life. . . . Nothing but this great pockmarked lump of gray pumice." And while he hoped to find "secrets of creation," Lovell confided, "the moon was void. . . . " Anders apologized for making "a few poets angry" with his banal descriptions of the lunar landscape, but admitted nonetheless that "the long ride out to the moon was, frankly, a bit of a drag." [44]

Meanwhile, as if to announce a total reversal of cultural sensibilities, a 1970 issue of *Life* ran a cover story on "Inner Space" that explored the new fascination with genetic engineering—yet another science founded on the principle of forming a "master race," this time through the colonization of the human body as opposed to celestial ones.[45] Indeed, by 1970, the era of the space race was officially in decline, and the Nixon administration's budget cuts would cap off the process. While the fascination with outer space has persisted with such spectacles as the *Star Wars* films, the fan culture around *Star Trek*, the catastrophe coverage of the Challenger, and the nostalgic visions of *Apollo 13*, space voyage has never achieved the heights that it did in the 1960s.

Now, as fantasies of outer space give way to the newer concept of cyberspace, we no longer think in terms of physical transport to another world so much as we accept "virtual" realities as a substitute for the dangers of hard science. Today we speak of software rather than hardware, and most space technology is developed for the movement of data rather than people. Still, despite these changes, one thing remains hauntingly familiar. Like outer space before it, cyberspace is also being populated mostly by elites who can afford the technology, and its parameters are developed mostly in the research labs of the global communications industry. Although its uses vary, the fantasies to which it gives rise are circumscribed by the research labs, government decisions, and industrial/consumer uses that necessarily support its foundational myths. In addition, our modes of imagining and speaking about the future of these technologies are subject to the same discursive rules that governed fantasies of outer space, television, and virtually all the transportation and communication technologies before them.

Indeed, predictions for cyberspace sound remarkably similar to what James Carey and John Quirk have called the nineteenth-century "mythos of the electrical revolution" in which technology in and of itself was seen to determine a better future. But, as they also suggest, technology does not cause social change on its own. Instead, it is shaped by social decisions and cultural fantasies that create it in the first place. Moreover, the mythos of electrical revolution obscures the social power hierarchies of class, race, and gender that give some groups access to technology while leaving others out. The language and images used to imagine cyberspace in our nation include a clear preference for colonizing it with white middle-class family values—the target consumer in the minds of the industries that want to adapt it for marketing services like home shopping, banking, education, and commercial entertainment. Meanwhile, consumer magazines present the public with luxurious model homes full of state-of-the-art electronics. So, as numerous critics have suggested, it seems likely that Americans who cannot afford to buy into the constituent components of this high-tech dream house will find themselves somewhere in the information ghetto.

The potential for "red-lining" in cyberspace is therefore both global and domestic in scope. Although I do not mean to suggest that cyberspace is without a joyful potential, it does seem useful to think about how its conception of utopia might differ from the white flight fantasies that took us to the moon. For this reason, looking backward at the space project and its representations in popular culture is not only an important corrective to the nostalgic tales of a future once lived. It also provides a way to think about the relationship between the community spaces that organize our everyday lives and the imaginary places that new technologies offer (only some of us) now.

Notes

1. Michael Curtin, *Redeeming the Wasteland: Television Documentary and Cold War Politics* (New Brunswick: Rutgers University Press, 1995).
2. Donna Haraway, *Primate Visions: Gender, Race, and Nature in the World of Modern Science* (New York: Routledge, 1989).
3. Office of the White House Press Secretary, "The White House Address of the President to the Opening Session of the 39th Annual Convention of the National Association of Broadcasters, Draft of Speech," 9 January 1961–25 May 1961, President's Office Files/Speech Files, Box 34, p. 1, John Fitzgerald Kennedy Library, Boston (hereinafter referred to as JFK Library).
4. In a press release he added, "I must say I think the presence of Commander Shepard and also Mrs. Shepard who, I think, is—I must say—when I saw her on television, I had a great satisfaction as a fellow citizen." Indeed, the President knew that astronauts —and importantly too their wives—made for good

television. Immediate Press Release: "The White House, Address of the President to the Opening Session of the 39th Annual Convention of the National Association of Broadcasters," 8 May 1961, Box 84, President's Office Files: NASA, JFK Library. The improvised portion of the speech is on film and housed at the JFK Library under the title "JFK Accompanied by Shepard," NBC, 8 May 1961. From the film clip, which appears to be edited, it is not clear whether or not President Kennedy actually read any of the written speech verbatim, but his comments are generally in keeping with its overall message.

5. Robert C. Seamans, Jr. , "Space—Friendly or Hostile?," Address before the Richmond Chamber of Commerce, Richmond, Virginia, 12 January 1961, NASA Public Relations Files, 1, Wisconsin Center for Film and Television Research, Madison.

6. I am thinking specifically of a minstrel song I found in the Smithsonian sheet music collection that featured a black minstrel on the cover and told the story of Parson Brown who promised his black congregation to take them to a utopian community on the moon. But when they got there they found they'd been duped because the moon was not utopia. See Gussie Davis, "I Just Got a Message from Mars," 1896, Devincent Sheet Music Collection, Box 94: 300, Smithsonian Institute, Washington, D.C.

7. For an analysis of the relations between private and public agendas in Cold War America see especially Elaine Tyler May, *Homeward Bound: American Families in the Coldwar Era* (New York: Basic Books, 1988) .

8. For a further discussion see Lynn Spigel, *Make Room For TV: Television and the Family Ideal in Postwar America* (Chicago: University of Chicago Press, 1992).

9. See Spigel, *Make Room for TV.*

10. For a discussion of this media panic see Walter A. McDougall, . . . *the Heavens and the Earth: A Political History of the Space Age* (New York: Basic Books, 1985), 141–156. It is clear that the Kennedy administration was interested in the popular media's representation of NASA because the president's files contain clippings of cartoons on this subject which date from December 8th 1957 (two days after the Vanguard I failure, and before he took office) to March of 1960. Almost all of these cartoons derive humor out of making women the butt of the joke or else likening women's sexuality to rockets. For example, a cartoon from the January 10th 1960 issue of *The Denver Post* titled "Snow White and the Seven Astronauts" depicts Snow White as a dormant rocket lying in bed (with the words "U.S. Space Program" written on her dress) and the astronaut dwarfs trying, so to speak, to "get her up." See Cartoon Clippings, 8 December 1957–21 March 1960, Box 362: Folder: Space Program General, JFK Library.

11. Contemporary intellectual and popular critics of suburbia include Lewis Mumford, *The City in History* (New York: Harcourt Brace Jovanovich, 1961); John Keats, *The Crack in the Picture Window* (Boston: Houghton Mifflin, 1956); William H. Whyte, Jr. *The Organization Man* (Garden City, NY: Doubleday, 1956).

12. William Atwood, "How America Feels as We Enter the Soaring Sixties," *Look*, 5 January 1960, 11–15. This survey was commissioned by the Gallup company and supplemented by *Look*'s staff.

13. In addition to the quiz show scandals and Minow's "vast wasteland" speech, television's public image was also under scrutiny in the Senate's violence hearings of the early 1960s. See William Boddy, "Senator Dodd Goes to Hollywood: Investigating Video Violence," in this volume. For more on the FCC -network relation in the 1960s see James Baughman,

14. Erwin H. Ephron, A.C. Nielsen Company Press Release, "News Nielsen: 40 Million Homes Follow Telecast of First U.S. Orbital Flight," ca. 21 March 1962, White House Central Staff Files, Box 655: File 054, 1, JFK Library.

15. As Wendy Kovel argues in her study of *Life* magazine during the Cold War, news stories typically used the rhetoric of public and private spheres in ways that produced faith both in American foreign policy and in the middle-class family ideal.

Family portraits often worked to sentimentalize American aggression overseas, suggesting this aggression was justified because it protected American family values. At the same time, Kozel argues, these portraits worked to naturalize the idea that everyone in America lived in or wanted to live in patriarchal nuclear family arrangements. While she does not discuss the space race specifically, Kozel's insights are germane to this case as well. See her *Life's America* (Philadelphia: Temple University Press, 1994).

16. Loudon Wainwright, "Comes a Quiet Man to Ride Aurora 7," *Life*, 18 May 1961, 32–41.

17. Miguel Acoca, "He's On His Way.... And It Couldn't Be Prettier," *Life*, 2 April 1965, 36–37.

18. "The Seer of Space," *Life*, 18 November 1957, 134–135; "How An Idea that No One Wanted Grew UP to Be the LEM," *Life*, 14 March 1969, 22.

19. Raymond Williams, *Television: Technology and Cultural Form* (Hanover, CT: Wesleyan University Press, 1992), 20–21.

20. Mike Featherstone, "Postmodernism and the Aestheticization of Everyday Life," *Modernity and Identity*, Scott Lash and Jonathan Friedman, eds. (Oxford: Blackwell, 1992), 265–90.

21. *Life*, 24 May 1963, 54–55.

22. "The Strange Boom at Cocoa Beach," *Look*, 24 June 1958, 24.

23. *American Home,* September 1964, p. 54; *American Home,* December 1962, 121; *House Beautiful,* June 1963, 129–130.

24. *Good Housekeeping,* September 1969, p. 232.

25. *The New York Times Magazine,* 1 May 1966, sec. VI, 77.

26. "TV Set Buyers' Guide," *TV Guide,* 18–24 September 1966, cover and insert.

27. "Should A Girl Be First In Space?" *Look,* 2 February 1960, 112–117.

28. Fredric Jameson, "Progress vs. Utopia: Or Can We Imagine The Future?" *Science Fiction Studies* 9:27 (1982), 151.

29. For more on this see Lynn Spigel, "From Domestic Space to Outer Space: The 1960s Fantastic Family Sitcom," *Close Encounters: Film, Feminism, and Science Fiction,* ed. Constance Penley, Elizabeth Lyon, Lynn Spigel, and Janet Bergsrom (Minneapolis: University of Minnesota Press, 1991), 205–235.

30. Tzvetan Todorov, *The Fantastic: A Structural Approach to A Literary Genre,* trans. Richard Howard (Ithaca, NY: Cornell University Press, 1970).

31. Mort Drucker and Stan Hart, "The Nilson Family," *MAD*, January 1966, 13.

32. Jeffrey Sconce discusses the representation of suburbia and its connections to outer space in his essay on the *The Outer Limits* in this volume. His readings of the programs foreground their allegorical critiques of rigid gender roles in the suburbs.

33. In 1967, *Star Trek* picked up the allegorical story-telling practices of these early anthology programs, presenting them in a series format. Unlike the anthologies, which tended to portray the dark side of the moon and of human nature, *Star Trek* usually had a more uplifting theme, suggesting that "strange new worlds" could be mastered by Americans (embodied by Captain Kirk) with the right diplomatic and managerial skills (as represented by Kirk's abilities to lead his multi-cultural crew, many of whom did not get along). Curiously, while it appeared after Kennedy's reign, *Star Trek* was probably more in line with the utopian ideals of New Frontierism than any of the programs that had actually appeared during the Kennedy years.

34. "Fashions in Orbit," *Ebony,* October 1965, 163–164.

35. *Ebony,* November 1969, 73.

36. bell hooks, *Black Looks: Race and Representation* (Boston: South End Press, 1992), 165–178.

37. It is interesting to note an ad in *Ebony* for the Greyhound bus company that shows a big picture of the moon and includes the caption, "Who goes to the

moon 5 times a day? . . . Nobody . . . but Greyhound does travel that far right here on earth." At a time *nobody* was going to the moon in the black community, Greyhound nevertheless reminded readers that they had conquered the bus system (and a smaller picture at the bottom of the ad displayed a picture of happy black passengers). *Ebony*, November 1962, 61.

38. Charles L. Sanders, "The Troubles of 'Astronaut' Edward Dwight," *Ebony*, June 1965, 35.

39. Hamilton Bims, "Rocket Age Comes to Tiny Triana," *Ebony*, March 1965, 106.

40. Rose Viega, letter to President Kennedy, 28 March 1962, White House Central Staff Files, Box 655: Folder O54, JFK Library. See also the reply from Ralph A. Dungan, Special Assistant to the President, 21 June 1962, White House Central Staff Files, Box 655: Folder 054, JFK Library. He told Ms. Viega that her letter was being forwarded to NASA "for whatever information they may be able to send you regarding the qualifications of a female astronaut." He also told her that the President was "dedicated to take every necessary and proper step to end discrimination."

41. Meanwhile, back in popular culture, the only representation of Hispanics on American entertainment/fiction television was the sitcom *The Bill Dana Show* (1963–1965) in which Hungarian-Jewish comedian Bill Dana starred in his stand-up comedy persona of Jose Jimenez , a poor Mexican hotel worker with dreams of being a real American. One of these dreams was Jose's wish to be an astronaut, which was pictured in the opening credit sequence as Jose is shown with fantasy-type comic strip "bubbles" around his head that contain, among other figures, himself dressed in a space suit.

42. Steven Morris, "How Blacks View Mankind's 'Giant Step,'" *Ebony*, September 1970, 33. See also commentary that compares the Moon Landing to Columbus's "rape" of America in "Giant Leap for Mankind?" *Ebony*, September 1969, 58.

43. "The New Priorities in Exploring Space," *Life*, 22 August 1969, 30.

44. Robert Lewis Shayon, "Cosmic Nielsens," *Saturday Review*, 9 August 1969, 40. "Our Journey to the Moon," *Life*, 17 January 1969, 26–31.

45. *Life*, January 1970, cover.

Kiss for a Killer

G. G. Fickling

HONEY WEST

TV'S Private
Eyeful in the
case of the
Eyes of
Death

Honey West paperback

nobody's woman?

three

honey west

and the

new sexuality

julie d'acci

In September of 1965 a slinky sleuth stole onto America's home screens and overturned television's seventeen-year history of confining female protagonists to situation comedies (often domestic ones), and at the end of the season, this sleuth silently stole away.[1] Was Honey West "Mickey Spillane in a skirt," or "James Bond in skirts—also slacks, evening gowns, leopard-skin bikinis, and pajamas?" Was she "for dad, unless mom likes to look at bikinis?" Then again, might audiences of the mid-1960s have been "just . . . ready for something like this?"[2] Wherever one comes down, then or now, on the merits of Anne Francis's prime-time private eye, her very inclusion in the 60s nighttime schedule provokes a number of questions: What exactly made such a rupture in TV's female depictions at the time even possible? Why were its effects on programming so muted (or camouflaged)? What does it tell us about the genealogy of "femininity," and for that matter, "masculinity" on U.S. prime time? And what does it reveal about the institution of 1960s network television itself?

Honey West, along with many other programs from the early and mid-1960s, negotiated massively shifting conceptions of masculinity, femininity, and sexuality. It also grew out of and helped to construct an emerging social category, a group of persons between "married adults" and recently fashioned "teenagers"—the new culture of young "swinging singles." As did *The Girl From U.N.C.L.E* and *The Avengers* a year later, it specifically involved the "new woman" of that culture, one whom Barbara Ehrenreich, Elizabeth Hess, and Gloria Jacobs describe as "urban, single, educated—who had to overcome both the puritanism of small-town America and the smothering conformity of suburban married life."[3] Furthermore, it sprang from network television's specific and ever-sharpening interest in target-audience baby boomers—a group whose first ranks were graduating from high school and forming the "cool set" (the swinging singles) of college campuses and metropolitan environments in the early and mid-1960s.

talk about a revolution

The break with conventions of TV femininity signaled by Honey West, a sportscar driving, martial-arts wielding, pet-ocelot toting "female dick," paralleled transitions in the social and economic spheres most often flagged by the phrase the "sexual revolution." Despite widely divergent interpretations and assessments of this phenomenon (especially regarding its "liberatory" effects for women), there is little doubt that such a revolution occurred in the United States between the 1920s and 1980s, with the 1960s forming a benchmark period.[4] And there is less doubt that it changed profoundly the ways many American women—ultimately of all classes, races, and ethnicities—experienced their sexuality.[5] The introduction of the birth control pill in 1960, the increased availability and acceptance of other birth control devices, and mounting agitation for legalizing the "third largest criminal activity in the country," abortion, all emerged from and contributed to the dramatic shifts in many women's sexual behavior during the decade.[6] And even though most African Americans considered the movement a white middle-class one, *Ebony* wrote in 1966 that it appeared to be affecting the young middle-class black woman who was "freed ... from many inhibitions imposed on her by a now outdated puritanical outlook on sex ... [and] like her white sister, has gained a new perspective on herself."[7] But despite the eventual effects of this revolution on all races, ethnicities, and classes, the early '60s construction of "singles" and "singles culture"—especially as a consumer and mass media phenomenon—was by and large aimed at the white middle class. And as we will see, the lion's share of cultural products depicted upwardly-mobile Caucasian characters and lifestyles.

The growing sexual freedom of many women (both single and married) in the middle of this century, and the diminution of the double standard between the sexes was, however, paralleled by a crisis of masculinity that had been unfolding, with different permutations, since the nineteenth century. In the 1890s, according to John Higham, a "cult of masculinity" developed in response to the degradation of white bourgeois American manhood after industrialization, to the "frustrations, the routine, and the sheer dullness of an urban-industrial culture." Among other things, this cult found expression in the rising popularity of sports and national bellicosity.[8] Margaret Marsh, however, details a concomitant rise in another expression of American maleness—"masculine domesticity"—a phenomenon of white middle-class turn-of-the-century suburban men who participated in companionate marriages and in leisure activities with their children (especially their sons). For Marsh, these domestic men kept the cult of masculinity alive in an "aggressive fantasy life," especially involving boxing, football, and adventure novels.[9]

In the post-World War II period, this continuing white male phenomenon took on added dimensions: the gnawing uncertainties of cold war hegemony, the memory of a successful women-powered wartime labor market, the humiliation of the Soviet-launched Sputnik, the ascendance of black men as the civil rights movement gained momentum, and the ever-increasing construction of middle-class white men in the traditionally "feminine" role of consumers. As Steven Cohan and Barbara Ehrenreich argue, masculine prowess was also threatened by the recently discovered "inadequacy" of men in fulfilling women's sexual needs, and the vulnerability of the male body to stress and heart disease.[10] One response to the crisis in the '50s was a revivified masculine domesticity, in which husbands and fathers took more part and power in family life, perhaps as compensation for a loss of authority in their public worlds.[11] Another response was for white heterosexual men to forsake the confines of marriage and the family altogether, to reclaim the domestic sphere for *themselves*, to embrace consumption, and become "playboys."[12]

Hugh Hefner's mushrooming industry not only grew out of these transitions in masculinity, but also exemplified one facet of the sexual revolution. As John D'Emilio and Estelle B. Freedman describe it, the revolution in the '50s and '60s was motored, on the one hand, by a political movement (the counterculture, exemplified first by the beats and then by hippies); and, on the other hand, by a consumer culture, with *Playboy* and advertising as preeminent examples.[13] The sex/consumer couplet, however, did not remain confined to play*boys* alone. Alfred Kinsey's 1953 report on female sexuality made only too plain that many women's sexual experience was infinitely more varied and "transgressive" than conventional assumptions and proscriptions would have it. And nine years after both the report and Hefner's first issue were published, an active sex life was openly, albeit more tamely, extended to unattached women in Helen Gurley Brown's book *Sex and the Single Girl*. This bestseller laid out a step by step plan for the single woman to forestall marriage, enjoy many sexual partners (including married men), have a job, and spend money on an apartment, furnishings, attractive clothes, and other goods to enhance her appeal.[14]

In discussing the Hefner and Brown prescriptions, we must also, of course, consider the ever-widening material bases for such sex-related consumption and singles cultures: Single working women, indispensable to the economic functioning of the postwar period, had gravitated in large numbers to major metropolitan areas; and young unmarried professionals and college students made up a six million dollar market by the mid-1960s, involving, among other things, singles clubs, bars, apartment complexes, and vacation trips.[15] We must further consider that as the decade progressed, the links between sex and consumption were only strengthened by the lifting of barriers against the straightforward presentation of sexual material in literature and the media.[16] It is clear that the revolution was—precisely because it was so imbricated in the nation's economy—widespread and deep. Given the ongoing crisis of masculinity, it is also clear that it was a revolution that pitted the needs, desires, injustices, and perceived threats of white middle-class men and women, in many instances, sharply against one another.

revolutionizing culture

Rock 'n' roll, novels, nonfiction books, Hollywood movies, and some prime-time TV from the mid-1950s and into the 1960s seethed with tensions between traditional and contemporary conceptions of the new woman, relations between the sexes, sex outside of marriage, and the new singles life.[17] Lyrics of a bolder female sexuality rang out in numerous songs from those of Connie Francis to Janis Joplin, to Diana Ross and the Supremes. Girl singers and girl groups, including Carole King, the Shirelles, the Crystals, and the Chiffons, may not only have testified to the sexual revolution but also, as Susan Douglas claims, influenced the women's movements.[18] And according to Ehrenreich, Hess, and Jacobs, girl Beatle fans in the mid-1960s were a full-scale manifestation of a powerful and increasingly open female desire.[19]

Nonfiction works, including Kinsey's 1953 *Sexual Behavior in the Human Female* and Masters and Johnson's *The Human Sexual Response* in 1966, were widely excerpted and debated in mainstream newspapers and magazines.[20] Betty Friedan's *The Feminine Mystique* similarly made plain that traditional gender roles were transforming, and that women would most likely be a formidable force in the public sphere of the coming decades. "Daring" 50s novels such as

Peyton Place and *The Group* paved the way for the explicit mid-60s bestseller *Valley of the Dolls*. Most significantly for my purposes, between 1957 and 1971 a group of eleven *Honey West* novels, by G.G. Fickling, featured a "sexsational private eyeful" who left absolutely no doubt that the public discourse on women's sexuality was undergoing change, even if such statements had roots immediately traceable to 1920s flappers and World War II pinups.[21]

Popular and pertinent films included *Peyton Place, Marjorie Morningstar, Butterfield 8, A Summer Place, The World of Suzie Wong, Lolita, Splendor in the Grass, Susan Slade,* and *The Sandpiper*. But it was the James Bond movies in the early to mid-1960s (*Dr. No* in 1962, *From Russia With Love* the following year, and *Goldfinger* in 1964, based, of course, on Ian Fleming's books first published in 1953) that brought the discourses surrounding the new woman, beleaguered masculinity, and the new singles culture together in powerful, far-reaching ways.

In their comprehensive work on the phenomenon, Tony Bennett and Janet Woollacott describe the cinematic figure of Bond, in the early to mid-'60s, as a hero of western capitalism and competitive individualism (during a time in which both, as well as the masculinity which undergirded them, were in crisis). The films themselves were mythic encapsulations of the new discourses of "swinging Britain" (classless and modern), and a masculinity and femininity that were "swinging free" from the constraints of the past.[22] They also see the films as contributing to the privileges (primarily western white male's privilege) to look and consume—"foreign sights, women, cars, cigarettes and liquor."[23]

Bennett and Woollacott describe the Bond movies of this period as "facilitating an adjustment" from one social model of sexuality to another, as working out and working over the terms of the sexual revolution. But they clearly assess the image of the "Bond girl" as one whose new sexuality was forged in the service of the patriarchy.[24] Whereas "the girl" was the subject of a "free and independent sexuality, liberated from the constraints of family, marriage, and domesticity"—and clearly no housewife—she was also fashioned according to the formula "equal but yet subordinate."[25] Her excessive independence or beyond-the-pale status needed to be "adjusted" by Bond (through sexual conquest,) and needed to be realigned to its proper place within the patriarchal order.[26] (Some of the Bond girls such as *Goldfinger's* Pussy Galore, leader of an all-female troupe of aviatrixes, reached the endpoint of transgression by being lesbians—overtly in Fleming's novels and thinly veiled in the films—and were in particular need of adjustment by the hero.) Bennett and Woollacott conclude that the freedom of "the girl" in these early movies was not much freedom after all. And the films themselves were essentially the playboy version of the sexual revolution, with swinging singles culture as the playground of the urbane, exciting, single stud, romping with an enticing, athletic, nondomestic and yet properly subalterned playmate. But their hugely popular success in the United States paved the way for explorations of such issues on the far more conservative and traditionally-domesticated American home screen.

home-screen revolutions

Mainstream U.S. television, especially since the late 1950s, had already begun to explore (although certainly in a much more covert and antiseptic way than the Bond films or the *Honey West* novels) *some* of this territory—the single-man part—with a spate of programs featuring the new hip and cool bachelor.[27] Beginning with *77 Sunset Strip* (1958–1963), Warner Bros. produced a battery of footloose-male-buddy detective programs such as *Hawaiian Eye* (1959–1963), *Bourbon Street Beat* (1959–1960), and *Surfside Six* (1960–1962). Other production companies joined in with *Peter Gunn* (1958–1961), *Checkmate* (1960–1962), *Michael Shayne* (1960–1961), and *Burke's Law* (1963–1966); still others offered nondetective dramas, with the same buddy-adventure premise, including *Route 66* (1960–1964), *Follow the Sun* (1961–1962), and *Adventures in Paradise* (1959–1962). The Bond-derived *Man From U.N.C.L.E.* (1964–1968) rejuvenated the form, adding a new twist of irony and spoof. Many of these programs were, of course, designed to attract women with on-screen hunks, and men with action and adventure—as well as the playmate who came and went every week. Other forms, such as the hospital dramas *Ben Casey* (1961–1966) and *Dr. Kildare* (1961–1966), similarly showcased "sexy" bachelors, and even adopted a more serial narrative structure, similar to that of the soap opera, as their series progressed. Situation comedies including *The Bob Cummings Show* (1961–1962), *The Tab Hunter Show* (1960–1961) and *Valentine's Day* (starring Tony Franciosa) also did their part to keep the swinging young playboy (or at least TV's version of him) in the public eye—particularly the eye of the female fan and consumer.

Only a couple of pre-1965 programs, however, (in the genre most hospitable to females, the sitcom) concentrated on representing the new single *woman*—the short-lived *Broadside* (1964–1965), about Navy WAVES, and the even shorter-lived *Harry's Girls* (1963–1964), about a vaudeville-type troupe touring Europe. (In this instance, *The Gale Storm Show* [1956–1960] may be seen as somewhat of a precursor.) One of the most daring and innovative forays into the subject matter of the sexual revolution (premiering a year before *Honey West*) was the TV version of *Peyton Place*. This prime-time soap was aired three nights a week and featured both female and male protagonists, portrayed the stories of both genders, and was an enormous hit with female viewers.

All of these conditions combined to pave the way for ABC's introduction of *Honey West* in 1965, and I will return to examine some of them in more detail shortly. But changing social discourses and practices, and other cultural products (even in tandem) would not have been enough to cause the networks to go out on the limb of featuring a single "new woman" protagonist in a prime-time dramatic program. The conditions of the TV industry at the time were absolutely fundamental to the eventual display of the "private eyeful" on the ever-cautious and wary home screen.

what did the webs want?

In 1965, 94 percent of the nation's homes had one or more television sets. Viewing was at a five-year high and averaged 5 hours and 38 minutes a day,[28] and the amount of time sold by networks and stations to advertisers was more than $1.7 billion—a 9.6 percent increase over 1964.[29] The impending move to all-color programs only promised more of the same.[30]

Although some series, such as Quaker Oats's *Bewitched* and General Foods's *Gomer Pyle*, were still fully owned and produced by sponsors, the networks had secured otherwise total control over licensing programs and selling advertising time. They had also achieved a high degree of rationalization and efficiency with regard to production. After the departure in 1964 of two anthology series (*Bell Telephone Hour* and *Kraft Suspense Theater*), prime time was essentially dominated by formulaic and cost-efficient filmed series, some music variety shows, Hollywood feature films, and a few news/documentary programs. CBS, NBC, and ABC had furthermore also begun to hedge their bets on new series. They extended only thirteen-week initial contracts, and engaged in the swift turnover of programs with lackluster ratings (sustaining a 35–45 percent failure rate for new series).[31] It was simply more lucrative for them to rapidly discard disappointments and try just as rapidly to hit upon new ratings winners.

Furthermore, even though there were many rumblings in the trade press about the FCC's concern with a possible network monopoly over programming, the Big Three were (at least temporarily) no longer worried about a reform-oriented FCC or even an active National Association of Broadcasters.[32] Since the demise of the "New Frontier," they essentially had the green light to produce whatever type of programming—no matter how commercial, "low-brow," or "mindless" and no matter how tinged with wasteland connotations—the market would bear.[33] Not only did they retreat from documentary and public affairs programs, but some critics also bemoaned their turn away from "meaningful dramas" such as *The Defenders* (1961–1965), *East Side, West Side* (1963–1964), and *The Nurses* (1962–1965); they claimed that the networks wholeheartedly rejected the "real world," and were moving primarily into fantasy situation comedies and "unmeaningful drama."[34] Other critics, however, threw their support behind those shows that captured the audience's imagination, and jumped to defend the "base" and commercial fare.[35] But for the Big Three unimpeded production of ratings-successful, assembly line, entertainment oriented, industrial culture, was a newly-secured goal—one they did not want jeopardized.

Among the networks themselves, the domination of CBS and NBC was challenged by an increasingly aggressive ABC. Because it was the youngest of the three, and because many of its affiliates were UHF rather than VHF stations (and consequently not widely available to the public), it had lagged behind its veteran competition.[36] It therefore had the least to lose and most to gain by taking sizable yet well strategized risks. By the 1960s, the onetime "mass" TV audience was increasingly conceived and researched as a "segmented" one, and ABC pursued the younger groups—both teens and the six million dollar market of professionals and college students who fueled the sexual revolution.[37] ABC's strategy paid off. Its stock climbed in 1964 as it grabbed 33 percent of the nation's audience and posed a real challenge to CBS's and NBC's ratings domination.[38] The trade press attributed its success to the "sensual appetite of young Americans."[39]

With the much touted success in 1964 of NBC's Bond-inspired, tongue-in-cheek *Man From U.N.C.L.E.* as the "favorite of the egghead set" (young, college-educated adults), and statistics that the "quality" segment of the audience—that same young, college-educated group—was at last beginning to watch more TV, ABC could afford to take a calculated gamble on *Honey West*.[40] Here was a series that fit in with the same proven trends, and potentially with the same camp, satirical, and pop characteristics that were bandied about in the trade press as key to attracting the coveted "war baby" audiences.[41] It was also a series that, like the Bond prototype, might appeal to both male and female "swingers." *Honey West*'s gamble was further calculated because it shared in the tried and true tradition of the swinging detective and was seen as employing some of the spoof and fantasy of the popular sitcoms of the time (simply by its woman-spy premise and its ironic tone).[42] It was also—unlike its sixty-minute male detective predecessors—simply, and therefore cheaply, a half-hour show, and, during a period in which conversion to color was underway, *Honey West* was filmed in black and white.[43]

Produced by Aaron Spelling for an independent production company, Four Star Television, *Honey West* made its debut in the Friday night schedule during a line-up of programs popular with teens and young women. (It followed *Tammy* and *The Addams Family* and preceded *Peyton Place*.) But it had the double advantage of potentially appealing to the "new woman" fantasies of power and the sexual fantasies of heterosexual men. The fact that one of its original sponsors (along with Breck, Norwich, and Pharmacraft) was Consolidated Cigar (with $60,000 in ad time) underscores the conscious conception of the show as, at least in part, a lure to target young men. As the season wore on, however, Consolidated Cigar disappeared in favor of a more uniformly women-oriented sponsorship which included Sunbeam, Standard Brands, U.S. Rubber, Diet Delight, General Electric, and Bristol-Myers.[44] The program, it seems, came to take its place, along with the rest of its line-up, as one primarily geared toward young female consumers.

But how would ABC finesse such an incendiary combination of elements—a single, sexual, woman detective/spy as the protagonist of a prime-time dramatic program? How, in other words, could the new woman's sexuality be dealt with on the conservative network prime-time schedule, which—despite the concurrent and actually quite tame *Peyton Place*—primarily featured women as mothers, wives, secretaries, nurses, singers, and variety show performers, and had virtually never showcased a woman as the main protagonist of a dramatic series?[45]

the private eyeful on the public airwaves

By the time that the sexual revolution and the new single woman came to 1965 prime-time TV, it had already been the subject of intense debate in popular journalism and had already given way to a series of fantasies in films, novels, and other popular media. Anxieties over its threat to traditional notions of sexuality, and struggles over the course this new sexuality might take, were continually expressed and negotiated in these media. *Honey West*, then, entered an ongoing dialogue on sexual revolution that had already proposed a set of discursive rules for speaking about sex. However, because the terrain was the home screen, innuendo, suggestion, and indirection were heavily relied upon. But as Lynn Spigel's work on the fantastic sitcom demonstrates, these elements actually characterized a good deal of 1960s prime time, and were not limited to programs grappling with too-hot-to-handle sex-related subject matter.[46] With *Honey West*, much of the initial suggestion and innuendo came from intertextual associations.

Even though she was a private eye and not an international spy, Honey was greeted and promoted by critics as "Jane Bond," "Jane Blonde," "James Bond in skirts," and the "Woman from A.U.N.T."[47] In addition, much was made of her Bond-like skills and accoutrements. The week the series premiered, *TV Guide* featured four action photos of Anne Francis in karate clothes performing feats of jujitsu, judo, and karate while taking lessons from her martial arts instructor.[48] Several months later another *TV Guide* piece listed Honey's tools of the trade, including a detonator compact, a frilly garter gas mask, tear-gas earrings, a lipstick microphone, earring radio receivers, a martini olive that transmitted conversations when dropped into a cocktail, and a cigarette lighter that doubles as a camera.[49] The episodes themselves similarly made occasional reference to "Bond" or "007," and always employed an array of electronic surveillance equipment reminiscent of that of a superspy, (although considerably more jerry-rigged). Though the TV network would never permit Honey to replicate the sexual elan of a female Bond or a Pussy Galore, the contradictory sexuality of the jet-set female spy (powerful, physical, bearer-of-the-look, dominatrix-like, deceptive femme fatale, to-be-conquered), the potential threat she might pose to men and the potential empowerment to women was insinuated from the outset.

Honey's swinging-detective ancestry reverberated with associations of the "cool set" American sexuality of her playboy brothers. She was first introduced to the TV audience on an episode of *Burke's Law*, wearing a low-cut slinky dress, bearing a pointed revolver, and hailed by the wealthy debonair bachelor Burke (played by Gene Barry) with, "Oh, private detective, girl type." The Honey of this pilot was, furthermore, more openly sexual than the one of the weekly series. Here she had two male pursuers (the ever-present Sam Bolt/John Ericson of the later program, and a lawyer named Chris whom she appeared to be dating and kissed romantically). Honey also remarked with flirtatious cheek when walking by a police detective, "You men are all so handsome." Explicit struggles between the new woman and traditional masculinity were additionally played out somewhat more explicitly in the pilot. For example, during a scene in which both Sam and Chris try to confine Honey to her apartment and not let her confront a dangerous assignment, Sam speaks for both men and shouts, "A woman's place is in the home." Honey retorts by trying to karate-flip Sam and telling Chris to "take off that suit of armor." When Sam finally overpowers her, Chris remarks, "we should never have given them the vote." The scene, however, is resolved as Honey fakes an injured hip, gets the drop on the men, and locks them both in her apartment while she flees to do her work.

Like her single men counterparts, this female private eye also drives a convertible sportscar (hers is a Cobra with a mobile telephone), wears sunglasses, uses state of the art firearms, and models upscale designer fashions (the program's wardrobe costs tallied $50,000).[50] In the series' intertextual associations with the TV detective genre, and a pilot more brazen than the episodes themselves, innuendos were floated that this female protagonist might control her own desires as well as the narrative, and might wield power in the public sphere along with cars and weapons.

The heroine's lineage from the private eye of G.G. Fickling's novels suggested a sexuality that would shatter the tubes of any self-respecting TV set of mid-1960s suburbia.[51] The pulp Honey is a blue-eyed "blonde bombshell," whose measurements, readers are often told, come in at "38–22–36." Furthermore, she wears no bra, and quips "I resemble that accusation" when a male admirer says she's "built like a brick road house." She smokes, drinks too many martinis, sports a blue garter holster with a pearl-handled .22, flirts shamelessly, and, we are strongly lead to believe, sleeps around. She is also totally fearless, a perpetual wise-cracker, and the object and subject of violent attacks; she usually ends up completely naked (in one instance wrestling a male intruder) in most of the books. Fans of the TV series had an increased likelihood of encountering the novels with Pyramid's republication of six earlier titles (*Girl on the Loose, A Gun for Honey, Girl on the Prowl, Honey in the Flesh, Blood and Honey,* and *Kiss for a Killer*) to coincide with the program's premiere. The covers and backs of these books featured pictures of Anne Francis as TV Honey and stills from the episodes. They also urged readers to "Follow Honey West's wild exploits (or "lethal saga," or "exciting escapades") in Pyramid's paperbacks and on ABC's sensational new TV thriller series." One book is, furthermore, dedicated to Julie London, "the symbol, the embodiment, and the fire of Honey."[52]

The series' sexual innuendo was also subtly heightened in the episodes themselves, and their publicity, by Honey's association with the cat. One of her most notable trademarks was a pet ocelot named Bruce, who was often seen on her sofa or in her sportscar, and who appeared with Francis/West on every front cover of the Pyramid paperback series (held in his mistress's right arm, while she pointed a gun with her left) and on every back cover (at the end of a leash gripped by a gun-toting Honey who wears black high heels and a long black V-neck dress with a kick slit up the front). On the level of association and myth, then, this protagonist was indirectly connected to other feline-linked females (like the comic book Catwoman)—women who are stealthy, unpredictable, surreptitious, wild (perhaps at the core), and, for men and masculinity, potentially lethal. As one TV critic perhaps hysterically described the heroine, "To complete the Jet Set image, she reins a *man-hating* ocelot on the end of a silver leash" (emphasis my own).[53]

The series' opening credit sequence is almost a microcosm for how these innuendos, and the negotiation of conflicting discourses about sexuality, would work in the series itself. It presents, however, much bolder sexual images than the episodes, and so encourages in its viewers a more explicit interpretation of the series' muffled sexuality. (It is also a stark contrast to the credit sequences for the male detective programs that focus mainly on action and adventure.) The sequence begins with an extreme closeup of Honey's lips filling the frame (they are slightly puckered and parted, and there is a "beauty mark" below the lower right one). It then cuts to another extreme closeup of Honey from just below her bottom lip to just above her eyebrows—she is looking out provocatively at the camera over sunglasses which are low on her nose. It cuts again to an extreme closeup of an unidentified man's ear (which fills almost two-thirds of the frame's left side) and Honey's mouth (lips parted, upper teeth showing, on the frame's right) almost touching the ear (as if getting ready to speak into it, blow into it, kiss it, or bite it), and then cuts again to an extreme closeup of the man's and Honey's lips almost touching, both parted and poised as if ready to kiss. Following twenty-two other shots (including Honey being attacked by another man and overpowering him in a head-lock, Honey in karate-chop poses, Honey pointing a revolver, and Honey beside her erstwhile boyfriend Sam, whose arm is around her shoulder), it cuts to a closeup of Bruce (the ocelot) looking into the camera. The shot then dissolves to a perfectly matched closeup of Honey looking into the camera, zooms out to her in medium closeup with a revolver tipped back in her right hand, dissolves to another medium closeup of her in a feminine and demure pose, and zooms out to a *plan American* shot which reveals her in a low-cut, formfitting, V-neck sleeveless gown, with exposed cleavage.[54]

The sequence neatly exemplifies the suggestive innuendo of prime-time drama's first outing with the new single woman, and the negotiation of different and often competing assumptions about female sexuality. It invokes the new woman's sexual subjectivity, female strength and power over men, a tamed female sexuality (encircled by her boyfriend's arm), a more conventionally fetishized female objectification (in the isolated lips and cleavage), and an ambiguously upper-class and white trash femininity. It also powerfully links the heroine with the wild cat (she literally merges with it in the superimposition preceding the dissolve), and because these shots are placed at the end of the sequence, it tacitly signals the centrality of a threatening sexuality to defining both the character and the new single woman.

But at the same time this new feminine sexuality was suggested, the episodes and publicity sought to tame it and make it safe. After all, if the big-screen Bond girls had to be adjusted to patriarchy, surely a small-screen "girl dick" could not appear wild on a Friday night in America's dens and family rooms. This domestication was, of course, part of the continual negotiation involving women's sexuality that occurred as the publicity and televisual texts frantically grappled with all the ramifications of the sexual revolution and the crisis of masculinity. Some critics sought to defuse the program's threatening dimensions by alluding to its fantasy character, or its "mock suspense" theme, or by describing Honey as "a female Peter Seller's role ... playing it for laughs." Others sought to assure readers that although Honey was adept at martial arts, she would "be very ladylike in her use of karate" and would not kill anyone with it.[55]

At the level of the narratives themselves, many moves modified the transgressive implications. First, as Richard Levinson and William Link (who wrote several of the episodes) tell it, it was nervousness on the part of the network that caused ABC to hedge its bets and cast John Ericson/Sam Bolt as Honey's costar and on-screen protector; one in whom her dying father had entrusted his daughter's care.[56] ABC then proceeded to advertise the show in *TV Guide* primarily with two shots of Francis and Ericson, giving them equal billing.[57] Honey was also not shown as living alone (with her pet ocelot) in a swinging single girl's apartment; instead—and Helen Gurley Brown would have shuddered—she shared an apartment with her Aunt Meg (played by Irene Hervey). Aunt Meg's "chaperoning" function went so far as to occasionally accompany Sam and Honey on dinner dates.

Furthermore, Honey's status as a conventional sex object was heavily played upon—flagging the new woman's sexuality but reinscribing it in traditional patriarchal terms. In the course of the series run, the heroine appeared in two-piece bathing suits; a wraparound towel (in a steam room); a tiger skin one-piece bathing suit with fish-net hose and black high heels; tiger skin, leopard skin, zebra skin, and snake-skin coats; many low-cut, formfitting evening gowns, often trimmed in sequins, beads, or sable; and a black leotard action-work outfit with black medium-heeled boots. Many of her "disguises" called for a sexual flair, including those of a dance hall girl, a bare-legged cigarette girl, a "Polynesian" waitress in a halter top, a "gypsy," and a German model; and during some episodes she also appeared in her bathtub.

In a number of instances this sexual spectacle was portrayed as directly controlled by Sam, who kept "his girl's" sexual display in line (or at least his line of vision) by perpetual surveillance. In one episode he watches her through binoculars while she lounges in a bathing suit on a boat. In another, he surveys her through a periscope in her tiger-skin bathing suit and fishnet hose, and in yet others he tracks her on closed circuit television. Moreover, despite Honey's martial-arts prowess, Sam often effects a last minute rescue, performing the most (and the messiest) of the fighting.

Finally, Honey was relentlessly depicted as stereotypically and safely feminine—high fashion, slim, blonde, glamorous, and heterosexually paired. Of the thirty episodes, most conclude with a whimsical epilogue which brings her and Sam together in a conventional dating scene. The swinging female detective/spy/catwoman ends each show; then, looking like anybody's upper-middle class, white, Anglo-Saxon girl next door, she and her escort dine out in fancy restaurants, dance at discos and nightclubs, or prepare (with Aunt Meg looking on approvingly) to go out on the town.

Despite this adjustment and taming of the female spy's sexuality (both

85

insinuated and more blatantly displayed), the series obviously abounded with conflicts. Sam was *considerably* less bright than Honey, and considerably more interested in a romantic relationship. Their dating status was utterly devoid of chemistry, and she always ignored his blustery rantings and orders. Furthermore, Honey often got to display her power, and occasionally in unadjusted ways. Weekly, viewers witnessed scenes of aggressive female subjectivity—the fearless, resourceful, willful, and adept action/adventure Honey talking her way out of scrapes, speeding off to solve cases, lowering herself on ropes into and out of precariously high windows, dangling from helicopters, and disposing of villains with kicks, chops, and flying leaps. Most notably, in an extraordinary episode called "The Grey Lady" (written by Link and Levinson), Sam is knocked unconscious while tracking Honey on his closed circuit TV. He stays that way for the whole program, allowing the female sleuth all the derring-do (including climbing up the side of a tall building and singlehandedly overpowering a jewelry thief in a no-holds-barred fight sequence). Such spectacles surely posed a challenge to conventional images of femininity.

Although I concur with Bennett and Woollacott about the adjustments that occur when masculinity in crisis wants to reassert itself against a burgeoning feminine sexuality, I fall short of accepting their ultimate conclusions about the Bond girls of the '60s and of applying them to *Honey West*. Rather than seeing either instance of femininity as, in the final analysis, wholly subordinated to patriarchy, or the films and programs as the ultimate, triumph of patriarchy over emerging feminine subjectivity, I see them as sites for the negotiation of conflicting discourses involving women's sexuality, the crisis of masculinity, and the sexual revolution. Although both surely scurry to mitigate and control it, neither representation, I think, closes down on the innovative or subversive dimensions of the new woman's power. As a surprisingly large number of women recounted to me after an initial presentation of this paper at the Society for Cinema Studies Conference in 1992, Honey West was a powerful heroine in their grade school, high school, and early college lives, and they had absolutely no recollection of Sam Bolt/John Ericson as even being a *part* of the program.

honey is history

Although hopes for Honey were high (it was touted as "promising" in a 1965 survey of ad agencies), the show was immediately clobbered by its competition from CBS's *Gomer Pyle*, which garnered a 26.1 rating and a 49 share (compared to *Honey West's* 13.2 and 25).[58] (However, *Honey West* actually did better than its lead-in, *The Addams Family*, which suffered due to competition from

86

CBS's *Hogan's Heroes*.) As the other networks "picked up the beat from the swingers at ABC," and as an outmoded Nielsen ratings sample continued to overweigh the preferences of rural and older viewers, CBS and NBC began to regain their ratings preeminence.[59] In a scramble to recapture lost gains, ABC weeded out its lowest rated series at mid-season. Still pursuing youth with camp, pop, and fantasy, ABC took a big chance in January on the innovative, *Batman* series. Honey West finished out her season as a sleuth, but was then forcibly retired from all future action and adventure. She gave way, the following year, to NBC's *Girl From U.N.C.L.E.*, starring Stephanie Powers as spy April Dancer (who also worked for only one year); and ABC's British import *The Avengers* costarring Diana Rigg as the action heroine Emma Peale (which played for three years—intermittently—and changed its female lead to Linda Thorson as Tara King in 1968).

Many factors contributed to Honey's demise and that of her short-lived NBC successor, as well as to the series' general lack of cloning. Surely in *Honey West*'s instance, competition from one of the top three programs of the year was a main reason for the failure. But I would also argue that it simply did not make good business sense for the networks to take the continued risk on a female-led dramatic program during a time in which they (and especially ABC) were rapidly replacing programs with weak ratings and in which situation and fantasy comedies were delivering 20-plus ratings in homes where advertiser's basic marketing target (women between 18–49) were present.[60] The networks found it more fiscally sound to channel their efforts involving the new single woman into cheaper, more formulaic, and more predictable situation comedies. ABC did just that with the introduction of *That Girl* in 1966. (Even the fantasy-drama *Wonder Woman*, which had been pitched for the 1967 season, would not make it to prime time until nine years later.)[61] The networks would also continue to let male-led programs (including all those I mentioned above, as well as their steady supply of westerns) continue to draw in their share of single (as well as married) female viewers.

Furthermore, the fact that "Batmania" hit not only high schools but college campuses in 1966 demonstrated that the young adult baby boomers—the new singles—would rally around a pop action-hero "kid's" program, as well as a more adult one like *Man From U.N.C.L.E.*. Such a turn of events worked, at least for a while, to further dampen the burst of dramatic programs featuring women protagonists. With the veritable explosion of movie and television-related toys and merchandise (in the wake of TV *Superman*, the more recent Bond films, and TV *Batman*), marketers began to dub 1966 the new age of the television "superhero."[62] And as one wrote, while outlining the specifications for these new cash marvels, "the child must be able to mimic his hero and thereby be on the side of the law, then he can fight and kill without punishment and guilt feelings. This eliminates ... [as merchandise-successful TV heroes] most women." Even though a Honey West doll was marketed, the momentum was clearly on the side of male action heroes, with women, once again channeled into situation and fantasy comedies (where indeed a lot of subversive work—however camouflaged—continued). In the seasons after *Honey West*, the industry, even the more daring ABC, discovered that other programs (such as *Bewitched, Batman, Man From U.N.C.L.E.,* and *That Girl*) would draw in the desired target audiences with much greater chances of being ratings hits than women-led dramatic programs. This was especially the case in the years just before the updating of the Nielsen ratings sample to chart the viewing habits of younger and less rural households, and before an organized women's movement gained force.

There are undoubtedly numerous other reasons why the series may have failed after only one year, including, as one critic put it, that *"Honey West* has all the getaway gadgets—including tear-gas earrings and a garter that converts to a gas mask—but she has not a chance of escaping the banalities of her script."[63] A further one I want to consider involves issues that I will only be able to touch upon here—issues that encompass the actual dimensions of TV's trailblazing depiction of the "new single woman." And this can only be discussed within the overall context of masculinity's representation on American television.

During a cultural scramble to shore up the cult of masculinity (or more precisely, its "fantasy") in '50s and '60s suburban America, an enormous number of television programs—particularly dramatic ones—virtually eliminated women altogether. These were TV's versions of turn-of-the-century adventure novels, popular tales for a masculinity in crisis—legions of westerns, detectives, and law and order programs. As in the *Playboy* philosophy, the heroes were men who lived and thrived without domestic bonds to tie them. Even though such manifestations as the swinging detective were "feminized" by an obvious attention to fashion and consumption and by the display of their bodies as spectacles (some heroes in the opening credit sequences of *Surfside Six* and *Hawaiian Eye* appeared in bathing suits), the routing out of females and children from their story worlds could work to ward off connotations of womanliness. The excessive deployment of masculine icons and behaviors—guns, sports cars, alcohol, cigarettes, and action/adventure—could also work to hold at bay implications of homosexuality. These heroes were clearly (or as the narratives battled to make clear) nobody's women. But in the fascinating twists and permutations of mainstream television narratives, the bonding with male partners ended up furnishing the "empathy" (a word invoked by critics of the time as fundamental to successful teleplays) necessary to draw in a heterogeneous audience, especially a women's and a suburban one. Such bonding could demonstrate to viewers the *potential* (however disavowed by other aspects of the text) for a tamed, relational man—for the *possible* "domestic male," not the fantasized cult one.

Despite her descendance from the mother of all Bonds, such strong and charged bonding was denied Honey and her *Girl From U.N.C.L.E.* successor. Even though both heroines were paired with male partners, they were not portrayed (as were the partners of male programs) as emotionally linked to them. In Honey's particular case, despite the series' epilogues, she spent a lot of energy ignoring and fleeing from Sam. Furthermore, her relationships with Aunt Meg, and even Bruce, were peripheral at best. It was, in 1965, and has remained so ever since, extraordinarily difficult to portray the new (hetero) sexual single woman on mainstream network prime time. From the outset, she could not be permanently bonded to any one man; could not be seen as a "sleepabout"; and could not be part of a conventional "family."[64] She also could not be paired with a woman partner, lest the threat from an emerging feminine power be exacerbated beyond endurance. A very important point about Honey (and *Girl From U.N.C.L.E.'s* April Dancer), is that they could not be seen as incapable of bonding. These early single women heroines were actually sent out to do what not even male protagonists could accomplish on a medium geared toward suburban domestic America—be substitute, wholly autonomous, fantasy males.

It would take nighttime TV nine years (and a full-scale women's movement) to dare to bring women buddies (however objectified) to prime-time drama (with the Aaron Spelling-produced, *Charlies' Angels*) and seventeen years to bring two non-objectified, fully-bonded, female partners (amidst cries and charges of lesbianism) with *Cagney and Lacey*. In mainstream U.S. television culture, when representing women (who have been socially constructed as primarily *relational*), it has been almost impossible to find the right mix when fashioning independent "autonomous" protagonists. Perhaps, along with everything else I have cited, this is one of the reasons that Honey West—nobody's woman—did not have a better chance of capturing the widespread popular imagination. It may also contribute to explaining why *The Avengers'* Emma Peale suggestively bonded to her partner (Jonathan Steed/Patrick Macnee) while she was legally bonded to her missing-in-action husband, yet never overtly compromised an overt relationship with either of them—and thus captured a large fandom and following. Audience members, in other words, had an immediate inroad for their own phantasmatic relationships with the character. (From ABC's point of view, this was a surely happy situation indeed—it did not have to bear the risk of producing the program, and the questionable, transgressive Mrs. Peale, was not a hometown American girl but a beyond-the-pale British one.)

Of course, as the comments from the women at the Society for Cinema Studies Conference testify, particular viewers will always find in popular images the stuff their hopes, desires, and imaginations require. In this specific instance, these were the hopes of young women and girls—in an America rising to a new wave of feminism—for empowerment, equality, and freedom. With such hopes and imagination, they had, it seems (or at least they remember having) no trouble making Honey West "their woman." And most likely, many urban young singles (whose viewing preferences were underrepresented in the ratings samples of the 1960s) similarly rallied around the program and its heroine. They were simply not joined by enough of the suburban, rural, and older viewers who (along with other young viewers) chose Gomer Pyle over Honey.

Honey West, along with many other cultural products, was generated from the sexual revolution, the emergence of the new single woman, the construction of singles culture, the anxieties around masculinity, and network television's (especially ABC's) pursuit of young adult baby boomers with camp, satire, fantasy, and "sexuals." It in turn negotiated the competing discourses involving these phenomena and contributed to shaping them in a variety of contradictory ways. Although, the depiction of the new and free single woman was fettered in the episodes, it did not prevent particular viewers from incorporating the image into the workings of their own unfettered desires. This is by no means an apologia for the constrained ways in which women have found what little representation they have in industrial television culture, nor a suggestion that the notion of dominant ideology involving masculinity and femininity is indeed dead. It is simply to echo Christine Gledhill in saying that into popular texts are locked both atavistic and utopian elements that engage in continuous battle, and they are drawn into the orbit of viewers' own interpretative and sometimes liberatory frameworks.[65]

notes

Thanks to Lynn Spigel and Antonette Paul.

1. "Slinky Sleuth" was the title above the cover photo of Anne Francis on *TV Guide*, 9 October 1965. *Honey West* was not the first dramatic program in television history to feature a woman protagonist. In 1951, Anna May Wong starred in the three-month run of a detective drama, *The Galley of Mme. Lui-Tsong*. Loretta Young also hosted an anthology series, *The Loretta Young Show*, from 1953–1961, and starred in each installment during the first two years. And *The Nurses* (from 1962–1964) starred Shirl Conway and Zina Bethune. This drama, although featuring two women in the title roles, was much more of an ensemble cast production, often showcasing male doctors or guest stars as the protagonists. The series, in fact, changed its name to *The Doctors and Nurses* for the 1964–1965 season. The 1957–58 *Decoy*, starring Beverly Garland as a policewoman, was a syndicated rather than a network program, and although an excellent example of a

woman-led, prime-time dramatic program, was not widely seen. Some people consider *Mama*, starring Peggy Wood, from 1949–1956 a drama, although most consider it a prototype of the domestic comedy. *Honey West* was the first dramatic episodic series, on network TV, lasting a full season, with a woman in the unequivocal protagonist position.

2. Barbara Delatiner, *Newsday*; Dwight Newton, *San Francisco Examiner*; Frank Wilson, *Indianapolis News*; Bob Williams, *New York Post*; Allen Rich, *Hollywood Citizen News*; all quoted in *Broadcasting* (27 September 1965): 69.

3. Barbara Ehrenreich, Elizabeth Hess, and Gloria Jacobs, *Re-Making Love: The Feminization of Sex* (New York: Anchor, 1986), 40.

4. See especially John D'Emilio and Estelle B. Freedman, *Intimate Matters: A History of Sexuality in America* (New York: Perennial Library, 1988), 239–343; and Linda Gordon, *Woman's Body, Woman's Right: Birth Control in America* (New York: Penguin, 1990).

5. D'Emilio and Freedman, 239–343; and Gordon.

6. D'Emilio and Freedman; and Gordon.

7. Ehrenreich, Hess, and Jacobs, 56.

8. John Higham, "The Reorientation of American Culture in the 1890s," in John Higham, ed., *Writing American History* (Bloomington: Indiana University, 1970), 79; quoted in Margaret Marsh, *Suburban Lives* (New Brunswick: Rutgers University Press, 1990), 75.

9. Marsh, 79–82.

10. Steven Cohan, "Masquerading as the American Male in the Fifties," in Constance Penley and Sharon Willis, eds., *Male Trouble* (Minneapolis: University of Minnesota, 1993), 212. Barbara Ehrenreich, *The Hearts of Men: American Dreams and the Flight from Commitment* (New York: Anchor, 1983), 68–87.

11. Lynn Spigel, "Seducing the Innocent: Childhood and Television in Postwar America," in William S. Solomon and Robert W. McChesney, eds., *Ruthless Criticism: New Perspectives in U.S. Communication History* (Minneapolis: University of Minnesota Press, 1993), 266.

12. For an interesting account of the Playboy phenomenon see Barbara Ehrenreich, *The Hearts of Men*, 42–51.

13. D'Emilio and Freedman, 277–307.

14. Helen Gurley Brown, *Sex and the Single Girl* (New York: Bernard Geis, 1962).

15. D'Emilio and Freedman, 41, 54, and 305.

16. D'Emilio and Freedman, 277.

17. For another look at some of these issues see Susan J. Douglas, "Will You Love Me Tomorrow? Changing Discourses about Female Sexuality in the Mass Media, 1960–1968," in Solomon and McChesney, 349–73.

18. Susan J. Douglas, 363–67.

19. Ehrenreich, Hess, and Jacobs, 10–38.

20. For an interesting account see Ehrenreich, Hess, and Jacobs, 39–73.

21. "G.G. Fickling" was the pen name for Gloria and Forrest E. ("Skip") Fickling, upon whose novels the *Honey West* TV series was in part based. Thanks to Lynn Spigel for presenting me with four of the rare novels as a gift.

22. Tony Bennett and Janet Woollacott, *Bond and Beyond: The Political Career of a Popular Hero* (New York: Methuen, 1987), 240, and 33–35.

23. Bennett and Woollacott, 247.

24. Bennett and Woollacott, 141.

25. Bennett and Woollacott, 35, 123, 242.

26. Bennett and Woollacott, 39, 114–127.

27. The earlier (1955–1959) sitcom, *The Bob Cummings Show*, featured Bob Cummings as a playboy-type fashion photographer.

28. "The Face of the Crowd," *Television Age* (22 November 1965): 20.

29. "Forecast '66," *Television Age* (3 January 1966): 22

30. "Through the Buyers' Eyes," *Television Age* (21 June 1965): 32.

31. "Shuffle at the Half-Way Point," *Television Age* (19 December 1966): 27–62. The five periods were September, December, January, March, and June.

32. James Baughman in *Television Guardians: The FCC and the Politics of Programming* (Knoxville: University of Tennessee, 1985), 137, writes that "between 1964 and 1966, the Federal Communication Committee went from being an industry nuisance to a regulatory non-entity ... [it] abandoned almost every vestige of the Minow era." He also writes that the NAB after 1965 "offered no realistic promise of a self-regulatory authority," (134). For mounting broadcasters concerns about a renewed FCC threat see, "Editorial: The FCC's Dominions," *Television Age* (15 March 1965): 20–21; and "FCC: Up from Slumber," *Television Age* (15 March 1965): 59–65, 108–114; and "A Program Man's Viewpoints," *Television Age* (29 March 1965), 39, 60.

33. A report in *Television Age* (30 March 1964): 39–43, 82, lists a number of reasons for the decline in regulatory fervor of the FCC since the Minow years: First, the TV industry had gained considerable respect during the coverage of the Kennedy assassination; second, LBJ was more conservative with regard to business regulation than was the New Frontier; third, the FCC had had its budget slashed; and fourth, Congress (angered that the FCC had been circumventing Congress's authority) was keeping the regulatory body in close check. James Baughman, p. 140, stresses LBJ's influence on the new and less zealous FCC, saying that even if Ladybird Johnson had not owned TV stations, and LBJ had not had close personal ties to both CBS and NBC, he still would have had a totally a relaxed attitude toward the FCC. According to Baughman, Johnson did not believe in an adversarial relationship between business and government and had assured business leaders in December, 1963, "we will not harass or persecute you." Baughman also argues that the civil rights movement was drawing attention away from television regulation (p. 140).

34. James Baughman, 147–49; "Three on a Seesaw," *Television Age* (21 June 1965): 28–31, 76.

35. "J.B.," "A Program Man's Viewpoints," *Television Age* (15 February 1965): 43.

36. Many television sets in the country were not equipped with UHF tuners, and even if they were, many locations had difficulty getting adequate reception. According to James Baughman (p. 155), in September of 1966, 24 of 137 ABC stations were UHF. (By 1964 all new TV sets had to have UHF tuners.)

37. See *Television Age* (14 September 1964): 55.

38. "Wall Street Report," *Television Age* (23 November 1964): n.

39. "Younger and Older," *Television Age* (18 January 1965): 55.

40. "In Camera," *Television Age* (21 June 1965): 78; "The Face of the Crowd," *Television Age* (22 November 1965): 22.

41. See "A Program Man's Viewpoints," *Television Age* (13 September 1965): 39; "Pop Goes the TV," *Television Age* (25 October 1965): 71–72; "A Program Man's Viewpoints," *Television Age* (6 December 1965): 47.

42. Cleveland Amory, "Review," *TV Guide* (23 October 1965): 12; "Would You Believe a Poison Ice-Pellet Flute-Shooter?" *TV Guide* (2 April 1966): 14–16; An ABC advertisement in *TV Guide* (12 November 1965): A-107, includes Honey West in a line-up of programs including *The Flintstones, The Addams Family, Tammy,* and *The Farmer's Daughter,* and urges viewers to "Follow the *Fantastic* [emphasis my own] Fridays on ABC!"

43. For its part, the series' production company, Four Star, reduced risks by specializing, to some degree, in detective/spy products including *The Detectives* and *Burke's Law,* along with *Honey West,* and distributing a package of eleven feature films, called the "International Super-Spy Action Group" to television. NBC cashed in on basically the same genre in 1965 with *Get Smart* and *I Spy,* and with the latter took a big risk of its own, this time, however, in casting an African American man—Bill Cosby—as the series' costar.

44. *Broadcasting* (14 June 1965): 66; "TV Age Network Programming Chart, Night-time," *Television Age* (30 August 1965): 51–55; *Television Age* (6 June 1966): 48.

45. See note 1.

46. Lynn Spigel, "From Domestic Space to Outer Space: The 1960s Fantastic Family Sit-Com," in *Close Encounters: Film, Feminism, and Science Fiction*, Constance Penley, Elisabeth Lyon, Lynn Spigel, and Janet Bergstrom, eds. (Minneapolis: University of Minnesota Press, 1991), 206–35.

47. "Show Business," *Time* (24 September 1965): 56; Cleveland Amory, "Review," *TV Guide* (23 October 1965): 12; Dwight Newton, *San Francisco Examiner*, quoted in *Broadcasting* (27 September 1965): 69; Amory, 12.

48. "This Lovely Star of 'Honey West' is Anne Francis and . . . She's MEAN," *TV Guide* (18 September 1965): 14–15.

49. "Would You Believe a Poison Ice-Pellet Flute-Shooter?" *TV Guide* (2 April 1966): 14–16.

50. Richard Warren Lewis, "Honey West's Earrings Explode, So Does Anne Francis," *TV Guide* (9 October 1965): 20.

51. See Kathleen Gregory Klein, *The Woman Detective: Gender and Genre* (Urbana: University of Illinois, 1988), 132–34, 234, for a look at the novels within the overall context of the woman detective.

52. See G.G. Fickling, *Blood and Honey* (New York: Pyramid, 1965).

53. Lewis, 20.

54. A *plan American* is a shot framed from the knees up.

55. *Broadcasting* (8 February 1965): 64; *TV Age* (28 September 1964): 32; "This Lovely Star of 'Honey West' is Anne Francis . . . and She's MEAN," *TV Guide* (18 September 1965): 14.

56. Richard Levinson and William Link, *Stayed Tuned* (New York: Ace, 1981), 153.

57. *TV Guide* (17 September 1965): 38; *TV Guide* (12 November 1965): A-107.

58. "Two Agencies Handicap 1965-66 TV," *Advertising Age* (13 September 1965): 138. "Ratings at the First Turn," *Broadcasting* (27 September 1965); 67.

59. "Shuffle at the Half-Way Point," *Television Age* (18 January 1965): 60.

60. "Everybody Counts, Everybody's Counting," *Television Age* (28 February 1966): 21.

61. "Tele-Scope," *Television Age* (7 November 1966). Greenway Productions was going to pitch *Wonder Woman* for the fall of 1967.

62. Mel Helitzer, "00TV: Licensed to Sell," *Television Age* (17 January 1966): 32.

63. "Show Business," *Time* (24 September 1965): 56.

64. Into the late 1980s, CBS expressed concern that Sharon Gless's Cagney from *Cagney and Lacey* would be considered a "sleepabout" if she had too many boyfriends.

65. Christine Gledhill, "Pleasurable Negotiations," in E. Deidre Pribram, ed. *Female Spectators* (New York: Verso, 1988), 87.

julie d'acci

93

The Patty Duke Show

four **girl watchers**

patty duke

and teen tv

m o y a   l u c k e t t

During 1965, teenage girls seemed to take over the airwaves: Patty Lane and her Scottish cousin Cathy as well as Gidget, Karen, and Tammy joined screaming Beatlemaniacs, girl singers, and the *Shindig* dancers as America fell under the spell of teenage girl culture. Although television had offered teen fare before *The Patty Duke Show* debuted in 1963, most of these shows were centered on aspects of male adolescence like the "many loves" of Dobie Gillis, the maturation of Ricky and David Nelson, or the problems of juvenile delinquents.[1] In contrast, *Patty Duke* focused on the consciousness of teenage girls, starting a trend that continued throughout the mid-1960s. While not a simple celebration of teenage femininity, *Patty Duke* certainly highlighted the values of its female protagonist(s) by contrasting her with the awkward figures of her vapid boyfriend Richard and her "geeky" bespectacled younger brother Ross, thus ensuring youthful audiences' identification with Patty—or her identical but more reserved Scottish cousin, Cathy.

During the mid-1960s femininity and teenage life both underwent major redefinition. Against the background of the civil rights movement, the popularization of feminist thought, and the JFK-led spotlight on youth, teenage girls found themselves facing a new future and at the center of public attention. Serenaded by the songs of New Jersey's Leslie Gore and entertained by the likes of *Patty Duke*, *Gidget*, and *Karen*, 1960s teenage girls participated in a culture that stressed the joys of self and same sex friendships. They were also taught to expect careers outside the home as they benefited from the more intensive education received as a result of the post-Sputnik drive to improve the nation's schools. As these teens anticipated a period of independence outside marriage and parental jurisdiction, new narrative possibilities became available and were quickly taken up by the media, especially television.

While the possibility of social change was unquestionably progressive, it created additional pressures for teenage girls that would be captured in the dilemmas and tensions represented in these girl shows. As a 1963 article in *Seventeen* noted:

> The question "Who am I?" has a far more special meaning for girls than it does for boys. Boys, from the time they are three or four, know in general terms what it means to be a man. It means to be brave, aggressive, decisive and logical—and above all it means to do *something*: a man *is* what he *does*. . . .Whatever his occupation, that is his *identity* . . . Not so for girls. As they grow up, they are never quite certain what their primary identity is going to be. Parents, teachers, friends, boys, novels, movies, and magazines all seem to be telling them so many different things, many conflicting things about who and what they are.[2]

After citing a number of letters from teenage girls detailing their identity crises, writer Morton M. Hunt suggested that this very confusion represented women's greatest strength. He argued that this was a reflection of women's multifaceted talents, a sign that teenage girls would be particularly suited to success in a modern, constantly changing world. Hunt's progressive message stands in contrast to other representations of teenage femininity from this period. For example, Grace and Fred M. Hechinger's best selling exposé, *Teenage Tyranny*, blames girls for most of the problems in teenage culture. Early marriage and excessive financial and social pressures on young men were all seen as consequences of the demands placed on boys by adolescent girls, rendering teen life a "girl-dominated society."[3]

Indeed, girls' influence would become more apparent as the decade progressed and the teen population of the United States exploded, bringing a new visibility to youth culture and making teenage girls increasingly valuable as consumers. By 1963, reports estimated teenage spending power at $10 billion annually, and by 1965 it had soared to three times this amount and showed no sign of decline.[4] Girls spent more than boys (who saved for large ticket items like cars), shopping regularly for clothes, records, makeup, books and magazines. Suddenly their tastes and activities really mattered, acquiring an economic importance that resonated outside the confines of their bedrooms.[5] These increases in teenage spending were accompanied by close and often critical media investigations into youth trends. Reports found feminine purchases and fads most bewildering, creating images of teenage girls as particularly erratic, incomprehensible, and often irresponsible—a reputation that would only be compounded by the rise of Beatlemania. Together, then, these phenomena suggested that there was some essentially "feminine" quality to teenage life at this time.

Unlike adult consumers, teenagers were that desirable rarity, a demographic with completely disposable income, a phenomenon that *Printers' Ink* described as "a fact sufficient to make any marketing man lick his chops with glee."[6] Nevertheless, despite manufacturers' seeming success in capturing this market, all reports testified to the problems of selling *any* particular product to this audience. Most consumer analysts agreed that the major difficulties were predicting and capitalizing on teen trends before they waned. *Newsweek* hinted that this problem might be traced back to teenagers' desire to keep their (sub)culture secret. Teens wanted to preserve this "generation gap," moving on from trends as soon as they were widely copied. Trying to keep pace, advertising agencies hired teenagers as part-time interviewers while major department stores like Macy's, Sears, and Chicago's Carson, Pirie & Co. appointed teen consultants to report on the latest high school fads.[7]

The problem of the unpredictability of teenage taste was also compounded by the brevity of teen life for, as a writer for *Newsweek* noted, "no one remains a teenager for very long."[8] This was somewhat solved by marketing the teen lifestyle to all consumer demographics. Teen tastes were widely disseminated through a variety of products including teenage fashion dolls marketed to younger children and "teen fashions" marketed to older adults. The press focused upon the success of Mattel's Barbie, launched in 1959 as a "teenage fashion model." During the 1960s, Barbie was accessorized with a host of friends, family, and fabulous fashions, all of which capitalized on little girls' desires to emulate teenage life through fantasy play with dolls, leading *Esquire* to comment:

> Barbie is no ordinary doll—no baby designed to let little girls
> play at being . . . adults, like Mummie and Daddy. Barbie is a dif-
> ferent kind of baby—a teenager with the proper physical mea-
> surements to inspire the desire for a training bra. Barbie has real

teenage needs—party and dating dresses, accessories, personal telephone, fur stoles.... From the point of view of preparing for teenage living and buying, nothing has been left out.[9]

Adults also sought a share of teenage style, purchasing clothes from the teen sections in department stores, copying teen dances, and listening to teen music. As *Esquire* observed:

> The youth cult—feeding on youth's better looks and greater freedom—is irresistible.... Mature men, addicted to gray-flannel suits or Brooks Brothers formality a few years ago, increasingly go for tight trousers and pointed shoes. Eugenia Sheppard, the *Herald Tribune*'s fashion editor, quotes "best-dressed" Vicomtess de Ribes: "The young married woman of—say—thirty used to be the most creative force in fashion not so long ago. Now everything begins with the teenagers."[10]

Although these strategies solved some marketing problems, they angered and further alienated many teenagers, who were repulsed by images of their parents or younger sisters acting as adolescents.

Manufacturers and the mainstream media soon found another solution: bypassing ephemeral teenage trends in favor of the industrially orchestrated "gimmick." Inventing gimmicks allowed department stores and television programmers to promote their wares as teen-centered without having to worry about fading trends. Gimmicks rapidly penetrated the heart of department store retailing and television programming. In 1965, for example, Macy's in New York opened up twelve "Young America" rooms, complete with suggestion boxes, a monthly newsletter entitled "The Pacesetters' Notebook," beauty workshops, and decorating sessions. Manufacturers followed with gimmick products such as Cutex's grape or cola flavored lipsticks, products they hoped would catch on in the teen community.[11]

By 1963, the networks were following a similar pattern. Led by ABC, whose interest in teen culture was largely in response to falling ratings, network executives aggressively courted teenage viewers with sitcoms like *Patty Duke* and *Gidget,* music shows like *Shindig,* and a variety of zany "gimmick shows" aimed primarily at youth audiences. By June 1965, *Variety* noted that to be successful, "You gotta have a gimmick," some novelty that would attract teenage viewers and distinguish the show from mundane, adult life.[12] These programs generally fell into two categories. One featured a fantastic world or character as seen in shows like *Bewitched, The Addams Family,* or *My Mother the Car.* The other capitalized on recent teen trends, such as surfing (*Gidget*) and the James Bond-inspired spy fad (*Get Smart, Honey West,* and *Batman*).

These programs were not met with universal acclaim. In October 1965, for instance, *Look's* senior editor reported that the new fall prime-time line up was slanted too heavily towards teenagers, leading to a dearth of "quality" adult fare.[13]

The Patty Duke Show was an early gimmick show, appearing one year before *Bewitched* and two years before the trend peaked with shows like *I Dream of Jeannie*. Besides technical gimmickry, its theme offered promotional opportunities to foreground the sitcom's quirkier aspects, including ABC's decision that Duke would use two separate dressing rooms—one for each cousin.[14] It also straddled both forms of gimmick show, showing its identical cousins participating in the latest teenage fads. This formula provided enough flexibility to carry the show through three years of rapidly changing teenage life. (In contrast, its sister show *Gidget*, which was centered around the surfing craze, only survived for one season.) Indeed, *Patty Duke* was the unexpected big hit of the 1963–64 season: its first episode rated number two overall and number one amongst new shows, with a "whopping 48 share." This success prompted the network to create a "teenage block" between 8–9p.m. on Wednesday nights, pairing *The Patty Duke Show* with *Shindig* (1964–65) and then with *Gidget* (1965–66) to consolidate its "girl-appeal."[15]

Although it was unquestionably lucrative, the whole concept of teen TV was fraught with problems. First of all, surveys of teenage habits showed that while children were avid television viewers, adolescents were not, preferring instead to listen to radio or to read specialist magazines. *Printers' Ink* suggested that this might have resulted from the general paucity of youth-oriented programming, observing that teens preferred media tailored to their specific interests.[16] Designing shows that corresponded to the details of teenage life was considered almost impossible, a difficulty compounded by the continual change of '60s youth culture. Despite the volume of research into youthful lifestyles during this time, there was increasing consensus that it was best to avoid attempts at "realistic" representation of teenage life insofar as any discrepancies and "adult" misapprehensions would be easily spotted. Gimmick shows, with their deliberate emphasis on fantasy and displacement, offered an attractive solution.

The Patty Duke Show's gimmick also provided one solution to the dilemma of representing the "unrepresentable"—a teenager and teenage life. Most shows aimed at teens sidestepped this problem, employing a cast of adult protagonists and relying on their fantastic properties for teen appeal. Teens were conspicuously absent from *Bewitched*, *The Man from U.N.C.L.E*, *Get Smart*, and *I Dream of Jeannie*, while, with the exception of the more adult Marilyn Munster, the children in *The Munsters* and *The Addams Family* were decidedly prepubescent. Although a center of attention, teenage life was not the central theme in family sitcoms like *Ozzie and Harriet* and *The Donna Reed Show*, easing some problems of representation. Likewise, the teen dancers on *Shindig* and *Hullabaloo*, two pop music shows modeled on British lines, were not narrative protagonists but instead offered background color.

When teens were presented at the center of a show, they were always white and middle-class. Working-class and ethnic teenagers were not simply ignored but unapologetically displaced from attention on the grounds they were not significant. As the 1962 exposé *Teen-age Tyranny* put it:

> We are fully aware that the mores and the problems of the underprivileged are quite different. But the truth of the matter is that ours is a society in which middle-class values set the pace and determine "normal" behavior.... That is why we have confined our scrutiny to the ways of middle-class teen-agers— without apology. They are setting the patterns. They are the models for those who after them will cope with the business of growing up.[17]

Consequently, these shows forwarded only a partial representation of 1960s teenage girl culture, one divorced from differences of race and class. Although this made them less controversial, it also resulted in images that would become so out of step with social changes that they could no longer engage the fantasy life of American youth. While many teenage girls enjoyed white middle-class lifestyles, their culture also incorporated elements from working-class and African American life, particularly expressed through popular music (girl groups and solo girl singers, for example) and from other foreign cultures (the British Invasion).

representing the teenage girl

Socially and culturally, then, teenage girls and their peculiar, ever changing tastes were deemed incomprehensible, unpredictable, and potentially unrepresentable. Yet, at the same time, these girls were a source of media fascination due to their unprecedented spending power and their new role as trendsetters. A series of representational strategies was thus mobilized to minimize the problems of portraying teen girls as protagonists. These strategies drew on observable aspects of girl culture and on older traditions of representing youthful femininity. For instance, the confessional strategies adopted by *Gidget* have been a trademark of much of the fiction centered around young women since the eighteenth-century publication of *Clarissa*, while the identical cousins gimmick used for *Patty Duke* was employed as early as 1933 in the juvenile novel *Dorothy Dixon and the Double Cousin*.[18] Just like the

cousins in *Patty Duke*, Dorothy and her cousin were physically identical, allowing them to pass for one another, but quite dissimilar in personality—
Dorothy was extroverted and talkative, whereas Janet was quiet and more
timid, a well-traveled, highly educated girl whose mother died when she was
very young. Like the cousins in *Patty Duke*, these girls were reunited at adolescence after a lifetime apart, discovering that they were doubles just as their
identity and sexuality started to become less certain. Both these confessional
and doubling strategies connote the fragmented and contradictory nature of
teenage girls' subjectivity, while emphasizing the important role that single
sex friendships play in girl culture. By adopting these well known conventions, these sitcoms were able to ease the problems of representing their
teenage protagonists, constructing them as "feminine" types through their
intimate but often confused relationships to themselves and their own subjectivity.[19]

The Patty Duke Show dealt with these problems by centering the narrative
around a doubling, a *disruption* of identity, thus representing the difficulty,
unpredictability, and protean nature of teenage behavior. Using the same
actress to play both Patty and Cathy implied the extreme mutability of the
teenage girl's identity. At the same time, this strategy suggested that both
Patty's modern teenager and Cathy's traditional young lady were extremes,
neither of which could be fully assimilated within mainstream adult society.
As Tzvetan Todorov has shown, the theme of the double in fantastic fiction
often functions as a sign of social disruption, a way to represent a censored or
"difficult" other: "the fantastic permits us to cross certain frontiers that are
inaccessible."[20] Here, the convention of the double allows *The Patty Duke Show* to
represent the "unrepresentable" 1960s teenager while multiplying the show's
appeal by offering viewers not one but two Patty Dukes. Crazy, popular,
trend-following Patty was the typical modern American teen, often neglect-
ing her schoolwork for her social life and spending much of her time fantasiz-
ing or engaging in outrageous schemes that inevitably placed her in trouble.
Physically identical to Patty (but in most other ways her opposite) was her
Scottish cousin Cathy, a quiet, cultured well-mannered scholar who did not
understand modern popular culture. While the zany Patty was clearly
intended as the ideal teen for youthful audiences, Cathy was offered as a sober
role model. As *Good Housekeeping* wishfully commented: "The essential point to
the show's millions of teenage viewers is that The Duke is in it, not just one
Duke but two. For the freshman and sophomore classes there is Patty, the
hep American kid. For the juniors and seniors, Cathy, the sensible, ladylike
cousin from Scotland."[21]

While *Gidget* focused on one teenager (surf-crazed Frances Lawrence, a.k.a.
Gidget) it used a similar tactic, this time employing narrational strategies to

"split" the heroine's identity. Gidget's voice-over started most shows (her implied authorship "authenticating" the program), and most episodes concluded with scenes where she playfully discussed events first with her father and then with the audience, using direct address to share her *real* feelings with her viewer-confidants. Whereas Patty has alter-ego Cathy to confide in, *Gidget* used confessions, diaries, direct address, and voice-overs to represent the *internal* contradictions of teen femininity. During one episode, "Dear Diary," Gidget decides her life needs spicing up. Turning to her diary for help, she invents exotic adventures for the next week. In the process of composing one entry—"And then, dear diary, I knew I had no choice but to give in. And he kissed me as he's never kissed me before and I sank into nothingness"—Gidget nearly faints with pleasure. Romantic music swells on the soundtrack both to underline and parody her bliss, signaling it as both a clichéd, adolescent fantasy and a true source of feminine joy. Unfortunately, her older sister reads her diary and is so shocked by Gidget's apparent sexual activity that she reports it verbatim to her suitably appalled father. When Gidget finally discovers why her family is treating her so strangely, she feels baffled and betrayed. Pointing to the date, she shows her father the entry and explains "*Tomorrow* I sink into nothingness, Friday I live a life of regret."

As Gidget's expression and subsequent refutation of her desires suggests, the taboo of female sexuality was central to the problem of representing teenage girls in a way that it never was for young men. These shows negotiated this by placing their heroines in innocent relationships with suitable boys whom they would probably marry at a much later date; by establishing their very close relationships with their families; and finally, and most importantly, by privileging female friendship above heterosexual relationships. Boyfriends were handled with particular care. While Patty and Richard flirted with the idea of marriage, they also dated other people. Cathy had her school work, which was punctuated by a series of faltering relationships, illustrating the traditional maxim that women cannot have both love and a career. Gidget had a steady boyfriend, Jeff (or, as he was known in surfing circles, Moondoggie), but he was conveniently three thousand miles away at Princeton, allowing her to date while ensuring that her important relationship remained suitably chaste.

Overall, however, fathers were the most important man in all three heroines' lives. Gidget's relationship with her father overshadowed her feelings for any man in her life and formed the show's structuring principle. As her mother had died and her older sister had married, Gidget and her father had to work harder to compensate for these losses, taking turns acting out the missing maternal role.

Patty and Cathy share similar relationships to their fathers (identical twin journalist brothers played by William Shallert). Like Gidget, Cathy is a motherless child, who sometimes takes on a compensatory maternal role. She is temporarily separated from her foreign correspondent father, although they plan to be reunited when Cathy leaves school (distancing her once again from marriage and heterosexual desire). Several episodes center on this theme, and some of the most emotional moments in the show occur when Cathy and her father have to part after a brief reunion. Patty is similarly close to her "Poppo," but while their relationship has emotional moments and its share of confessions, Patty is not her father's confidant, ally, and closest friend. Patty has a mother, so she can slide more easily into the role of modern, teenage daughter. Consequently, she can immerse herself more fully in youth culture, leaving her father to take on the role of beneficent patriarch. As the sympathetic, well-meaning father who often fails to understand his daughter's tastes, behaviors, and slang-ridden speech, Martin Lane also provides a point of identification for other similarly confused parents.

Unlike her cousin, Cathy has no steady boyfriend, and most of her dates are one dimensional characters. One of the few episodes centered around her romantic life, season one's "The Princess Cathy," *reverses* the show's standard narrative structure by coupling Cathy with an unpredictable boy. This unpredictability is, however, voiced in terms of ethnic and cultural difference as Cathy falls in love with Kalmir, the teenage Crown Prince of Bukhanistan who is visiting this country to learn "American know-how." She agrees to marry him and together they plan schemes to irrigate his homeland to relieve poverty and hunger. One day before she is due to sign the wedding agreement, Kal's uncle visits her to explain their prenuptial contract. After specifying the number of water bison that constitute part of her dowry, he casually announces that the agreement is complicated because it deals with the *first* wife. When the shocked Cathy asks for an explanation, his uncle tells her "It is a small point. In our country a man can have as many wives as he can afford." Kal states that his father had fifteen wives, and when she protests that this is not what she considers marriage, he replies that he assumed she knew their customs. The threat of marriage is thus expelled from the text, leaving Cathy single and mourning for her one serious relationship. Here, the teenage boy is allowed to act strangely partly because he is an exotic "other" and partly because Cathy, despite her tender years, is not represented as a typical teenage girl. Unlike Gidget, or her perky, fad-following, trend-setting cousin, Cathy is a serious, cultured young *woman*, brought up in an older European tradition.

All these narratives ultimately expel male figures in order to underline the importance and pleasure of female bonding, a move which is intensified by the representational strategies that position Patty, Cathy, and Gidget as more desirable than any of their potential male friends. As Alexander Doty has observed, this structure is characteristic of lesbian narratives which invite viewers to take up a "queer position" in relation to the text.[22] These lesbian/queer pleasures (such as female friendship and the pleasure of looking at other women) are also a fundamental part of (heterosexual) girl culture, usually accounted for and dismissed as a sign of immaturity. In order to gain respect in Western culture, teenage girls are supposed to "grow up," replace best friends with boyfriends and husbands, renounce their girlish tastes and deflect their objects of desire and sexual aims away from the feminine and towards men (with the concomitant realization that this also means sacrificing homosocial freedom for heterosexual stability and a recognized social position). Although not as marginalized as gay culture, girl culture is certainly on the cusp, identified as a potentially embarrassing, somewhat humorous phase, accepted only because it is in some sense considered "natural" for girls of a certain age (just as it is equally "natural" for them to reject its pleasures after adolescence).

This tension (or overlap) between homosocial and heterosocial relationships not only structures the world of girl culture, but suggests two reasons why adolescent femininity might have been considered a representational minefield. Because of their youth, marriage is not a possibility for middle-class girls like Patty, Cathy, or Gidget. As if to reinforce this point, several episodes of *Patty Duke* feature Patty contemplating marriage. After experiencing nightmarish visions of domestic suffocation (in "Fiancé for a Day"), she decides to steer clear of commitment until she matures. Yet this renunciation also has more problematic undercurrents. Rather than simply indicting Patty as an unstable, unformed youth, unable to cope with the greater pressures and joys of adult life, her rejection also undermines marriage itself as her nightmarish visions reveal its constraints but never its pleasures.

Complete endorsement of same sex friendships was also somewhat problematic, however, precisely because they might be seen as an alternative to heterosexual romance. Even though this drew on homosocial elements of teenage girl culture, it still demanded careful treatment. After all, despite the presence of numerous male suitors and loyal boyfriends, Patty's friendship with Cathy was finally positioned as the central romance. As if to compensate, 1960s television offered images of excessively feminine teenage girls. The likes of Patty, Cathy, and Gidget dress in skirts, enjoy fashion, wear bows in their hair, and are accomplished in feminine skills like cheerleading, dancing, making-up, fashion designing, and poetry writing.

Yet all these girls are also strong, active heroines: the ambitious Cathy privileges her studies and her career, while Patty and Gidget scheme in order to control others and become masters of their environment, placing them outside balanced gender norms and hierarchies. The combination of their hyperfemininity and more (culturally coded) masculine/active desires ultimately produces an uneasy sexuality. These teenage girls thus come to occupy a sexually marginal space—like lesbian characters, they are simultaneously too masculine and too feminine to occupy traditional narrative roles. Nevertheless, because their sexuality is "unfinished" and in process, these teenage protagonists can be more openly configured, although these narratives often have problems presenting a safe social and sexual resolution to the teenage problem.

The issue of teenage sexuality is perhaps most openly addressed in the feature film *Billie* (1965) that Patty Duke made during her show's second season hiatus. Tomboy Billie is a talented runner, the star of her high school's otherwise all-male track team. At the beginning of the movie, she meets a boy who also qualifies for the track team but lacks her athletic abilities. While coaching him, she falls in love, tries to throw races so he can win, and is predictably confused by her emotions. She is more troubled, however, by his inability to think of her as an equal rather than a girl (as her coach comments, she has invented a third sex—men, women, and equals). In the midst of her dilemma, Billie retreats to her room and sings "Lonely Little In-Between," a song lamenting her uncertain sexual identity. After winning every event at the year's most important track meet, earning everybody's respect and proving herself more than an equal, Billie gives up track, enters into a steady relationship with her suitor (with the future promise of marriage), and finally accepts her role as a girl, although she still insists on gender equality—albeit within a stable heterosexual relationship.

Due to the different narrative demands of motion pictures, Billie's metamorphosis from an "in-between" to a romantic girlfriend is more rapid and straightforward than television's portrayals of teenage femininity. *Billie* diagrams the "normal" pattern of teenage development. Adolescent feminine sexuality starts out as a problem, but both its excessive masculine and feminine tendencies are blunted as the girl matures and adopts her traditional role. In contrast, television shows needed to prolong their heroine's "problem" stage, endlessly deferring marriage and commitment.

While Billie's in-between nature and sense of incompleteness are easily remedied through heterosexual coupling, Patty, Cathy, and Gidget's identity crises are expressed through doubling and same sex friendships. These shows suggest that female partners might complete each other, compensating for each other's deficiencies. *Patty Duke*, for example, proposes that together its two ordinary but opposite girls could be something special, a premise clearly voiced by Patty Lane in the show's unaired pilot:

Separately we're two girls who have a few talents—just like anyone else. You're a brain—I like sports. You like opera—I like to dance. But together we'll really be on the beam. We can be in two different places at the same time. Take school. My teacher says I'll probably flunk Latin—its all Greek to me. But with you here, I don't have to know Latin. You can take my tests for me.[23]

As this quotation implies, these all-female unions only produce a temporary solution as they effectively cheat and short-circuit the social order, resolving problems in an underhanded way and producing illicit pleasures.

Clearly, however, part of *The Patty Duke Show*'s appeal lay in its celebration of contradictory identity, displacing the anxiety of teenage girls' uncertainty into a celebration of its positive, fantastic, and underhanded possibilities. In the episode "Partying Is Such Sweet Sorrow," Patty masquerades as Cathy in order to sing at a party to which she was not invited, while the pilot show found Cathy impersonating her cousin in order to reunite her with her wandering boyfriend, Richard. The show repeatedly celebrates those moments when Patty performs as Cathy, as she runs to a mirror to comb her hair in her cousin's style, rehearses her correct grammar, and removes her lipstick—all to the accompaniment of the same jaunty music. In "Double Date," Patty changes from Patty to Cathy no less than nine times during the course of an eleven-minute party sequence, in an attempt to keep both the sick Cathy's and her own dates, becoming so confused that she identifies herself as "Pathy . . . no, Catty." In "The Perfect Hostess" Duke played three roles: cousins Patty, Cathy, and Betsy Lane (described in ABC's publicity as "a distant cousin . . . from Chattanooga, a platinum blonde with honeysuckle accents").[24] This profusion of identities is further celebrated as Patty impersonates Cathy mimicking Betsy's accent, but the final commentary on her performance is found in the closing credits, which list "Guest Star Patty Duke as Betsy."

These multiple masquerades not only signify a certain feminine excess and a fragmentation/dissemination of identity (particularly when we consider that all these characters and performances originate from one actress), but also suggest that these characters are all at some level engaged in *passing*. Although these performances do not serve the same protective function for adolescent girls as they do for gays and lesbians, this interpretation is suggestive nonetheless, underlining the way teenage sexuality, with its focus on heterosocial activity and narcissistic looking, represents a devalued, abject phase of sexual development. After all, Patty and Cathy's coupling is often associated with cheating and deception, offering an easy and immature way to handle social problems. Yet Patty's drag simultaneously celebrates and rejects the mutability of sexuality and identity, at the same time seemingly maximizing the possibilities of her in-between nature (through her performance of alternate identities). She short circuits these possibilities, though, by emphasizing that there is minimal difference between her "real" and "performed" selves.

These performances play a pivotal role within girl culture. Patty's impersonations of her mirror-image cousin suggest the importance teenage girls attach to looking at oneself, the pleasure in examining one's own face and body. After all, to make a successful copy, each girl has to be familiar with the smallest detail of the other's looks. A series of tie-ins invited the show's viewers to participate in this imitation, transforming their bodies into Patty's, a performance that encouraged them to pay even greater attention to both Patty's and their own images. Advertisements in television fan magazines sold pin-up photographs of Duke to her estimated 6.5 million teen and pre-teen fans, suggesting that readers "Paste them in your locker, treasure them!" The Whitman Publishing Company published a line of *Patty Duke Show* novels for younger readers; a Patty Duke doll was available during 1964–65; and Milton Bradley games produced a *Patty Duke Show* board game for Christmas 1964.[25] Tie-in clothes, jewelry, and beauty tips included Breck's 1965 Patty Duke earring wardrobe promotion that contained her hair-styling advice, plus five pairs of Coro earrings in a miniature hatbox for $2.75 and one proof of purchase. Most significantly, fall 1964 saw the launch of the Juniorite Patty Duke clothing line, a selection of junior petite dresses designed by *Patty Duke* designer Erika Elias; these were dubbed the "Patty Duke Jumpers 'Round The Clock."[26] Now teen and pre-teen girls could watch Patty and Cathy on TV once a week, read their fictional adventures, play the Patty Duke game with their friends, follow Duke's "real-life" exploits in teen and fan magazines, and, if they were fortunate enough to stand 5′1″ or under, dress like Patty Lane herself.[27]

from patty lane to penny lane

Images of adolescent female sexuality could thus be somewhat contained, as long as their desire for young men was undermined and their potentially erotic homosocial look (whether at the self or other girls) framed as immature, duplicitous, and/or directed at the acceptably "feminine" activities of shopping and dressing up. Producers were confronted with a new series of problems in early 1964, however, as images of teenage girls were forever altered by the rise of the Beatles and the corresponding "British Invasion." The Beatles played their first American concerts and appeared on *The Ed Sullivan*

Show in January and February 1964, and were met by throngs of "hysterically" screaming teenage girls at each location—a phenomenon as newsworthy as the teen idols themselves. These events were significant as they affected all representations of youth culture, presenting new images that foregrounded teen girls' erotic look at the *male* body.

Although earlier icons like Elvis Presley, Frank Sinatra, and Rudolph Valentino had previously stimulated excessive displays of female desire, Beatlemania was different. With Elvis, there was the inescapable sense that his sexuality created these socio-sexual disturbances in otherwise innocent women. Female reactions to Elvis thus suggested that society had failed in its mission to protect women, leading to the subsequent censoring of his television performances. Consequently, these women's responses were framed not as signs of aggressive female desire, but as symptoms of their weakness in the face of an excessive masculine sexual stimulus. In marked opposition, Rudolph Valentino had earlier attracted women who responded to his exotic and "deviant masculinity."[28] According to Miriam Hansen, femininity was central to the Valentino cult, whether at the level of the actor's appearance, star persona, or his fans' response.[29] Even at the time, his star persona and his cult appeared to be the creation of women, making Valentino himself seem less powerful than either his fans or his entourage of lesbian Svengalis.[30] Rather than symbolizing the strength of women's desire for men, Hansen observes that "the Valentino cult gave public expression to a force specific to relations *among* women."[31]

While aspects of Beatlemania (particularly the teen girls' screams during concerts that obscured the band's music) suggested a similar form of homosocial communication, this phenomenon was more driven by heterosexual desire. Despite their shockingly long hair, the Beatles were not as easily feminized as Valentino, nor were they pronounced sexual aggressors like Elvis. Their sexuality was not on display but instead accented—if not created—by the reactions of teenage girls. Beatlemania was notable, then, because it placed teenage girls as sexual aggressors while suggesting that their ideals of sexual desirability were distinct and incomprehensible. As the Beatles' sex appeal was not immediately evident to their elders, it suggested that teenage feminine desire operated according to its own logic. This provoked fears, for it implied that teenage girls' distinct tastes could circumvent censorship by producing their own idols, creating their own sexual stimuli.

The Patty Duke Show was in the middle of its first season when the Beatles first appeared on television. It quickly and superficially responded with an episode centered on the new popular music. "Leave It To Patty" (April 29, 1964) finds Patty, the head of the prom committee, looking for a band to entertain her classmates. Cathy's British connections come to the rescue as Patty discovers that her current favorite singer, Bertram "Binky" Bristol (also known as "The Mop"), is not only an ex-classmate of Cathy's but also a former admirer. When Binky comes to New York, Patty, disguised as Cathy, persuades him to sing at the prom. This episode is opportunistic. Bristol is played by an actor who is clearly in his thirties, wearing a badly fitting "mop top" wig. His songs are written by producer Sidney Sheldon and theme song composer Sid Ramin, and the cover of his record reveals uneven lettering and obvious paste-up marks. The show's second season was more clearly influenced by the British Invasion and the changed image of the teenage girl. Pop music trends were more accurately represented as Patty was teamed with "genuine" British Invasion singers Chad and Jeremy.[32] More fundamentally, the show's focus shifted. While the first season was more concerned with such "traditional" girls' pursuits as slumber parties, boy trouble, and school plays, the second season foregrounded Patty's engagement with the latest fads. More significantly, its representation of its teenage protagonists changed in response to Beatlemania and the British Invasion.

One of the most important aspects of the British Invasion was the way it highlighted teenage girls' responses to popular music.[33] According to the mainstream media, the typical Beatles fan was a (white) teenage girl, excessively emotional but inarticulate and hopelessly confused. Media representations of hysterically screaming girls presented older audiences with images of a psychopathology that was beyond their experience, images that cried out for analysis but could not be understood. In February 1964, *Science News Letter* reported that "Psychologists are just as puzzled as parents over the explosive effect the Beatles are having on American teenagers," explaining that "there has not been enough serious study on mass adolescent reaction to explain the impact of these four mop-headed British youths on the hearts—and the vocal chords—of a good segment of the younger generation."[34] Even the Beatles fans quoted in the mainstream media could not articulate their feelings or explain their behavior:

> The girls who shriek when they see the Beatles are not very well able to explain why they feel the way they do. "They move me," said one. "They give me a new feeling of youth," said another. "They're cool, man," said a third.[35]

The New Republic cited a doctor who suggested that "this type of activity was important for young women because it made the pains of pregnancy easier for them when they grew up and got married."[36] Even that bastion of middle-aged, middle-class, middle-brow culture, *The Saturday Evening Post*, offered its interpretation. After describing the latest pop music as gimmick-laden "noise," writer Alfred G. Aronowitz patronizingly described its typical consumer. She was:

> ... a sometimes tomboyish and sometimes entirely feminine creature with an identity as vague as her years and as elusive as her tastes. *Billboard* ... says she is about 14 or 15 years old. Other market surveys show her to be 13 and getting younger. One magazine describes her as "desperate, unhappy, twelve years old." Desperate and unhappy though she may be, she still contributed the major share of the $161 million that the pop-record business collected for the 210 45-rpm records it sold last year.[37]

Beatlemania thus came to represent an unfathomable expression of young women's problematic sexuality and its expression through pop music and consumption.

It is interesting that at the height of this craze, the producers of *Patty Duke* did not decide to update Cathy to capitalize on the British Invasion. This would not have been unbelievable, as the show's first season traced the increasing modernization (or Americanization) of Cathy. Patty was, of course, the catalyst, teaching Cathy the latest dances, helping her date boys, introducing her to her friends at the Shake Shop, and updating her clothes and hairstyle. In "The Cousins," the final episode of the first season, Patty and Cathy reminisce about Cathy's first year in America. Flashbacks reveal that she has become more fashionable and assured as a result of her exposure to Patty and U.S. culture. When Cathy sees a frumpish photo taken shortly after her arrival, she denies its likeness, stating, "Why I look so—so foreign."

Rather than continuing to Americanize and modernize Cathy after the first season, *The Patty Duke Show* did the opposite, suggesting that (young) America did not necessarily consider Britain as the hotbed of mod culture. Indeed, as Herbert J. Gans suggested in a 1965 article in *Vogue*, Americans interpreted the British Invasion more as a projection of their needs rather than a reflection of a new—or previously ignored—British sensibility. As he notes, "every alteration in the British image seems to have been followed by a change in America's attitude about herself.... This process [the modernization of British culture] may well have nothing to do with what is really happening in Britain, but then foreign images are only created for domestic purposes anyway."[38] In short, he proposed that the British Invasion was based around a fantasy of a new British culture in order to ease America's more "real" transition into modernity. According to this logic, England was really the old-fashioned culture and America the new: the British Invasion was not the sign of the impending Anglicizing of U.S. culture, but instead a sign of

America's increasing hegemony manifested through these new British imports, which owed their modernity to the United States:

> In support of this theory, it is relevant to note that the subjects of this new British image all have some American connection which has helped bring them to prominence here. The Beatles have used musical styles that owed as much to America's Negro musicians and the publicity techniques of Tin Pan Alley as to London's Denmark Street, while Richard Burton gained his new prominence through his involvement with America's ruling sex goddess.[39]

Gans's comments reveal an implied national refusal to acknowledge that "jolly old England" could *ever* be more modern than the United States, as seen in American-produced images of British tradition (represented, for example, by Cathy Lane) which persisted, despite the influx of young English stars and wild fashions. Television and the popular press continued this paradoxical project of touting English culture as hypertrendy, while also subtly suggesting that its very modernity was due to its transplantation onto U.S. soil, granting these imports a new and "exotic" identity. While London, and perhaps Liverpool, were central to the mythos of the British Invasion, these spaces were constructed as central nodes of a mod fantasy, exotic locales rather than social contexts producing specific forms of popular culture. Consequently, descriptions of the Beatles stressed their debt to indigenous American music rather than the working-class culture of Northern England, while the business of "discovering" new British stars became an American task.

Several episodes of *Patty Duke* reinforce these ideas, suggesting that imported British culture was actually more "American" because of its modernity and its welcoming reception on these shores.[40] Although Patty "has only seen the sights a girl can see from Brooklyn Heights," she has a greater familiarity with British Invasion culture than her cousin precisely because she is a modern *American* girl.[41] This paradox is explored in 1964's "Leave it to Patty," where Cathy is blind to the merits of her friend, British singing star Binky Bristol. Although he is met by hoards of hysterical American girls wherever he goes, Binky is actually pretty traditional, a "typical" Englishman who drinks tea made in a silver teapot, who has a crush on Cathy, and is baffled by his fame. American girls perceive his star magic, responding hysterically to him: one girl is mesmerized, holding her arm out in front of herself as she mutters, "He shook my hand."

Nevertheless, as the series progressed, the tensions of maintaining Cathy's image as a staid, British teenager became more manifest. Even though Beatlemania showed no signs of abating, Cathy paradoxically appeared in fewer shows, despite changes in the image of British culture resulting from young English women like Twiggy, Petula Clark, Diana Rigg, and Julie Christie finally achieving stardom in the United States. Cathy's prim image possibly seemed less plausible once juxtaposed with these new stars, but the British "mod queen" also posed a problem for *The Patty Duke Show* that depended on the differences between its two girls. If Cathy was transformed into a modern teen, the sitcom's textual system would collapse as the two girls merged into one.

The appearance of the British girl stars also had more far reaching implications. Early British stars were male, enabling the media to construct sexual difference crudely along national axes—modern teen girls were American and British stars were men. British girl stars disrupted the "masculinity" of British culture and, in the process, foregrounded Beatlemania's undercurrents of latent femininity. Aspects of the Beatles' appearance, particularly their long haircuts, were seen as girlish, suggesting that their attraction involved a combination of masculine and feminine elements. This infusion of femininity within British culture and its icons thus complicated the stalwart (if excessive and unfathomable) heterosexuality of teen girls' look at the Beatles, suggesting that adolescent feminine desire still vacillated between genders.

These developments undermined *The Patty Duke Show*'s representation of Patty as the modern teen, while suggesting that modern teenage culture did not completely uphold established boundaries of sexual difference. The British Invasion highlighted the flexible sexual aims and object choices entailed in teenage girls' desire. Caught within this logic, Patty and Cathy's relationship increasingly ran the risk of being reconfigured as another American-British romance.

from girl heroines to boy idols

Faced with the British Invasion-induced turmoil over teenage desire, *The Patty Duke Show* gradually changed its textual strategies. During the second season, Cathy's role was somewhat reduced, only to be almost eliminated during the third and final season. As *Variety* commented in their review of the second season opener, "The gimmick of Miss Duke in a dual role . . . could be a waste of production time. At least in the initialer last week, the quiet cousin was completely irrelevant."[42] By the final season, her role had been reduced to such an extent that one episode, "Sick in Bed," was even *promoted* as the first show without Cathy. With less screen time devoted to Cathy, Patty's character was reformulated. By the third season, both her on-again, off-again relationship with Richard and her partnership with her cousin were downplayed, placing her in a more traditional role as a teenage daughter. Increasingly, the show dropped its engagement with teenage popular culture to become a family-oriented sitcom. Now Patty's "teenage problems" were rewritten from an "adult" perspective: the vagaries of teen culture lampooned rather than celebrated, and ultimately represented as infantile fads. Correspondingly, Patty's performance became more centered around broad physical comedy, positioning her as a clownish younger daughter—an older female Beaver Cleaver—rather than a teenage queen.

Clearly, these strategies helped evade some of the problems of representing a vacillating and troublesome teenage sexuality. While Cathy was not entirely displaced, her relationship with Patty was reconfigured. Although they remained close friends, Cathy increasingly distanced herself from Patty's antics, often serving as the mature voice of reason, warning her cousin about the folly of her increasingly juvenile schemes.

Cathy Lane was not the only teenage girl to disappear from the small screen. By the spring of 1966, *Patty Duke, Gidget, Shindig, Tammy,* and NBC's *Hullabaloo* had been canceled. After its success during the 1964–65 season, ABC found itself stranded at the bottom of the ratings by November 1965, with all its teen programs performing badly. On the surface, it appeared that the vogue for teen programming was on the eclipse, although teenage television viewing had seemed to be ascending during 1965.[43] This decline was not a reflection of teenagers' sudden loss of interest in television, but instead resulted from Nielsens' sudden loss of interest in teen viewers:

> Following the 1963 TV ratings hearings, Nielsen adjusted its sample to make it more representative. Originally, the service had been criticized for overrepresenting older age groups. So last season, the sample was loaded with families with children. Competitors say ABC gained because of its strong appeal to younger age groups. This season, Nielsen, trying to hit national norms on the button, reduced representation of homes with children. Result: ABC's ratings dropped.[44]

The issue of why Nielsen decided to reduce the number of teenage homes sampled remains a pressing one. Despite the continued spending power of teen girls, it appears that this demographic was no longer as desirable.

The 1965–66 season did not see the end of all teenage shows, but represented the demise of the middle-class teen girl protagonist, suggesting that these images were now somewhat out of touch. Teenage fashion, fads, and music had all changed rapidly throughout 1966 as the British mod scene had an impact on contemporary style. Teen shows premiering in fall 1966, such as *Batman* and *The Avengers*, revealed this new mod style. These changes abruptly dated most of the teen shows, as Gidget's fascination with surfing and Cathy's romantic problems seemed suddenly to have little to do with "real" teenage life.

While at first sight it appears that *Patty Duke* was canceled because it was no longer contemporary, the reasons for its demise are more complicated. Summer 1965 saw Patty Duke the actress rebelling against her on-screen "nice girl" persona, while October 1965 brought the announcement of her engagement to thirty-two-year-old Harry Falk Jr., the divorced assistant director of *The Patty Duke Show*. *Newsweek* speculated that this would destroy Duke's credibility with her fans, citing one reaction: "'I just can't believe it,' said one 13-year-old, sobbing into her milkshake. 'Not Patty.'" Producer Bob Sweeney announced that it would not be written into the show: "Her audience is 5 to 15 . . . They wouldn't identify if the engagement was written into the script."[45]

Despite these cancellations, the networks continued to cater to the lucrative teenage girl audience. But rather than producing shows starring teenage girls to appeal to young women's more narcissistic and identificatory desires, they drew on Beatlemania and the British Invasion to reconceive the young girl as a spectator as opposed to a protagonist. This allowed them to sidestep problems of representing teenage feminine desire, while still attracting the lucrative teen girl consumer. New teen shows featured young male would-be teen idols such as NBC's *The Monkees*, which premiered in fall 1966. Even *Star Trek*, starring potential teen idol William Shatner, was reworked after its first season, dropping the young Yeoman Janice Rand and adding Ensign Pavel Chekov (a would-be Monkees/Beatle lookalike) to bolster the show's appeal among teenage girls. Even though the British Invasion had arguably peaked, its legacy remained, transforming the image of teen girls, stressing the more aggressive, heterosexual aspects of youthful feminine desire. In turn, television's accent on the specularized male pin-up accented the more heterosexual aspects of Beatlemania, distancing teenage girl desire from its more troublesome homosocial impulses. The explosion of feminine desire, pivotal to the success and central to all media representations of the British Invasion, contributed to the temporary disappearance of teen girl protagonists on U.S. television. This erasure of the precocious teen girl encapsulated the difficulties of representing youthful feminine sexuality. These developments suggest that if teenage feminine desire was to be directly addressed, it had to be in the guise of spectatorship (mimicking, once again, the structure of British Invasion culture, where American girls looked and screamed at male bands rather than directly participating in these cultural events themselves). Ironically, then, just as young women forced their way into visibility, they were made to replay their role as "girl watchers," forever "just looking on" and hidden once more from the public eye.

notes

1. Exceptions to this included NBC's short-lived *Too Young To Go Steady* (14 May—25 June 1959), which was centered around the romantic awakening of fifteen-year-old Pamela Blake.

2. Morton M. Hunt, "Are you the NEW KIND OF GIRL who fits in the NEW KIND OF WORLD?," *Seventeen* (October 1963): 86.

3. Grace and Fred M. Hechinger, *Teen-age Tyranny* (Greenwich, CT: Crest Books, 1962, 1963), especially 46—72.

4. "Specialized Media and Spending Money Both Growing Factors with Teenagers," *Printers' Ink* (20 September 1963): 27. By November 1964, *Newsweek* estimated that the youth market (a slightly expanded demographic covering the thirteen to twenty-two age group) would be worth around $25 billion for 1964, up from $10 billion in 1963. "The $25 Billion-a-Year Accent on Youth," *Newsweek* (30 November 1964): 81; Penelope Orth, "Teenager: What Kind of Consumer?," *Printers' Ink*, (20 September 1963): 67.

5. Susan J. Douglas has suggested that as teenage girls gained power as a consumer demographic during the early 1960s, girl culture was bolstered because young women were addressed as important members of society. See *Where the Girls Are: Growing Up Female with the Mass Media* (New York: Times Books, 1994), 14—15, 17, 23—26, 90—96.

6. "Teenager: What Kind of Consumer?," 67.

7. "The $25 Billion-a-Year Accent on Youth," 81; Grace and Fred M. Hechinger, "In the Time it Takes You to Read This, the American Teen-Ager Will Have Spent $2,378.22," *Esquire*, special issue on teenagers (July 1965): 68.

8. "The $25 Billion-a Year Accent on Youth," 82.

9. "In the Time it Takes You to Read This, the American Teen-Ager Will Have Spent $2,378.22," 65.

10. "In the Time it Takes You to Read This, the American Teen-Ager Will Have Spent $2,378.22," 114.

11. "In the Time it Takes You to Read This, the American Teen-Ager Will Have Spent $2,378.22," 68, 113.

12. "You Gotta Have A Gimmick: Teens Dictate Adult 'Culture,'" *Variety* (2 June 1965): 35, 48.

13. Joseph Roddy, "The Networks Turn To Teen-Agers," *Look* (5 October 1965): 34—39.

14. Patty Duke and Kenneth Turan, *Call Me Anna: The Autobiography of Patty Duke* (New York: Bantam Books, 1987), 122.

15. "30 Cities Appraise 31 New Shows," *Variety* (23 October 1963): 24; "It's 30 Share or Drop Dead," *Variety* (16 October 1963): 34, *Variety*, (8 April 1964): 36—37.

16. "Specialized Media and Spending Money Both Growing Factors with Teenagers," 27.

17. Hechinger, x—xi.

18. Dorothy Wayne, *Dorothy Dixon and the Double Cousin* (Chicago: The Goldsmith Publishing Company, 1933).

19. These strategies are still widely used in television's representation of teenage girl protagonists. For instance, *Twin Peaks'* Laura Palmer, the unknowable teen girl *par excellence*, had her own identical cousin, Maddy, and confided her intimate thoughts in a secret diary (later merchandised through Pocket Books); Nickelodeon's Clarissa (from *Clarissa Explains It All*) shared her insights with her viewers, *Gidget*-style, through a series of direct address monologues from her bedroom; and ABC's *Sister-Sister* (promoted as a *Patty Duke* for the 1990s) centered on identical twin sisters reunited at adolescence after a lifetime apart.

20. Tzvetan Todorov, *The Fantastic: A Structural Approach to a Literary Genre*, trans. Richard Howard (Ithaca: Cornell University Press, 1975), 158. Following Todorov, Lynn Spigel argues that some 1960s sitcoms use fantastic tropes (housewife-witches, genies, vampiric families) to articulate somewhat controversial issues of gender,

race, and ethnicity that could not be addressed on TV in an undisplaced form. Spigel, "From Domestic Space to Outer Space: The 1960's Fantastic Family Sitcom," in *Close Encounters: Film, Feminism, and Science-Fiction*, ed. by Elizabeth Lyon, Constance Penley and Lynn Spigel (Minneapolis: University of Minnesota Press, 1991) 205-35.

21. Alfred Gillespie, "The Double Life of Patty Duke," *Good Housekeeping* (April 1964): 52.

22. Alexander Doty, *Making Things Perfectly Queer: Interpreting Mass Culture* (Minneapolis: University of Minnesota Press, 1993), 1–16, 39–62, 118–9.

23. Sidney Sheldon, "The Patty Duke Show," Pilot, Final shooting script, 15 August 1963, 28, Box 1, The Sidney Sheldon Papers, Wisconsin Center for Film and Theater Research State Historical Society of Wisconsin, Madison, WI.

24. "Patty Triples," and "One for Three," caption on the back of promotional photographs, ABC Photo Division Press Information, Wisconsin Center for Film and Theater Research.

25. Advertisement in *TV Star Parade* (March 1964): 70; "Aaaaaaahh-Wow!," *Newsweek* (18 October 1965): 106.

26. Advertisements in *Seventeen* (August 1964): 324–25 and (October 1964): 43–44.

27. Interestingly, the Patty Duke Game was based on matching pairs of cards of Patty and Cathy performing the same act. When a player matched cards of the cousins, they could discard them. The first person to lose all their cards won.

28. Miriam Hansen, *Babel and Babylon: Spectatorship in American Silent Film* (Cambridge: Harvard University Press, 1991), 18.

29. Hansen, 252–66.

30. Hansen, 261.

31. Hansen, 260.

32. Chad and Jeremy were the most opportunistic stars of the British invasion and were also featured on other, less teen-oriented shows such as *The Dick Van Dyke Show*.

33. See Barbara Ehrenreich, Elizabeth Hess, and Gloria Jacobs, "Girls Just Want To Have Fun," in *The Adoring Audience: Fan Culture and Popular Media*, Lisa A. Lewis, ed. (New York: Routledge, 1992), 84–106.

34. "Beatles Reaction Puzzles Even Psychologists," *Science News Letter* (29 February 1964): 141.

35. "The Feeling of Youth," *The New Republic* (22 February 1964): 6.

36. "The Feeling of Youth," 6.

37. Alfred G. Aronowitz, "The Dum Sound," *The Saturday Evening Post* (5 October 1963): 91.

38. Herbert J. Gans, "Who's O-O-Oh in America," *Vogue* (15 March 1965): 151.

39. Gans, 151.

40. The idea that imported British culture can be considered more truly American was not new. As Lawrence W. Levine has shown, Shakespeare's plays were accorded the same reception in the U.S. in the early nineteenth century. See Lawrence W. Levine, *Highbrow/Lowbrow: The Emergence of Cultural Hierarchy in America* (Cambridge: Harvard University Press, 1988), 30–69.

41. Despite Cathy's European upbringing, she is still American by birth, and thus she does not counter the idea that teenage femininity is synonymous with America even though her Scottish education has stripped her of her American customs and tastes.

42. Review of *The Patty Duke Show*, *Variety* (23 September 1964): 40.

43. "The Habit," *Time* (26 March 1965): 52.

44. "Upheaval in the networks," *Business Week* (13 November 1965): 46–7.

45. "Aaaaaaahh-Wow!," 109.

Jay North and Herbert Anderson in *Dennis the Menace*

dennis the

menace,

"the

all-american

handful"

h e n r y   j e n k i n s

Physically, he is sturdy, active, agile, tireless, and hard-to-catch. Mentally he is lively, inquisitive, imaginative, and of an experimental turn of mind, which frequently leads him into situations he can't always control. Add an unruly shock of hair, freckles, a smudge on his nose, dirt on his pants and traces of paint and chocolate on his hands, and you have Dennis, the All-American Handful."

—Hank Ketcham, Creator of *Dennis the Menace*
The Merchant of Dennis the Menace (New York: Abbeville Press,), p.110.[1]

Permissiveness is an attitude of accepting the childishness of children. It means accepting that "boys will be boys," that a clean shirt on a normal child will not stay clean for long, that running rather than walking is the child's normal means of locomotion, that a tree is for climbing and a mirror is for making faces.

—Dr. Haim G. Ginott, *Between Parent and Child*[2]

Alice is watching a soap opera on television when Dennis returns home. Immediately, he begins to lecture her, "Hey, Mom ... don't you know too much telebision is bad for your eyes?" At first, she tries to ignore him; "Mmm." But he continues, citing the fact that "there's a lotta JUNK" on television, that television violence "learns ya a lotta BAD stuff," and that she should be doing something better with her time. She finally gets up and turns off the set before asking Dennis what he thinks she should be doing instead. "Bakin' cookies! The cookie jar's clean empty!"

This exchange from a 1964 *Dennis the Menace* comic book follows familiar logic.[3] As Lynn Spigel has shown, the place of television within the American domestic space—and specifically, its influence on family interaction—had been debated and negotiated for more than a decade.[4] Here, however, the power relations within the debate have been inverted for comic effect. The boy now rules the home, scolding his mother on her bad TV habits.

These inversions of traditional adult authority reflect the anxieties and tensions surrounding the child-centered doctrines of permissive parenting. Often defended as more "democratic" than prewar paradigms, permissiveness outlined a form of parenting that ideally allowed the child to develop into a spontaneous, creative, exploratory human being without fear of trauma and repression. Its critics warned that it put the parents, especially the mother, at the mercy of the child, who often became a spoiled brat and a domestic tyrant.[5]

Although proponents such as Benjamin Spock and Margaret Mead worked hard to "naturalize" core assumptions about childhood through appeals to "common sense" and biological determinism, the "birth" of the permissive family was not a simple or painless process. Parents were raising their children according to principles dramatically different from the more authoritarian and behaviorist approaches which dominated the prewar period of their own childhood, and this shift produced a high degree of confusion and uncertainty. Permissiveness was also bound up with the shifting gender politics of the American family, linked to the domestic containment of women and the emergence of a more playful mode of paternalism in the postwar period. Never an absolute ideal, more often simply a reformist tendency, permissiveness involved a constant negotiation between the interests of adults and children, between the internalized restraints of the previous era and the conscious reformation of domestic relations, and between traditional and emergent forms of gender relations.

The stakes in these debates were high. Postwar Americans married earlier, and had more children at an earlier age than any other point in the twentieth century. By the end of the 1950s, 70 percent of all American women were married by the age of twenty-four, in contrast to just 42 percent in 1940 and

50 percent today. Nearly one-third of all American women had their first child before they reached their twentieth birthday.[6] At the same time, suburbanization shattered the extended family, leaving these young women isolated from traditional sources of childrearing information and increasingly dependent upon guides, such as Spock's phenomenally successful *Common Sense Book of Baby and Child Care*. Such a situation allowed for a more dramatic change in parenting styles than would have been conceivable in a more rooted community.[7]

Although for some he may stir only faint memories today, *Dennis the Menace* was an important part of that cultural environment, speaking to postwar parents and children about the nature of masculine experience. Hank Ketcham's *Dennis the Menace* first appeared in March 1951, just two years after the initial publication of Spock's *Baby and Child Care*. By 1953, Dennis was appearing daily in 300 newspapers, featured in his own comic book, and linked to a diverse range of merchandise.[8] A CBS sitcom based on the character ran from 1959 to 1963. In the midst of debates about permissiveness, Dennis, "The All-American Handful," was perhaps the best-known child in the country, a figure comparable in his cultural impact to Bart Simpson's place in contemporary popular culture. Ketcham remarked in 1953 that Dennis was "typical of almost every American boy in this particular age bracket." Far from unique, "There are literally millions of 'menaces,' the boys making their own surprising and spontaneous reactions to a sometimes hostile and incomprehensible grownup world."[9] While Ketcham saw Dennis as representative of all permissive children (or at least of all boys), he actually constituted a particular articulation of permissive discourse, one which used the generic tradition of Bad Boy comedy to express male anxieties about domestic containment and the challenges of fatherhood. For Ketcham, as for many postwar children's writers, the model permissive child was male, and the problems he confronted centered on the formation of masculine identity.

genre and gender in *dennis the menace*

> Between the innocence of babyhood and the dignity of manhood we find a delightful creature called a boy.... A boy is truth with dirt on its face, beauty with a cut on its finger, wisdom with bubblegum in its hair, and the hope of the future with a frog in its pocket.... A boy is a composite.
>
> —Press release, *Dennis the Menace*, circa 1953[10]

> He is not a Katzenjammer kid. He is a totally well-meaning, totally honest little boy. Everything he does is out of curiosity, energy or just because he is being helpful—in short, all the things that are normal in a young animal.
>
> —Hank Ketcham[11]

Far from a "menace," Dennis was simply an adventurous young boy who wanted to explore and understand the adult world. Dennis was part of an army of tow-headed boys in striped shirts and blue jeans who romped through postwar American popular culture. Dennis's sandy-topped comrades turned their parents' bedrooms upside down or talked back to kings or took charge of zoos and circuses in the pages of Doctor Seuss's bestselling books. They were rescued by Lassie or led astray by Flipper, or had adventures around the world in *Johnny Quest*. The boys in their striped shirts sought appropriate new moms in *The Courtship of Eddie's Father* or helped their dads escape the pitfalls of corporate life in *A Thousand Clowns*, witnessed crimes in *The Window*, ran away from home in *The Little Fugitive*, or fought the onslaught of aliens in *Invaders From Mars*. In each case, the protagonist knew more than he should about the adult world, questioned or disobeyed his parent's dictates, but somehow, set things right in the end and, in some cases, solved crimes or saved the Earth.[12]

Permissiveness had ushered in the era of what Leslie Fiedler called "The Good Bad Boy." As Fiedler notes, the Good Bad Boy's badness is "a necessary spice to his goodness," with his mischievousness and disrespect for the established order a mark of his masculinity.[13] The Good Bad Boy, for Fiedler, represented America's self-perception as "crude and unruly . . . [but possessing] an instinctive sense of what is right." What a previous generation might have regarded as the worst kind of misbehavior or as horrifying disrespect was here tolerated and even celebrated as "natural" and "normal" parts of growing up.

Not all writers of the period, however, embraced this benign conception of the permissively reared child, evoking instead the image of "wild Indian kids bucking control—outstanding in wilfulness but flunking in perseverance—natural candidates, all, for juvenile delinquency."[14] Jules Henry's *Culture Against Man* warned that permissiveness had reconfigured the Oedipal conflict, with the mother and father competing with each other for the attentions of the child.[15] Henry's anxiety about child rule is vividly represented in Jerome Bixby's acclaimed 1953 science fiction short story, "It's a *Good Life*," later adopted as an episode for Rod Sterling's *The Twilight Zone*.[16] Here, not only the parents but the entire community cower before the fickle will of a psychically powerful brat. Whatever he demanded was judged "good" by the adults, since otherwise he will punish them with his superpowers.

Dennis the Menace straddles the line between Leslie Fiedler's "Good Bad Boy" and Jules Henry's domestic tyrant. In early comic strip panels, Dennis *was* sometimes demonic, as in one where he teaches a neighborhood kid how to make a pretty effective weapon by filling a sock with sand. An early publicity picture of the real-world Ketcham family shows Dennis clubbing his parents with a baseball bat. As Ketcham developed a firmer sense of the character, he increasingly set limits on Dennis's conduct. By the time the comic strip came to television in the 1959–60 season, the neighborhood has "mellowed" towards Dennis, just as the society at large had embraced a permissive culture.[17] Jay North played Dennis as such a clean-cut, good-spirited, and polite boy that the other characters often found it difficult to dislike him. Joseph Kearn's George Wilson is at times a cranky killjoy, but one who is consistently linked to adult consumption and recreation, spending his days trying to put his stamp and coin collection in order, outraged over the constant destruction of his flowerbeds. He also displays a good deal of affection for the boy next door, helping Dennis build a soapbox derby and participating in July 4th competitions. Assuming the central role following Kearn's death, John Wilson (Gale Gordon), George's brother, adopts an even more benign view of Dennis. Himself more active and outgoing, John respects Dennis's spunk and considers him a friend. Dennis seemed much less a menace than the "all-American" boy who was the pride of his community, and whose innocent curiosity could be taken in stride.

The ambiguity surrounding Dennis's "menace" was tied to the shifting composition of his audience. Ketcham, himself a new father, initially saw the comic strip as appealing to "the babysitting age"—young adults, particularly parents, in their twenties and thirties. Much of the earliest *Dennis* merchandise, such as BBQ aprons, cocktail glasses, and matchbooks, were aimed at adult consumers. Quickly, however, Ketcham discovered that the strip had tremendous appeal to children, who imitated Dennis's antics "much as they would play cowboys and Indians."[18] Here, the "menace" becomes a role model and, therefore, Ketcham responded to greater pressure to make his behavior comprehensible and sympathetic (not to mention, a little less demonic).

The television series was pitched to this same double audience of menaced adults and "happy half-pints." Series writer Bill Cowley told the *LA Mirror:* "We don't consider *Dennis* a show for children. It gives adults a chance to recapture their childhood. We think a great many sophisticates watch *Dennis* for relaxation. Don't forget that Albert Einstein used to play the violin and that the late secretary Foster Dulles polished pots and pans as a hobby." A disgruntled Hank Ketcham scribbled in the margin of his scrapbook, "What has this got to do with watching a kiddie show?"[19] After all, this program for "sophisticates" was scheduled immediately following *Lassie* on Sunday nights.

Such ambiguities about the relations between adult and child audiences had long surrounded the "Bad Boy" genre. Anne Trensky has identified two icons of American childhood emerging in nineteenth-century literature aimed at both children and adults. On the one hand, there was the "saintly child" of feminine fiction, the sentimental ideal whose virtue and innocence redeems the adult world; born martyrs, these children are ultimately too good to live and must die in the books' melodramatic conclusions. The saintly child was most often a girl, and was depicted with "pale skin and golden curls."[20] On the other hand, there was the "bad boy" of the masculine imagination, the puckish protagonist of such books as *Story of a Bad Boy* (1870), *A Boy's Town* (1890), *Tom Sawyer* (1876), *The Real Diary of a Real Boy* (1903), or *Being a Boy* (1877). The Bad Boy books, she suggests, parody the "sentimental and pious child literature," pitting an aggressive, free-spirited boy against maternal authority, not to mention saintly but spoiled siblings.[21] The bad boy was "rough and tough, quick to play and quick to fight," a shrewd judge of character, intolerant of adult hypocrisies. His pleasure often came in escaping adult control (playing hookey, going barefoot, sneaking off to the river for a swim, or steeling apples from the neighbors yard). If the "saintly child" stories are part of the process Vivianna Zelizer calls the "sacralization" of the child,[22] the "bad boy" literature represented the carnivalization of the child, the celebration of boyhood as a liminal and ludic moment still free from stifling civilization. Interestingly, both genres were written to be read by both children and adults, the saintly child aimed at the adult female reader of sentimental fiction and the bad boy devised for an adult male interest in comic freedom.

Arguably, the two genres were responsive to the same historical shifts; specifically, the increased isolation of the middle-class family home from the realm of production. As the agrarian and crafts-based economies of the late eighteenth and early nineteenth century gradually gave way to an industrial and factory-based economy, the husband, the principle breadwinner, left the home to work, resulting in the mother's increased domestic authority. The saintly child lives comfortably within this new feminine-centered middle-class household, an embodiment of maternal culture and true womanhood, her emotional values making up for a loss in the economic value of children. The bad boy inhabits what E. Anthony Rotundo describes as "Boy Culture," existing just outside the mother's watchful eyes.[23] While boys no longer had easy access to the professional world of grown men, Boy Culture allowed them to develop the daring, autonomy, and mastery needed to function in a world apart from women, offering an informal and unstructured "course of training for manhood."[24] However, the spontaneity of Boy Culture contrasted sharply with the duty and responsibility awaiting the adult male. With the shift from agrarian to urban (and later suburban) lifestyles, free play gave way to structured organizations for boys such as the YMCA, the Little League, or the Boy Scouts, which more consciously convey an adult sense of responsibility rather than the pleasures of romping barefoot in the grass.

By the early twentieth century, more pathologized Bad Boys appeared in countless early prank films,[25] early comic strips (such as *The Yellow Kid* or *The Katzenjammer Kids*), or the popular *Peck's Bad Boy* books. If the nineteenth-century Bad Boys came from middle class, rural, or small town backgrounds, the early twentieth-century Bad Boys were working-class street urchins, often from Irish or "Dutch" immigrant families. Their pranks reflect overt hostility towards adults rather than a desire to simply escape their control. As the advertising slogan for the Peck books suggested, "One such boy in every community would retard the march of civilization. One such boy in every family would drive the whole world mad."[26] *Peck's Bad Boy* (1883) consistently sought to cause his "pa" physical injury, to expose him to public ridicule, or to reveal his drunkenness, gambling, and womanizing to his moralistic mother. If such works reflect a growing horror at children's misbehavior and a fear of their sexual precociousness consistent with prewar authoritarian parenting, George Peck still imagined essential masculine traits in the Bad Boys, whose "innocent jokes" contain the makings of "first class business men."[27] However, most often, these stories end with the Bad Boy receiving much deserved, often corporal, punishment for his transgressions, restoring appropriate discipline and proper authority.

The debut of *Leave It to Beaver* on CBS's 1957 prime-time schedule signaled the emergence of a tamed, domesticated, and suburbanized conception of the Bad Boy, one well-suited to the comic realism of the American sitcom tradition; Beaver's popular exploits paved the way for the network appearance of *Dennis the Menace*. The good-natured representation of the Bad Boy found in *Dennis the Menace* or *Leave It to Beaver* had more in common with the nostalgic tales of nineteenth-century small town life than the brutal slapstick of twentieth-century urban comedy. As Ketcham stressed, Dennis was *not* a Katzenjammer Kid. Living in a world which brought them constant and often unwelcome attention from adults, Dennis, Tommy, and Joey resurrected Rotundo's Boy Culture amidst the grassy lawns, parks, and vacant lots of American suburbia. If the nineteenth-century Bad Boy primarily sought a refuge from his overly protective mother, and the early twentieth-century Bad Boy sought vengeance on his disciplinarian father, Dennis wanted acceptance and understanding from the adult male community. If the problem which led to the rise of the Bad Boy figure was the isolation of the realm of adult male activity from the domestic scene of childhood, Dennis's actions reintegrated the space of boys and the space of men. Many of the television episodes are set in late afternoon or on the weekends, at times when Dennis's father is likely to be at home and thus capable of being drawn into the commotion.

As Jay North's Dennis barges past closed doors and snoops into closets, he unearths much that went unsaid about the experience of "Organization Men" and suburban-dwellers, and about the great gender divisions that separated male and female experience. Dennis's antics reveal deep-rooted fears about the potential loss of male autonomy and heroic stature as men became corporate cogs and suburban homeowners. "The Pioneers" episode opens with Wilson huffing and puffing over a newspaper editorial that claims "the men of this town are a generation of weaklings" compared to their pioneer fathers. After Wilson writes a heated response, the newspaper challenges him to live off the land for a weekend and thus "prove to the world and our readers that modern man is not a cream puff." When Martha wisely refuses to accompany him on this "great adventure," Wilson drags along Henry and Dennis. Much of the episode centers around their clumsy attempts to hunt, fish, set up camp, and survive in the wilderness under the watchful eye of Dennis and the newspaper photographer. The sad truth, the episode suggests, is that suburban men *are* poor imitations of frontiersmen and might be better off staying at home watching *Maverick* (the popular western which was *Dennis's* prime-time competition).

Consistently, the series' male protagonists fall short of their hypermasculine fantasies, often "infantalized" by their close and persistent contact with Boy Culture. Jules Henry had warned that the loss of traditional masculine authority was one of the negative consequences of permissiveness: "The American father can no longer stand for a Law or for a Social Order; he often can neither explain nor defend sensibly against the challenges of his wife and children.... It seems to him better to relax and have fun." A *Parents* magazine ad for a series of childcare books summarizes the problem: "Every Dad wants to be a *Pal* as well as a good disciplinarian—but how to be *both* when your time with your child is so limited? How to win his *love* and *respect* as well as his obedience?"[28]

If traditional patriarchal authority was breaking down, permissive discourse encouraged a more playful mode of fathering. Child expert Dr. Benjamin Spock notes that "a boy needs a friendly, accepting father. Boys and girls need a chance to be around with their father, to be enjoyed by him, and if possible, to do things with him." Spock stressed the importance of fathers helping their sons to learn how to become a man: "Give him the feeling he's a chip off the old block, share a secret with him, take him alone on excursions sometimes."[29] The image of the father as pal, often wallowing on the ground with his kids or allowing them to "play horsey" on his back, recurs throughout permissive era advertising. Yet, as Robert L. Griswold notes, the new postwar conception of fatherhood represented a reform, rather than a radical shift, in family structure.[30] The mother still maintained primary childcare responsibilities, while the father retained primary and often exclusive responsibility as breadwinner. Men were learning to play catch with their sons and sip tea with their daughters, but they still weren't changing diapers or cooking their meals (aside from the occasional backyard cookout).

The problem, then, is how to bridge the gap between the father's world and the son's. The most common solution was for the father to join into Boy Culture, as Henry and Mr. Wilson consistently do in *Dennis the Menace*. Jules Henry notes that fathers were most often liked because they were willing to participate in the son's activities rather than because they included their sons in their adult interests. Far from preparing the boy for manhood, permissive fatherhood, Henry feared, reinforced adult men's retreat from "the hostility, competition and strain men experience in their occupational lives" back into boyhood security and pleasures.[31] Television's *Dennis the Menace* centers not only around Henry's playful attempts to become an active participant in his son's life, but also the ways that Dennis's playlife bears strong parallels to the anxieties of Henry's professional life. Here, the world of adult men is marked by the ongoing conflicts between insecure yes-men and bragging bullies. The program frequently links Henry's workplace competition against the self-important Mr. Brady and Dennis's schoolhouse feud with the bully, Johnny Brady. Most often, the adult antagonisms are played out through the boys as the two men try to best each other at egg tosses, Little League games, and soap box derbies. "The Club Initiation" contrasts Dennis's initiation into the Scorpions, a gang of older boys, with Mr. Wilson's potential acceptance into the local country club; Dennis's pranks, such as keeping a live goat overnight in Wilson's garage, push the adult to more and more erratic behavior. Dennis ultimately rejects the exclusive Scorpions to form his own club with his friends, which, Wilson, having been rejected from the country club, is invited to join.

If they are prepared to take on more parental responsibilities, Henry and Mr. Wilson hunger for something beyond the safety and security of their suburban homes. Episodes like "Dennis in Gypsyland" (where Mr. Wilson plans to run off with a gypsy caravan) or "Henry's New Job" (where Henry plans to quit his job and build bridges in the Indian jungles) cast the adult males in the ranks of Barbara Ehrenreich's "gray flannel dissidents". While men underwent intensified pressure to become fathers and breadwinners in the 1950s, they also expressed increased frustration and dissatisfaction in these roles, pointing towards a flight from domestic commitment which would reshape the American family over subsequent decades.[32]

Almost any event might spark the male hunger for "something more" than washing the stationwagon or cutting the lawn. When Wilson purchases an old chest at a local auction in "The Treasure Chest," both boys and men believe it is a pirate's box. Dennis and Tommy use the old coat and spyglass Wilson finds in the box to play pirate, making a pretend map and stuffing it into the vest pocket. When Wilson finds the map, he is convinced it's real and ropes several of the men, including Henry and the town banker, into financing a boat trip to Marsh Island to recover the buried loot. The "practical" Alice and Martha question the men's boyish pleasure in treasure-hunting, but the men disregard them: "Women have no sense of adventure." The men are portrayed as overgrown boys and their wives as nurturing and forgiving mothers. Ultimately, the men's pirate fantasy is shattered when they learn that the map is fake. As Ehrenreich wrote of their contemporaries, Henry "stayed where he was because he could not think of anywhere to go. If he blamed the corporation for his emasculation, he was not about to leave his job.... If he blamed women, he was not about to walk away from the comforts of home."[33] The result was a male culture seething with resentment and boiling with misogyny. If men were trapped in nowhere jobs and conformist lifestyles, women were their jailers—their "ball and chain"—or so the mythology went.

Just as the nineteenth-century Bad Boy genre embraced a Boy Culture that defined itself in opposition to maternal constraint, the male protagonists in *Dennis the Menace* struggle against the encroachment of women. Misogynistic conflicts surface everywhere, from Mr. Wilson's ongoing antagonism with the spinster Miss Elkins and her cats, to Dennis's attempts to dodge Margaret's persistent invitations to "play house." Margaret's efforts to domesticate Dennis are constantly rebuffed, often with a crisp line drawn between masculine—and feminine—appropriate activities. In "Junior Pathfinders Ride Again," Dennis expresses chagrin that the troopmaster has allowed Margaret to be a "squaw" in their fire-starting demonstration: "You just stay out of the victory dance." Margaret obliges, turning around to reveal a doll papoose on her back. "How could I dance with a little one to take care of?" Tommy, however, remains suspicious: "If the pathfinders are letting girls in, I'm going to desert and become a cowboy!"

Having made remarkably little progress towards bridging that gap, the confrontations between Margaret and Dennis constitute a contemporary restaging of the nineteenth-century encounters between the feminine "saintly child" and the masculine "bad boy." The curly-haired, pale-faced Margaret shares many attributes with her predecessors, including piety, obedience, booklearning, cleanliness, good manners, and an unwavering sense of appropriate femininity. Just as the earlier Bad Boy books parodied this sentimental fiction, Ketcham has no sympathy for her domesticating impulses:

> There is a Margaret in every man's life.... Threatening, bossy, superior, always pursuing, the incipient castrator. Some of us marry her, some escape, and others are rescued.... Perhaps she perceives his freedom in speech and action as a challenge to be met. But more likely, the vitality and disorder of his very male personality appeal to her as a Woman's Problem: an untidy room to be cleaned up and put into order.[34]

Dennis escapes from the threat of domesticity into heroic male fantasies of "Cowboy Bob," who never kisses anyone other than his horse and who knows how to enjoy the manly freedom of the frontier. An early 1960s children's record based on the TV *Dennis* series explicitly links these cowboy fantasies with male flight from domesticity and commitment: "When Margaret cries, 'Dennis, let's play house,'/ I say/ 'Okay'/ But I'm a cowboy with a range to ride/and so I'm leavin' ya', my blushing bride/ I'm gonna ride all night/ I'm gonna ride all day/ I'll never marry, Margaret/ She won't catch me/ I'm leavin', I'm gettin' away." However, Dennis can never fully escape. A recurring theme in both the comic strip and the television series was Dennis's attempts to run away from home, to enjoy the life on the open road as a hobo, only to return again when he ran out of food or developed a fear of the dark. Like the adult males, he hungers for freedom while desiring to be mothered.

If permissive discourse saw gender differences as a set of natural biological attributes (rough-house in boys, domesticity in girls), it also expressed anxiety that sexual identity might be negated by poor socialization (or, as in many misogynist formulations, by too much mothering). Ginott's *Between Parent and Child* (1965) advises that:

> Both boys and girls need help in their progress toward their different biological destinies.... Boys should not have to bear feminine names, or to wear restrictive clothes, or to grow girls' curls. They should not be expected to be as neat and as compliant as girls, or to have ladylike manners.[35]

The most ambivalent figure in *Dennis the Menace*, Joey is constantly torn between playing house with Margaret and playing cowboys with Dennis. In one story from an early 1960s comic book, Margaret convinces Joey to become a "little gentleman" who is "nice and polite and clean" and shuns Dennis's company. Joey rejects Dennis's play as too "rough ... an' noisy," until Dennis tricks Margaret into a long anticowboy tirade. "See? She don't know nothin'! So lets play!," Dennis exclaims before the two boys engage in a backyard gunfight.[36] Despite his allegiance to the cowboy mythos, Joey is a "sissy." The Gesell Institute's *Child Behavior* (1955) offers a description of a boy very much like Joey:

> This is the boy who from the beginning prefers feminine activities and shuns anything rough and tumble. He prefers to play with girls. He favors such activities as painting, singing, play-acting, dressing dolls. He himself loves to dress up in girls' clothes.

Permissiveness rejected the notion that scolding or ridiculing such a child might push him back into gender-appropriate conduct: "The best treatment seems to be to permit these favored activities within certain bounds." For example, one recommendation taught the young boys how to closet their desires: "No lipstick and no flowers in the hat *outside the house* [emphasis in original]."[37] Ultimately, most such boys would "grow up to lead perfectly normal personal lives," and might "eventually become outstanding as artists, musicians, or as actors, costume designers, playwrights"—professions linked with homosexuality.[38] A "Mama's boy" like Joey confounded permissiveness's attempts to naturalize gender differences. Even Dennis seems at times confused about appropriate gender behavior in his presence, as in a 1950s cartoon where Dennis asks, "Mom, would you explain to Joey why boys don't play with dolls? I forget." Given the potential "queerness" of this character and his poor fit within the gender-segregated world of *Dennis the Menace*, it is hardly surprising that the character appeared infrequently on the television series. His function as Dennis's pal is replaced by the more traditionally rough-and-tumble, girl-hating Tommy, helping to keep the suburban frontier safe for "Cowboy Bob" and his posse.

the bad boy as political allegory

> Taking the so-called "Menace" out of Dennis might prove to be
> a real job of subversion and a truly un-American activity....
> Dennis may be hard to live with at times. Free people are always
> harder to live with than slaves.
>
> —Dr. James L. Hymes Jr.[39]

Children—their bodies, their impulses, their imaginations—had always carried tremendous political significance within permissive discourse. The architects of the postwar permissive culture had mostly been veterans, many of them involved in the management of American opinion during the war.[40] Early permissive books saw their approaches as fostering "democracy" within the home and contrasting sharply with the authoritarian regimes of the Germans.[41] Arnold Gesell and Frances Ilg's *Infant and Child in the Culture of Today* (1943) argued that German Kulture "fosters autocratic parent-child relationships, favors despotic discipline ... [and] is not concerned with the individual as a person"—traits also linked to the prewar paradigm. A more democratic approach to childrearing, on the other hand, "exalts the status of the family as a social group, favors reciprocity in parent-child relationships and encourages humane discipline of the child through guidance and understanding."[42] The rules that structured the family and their enforcement constituted the child's first exposure to democracy; they should be applied in a fashion that left the child feeling a full participant in the family's decisionmaking, and that allowed the growing boy or girl a sense of their own freedom and autonomy.

For editorial writers of the 1950s and early 1960s, Dennis became the embodiment of what was right about America. Dennis's attempts to explore the adult world might cause a few problems, but, as James L. Hymes suggested, it was "a wonderfully American kind of response: open, trusting, friendly, cheerful." Dennis possessed qualities that were "inherent in the American way of life," including a strong sense of his own value and an insatiable curiosity about the world, "the very qualities we would prize in him twenty years from now in a laboratory."[43] Speaking in 1958, Hymes saw Dennis as the perfect response to the Sputnik crisis and to growing anxieties about the American education system. As Lynn Spigel argues in her work on postwar kidstrips, Dennis was marketed as an "ambassador of mischief," and, like other "kids" of the period, was put to the service of symbolizing the superiority of the American way abroad.[44]

The television series came to the air in the midst of increasing American concern about children's "readiness" to compete in the space race. If the comic strip Dennis was most closely associated with the frontier mythology of Cowboy Bob, television's Dennis just as often was shown playing Spacemen. As Dennis remarks in "Trouble From Mars," "we've decided to desert six shooters for space-guns." Like the traditional Boy Culture, space becomes a training ground for masculinity and a "frontier" beyond the reach of feminine domesticity. NASA had rejected the idea of female astronauts, and so for the immediate future, space might be the one place where men could escape feminine influence. But in *Dennis*, outer space only offered pleasure for the young; space baffled adults. When they dress up as astronauts in "Trouble From Mars," Dennis and his friends frighten the neighbors, who are filled with pulp science fiction fantasies, and become convinced that the boys are "men from Mars." Scheduled to be photographed for *Graceful Living* magazine, Mr. Wilson accidently gets stuck in Dennis's astronaut helmet, his adult head not suited for a spacesuit. "The Junior Astronaut" opens with a dream sequence depicting Dennis as an astronaut and Mr. Wilson as mission control. Just as Dennis is preparing for a rocky re-entry, his parents wake him up, and we discover that he has fallen asleep over his math book. Dennis boasts that he will be an astronaut when he grows up, and his father responds, "You might as well be. You're always in orbit anyway!"

The post-Sputnik educational campaigns, with their emphasis on math and science, are often represented as a repudiation of permissive educational and childrearing practices. Too many American youngsters were falling asleep over their math books. Yet Dennis's dream reminds us that there were strong continuities between Sputnik era appeals to science and exploration, and permissiveness's focus on children's creativity and imagination. Much like television's *Mr. Wizard*, childrearing articles taught parents how to turn preschool science and math readiness into fun and play by holding parties with spaceman themes, launching expeditions to better understand the "outer spaces" of nearby meadows, and learning to use magnifying glasses and microscopes.

Appropriately enough, Dennis, the "eighth Mercury Astronaut," became the mascot for the United States Junior Astronaut program, which encouraged children to buy savings bonds to help pay for the space program; this promotion, which mobilized Dennis's newspaper strip, comic book, and television program, effectively linked the permissive child with the exploration of deep space. "Someday," a song on the Dennis record, centers specifically around his hopes that the president will choose him to be the "first boy on the moon." Dennis would be more broadly linked to education in the coming decade, as Ketcham produced a series of comic books dealing with the boy's adventures around the world, comics designed to direct children's exploratory impulses towards a greater awareness of America's global mission. If the Bad Boy of the nineteenth century took great pleasure playing hookey, Dennis, the Bad Boy of the postwar period, was leading the way into the classroom.

Dennis's "Someday" never quite arrived. The President never called him to become the "first boy on the moon." In the real world, the tow-headed youths of the 1950s entered into the "Age of Aquarius" and struggled with their consciences in response to the Vietnam War. If Dennis had been born a real boy in 1951, he would have arrived at draft age in 1969. Would he have traded in his "Cowboy Bob" buckskins and his Junior Astronaut badge for Army fatigues and a M16, or would he have been one of the "Good Bad Boys" who occupied ROTC buildings and went to Woodstock? (Or perhaps we might have read a new comic adventure, *Dennis the Menace Goes to Canada*.) In the eyes of conservative critics, such as Norman Vincent Peale or Spiro Agnew, "permissiveness" was to blame for the youth rebellion. Far from bringing about a new era of democracy, Spock's advice, *The New York Times* claimed, had "turned out a generation of infants who developed into demanding little tyrants.... The small monsters have grown up to be unkempt, irresponsible, destructive, anarchical, drug-oriented, hedonistic non-members of society."[45] This rhetoric evokes the persistent fears of permissive-raised children becoming domestic monsters, or, to use Hank Ketcham's suggestive term, "Teacher's Threats."

But, as we know, Dennis remained an eternal child, living in his old suburban neighborhood, still pestering good ol' Mr. Wilson, still being raised by permissive principles. Dennis appears in hundreds of American newspapers, the subject of nostalgia for parents and children of the baby boom. Children of the 1990s can watch black and white reruns of *Dennis* on Nickelodeon, catch a new animated version of the character in syndication, see Dennis on ads for Dairy Queen, or rent the 1992 John Hughes feature film comedy about the boy's antics. Dennis came of age with permissiveness, embodying both its aspirations and its contradictions, but he has outlived it.

In the 1950s and early 1960s, however, Dennis enjoyed greater cultural resonance, an important representation of the permissive child. Hank Ketcham had reworked the Bad Boy comic tradition to gain new relevance during a transitional period in the history of the American family. Dennis spoke to parents about their uneasiness in abandoning prewar disciplinary approaches for the new and still untested methods of permissiveness. Dennis also spoke to boys and their fathers about shifting conceptions of gender, about male fears of a loss of heroic status, the adoption of greater childrearing responsibilities, flight from domestic containment, and anxieties about the formation of gender and sexual identities. Dennis embodied a particular conception of American nationhood based on exploration and democracy, and he became a spokesman for America's space mission and for the new focus on science education. Within this context, Dennis stood for the permissive child who was always a boy, always an American, and always a handful.

notes

1. Hank Ketcham, *The Merchant of Dennis the Menace* (New York: Abbeville Press,), 110.
2. Dr. Haim G. Ginott, *Between Parent and Child: New Solutions to Old Problems* (New York: MacMillan, 1965), 93.
3. "Down With Telebision!," *The Best of Dennis the Menace*, no. 21, 1964, unnumbered pages. Thanks to Nic Kellman for assistance in getting access to vintage *Dennis* comics.
4. Lynn Spigel, *Make Room For TV: Television and the Family Ideal in Postwar America* (Chicago: University of Chicago Press, 1992). See also Lynn Spigel, "Seducing the Innocent: Childhood and Television in Postwar America," in William S. Solomon and Robert W. McChesney eds. *Ruthless Criticism: New Perspectives in U.S. Communication History* (Minneapolis: University of Minnesota Press, 1993), 259–90.
5. For feminist critiques of permissiveness, see Nancy Pottishman Weiss, "Mother, the Invention of Necessity: Dr. Benjamin Spock's *Baby and Child Care*," in N. Ray Hiner and Joseph M. Hawes eds. *Growing Up in America: Children in Historical Perspective* (Chicago: Chicago University Press, 1985), 283–303; Barbara Ehrenreich and Deirdre English, *For Her Own Good: 150 Years of the Expert's Advice to Women* (New York: Doubleday, 1978). For additional information on Spock's cultural influence, see William Graebner, "The Unstable World of Benjamin Spock: Social Engineering in a Democratic Culture, 1917–1950," *The Journal of American History* 167: 3 (Spring 1980): 612–29.
6. Figures from Steven Mintz and Susan Kellogg, *Domestic Revolutions: A Social History of American Family Life* (New York: Free Press, 1988), 177–82. For other useful discussions of the "baby boom," see Arlene Skolnick, *Embattled Paradise: The American Family in an Age of Uncertainty* (New York: Basic Books, 1991); Charles E. Strickland, "The Baby Boom, Prosperity and the Changing Worlds of Children, 1945–1963"

in Joseph M. Hawes and N. Ray Hiner eds. *American Childhood: A Research Guide and Historical Handbook* (Westport: Greenwood, 1985), 533–85.

7. Contributing to Spock's success was the fact that the PocketBook edition was released simultaneously with the hardback edition, making the book widely accessible and affordable. The paperback edition outsold the hardback at a ratio of ninety to one, with paperback sales reaching one million within the first three years of publication. Spock's book ranks with The Bible and the collected works of Shakespeare as the world's all-time bestseller. The actual sales of the book are a meager measure of its impact, since copies were often passed from mother to mother as one's child outgrew Spock's advice and another was born. Nancy Pottishman Weiss, ("Mother, the Invention of Necessity," 283–93), notes that many mothers, only half jokingly, referred to Spock's book as the "Bible" or the "Gospel" around which they ran their households.

8. "Dennis the Menace is Big Business," Press Release, Hank Ketcham Papers, Boston University, Box 69, Boston, MA. (All subsequent references to these materials will be identified as HKP.) See also "Ketcham's Menace," *Newsweek* (4 May 1953): 57. By 1961, Dennis ran in 700 daily and Sunday newspapers. "From Cartoon to Big Business with *Dennis the Menace*," *Publisher's Weekly* (HKP): nn.

9. Hank Ketcham, "There are Millions of Menaces," *McClurg Book News*, November 1953 (HKP).

10. The statement seems to have been written by Alan Beck for the New England Life Insurance Company. Ketcham distributed it as part of the promotional materials for the comic strip, sometimes with, sometimes without attribution (HKP). One presumes that Ketcham felt it summarized something of the quality of "boyhood" as he represented it in *Dennis the Menace*.

11. Donald Freemman, "Dennis the Menace to Make TV Debut with Fall Series," *San Diego Sunday Morning* (16 August 1959): 6 (HKP).

12. As Jacqueline Rose notes, society often represents childhood innocence in universalized terms which ignore the "local" problems of race, class, gender, and sexuality. Here, the popular image of the boy in the striped shirts seems to stand in for all children despite, and probably because of, the image's specificity as white, middle class, and male.

13. Leslie Fiedler, "The Eye of Innocence," in Leslie Fiedler, *No! In Thunder: Essays on Myth and Literature* (Boston: Beacon Press, 1960), 263.

14. Puner, 39.

15. Jules Henry, *Culture Against Man* (New York: Vintage, 1963). Henry's primary targets in the book are permissive parents, progressive educators, and "the merchants of toyland," advertisers who target children as consumers.

16. Jerome Bixby, "It's a *Good Life*," in Robert Silverberg ed. *The Science Fiction Hall of Fame*, Volume One (New York: Avon, 1970), 523–42.

17. Ketcham discussed this "mellowing" of the character relationships in "Complacency, the Real Menace," *CA, The Journal of Commercial Art* (August 1959): 17 (HKP).

18. Hank Ketcham, "There are Millions of Menaces," *McClurg Book News* (November 1953) (HKP).

19. Hal Humphrey, "Dennis Is Only a Menace to Maverick," *LA Mirror* (27 January 1960) (HKP). Sarcastic comments are written in the margins of the newspaper article. Ketcham clearly lost faith in the television series early in its run; he makes no explicit reference to it in his autobiography, and there are very few materials relating to it in the Hank Ketcham papers at Boston University.

20. Anne Tropp Trensky, "The Saintly Child in Nineteenth-Century American Fiction," *Prospects* (Vol. 1, 1975): 389. See also Mary Lynn Stevens Heininger, "Children, Childhood and Change in America, 1820–1920," in Mary Lynn Heininger et al. eds. *A Century of Childhood 1820–1920* (Rochester: Margaret Woodbury Strong Museum, 1984), 1–32. I am grateful to Peter Kramer for calling Trensky's work to my attention.

21. Anne Trensky, "The Bad Boy in Nineteenth-Century American Fiction," *Georgia*

Review (Vol. 27, 1973): 503–17. See also John Hinz, "Huck and Pluck: 'Bad' Boys in American Fiction," *South Atlantic Quarterly* (Vol. 51, 1952): 120–29; Jim Hunter, "Mark Twain and the Boy-Book in Nineteenth-Century America," *College English* (Vol. 24, March 1963): 430–38; Evelyn Geller, "Tom Sawyer, Tom Bailey and the Bad-Boy Genre," *Wilson Library Bulletin* (November 1976): 245–50.

22. Viviana A. Zelizer, *Pricing the Priceless Child: The Changing Social Value of Children* (New York: Basic Books, 1985). See also Spigel, "Seducing the Innocent."

23. E. Anthony Rotundo, "Boy Culture: Middle-class Boyhood in Nineteenth-Century America," in Mark C. Carnes and Clyde Griffen eds. *Meanings for Manhood: Constructions of Masculinity in Victorian America* (Chicago: University of Chicago Press, 1990), 19.

24. Rotundo, 31.

25. On the prank films, see Tom Gunning, "Crazy Machines in the Garden of Forking Paths: Mischief Gags and the Origins of American Film Comedy," in Kristine Karnick and Henry Jenkins eds. *Classical Hollywood Comedy* (New York: Routledge, 1994).

26. Hinz, 123.

27. George W. Peck, *Peck's Bad Boy and His Pa* (New York; Dover, 1958), 28.

28. Advertisement, *Parents*, (April 1959): 140.

29. Benjamin Spock, *Dr. Spock Talks about Problems of Parents* (New York: Crest, 1962), 254–55.

30. Robert L. Griswold, *Fatherhood in America: A History* (New York: Basic, 1993).

31. Henry, 143.

32. Barbara Ehrenreich, *The Hearts of Men: American Dreams and The Flight from Commitment* (Garden City, NJ: Anchor, 1983).

33. Ehrenreich, 39–40.

34. Ketcham, *Merchant*, 136.

35. Ginott, 171–72.

36. "Miss Behavior," *The Best of Dennis the Menace*, no. 21 (1964), pages unnumbered.

37. Ilg and Ames, 62–64.

38. For a useful discussion of the sissy's problematic place in childrearing discourse, see Eve Kosofsky Sedgwick, "How to Bring Your Kids Up Gay," in Michael Warner ed. *Fear of a Queer Planet: Queer Politics and Social Theory* (Minneapolis: University of Minnesota Press, 1993): 69–81.

39. "Educator Cites Comic, Sees No 'Menace' in Dennis," *Honolulu Star-Bulletin* (23 July 1958): 23 (HKP).

40. Dr. Seuss and D. Eastman, two of the most popular children's writers of the permissive era, had served in Frank Capra's propaganda unit, working along with animator Chuck Jones on the *Private Snafu* carton series. Hank Ketcham drew cartoons for *Stars and Stripes*. Benjamin Spock drafted his baby book while serving as a navy doctor.

41. *The Mechanical Baby*, 172–86.

42. Arnold Gesell and Frances Ilg, *Infant and Child in the Culture of Today* (New York: Harper and Row, 1943), as quoted in *The Mechanical Baby*, 174.

43. "Educator Cites Comic," 23.

44. Lynn Spigel, "Innocence Abroad: The Geopolitics of Postwar Kidstrips," in *Media and Childhood*, Marsha Kinder, ed. (Durham, NC: Duke University Press, 1996).

45. Cited in Ehrenreich and English, 261.

institutions

of

culture

On the set of *Alfred Hitchcock Presents*

Alfred Hitchcock Presents

the

independents

rethinking the

television studio system

mark alvey

By 1960 American television was, by and large, Hollywood television. The three networks had solidified their control over prime-time programming during the previous decade, in the process delegating the bulk of production matters to motion picture makers. By the mid-1950s most of the major movie studios were involved in producing series for the small screen, and when the 1960 prime-time schedule was unveiled, over 80 percent of it was generated in Hollywood.[1] With the network-Hollywood alliance cemented, telefilm production established as an integral part of the American film industry, and the filmed series set as the fundamental form of television, the late 1950s has been seen as a period of stabilization, setting the stage for the stasis—both industrial and creative—of the 1960s. As one historian put it, "The economic and programming trends within the TV industry climaxed at the end of the 1950s, giving American television a relatively stable set of commercial structures and prime-time program forms."[2]

Yet the dawn of the 1960s did not mark a point of closure and inertia for commercial television, but rather a transition into another stage of the medium's development, a stage characterized by continuing transformation and redefinition. Indeed, the new decade arrived on the heels of quiz show scandals, a perceived programming crisis, and mounting criticism from both inside and outside the television community. It was virtually inevitable that the industry would enter the new decade in a flurry of conscious and explicit change.[3] This atmosphere of crisis and criticism intensified the creative and commercial stakes in an already competitive arena, and played into the industry's inherent quest for apparent novelty and regulated difference.

Certainly the 1960s witnessed further consolidation of the networks' control over programming—but against a backdrop of shifting Hollywood power relations, marked by the growing status of independent producers, the rise and fall of various major program suppliers, and ongoing struggles for survival among telefilm majors and independents alike. The central role played by the independents has been largely overlooked in the standard scenario of the telefilm's development as essentially a continuation of the Hollywood factory system. Tino Balio, for example, writes that "after the majors entered telefilm production the market underwent consolidation as independent producers either went out of business or merged with larger firms."[4] In fact, independent producers dominated television production during the 1960s. It was in the interests of the networks and indeed the major studios themselves to subcontract production duties, delegating the nuts and bolts of program creation to independent producers, while retaining the considerable financial benefits of distribution—a logical expectation, since the Hollywood majors had shifted to precisely the same model for features. Such a process of "vertical disintegration," as one critic has put it, is a function of "both the externalization of risk and the attempt to exploit a maximum variety of creative resources."[5] By drawing on a range of independent suppliers, the American television industry could re-invigorate programming while minimizing risk and exploiting the established rewards of distribution. The creative tensions of the telefilm era and the competitive dynamics of Hollywood TV, informed by the enterprising efforts of independent producers, ordained that the terrain of 1960s television would be not a sterile expanse of banality, but rather a diverse field for cultural expression, marked by both imitation and invention, convention and creativity.

the network-hollywood axis

Television's shift from a predominantly "live from New York" operation to a largely filmic medium, and the associated rise of Hollywood as the center for television production, has been well-documented over the past decade. A rich body of scholarship has demonstrated the symbiosis between Hollywood and television, and clarified the impact that the small screen had on the movie business. In 1959, *Broadcasting* magazine claimed: "To the movie capital, the dreaded destroyer that they thought TV would be has turned out instead to be the good provider."[6] The reasons for telefilm's rise to dominance are many, but the most important can be summed up in one word: residuals. Where live production was generally a one-shot event, forever lost in the ether, the filmed series was a durable product—with a durable profit potential via syndication. This revenue potential was significant for the networks as well as producers, and proved to be a pivotal factor in the development of the telefilm.

In addition to the promise of residuals, the rise of the Hollywood film industry as the dominant source of television product was also a function of increasing network control over prime-time programming. Throughout the 1950s the networks had gradually been consolidating their hegemony over program scheduling and selection, and the telefilm series offered the networks a greater opportunity for program control, since it could be brokered by networks to sponsors, rather than the reverse (the dominant practice for live shows). By ordering programming from outside producers, networks left the cost and complications of production to an industry already equipped with the infrastructure and resources to produce a polished entertainment product.[7] Both NBC and CBS increased their reliance on filmed series during the late 1950s, cutting back on in-house programming. ABC had already embraced the telefilm, achieving its earliest successes with filmed programming from Disney and especially Warner Bros., which produced a steady diet of westerns and detective series exclusively for that network (e.g., *Cheyenne*, *Maverick*, *77 Sunset Strip*, *Hawaiian Eye*). NBC went on to establish a similar relationship with MCA's Revue studios, leading to the oft-cited tale of one NBC executive's instructions to a Revue studios vice president: "Here are the empty spots, you fill them."[8] The quiz scandals of 1958 and 1959, coming on the heels of a widely-lamented "crisis" in programming quality, afforded the networks an occasion to further tighten their grip with much rhetoric of "cleaning up" and "taking charge."[9] By dumping the largely New York-based quiz shows, the networks further increased Hollywood's stake in prime time, helping it reach the 80 percent-plus mark noted above.

Once masters of their own time slots, and sometimes producers of their own shows, advertisers were effectively squeezed out of program production and ownership in favor of "participation sponsorship." There can be little doubt of the networks' calculation in this regard, yet there is also no doubt that the economics of the industry played into their hands. Program costs were ever increasing, especially as hour-long shows became more widespread, and the higher costs helped to strengthen the practice of multiple sponsorship. With the price of an hour-long show at $100,000 or more by 1960, few sponsors could afford "a week-in, week-out ride on a 60-min. show," as *Variety* put it. Even those that could came to embrace the wisdom of spreading advertising dollars across several shows. While this strategy sacrificed traditional single-sponsor identification, it minimized risk by increasing the odds of being attached to a hit, and promised a potentially greater audience "reach."[10]

Whatever its ostensible benefit to advertisers, of course, the move to multiple sponsorship further tightened the networks' grip on programming. A few sponsors retained some control over programming in the early 1960s, but shows owned by advertisers were a disappearing breed, *The Andy Griffith Show* and *The Rifleman* being among the last surviving examples. There is no question that sponsors still meddled in production matters and asserted some influence over time slots and content well into the decade, even in shows they did not own.[11] Nevertheless, this influence was relative, and it was quite clear by this time that the networks held ultimate power in programming— not only in terms of scheduling, but, increasingly, in program production matters as well.

As they solidified their control over the schedules, the networks increasingly demanded ownership interests in the series they aired. Typically, they would underwrite pilot and/or series production in return for shares of both first-run and syndication profits. As early as the fall 1960 season, the networks had ownership positions in 62 percent of their prime-time offerings, and the practice became more and more common as the decade progressed.[12] Here again one could argue—as the networks unfailingly did during FCC inquiries into program procurement—that network involvement worked to the benefit of producers and sponsors by reducing their financial risk in pilot production, and that the networks' profit participation was justified by their shouldering of the risk in program development.[13] Of course, their "risk" was relative. If a network-financed pilot was not picked up as a series, the network's investment could be written off; its interests in the rest of the prime-time line-up would offset the expenditures on unsold pilots (and the network's risk was further minimized in those cases in which it chose not to commission a pilot at all).[14] As for the benefits of such arrangements, the payoffs in domestic and foreign syndication, as well as possible merchandising tie-ins, ultimately proved quite lucrative. Clearly, the network position in all such arrangements was reasonably safe and highly profitable.

The networks' reliance on outside program packagers continued during the 1960s, and their insistence on profit participations increased, although the network-producer relationships shifted as each of the three "webs" pursued its own strategy of dealing with its suppliers. For the 1964 season *Variety* observed that CBS was casting its "non-patronage plague" on the studios in favor of independent producers, contrasted with ABC's "reliance on the same giant production companies" it had always favored. NBC, on the other hand, was striking a relative balance between independents and "Hollywood factory" deals.[15]

Although by this time the distinction between independents and "majors" in some cases was ambiguous or academic, it is important to recognize that independent producers maintained a significant role in telefilm production in the 1960s. While Hollywood's move into the telefilm business is often reductively glossed as a perpetuation of the old mass-production studio system, or an extension of "B" movie production, the production systems and financial arrangements of the telefilm industry beyond the mid-1950s replicated the new realities of the motion picture business. The telefilm was inextricably bound to the Hollywood system, but it reflected the package-oriented structure of the contemporary film industry more than the studio system of old.

from minor-leaguers to "tv majors": the independents

Independent production had long been a component of the Hollywood system, but the "Paramount decrees," which forced the major studios to abandon the exhibition side of the film business after 1948, led to its solidification. As a result of divestiture, the "factory" system of film production was replaced by a decentralized model wherein each film was created as an autonomous project. As Thomas Schatz has written, "the studios became primarily *distribution companies,* financing independently produced films ... shot on sound stages and lots rented from the studio by the independent producer."[16] The same held true for the telefilm. By 1960 the telefilm business was dominated by various forms of independent production and the "packaging" of series on a project-by-project basis, with the major studios serving more often as financiers and distributors than as strict producer-owners.

In feature production an independent was traditionally defined as a firm that was neither owned by a distribution company, nor owned a distribution arm.[17] In television production, the term generally was used to designate firms devoted solely to TV production, or sometimes more narrowly defined as companies that owned no studio facility.[18] Independent television production in the 1960s was characterized by two main systems, primarily distinguished by their respective financing and distribution arrangements: the self-contained firm, and the coproduction deal with an established studio (which might involve one or multiple projects). While the term "independent" does bear some qualification in terms of the power relationships that obtained during this period, in the context of the 1960s telefilm it served to distinguish a new breed of independent operator from the old Hollywood majors.

The earliest of telefilm pioneers were independents in the truest sense of the term—small, entrepreneurial, and unaffiliated with the big studios. During the late 1940s and early 1950s, while the major studios were investigating co-optation strategies such as theater TV and subscription TV, enterprising producers from the margins of the movie industry and related entertainment fields moved into telefilm production, establishing a niche in network and syndicated programming with half-hour anthologies or genre-based series. Most of the self-contained independents shot in rented studio space, financed their own projects (sometimes with network assistance), and distributed their own product under their own logos.[19] Many independents established a solid foothold in production before the motion picture majors entered the field in 1955.

While not all of the pioneering independents survived (e.g., Jerry Fairbanks Productions folded, Ziv Television was absorbed by United Artists), many thrived. Desilu, for example, went from shooting the *I Love Lucy* pilot on a rented soundstage in 1951 to purchasing the entire RKO studio facility in 1957, becoming one of the medium's top suppliers by the early 1960s with shows such as *The Untouchables, The Lucy Show, The Greatest Show on Earth,* and *The Lineup.* Four Star was dubbed a "TV major" by the trades in 1962, with six shows in prime time (down from a peak of twelve in 1960); its output included *The Rifleman, Burke's Law, Honey West, The Rogues,* and *The Big Valley.*[20] Many other early independents also retained a solid presence as telefilm manufacturers well into the 1960s and beyond, in some cases launching distinctive program dynasties, e.g.: Bing Crosby Productions (*Ben Casey, Breaking Point, Hogan's Heroes*); Danny Thomas/Sheldon Leonard's T and L Productions (*The Danny Thomas Show, The Dick Van Dyke Show, The Andy Griffith Show, I Spy*), and Filmways (*Beverly Hillbillies, Mr. Ed, Petticoat Junction, Green Acres, The Addams Family*). Smaller companies with smaller inventories also continued to operate in the shadow of the major film studios during the decade, among them Rod Serling's Cayuga Productions (*The Twilight Zone*), Herbert Brodkin's Plautus Productions (*The Defenders, The Nurses*), Jack Chertock Productions (*My Favorite Martian, My Living Doll*), Don Fedderson Productions (*My Three Sons, Family Affair*), and Jack Webb's Mark VII (*Dragnet '67, Adam-12*). The fortunes of such unaffiliated operators shifted during the decade, but they maintained a steady and important role in the industry, holding their own with the majors to account for a significant share of prime-time product.

As such self-contained independents flourished, others found success through coproduction with established Hollywood powers. Many of the majors opened their doors to independent partnerships in the mid-1950s, mirroring the increasingly dominant practice in feature production, a practice that bloomed in the 1960s. In such cases the studio provided financing, studio and office space, postproduction facilities, and distribution services, while the outside producer supplied the concept, hired the talent, and coordinated the production. Columbia's TV division, Screen Gems, first adopted this practice in 1954, about the same time as the leading TV major, Revue; MGM and United Artists followed around 1960, as did 20th Century-Fox in 1964. Of the Hollywood movie studios active in television production, only Warner Bros. remained closed to independent deals until the mid-1960s. It should be stressed that Screen Gems, MGM, Fox, and Revue continued to produce and distribute wholly owned projects as well, while United Artists confined its television output exclusively to coproductions (as it did with its features). In-house independents during the 1960s included Herbert Leonard, whose *Route 66* and *Naked City* were distributed by Screen Gems; Norman Felton's MGM-based Arena Productions (*Dr. Kildare, The Lieutenant, The Man from U.N.C.L.E., The Eleventh Hour*); Irwin Allen's science fiction factory (*Lost in Space, Voyage to the Bottom of the Sea, Land of the Giants*), associated with 20th Century-Fox; Leslie Stevens's Daystar, distributing through United Artists (*The Outer Limits, Stoney Burke*); and of course Alfred Hitchcock, whose Shamley Productions (*Alfred Hitchcock Presents, Suspicion*) was headquartered at Revue. The prolific Quinn Martin (QM Productions) was more explicitly "independent," striking three co-production deals with three different studios for 1965: *The Fugitive* with UA-TV, *Twelve O'Clock High* with 20th Century-Fox, and *The F.B.I.* with Warners; likewise, David Susskind's Talent Associates teamed up with various partners during the 1960s, including UA (*East Side, West Side*), Paramount (*Get Smart*), and CBS (*He and She*).

To further qualify the relative independence of these producers, one could distinguish between those that used talent agencies to handle the selling of their products (e.g., Talent Associates, Arena, Daystar) and those that didn't (e.g., Leonard, Martin). While talent agents had been involved in the packaging of series from television's earliest days, they became key players in the 1960s, as they were hired with increasing frequency as packagers and/or selling agents for self-contained firms and writer-producers. After 1960 it became increasingly common for independent producers to retain talent agencies to broker their network deals, and/or put together entire series projects—another byproduct of divestiture and "the package system." In the feature film arena, the agency "came to perform the same function as the studio of old," writes Schatz, as mass production gave way to individual packages, with writers, directors, and actors no longer bound to studio contracts.[21] Although the agencies did not consolidate their power in features until the mid-1960s, agency packaging of television series was well in place by the beginning of the decade as unaffiliated producers and small independents struggled to maintain a stake in the industry. Moving beyond mere talent representation, agents now brought together producers, writers, and performers in series packages, or in some instances represented existing packages to networks, in return for a ten percent commission on the entire package price (around $100,000 per episode for a one-hour show in 1960).

Although they were less visible to the public, the agencies became as powerful in the telefilm business as the Hollywood majors. As the parent company of Revue Productions since 1952, MCA was the largest de facto agency-packager in the business (and remained so until a 1962 consent decree forced the firm to divest its talent arm). And as early as 1957, William Morris and General Artists together represented over fifteen hours on the air. In some cases, talent agencies even brokered coproduction projects for producers in league with established Hollywood powers (e.g., Arena at MGM and Daystar at UA), especially when one or more of their clients were involved as above-the-line personnel.[22] The agencies also were recruited by some of television's key independent "majors": Four Star signed William Morris as selling agent for its entire product line in 1956, and four years later the venerable agency had twenty-five shows booked in prime time (nearly half of them Four Star entries). Similarly, General Artists was hired to represent Desilu's program sales beginning in 1961.[23] Ashley-Steiner, with an established reputation as a "literary" shop, concentrated on putting together prestige packages such as The Twilight Zone, Dr. Kildare, Mr. Novak, and The Defenders, going on to become one of television's leading packagers after MCA's 1962 breakup. By 1963 the talent agencies' television divisions were their biggest and most profitable components. The Morris agency estimated that it drew 60 percent of its commissions from its television projects (including talent and packaging), while Ashley-Steiner confirmed that its television division was the firm's largest, and its major source of income.[24]

By the early 1960s, television was dominated by independent production and "package deals," accounting for nearly 70 percent of prime-time fiction shows by 1963.[25] Admittedly, as small outfits like Desilu and Four Star became top suppliers of prime-time product, and as producers teamed up with old-line majors or powerful agents, the term "independent" became more and more ambiguous, and sometimes meaningless in any "alternative" sense. Likewise, the ostensible autonomy of any producer during the 1960s was further qualified by network financing and ownership interests in many shows, and strong relationships between particular suppliers and networks. Independent producer Lee Rich (Mirisch-Rich), for example, argued that indepen-

dent firms like Filmways and Talent Associates were in fact "house companies" because of their close relationship with CBS.[26]

Still, neither a partnership with a major studio nor a network development deal guaranteed longevity in the television production game. Under
network deficit-financing arrangements (whereby a producer sold a show
below cost in anticipation of residual revenues), even "house companies"
were gambling—and the syndication profits they hoped for, of course, were
increasingly being divided with the networks. Independent suppliers operated at the whim of the market, and it was a market that had only three buyers. Producer-network relationships were notoriously tenuous and network
buying patterns could be unpredictable. A self-contained firm was only as stable as its last hit, and one package sale did not guarantee another. Rod Serling's Cayuga Productions managed to mount only one post-*Twilight Zone*
series project during the 1960s. Perhaps as a result of its long-standing refusal
to cut the networks in on foreign and domestic syndication, Four Star went
from being a "TV major" with twelve network shows in 1960, to a single
prime-time slot in 1963, to receivership in 1967. Filmways found itself with no
program base when CBS "purged" its rural-slanted programming in 1970,
ending the studio's bucolic sitcom reign. (On the other hand, David Susskind
of Talent Associates went from damning the networks in the 1950s when his
programming was "out," to praising their vision in the mid-1960s when he
had several shows in prime time. Within a year of forecasting oblivion for
independent producers, Lee Rich himself had formed Lorimar Productions
and went on to great success in the 1970s and 1980s with shows like *The Waltons*
and *Dallas*.)[27] By the end of the 1960s, all of the powerful movie giants, as well
as telefilmeries like Desilu and Revue, were involved in coproduction ventures with "in-house" independents.

the open-door policy: the majors

Although their fortunes fluctuated from year to year, the major studios
not only survived but flourished in the 1960s; yet the fact that those familiar
Hollywood logos continued to mark a significant share of television fare during the decade was due in large part to the fact that they opened their doors
to independents. It had not always been so. During the mid-1950s the studios
conceived of television as an adjunct to the feature film business, rather than
a site for autonomous, differentiated texts. The earliest TV projects from the
majors—for example, *MGM Parade*, *Warner Bros. Presents*, *20th Century Fox Hour*—
promoted the studios' new big-screen releases and/or offered small-screen
remakes of old features. The film factories' blindness to the need for innovation is not surprising, perhaps, when we recognize that the studio era was

just winding down, and the majors were just beginning to shed the residual practices of their mass production days.

The telefilm track record of these three Hollywood majors is revealing. MGM and Fox first tested the TV production waters in 1955, but their earliest efforts were short lived, and the two studios subsequently sold fewer than a half-dozen series combined by the end of the decade.[28] Significantly, both of these Hollywood powers opened their doors to coproductions as part of their retooling efforts, supporting both in-house projects and joint ventures. MGM geared up in 1961 under a new television production chief, making several network sales. Its single hit that season, Arena Production's *Dr. Kildare*, helped turn around the television division's fortunes, and by 1963 MGM ranked among TV's top suppliers. As for Fox, most of its remaining prime-time inventory was canceled in 1961; soon after, the entire studio underwent reorganization, and for the next two years the studio's role in television production was that of a rental space. But in 1964 the studio staged a comeback with a program line-up that included *Daniel Boone*, *Voyage to the Bottom of the Sea*, *Twelve O'Clock High*, and the seminal prime-time soap opera *Peyton Place*.[29]

Warner Bros., on the other hand, became the definitive example of the dangers of "assembly line" thinking, as it continued its factory system of production, maintaining its roster of contract players, writers, directors, and producers, eschewing outside deals until the late 1960s. Rigidly bound to its conception of television as a formula-genre medium, Warners stuck to its original telefilm path of westerns and private eyes until it was too late. Admittedly, much of the responsibility for the studio's rigid reliance on the same formulas was the conservatism of its network partner, ABC, which demanded almost literal carbon copies of previous hit shows. By 1963, after ABC had begun to broaden its programming menu, Warners had only two series in production (a western and a private eye yarn). The studio made an ill-fated attempt to diversify into the sitcom arena in 1965; its single success, the cavalry-and-Indians sitcom *F-Troop*, was canceled in 1967, the same year the studio was acquired by Seven-Arts, a television distributor. By the end of the decade the only program being distributed under the familiar Warner Bros. banner, *The F.B.I.*, was in fact a coproduction with independent Quinn Martin.[30] If nothing else, the Warner's example suggests that the assembly line approach to television production was outmoded, and that its closed system limited the studio's potential for innovation.

The telefilm fortunes of the other major film studios fluctuated during the 1960s, but most maintained a fairly successful output. Columbia-Screen Gems, the first of the Hollywood majors to embrace full-scale television production, maintained a steady spot in the upper ranks of telefilm producers throughout the decade. In contrast to Warners, the varied menu of programming offered by Screen Gems through its coproductions (*Father Knows Best, Rin-Tin-Tin, Naked City, The Donna Reed Show, Route 66, The Flintstones*) and its wholly-owned shows (*Bewitched, The Flying Nun, The Partridge Family*) suggests that inviting joint ventures offered more variety to a studio's output than maintaining a closed system of in-house production. MGM and Fox, after their initial struggles, solidified their positions among the top telefilm producer-distributors, with MGM going on to produce or coproduce hits like *Medical Center* and *Flipper* (as well as misses like *Please Don't Eat the Daisies* and *A Man Called Shenandoah*), and Fox turning out (solely or in partnership) such projects as *Julia, Room 222, Judd for the Defense,* and *The Ghost and Mrs. Muir.* Paramount, barely active as a telefilm supplier during the early 1960s, save as a partner in David Susskind's Talent Associates (and later, Herbert Brodkin's Plautus Productions) and as a rental studio (notably for NBC's *Bonanza*), did an about-face in 1967, when its new parent conglomerate, Gulf+Western, bought Desilu. Paramount very soon became a significant force, playing host to a mix of wholly-owned projects and joint ventures, including *Star Trek, Mission: Impossible* (both inherited from Desilu), *Mannix, Get Smart,* and *The Brady Bunch.*[31] By contrast, when United Artists merged with Transamerica Corp. the same year, it was already out of the telefilm business, having begun to phase out its television production activities after all of its proposed series were rejected by CBS in 1965.[32]

The one constant among the majors during the decade was the presence of MCA's Revue studios (known as Universal TV as of 1964) at or near the top of the hierarchy of powerful telefilm producers. An observation made by *Television* magazine in 1963 held throughout the decade: "In Hollywood the major film studio always has been known as the big one. Revue studios is the big one in Hollywood these days and it's getting bigger all the time."[33] The studio, which had pioneered hour-long shows in the 1950s, and the 90-minute format in the early 1960s (*Wagon Train, Arrest and Trial,* and *The Virginian*), also generated hit sitcoms (*McHale's Navy, The Munsters*), while remaining the industry's leading supplier of drama series throughout the decade with such programs as *The Name of the Game, It Takes a Thief, Ironside, Marcus Welby, M.D.,* and *The Bold Ones.* Universal initiated an even greater lock on prime-time hours in 1966 when it developed made-for-TV movies for NBC.[34]

Despite being "the big one," Universal's television division was far removed from the Hollywood factory system of old. It, like MGM, Fox, and Screen Gems, retained a vital role in the industry by embracing rather than eschewing coproduction, benefiting the studios with an infusion of ideas—as well as overhead—not possible under the factory system preserved by Warners. As Christopher Anderson has suggested, the other studios thrived because they diversified their programming, distribution methods, and financing and production arrangements, while Warners, with "an astonishingly narrow definition of the television business," continued to rely on one type of product, one customer (ABC), and one system of financing and production.[35] Acting as partner-distributors for a variety of independent producers, the old guard Hollywood studios as well as TV majors like Desilu and Four Star were able to reap the benefits of a more diverse product line in a highly competitive market.

independents and innovation

While imitation is a staple strategy in popular culture production— nowhere more obvious than in television—product differentiation is also essential to market strength and profitability, in television as in any industry. Media scholar Joseph Turow, drawing on organizational and "production of culture" sociology, has suggested that "a firm is much more likely to produce innovative products when it or its environment experiences tension-inducing changes"—in competition, technology, distributors' demands, and government policy.[36] No industry is fraught with more such tensions than the television industry, and no period in the medium's history is more apt an example of such an environment than the late 1950s and early 1960s. As *Variety* reported in late 1959, networks and producers were busily seeking alternatives that would free them from "the quiz-violence-western hook."[37] In the prevailing climate of the television industry as the 1960s began, the calls for innovation could not be ignored. This atmosphere of change and differentiation established a tenor that would characterize the evolution of programming throughout the decade. Reaction to the Warner/ABC-inspired western-crime formats sparked a shift from the action-adventure to "people drama," in the words of one trade reporter, as producers and networks embraced character study, social realism, and topical issues (*Naked City, Route 66, Bus Stop, The Defenders, Dr. Kildare, Slattery's People,* and *East Side, West Side*). Many producers were "presenting anthologies in the guise of more orthodox series" in an attempt to "circumvent" continuing-character conventions, according to *Television* magazine—a form dubbed the "semi-anthology" by *Variety*. The early 1960s even saw a "modest renaissance" in New York production, sparked by an easing of bureaucratic and union restrictions, improvements in studio facilities, and most of all, the success of *Naked City* and *The Defenders*.[38] The medium's more frivolous fare also changed, as the wholesome, well-scrubbed sitcom families of the late 1950s were replaced by a host of bizarre, supernatural or surreal clans (*The Beverly Hillbillies, The Addams Family, Bewitched*), and the heroic marshalls and trailhands gave way to suave spies (*The Man from U.N.C.L.E., I Spy*) and caped crusaders (*Batman, The Green Hornet*).

Granted, most of these innovations were incremental, and aside from contro-versial or "downbeat" social dramas like *The Defenders* and *East Side, West Side,* most were safely commercial. But they were innovative nonetheless.

Admittedly, the concrete strategies for upgrading and diversification of television fare were constrained by the conservatism inherent in the medium. While the industry condemned imitation, it also feared radical innovation. Producers tended to place most of the blame for the imitation problem at the feet of networks and sponsors, who (the suppliers argued) tended to reject the new and different and stick with the tried and true. Yet at the same time producers understood sponsors' reticence to stray too far from established successes, given the large sums at stake.[39] The producers, on the other hand, had more to gain by gambling with innovation, to set themselves apart from the crowd of concepts and pilots being pitched each season.

It is evident that the entry of independent producers on the telefilm scene contributed a measure of innovation and diversity when compared to the rigidly controlled factory mode of production like that at Warners. Even early independent products like *I Love Lucy* and *Dragnet,* while hardly radical—both were, in fact, radio spinoffs—were nonetheless stylistically and formally groundbreaking for their time. Whether driven by creativity or desperation, independents—both in feature films and telefilms—were willing to take chances that the convention-minded and tradition-bound studios often were not.

This view was affirmed within the industry. Dick Dorso of United Artists, which was devoted exclusively to independent projects, cited diversity of product as a key benefit of the coproduction system. "The independent pro-ducers make it possible to attain a full dramatic spectrum of production, from comedy to documentaries to hour-long dramas," Dorso claimed. In addition, he argued, the independent coproduction arrangement appealed to "talented producers" because deals were made on the basis of specific pro-jects, generally of their own conception, unlike the studio contract system "where producers are assigned to projects they may or may not have enthusi-asm for."[40] With the studios acting primarily as distributors, the independent producers retained a degree of creative autonomy from the front office— sometimes total, often contractually guaranteed—promising at minimum the freedom from a conservative "house format" (à la Warners), and at best, the freedom to take chances.

CBS-TV president James Aubrey, who favored independent packages dur-ing his tenure (1959–1965), framed the independent producers' inducements for quality and creativity in more practical financial terms. "Independent pro-ducers are not more capable than major studios," he argued. "But individuals who are involved with the creation of a show tend to remain with that show.

And if they have an ownership deal, they have an incentive to devote more time and energy to its success than if they were on the staff of a major studio." In Aubrey's view, "the factory process cannot work in creative areas."[41]

While we should be cautious in attaching to "independent" producers any mythic implications of rebellion or artistic commitment, it is important to interpret the independent label, as it was used in the 1960s, as a marker of distance and autonomy from the feature film majors. If nothing else the term signals a recognition of significant changes among the studios and the "outside" producers, and an acceptance of the new configuration of the industry in postwar Hollywood.[42] Further, there can be little doubt that much of the change and innovation that marked the industry during the 1960s was due in great part to the competitive efforts of independents.

Hollywood has always been adept at exploiting "conventional innovation." As David Bordwell has written, "Hollywood itself has stressed differentiation as a correlative to standardization."[43] In the context of 1960s television, innovative practices and strategies must be viewed primarily as attempts at product differentiation aimed at achieving competitive advantage in the program-selling marketplace. The independent producer had to differentiate to survive, had to distinguish his product from the competition. Granting that independent production is an avowedly commercial enterprise, concerned with producing popular texts for a large audience, the evidence suggests that the independents were testing the limits of convention and expanding the horizons of popular television entertainment, albeit within fairly circumscribed formal limits. At minimum, independent production can be said to have broadened the creative possibilities within the given narrative and ideological constraints of the industry at the time. Indeed, the "programming crisis" of the late 1950s was due in some measure to the entrenched ideologies and practices of the old studio system (e.g., Warner's western/action cycles), while the drive for differentiation was in large part a function of the "New Hollywood."

fade-out

As the 1960s drew to a close, majors and independents alike were competing in a business driven by the Nielsen ratings and programmers' whims. The market for series had actually been shrinking throughout the 1960s due to the increase in longer-form programs and the growing population of feature films and made-for-TV movies on network schedules. Five network "nights at the movies" by 1966 meant ten less hours of prime time for television producers to fill, and although some observers declared that the studios' feature packages were competing with their own series products, the profits from an extant feature film library obviously held many advantages by comparison to the uncertainty involved in developing new series projects.[44]

As available time slots shrank, network power grew. The major studios had a hand in generating much of what America watched on prime time during the 1960s, but even these titans of tinseltown had to pay their tribute to their de facto "partners," the networks. As the decade wore on, the networks not only tightened their hold on scheduling, but expanded their authority in program ownership and even production. By 1964, for example, CBS was not only insisting on profit positions in most of the programs it carried, but creative control as well. Network profit participation in prime time was nearing saturation. Whereas in 1960 the networks held profit participations in 62 percent of their prime-time line-ups, by mid-decade the figure had risen to 91 percent.[45] In 1965 the FCC issued a proposal, known in the industry as the "50−50 rule," that would have barred the networks from owning or controlling more than 50 percent of prime-time non-news programming, prohibited them from owning interests in independently produced shows, and severed their involvement in domestic syndication. The rule was debated by the commision, networks, producers, and advertisers throughout the latter half of the decade, ultimately taking shape in 1971 as a set of restrictions known as the Financial Interest and Syndication Rule.[46]

Even with the network's monopolistic grip on programming, and despite some pessimistic prognostications, the independents survived. By the fall of 1971, the bulk of prime-time series were still being generated under familiar Hollywood banners—Universal, 20th Century-Fox, Paramount, and Screen Gems—but all were in league with independents. Smaller firms continued to play a significant role in the new era, although many of the names had changed: Filmways, T & L, and Talent Associates had given way to the likes of Leonard Freeman (*Hawaii Five-0*), MTM Enterprises (*The Mary Tyler Moore Show*), Tandem/TAT (*All in the Family*), and James Komack (*Welcome Back, Kotter*).[47]

Television programming at the end of the 1960s looked very different from the way it had at the beginning, in some respects. The decade was, admittedly, a time of continued imitation and business-as-usual as well as innovation and change. Action-adventure flourished on ABC throughout the decade, western heroes still wandered the video frontier (albeit in smaller numbers), and *Dragnet* even returned in 1967. Lucy, Matt Dillon, and Ed Sullivan all survived well into the 1970s. Time, and television, bore out critic Gilbert Seldes' 1956 observation that "the seesaw between repetition and originality will probably be a permanent characteristic of television."[48]

Nonetheless, the 1960s was a period of flux for American television, both formally and industrially. The structural changes in the motion picture industry influenced the evolving systems and shifting fortunes of independent producers and established Hollywood majors as they struggled to maintain a viable presence in program production. The prevailing climate of crisis in which the decade had begun, fraught with perceived mediocrity and genre overload, and the industry's self-imposed sense of responsibility, resulted in explicit ongoing attempts at differentiation in the telefilm series. As it was in the 1950s, and as it is today, television's forms and the television industry were in transition.

Television, then as now, was a business of regulated innovation, and nowhere is this more clearly evidenced than in the evolution of television's storytelling strategies. The economic mechanisms that determine the life and form of popular TV narrative dictate that television must change in order to survive. Producers and networks are involved in a constant process of redefinition, attempting to strike the right balance of entertainment and ideas, familiarity and innovation, continuity and flexibility. The simple imperative of product differentiation, driven by a belief in the audience's desire for novelty, decreed that the telefilm circa 1960 had to diversify. Innovation in this environment was borne of industry pressures and desperation, a product of brainstorming, spitballing, recombination, imitation, theft, *bricolage*, and, on occasion, originality and creativity. And at the end of the decade television was still in flux, reinventing its dramatic forms as part of its ongoing efforts to navigate the creative and commercial imperatives of standardization and innovation. To say that the early 1960s was a period of differentiation is to isolate one moment in the ongoing process of differentiation that characterizes the entire history of television storytelling. To propose that the decade was dominated by the Hollywood telefilm demands the recognition that the telefilm itself was a varied textual phenomenon, and that it continued to evolve.

As yet there has been little in the literature to indicate that American television between the late 1950s and early 1970s was anything but homogeneous, formulaic, static, violent, and/or idiotic. Not so distant historically, and still so familiar via syndication, '60s TV is easy to take for granted. As we tend to accept received assumptions about program forms (e.g., 1960s as escapist wasteland), so do we affirm too easily stock accounts of television's development. Claims of the stability of the industry and its programming after 1959 give only the broadest outlines of the processes and practices at work during a remarkable period of change. Television was stable insofar as Hollywood largely dominated the telefilm, but still quite dynamic in terms of who dominated Hollywood. Obviously, this is complicated territory, which will be fully understood only cumulatively, one step—one case study—at a time. At this stage it may be enough to acknowledge the overarching hegemony of the networks while recognizing the significant role of independent producers and the shifting power relationships within the industry during the 1960s. The questions that emerge as we look more closely at the industry and its products suggest that there is still much to discover about what 1960s television—as industry and as artifact—really was.

notes

1. Morris J. Gelman, "The Hollywood Story," *Television* (September 1963): 33.
2. William Boddy, *Fifties Television* (Urbana: University of Illinois Press, 1990): 2.
3. "Is There a Programming Crisis?," *Television* (February 1957): 50–52, ff.; "A Need for Innovation: Levy," *Variety* (30 September 1959): 23; "Aubrey of CBS: A New Era Ahead," *Television* (September, 1959): 58 ff.; Murray Horowitz, "Vidfilmeries' Soul-Searching," *Variety* (29 November 1959): 31; Harold Hackett, "A Plea to Widen TV's Horizons for More Creativity," *Variety* (1 January 1960): 80.
4. Tino Balio, ed. *Hollywood in the Age of Television* (Boston: Unwin Hyman, 1990): 35
5. Kevin Robins, "Reimagined Communities? European Image Spaces, Beyond Fordism," *Cultural Studies* 3 (May 1989): 152. Also see Michael Curtin, "On Edge: Culture Industries in the Neo-Network Era," in Richard Ohmann, ed., *Making and Selling Culture* (Hanover, NH: Wesleyan University Press, 1996).
6. "Hollywood in a Television Boom," *Broadcasting* (26 October 1959): 88–90. Some important recent scholarship on Hollywood-TV symbiosis includes: Robert Vianello, "The Rise of the Telefilm and the Networks' Hegemony Over the Motion Picture Industry," *Quarterly Review of Film Studies* 9 (Summer 1984): 204–18; William Boddy, "The Studios Move into Prime Time: Hollywood and the Television Industry in the 1950s," *Cinema Journal* 24 (Summer 1985): 23–37; Douglas Gomery, "Failed Opportunities: The Integration of the U.S. Motion Picture and Television Industries," *Quarterly Review of Film Studies* 9 (Summer 1984): 219–28; Michele Hilmes, *Hollywood and Broadcasting* (Urbana: Illinois, 1990); Tino Balio, ed. *Hollywood in the Age of Television* (Boston: Unwin Hyman, 1990); and Christopher Anderson, *Hollywood TV: The Studio System in the Fifties* (Austin: University of Texas Press, 1994).
7. As Vance Kepley has noted apropos of NBC, that company's emphasis on outside suppliers allowed it to minimize risk, cut overhead costs, and streamline its operations. Vance Kepley, "From Operation Frontal Lobes to the Bob and Bob Show," in Balio, ed., *Hollywood in the Age of Television*, 54. On the similar CBS strategy see William Boddy, "Building the World's Largest Advertising Medium: CBS and Television, 1940–1960," in the same volume, 78–80.
8. The "empty spots" story is repeated in Boddy, *Fifties*, 238; Hilmes, 66; Kepley, 55; Laurence Bergreen, *Look Now, Pay Later* (New York: New American Library, 1980), 229; James Baughman, *The Republic of Mass Culture* (Baltimore: Johns Hopkins, 1992): 88.
9. See, for example, "CBS Eye on 3 Areas," *Variety* (18 November 1959): 27.
10. "Plateau on Hour Film Shows," *Variety* (24 February 1960): 27. See also "King-Size 'Bread & Butter'," *Variety* (13 February 1957): 29, 71; Murray Horowitz, "Hour Vidpix Yen Still Hot," *Variety* (4 November 1959): 27; "Why the Rush to Hour-Long Shows?," *Broadcasting* (17 April 1961): 108–9.
11. George Rosen, "Kintner: We'll Take Charge," *Variety* (11 December 1963): 21. See also "Magazine Concept a Panacea for Program Evils? Hardly," *Variety* (25 November 1959): 32; "Who Controls What in TV Films," *Broadcasting* (17 October 1960): 29–36.
12. See also "Co-Financing on Pilots Continues to Pose Problems," *Variety* (18

November 1959): 30. On network control and ownership see "CBS: If We Play 'Em, We Own 'Em," *Variety* (30 March 1960): 25; "The Swing to Network Control," *Broadcasting* (16 May 1960): 92.

13. For the network line on their "risk" in program development see "Swing to Network Control," 93; "For TV Networks: A Long Day In Court," *Television* (March 1962): 72–102.

14. For the fall of 1964, CBS-TV president Aubrey ordered only eight pilots (compared to 20-plus at the other networks), and was considering most series on the basis of scripts or treatments. George Rosen, "A to Z: (Aubrey to Zanuck)," *Variety* (4 December 1963): 17. Richard Oulahan and William Lambert, "The Tyrant's Fall That Rocked the TV World," *Life* (10 September 1965): 96. According to Kepley, NBC eventually began ordering MCA product without pilots. With the right track record, a producer might sell a series without a pilot; see Deborah Haber, "In the Wings," *Television* (January 1964): 38–41, 68–70.

15. Rosen, "A to Z."

16. Thomas Schatz, *Old Hollywood/New Hollywood: Ritual, Art and Industry* (Ann Arbor: UMI Research Press, 1984): 172. For an essential examination of independent feature production before and after the decrees see Janet Staiger, "Individualism vs. Collectivism," *Screen* 24 (July-October 1983): 68–79. Also see Staiger's Chapter 24, "The Labor Force, Financing, and the Mode of Production," in David Bordwell, Janet Staiger, Kristin Thompson, *The Classical Hollywood Cinema* (New York: Columbia University Press, 1985): 317–19, and Chapter 26 on the Package Unit system, 330–337.

    David Bordwell, Janet Staiger, Kristin Thompson, *The Classical Hollywood Cinema* (New York: Columbia University Press, 1985): 70.

17. Staiger, "Individualism vs. Collectivism," 68–69.

18. Thus the designation excluded the feature film "majors," but included producers partnered with the majors in financing and distribution deals. See Edwin H. James, "The Boss is His Brightest Star" *Television* (September 1962): 50; and "Six Studios Big in Network TV," *Broadcasting* (13 August 1962): 59.

19. Early independents included the likes of Hal Roach (Laurel and Hardy and *Our Gang* veteran), Frederick Ziv (radio syndicator), Jerry Fairbanks (Paramount short subjects producer), and General Television Enterprises (former movie executives). Performers-turned-producers also entered the field around 1951–52, with notable success: Desi Arnaz and Lucille Ball's Desilu, Jack Webb's Mark VII Productions, Bing Crosby Enterprises, Ozzie Nelson's Stage 5 Productions, and Four Star Television (formed by Dick Powell, David Niven, and Charles Boyer). On early independents see Hilmes, *Hollywood and Broadcasting*; Balio, ed. *Hollywood in the Age of Television*; Boddy, "The Studios Move into Prime Time"; Anderson, *Hollywood TV*. Trade sources on independent TV production, in addition to those cited above, are Gelman, "Hollywood Story"; *American Cinematographer*, especially "Television Filming Activities" and "Current Assignments" columns, 1949–1968; and Broadcasting magazine's "Detailed Look at Fall Schedules" columns, 1960–1965.

20. "Six Studios Big in Network TV," 59. For a useful account of Four Star's genesis, via a profile of Dick Powell, see James, "The Boss is His Brightest Star."

21. Schatz, *Old/New*, 172.

22. "Above-the-line" denotes the creative talent involved in a project: writers, directors, performers, producers. "Below-the-line" personnel are the craftspersons and technicians.

23. Background on the talent agencies' role as TV packagers is derived from "Who Controls What in TV Films," 29–36; "How the Big Talent Agencies Operate," *Broadcasting* (24 October 1960): 70–81; "Financial Outlook 'Good' for Film Production Companies," *Telefilm* (September 1961): 10; Albert Kroeger, "Veni, Vidi, Vici. [Closeup: Ted Ashley]," *Television* (April 1963): 67–80; Deborah Haber, "The Men From Morris: All the Talent Isn't on Stage," *Television* (September 1964): 2–7.

24. "The Men from Morris," 3; Kroeger, "Vini," 70.

25. "A Detailed Look at Fall TV Schedules," *Broadcasting* (27 June 1960): 34–5; "Who Controls What in TV Films;" Gelman, "Hollywood Story."

26. "TV Film Makers Headed For Oblivion?," *Broadcasting* (3 April 1967): 110.

27. On Four Star see James, "Boss is His Brightests Star," 62; "Four Star Goes to Syndicate," *Broadcasting* (21 August 1967): 58; on Cayuga see Joel Engel, *Rod Serling* (Chicago: Contemporary, 1989); on the CBS rural purge see Les Brown, *Television: The Business Behind the Box* (New York: Harcourt Brace Jovanovich, 1971); Susskind is interviewed in "Says the Critic," *Television* (April 1963): 58–9, 90–100.

28. In addition to *20th-Century Fox Hour*, Fox produced *My Friend Flicka* in 1955, followed by *Dobie Gillis*, *Adventures in Paradise*, and *Five Fingers* (all 1959); the 1960 and '61 Fox menu included *Hong Kong*, *Follow the Sun*, *Margie* and the widely excoriated *Bus Stop*. After *MGM Parade*, Metro sold two feature retreads, *The Thin Man* (1957), and *Northwest Passage* (1958), followed in 1960 by *National Velvet* and *The Islanders*. MGM's other 1961 offerings were the short-lived *Cain's Hundred*, *Father of the Bride*, and *The Asphalt Jungle* (Spring '61 only).

29. Deborah Haber, "The Studio That Came in From the Cold," *Television* (September 1965): 32; Gelman, "Hollywood Story"; *American Cinematographer* columns, 1949–1968; *Broadcasting* "Detailed Look" columns, 1960–1965.

30. "Who Controls What"; Gelman, "Hollywood Story." The whole Warners TV story is told in fascinating detail in Anderson, *Hollywood TV*.

31. "Desilu, Famous Players to G & W," *Broadcasting* (20 February 1967): 71.

32. Les Brown, ed., *Les Brown's Encyclopedia of Television* (New York: Zoetrope, 1982): 129.

33. Gelman, "Hollywood Story," 38.

34. Morris Gelman, "A $15-Million Gamble on Movies Made for TV," *Television* (December 1966): 42, 54–62.

35. *Hollywood TV*, 257.

36. Joseph Turow, "Unconventional Programs on Commercial Television," in *Individuals in Mass Media Organizations*, ed. James S. Ettema and D. Charles Whitney (Beverly Hills: Sage, 1982): 108.

37. "Situation Comedy Comeback," *Variety* (18 November 1959): 29.

38. On "people drama" and New York TV see Morris Gelman, "New York, New York," *Television* (December 1962): 39–45, ff. On the "semi-anthology" see Gelman, "The Hollywood Story," 51; George Rosen, "TV Debut: 'No Mischief' Season," *Variety* (5 September 1962): 1, 30; "TV Anthologies Hit Peak With 8 in 1963–64," *Variety* (26 June 1963): 27

39. See, for example, Leon Morse, "The Hollywood Viewpoint," *Television* (May 1960): 77.

40. Gelman, "Hollywood Story," 53.

41. Albert R. Kroeger, "Iron Fist Less Velvet Glove," *Television* (March 1964): 52.

42. It should be stressed that "independent production" in this context refers to a form of production that is firmly implicated in the structures and practices of the Hollywood movie-making business—what might be termed mainstream independent production—rather than the current usage of low-budget, self-financed, alternative filmmaking, operating outside of and sometimes in opposition to mainstream business and formal practice. Mainstream independent production is an alternative to the studio system, but it is not an alternative to the Hollywood mode of production; rather it is a component and a version of it, and it operates within the conventional and qualitative norms of dominant commercial filmmaking. As Janet Staiger has pointed out, commercial independent production "has reproduced the dominant practices of Hollywood." "Individualism vs. Collectivism," 69.

43. *Classical Hollywood Cinema*, 70.

44. "Hollywood's Hot New Romance," *Broadcasting* (10 January 1966): 27–30; "$93 Million Week's Film Jackpot," *Broadcasting* (3 October 1966): 25–27.

mark alvey

157

45. "CBS Control: Not So Remote," *Variety* (19 February 1964): 27; "Aubrey's Show Business Credo," *Variety* (25 March 1964): 26; "Swing to Network Control," 92; "The 'Three Men' Theme," *Time* (12 March 1965): 81.

46. See: "'Three Men' Theme"; "In Defense of Network Programming," *Broadcasting* (7 March 1966): 31—33; "Another View on 50—50 Rule," *Broadcasting* (7 March 1966): 34—35; "50—50 Rule gets a Lashing," *Broadcasting* (2 May 1966): 36—38; "Coup d'e-tat for 50—50 Proposal?," *Broadcasting* (6 June 1966): 52—54; "50—50 Fades," *Broadcasting* (27 February 1967): 5. On the "fin-syn" rules see "FCC Ruling a Boon, But . . .," *TV-Radio Age* (1 June 1970): 23; J. Fred MacDonald, *One Nation Under Television: The Rise and Decline of Network TV* (New York: Pantheon, 1990): 184—6.

47. Brown, *The Bu$iness Behind the Box*, 358.

48. *The Public Arts* (New York: Simon and Schuster, 1956): 181—82.

Robert Stack in *The Untouchables*

senator dodd

goes to

hollywood

investigating

video

violence

william boddy

At first glance, the U.S. television industry's position of prosperity and security by the early 1960s seems unassailable. By 1963, 91 percent of U.S. households owned at least one television set, and network television had achieved unprecedented audience levels and advertising revenues within commercial and regulatory structures that would remain generally stable for most of the two subsequent decades.[1] The early 1960s also witnessed the confident march of American television program exporters into a booming international market and saw new demonstrations of the powerful role of television in U.S. domestic political life in the famous Nixon-Kennedy 1960 Presidential debates.

But the early 1960s also saw unprecedented congressional and public criticism of the content of prime-time network programming, centered on television violence and its alleged effects upon young people. The forum for some of the most heated denunciations of network program practices, the Senate

Judiciary Committee's Subcommittee on Juvenile Delinquency, held several rounds of high profile public hearings over a three-year period, subpoenaed proprietary industry records, and generated thousands of pages of public testimony from social scientists, industry officials, and members of the public. This lengthy congressional investigation of violent prime-time programming was led by a freshman Democratic Senator from Connecticut, identified by *Variety* at the start of the hearings as the "little-known, hard-to-figure Senator Thomas J. Dodd."[2] Only a few years after quiz show hero Charles Van Doren's spectacular public confession of fraud to a packed congressional committee room, Dodd's 1961 television violence hearings produced "the juiciest headlines on TV out of Capital hill since the quiz scandals," according to one journalist.[3] Though Dodd's intermittent public hearings between 1961 and 1964 produced no new legislation or regulatory reform, the thousands of pages of testimony and exhibits, including material generated by the unprecedented subpoena of hundreds of confidential business documents, provide a valuable portrait of the commercial television industry and its contested place in American life.

While the chief early target of Dodd's Subcommittee was ABC's *The Untouchables* (1959–63), a popular crime series featuring the fictionalized Prohibition-era exploits of U.S. Treasury agent Eliot Ness and gang leader Al Capone, several other action-adventure series on all three networks attracted congressional scrutiny and public criticism in the early 1960s for their depiction of violence and other transgressions of public taste. At the same time, these action-adventure film series also signaled the growing ties between the Hollywood studios and the television networks, and the increasing power of the television networks in relation to their sponsors and local affiliates. The hearings came at a time when prime-time programming was moving from the 1950s model of New York-based live drama and single sponsorship to a highly rationalized structure of network-licensed, Hollywood-produced telefilms supported by multiple sponsorship. The Dodd hearings thus offer not only a documentary snapshot of the shifting modes of production and relations of power in prime-time television during a crucial era of transition, but also provide an arena for examining wider cultural and political anxieties about commercial television's social role in the United States. The crusade against violent television programming in the early 1960s brought together an unlikely coalition of long-standing broadcast reformers, public morality campaigners, and an army of social scientists eager for government and industry research funding. For the Juvenile Delinquency Subcommittee and some of its more alarmist witnesses (notably Dr. Frederic Wertham, author of the 1953 anti-comic book broadside *Seduction of the Innocent*), the television violence debate promised a reprise of the successful campaign against comic

162

books of the early 1950s. Senator Dodd rode the television violence hearings into national prominence as feverish congressional testimony spilled into *Ladies Home Journal*, *TV Guide*, and the quality press, providing a taxonomy of popular and expert accounts of the social effects of popular media. At a time when the networks were reeling from the quiz scandals and critical attacks for the precipitous decline of "golden age" live drama, the industry's reactions to the television violence controversy underscore the networks' new economic practices and public profile. The debate inevitably, if often inadvertently, raises questions about the larger relationship between commercial media and public accountability in the United States. It also provides a portrait of the prevailing representations of commercial broadcasting's public responsibilities at a time when American commercial television was enjoying new domestic and international prosperity and power. Yet the committee failed to deliver promised reforms, and by the mid-1960s, Senator Dodd's television violence investigation collapsed amid growing scandal. Nevertheless, the Dodd hearings provide a revealing glimpse of both the programming operations of the network television industry and of the popular discourses that have represented commercial television in American culture. The television violence probes of the early 1960s thus illuminate both industry practices as well as the complex moralistic, social scientific, and political discourses they engendered, discourses which still hold considerable sway in the worlds of television in the United States and abroad.

troubled times for network television

The Dodd investigation came at a time of transition and crisis for the American television industry. The hearings provoked a unique condensation of industry, regulatory, and public anxieties about the role of commercial television domestically and globally. While congressional probes of violent and objectionable television programming had been conducted in the House of Representatives in 1952 and by the Senate Subcommittee on Juvenile Delinquency (led by Republican Senator Robert Henrickson in 1954 and by Democrat Estes Kefauver in 1955), the Dodd hearings were longer, wider ranging, more critical of network practices, and more widely reported. Well before Dodd assumed leadership of the Subcommittee, a ritualized drama of sternly-raised eyebrow and limited public contrition had been constructed by congressional interrogators and industry witnesses. The 1952 House hearings prodded the early television industry into adopting a censorship code modeled after the Hollywood Production Code, and the Senate hearings of 1955–56 elicited from network witnesses both promises of increased sensitivity to "responsible" programming and disclaimers of social scientific proof of any deleterious social effects of violent television programs.[4] While the first round of the Dodd hearings promised a similar agenda, the unsettled conditions of the television industry at the beginning of the 1960s, an emboldened antiviolence coalition, and the frequently hostile attitude of Senator Dodd, together produced an unusually prolonged and acrimonious confrontation between network leaders and elected officials.

There was already a great deal of anxiety in the television industry in the spring of 1961 when Dodd initiated the congressional hearings into television violence and juvenile delinquency. Allegations of the rigging of the phenomenally popular prime-time quiz programs smoldered in the national press more than a year before exploding with the spectacular public confession of star contestant Charles Van Doren before a congressional committee in the fall of 1959. The scandal brought new attention to long-standing charges of coercive network business practices from some television program producers and sponsors. Moreover, several prominent television writers and critics related the quiz show fraud to the decline of prime-time live drama and what they saw as the increasingly heavy hand of commercial censorship in entertainment programming. The complaints of program producers and syndicators sparked a series of congressional and regulatory investigations of network business practices, including an inquiry by the FCC's Office of Network Study that produced tens of thousands of pages of public testimony and exhibits between 1955 and 1962. Thus, by the time the Senate hearings on television violence began in the summer of 1961, the industry was facing criticism from four sides: from program producers and sponsors unhappy with coercive network practices; from disaffected television writers, critics, and drama producers; from Senator Dodd and a chorus of prominent critics of television violence, and from President Kennedy's new FCC Chairman Newton Minow.

Appointed after several years of inefficiency and corruption at the FCC under President Eisenhower, Kennedy's new FCC Chairman used the May 1961 annual meeting of the National Association of Broadcasters to call commercial television program schedules a "vast wasteland." The impact of Minow's speech was immediate; one industry observer reported that Minow's NAB audience "resembled refugees from an atomic bomb blast," and the FCC Chairman's phrase quickly entered the popular lexicon and encouraged other critics of U.S. commercial television. Shortly thereafter, Writers Guild of America Chairman David Davidson told the FCC Office of Network Study that "never in history have so many writers been paid so much for writing so badly," and television industry pioneer and former network operator Allan B. DuMont complained to an industry audience that he had helped create a "crassly commercial Frankenstein" in the modern television industry.[5]

In addition to this criticism there were the rising industry tensions resulting from unprecedented three-network ratings competition, as the perennial also-ran ABC rode the success of a string of late-1950s Westerns and action adventure series like *Maverick* and *The Untouchables* into ratings parity in three-station local markets. The trade press announced that 1959 would be the first television season of full 3-firm network competition.[6] "With so much at stake in so infinitely tougher a competitive condition than has existed before, the program plans of each network take on life-or-death meaning," *Broadcasting* wrote in 1959.[7] By 1960 ABC was claiming number-two rating status in markets where all three networks had equal affiliate access, and the two larger networks reacted sharply to the new competition. At the annual meeting of NBC affiliates in November 1960, NBC President Robert Sarnoff blasted ABC as a "narrow-gauge network," accusing it of manipulating audience figures and committing other unethical business practices. Noting ABC's dependence upon the action adventure genre, Sarnoff pointed to ABC's special vulnerability to rising criticism of television violence and boasted that NBC "will not put all of our eggs into one basket that stands for a single narrow segment of programming—especially when it happens to be the kind that is under the heaviest attack." However, one advertising executive dismissed Sarnoff's speech as "sour grapes," and another argued that "none of the networks is clean."[8]

Responding to Robert Sarnoff's criticism of ABC's "narrow gauge" programming, ABC program head Oliver Treyz accused the other two "old-line networks" of wholeheartedly imitating ABC's successful action-adventure formula. Treyz told an advertising group in the spring of 1961: "Unfortunately, in the wake of ABC's success, the old-line networks started to abandon their established areas of achievement in live drama, variety and comedy shows to attempt to parallel us." Treyz perhaps disingenuously suggested that since no single network could be all things to all viewers, the other two networks should collectively undertake to provide program balance by counterprogramming ABC with less popular "Golden Age" genres instead of competing with ABC in action-adventure.[9]

In this context of declining program diversity, feverish ratings competition, and increasing public scrutiny of program content, complaints from television writers and critics of growing commercial influence over prime-time programming attracted a great deal of public attention. The Office of Network Study's public interrogation of television advertisers in the fall of 1961 produced a litany of sponsor program taboos ranging from the comically trivial to the breathtakingly heavy-handed.[10] The advertising vice president for General Foods told the FCC panel that any program it sponsored "must be light, it must be pleasant." Television's largest advertiser, Proctor and Gamble, revealed its formal program content guidelines to the Office of Network Study:

> The writer should be guided by the fact that any scene that contributes negatively to the public morale is not acceptable ... There will be no material in any of our programs which could in any way further the concept of business as cold, ruthless and lacking in all sentiment or spiritual motivation ... The moral code of the characters in our dramas will be more or less synonymous with the moral code of the bulk of the American people. The usual taboos on sex subjects will be observed. Material dealing with sex perversion, miscegenation, and rape is banned, as are scenes of excessive passion and suggestive dialogue.[11]

Such sponsor pressure was widely viewed as one nail in the coffin of naturalistic live drama in network prime time. J. Edward Dean, director of advertising for DuPont, told the FCC that the well-done serious drama was not as "well liked as other shows which were less stressful, and that the message that was taught through our commercials was not as well learned as in those shows which were ... lighter, happier—had more entertainment value." He told the panel that his company was not interested in "controversial" programs, which he defined as programs where "there is one group in conflict with another."[12] One advertising executive summarized the sponsor's attitude:

> A large corporation is expending a lot of dollars to bring entertainment to the viewer, and this corporation does not desire to bring such entertainment that, when it's all over, the viewer is pretty sad and depressed about the state of the world—in other words, where the script might be built around one-tenth of one percent of the misery and desolation of the country ... [13]

The head of the Writers Guild of America-East told Dodd's Subcommittee the same year that sponsors and advertising agencies were likewise to blame for violent program content and that "writers had lost practically all control over what appears under their name on television."[14]

Many critics viewed the rise of action-adventure as a partial result of growing sponsor pressure on program content; in 1961 ABC executive Daniel Melnick explained that the new action-adventure programs required "a different type of television writer, one who doesn't have a burning desire to make an original statement."[15] The Office of Network Study's 1965 report concluded: "As a general proposition, sponsor aversion to controversy, thought-provoking material, 'downbeat' material, etc., permeates and shapes the production of 'formula type' program series from start to finish."[16] While many industry observers found a conflict between the marketing aims of consumer good manufacturers and the naturalistic live drama as prime-time advertising vehicle, some saw a special compatibility between mass-market merchandising and the new action-adventure programs, despite their use of violence and horror to attract audiences. Albert Shepard, the executive vice president of the Institute for Motivational Research, a television industry consulting firm, contended:

> Commercials can be worked into even the most horrifying of the horror shows. The institute has discovered that the audiences for violence and horror have above-average tension levels. They have repressed violent tendencies that are in a way eased by the program in question. Therefore, if you have a product which would appeal to the insecure—mouth wash, deodorant, a soap with a body-odor pitch—this would be the sort of thing for violence and horror programs.[17]

Notwithstanding such claims for the general compatibility of violent programming and advertising efficacy, the ABC Continuity Acceptance Reports concerning *The Untouchables* subpoenaed by Dodd's Subcommittee contain numerous concerns passed on from the program's sponsors, which included a cigarette company, ranging from the specific—"Don't have too many dirty ashtrays full of cigarette stubs (sponsor objection)," to the general—"Delete the way Johny kills Mrs. Zagano. As described it is not acceptable. If we don't see the cord he uses, if his back covers the action and she drops to the floor we can try it. Delete the scream and any gurgles. There's a commercial coming up."[18]

Beyond the early 1960s controversies over television program content and commercial censorship, the networks were also nervous about possible federal legislative and regulatory reforms triggered by complaints over the networks' increasingly tight control of the television programming and advertising markets. By 1961 economic power in the American television industry had become concentrated in network hands: of a total of 546 network and station operators in the United States, the three networks took nearly half of industry revenues and 40 percent of total industry profits.[19] The networks' control of the prime-time program market nearly extinguished the business of first-run syndication (the production of original programs for the non-network market), reducing the number of potential customers for program producers from scores of national advertisers which had previously licensed programs themselves to the three networks selling advertising minutes to participating sponsors. One distributor told *Television* magazine in 1961:

"Today, with regionals pulling out of syndication like there's no tomorrow, with time periods as tight as A-bomb security in Siberia, with ... bankruptcies, this business plain stinks."[20]

In April 1961 veteran *Variety* reporter George Rosen warned the networks of the rising danger of years of accumulating complaints from program producers and television sponsors about network business practices; the networks "could be looking for trouble" with their coercive strategies in the new context of public and official complaints of violent television programming, especially given "the growing practice of the networks in demanding an equity on outside film shows that are given a berth on the webs."[21] Elsewhere in the same issue, *Variety* reported that 80 percent of the fall 1961 television series contained provisions for network profit participation, up from an estimated 50 percent the previous season. In light of the increasing difficulty of producers in getting access to network schedules, *Variety* reported that, with "a few pretty raw exceptions," networks were demanding an equity share in exchange for a degree of pilot financing; merchandising rights and foreign rights were also up for network grabs. *Variety* concluded:

> Privately, vidfilm production-distribution execs may howl about the state of affairs, talk darkly of 'monopoly' with only three possible outlets, etc.... What brings on many of the howls is the hard bargaining by the webs to up their rights, to encompass greater financial interests in the possible success of a series.[22]

Figures presented to Dodd's Subcommittee by CBS revealed a pattern of declining single sponsorship and network in-house production and increasing network licensing of independently-produced telefilms, a common trend across all three network schedules.[23] CBS executives described to the Subcommittee the typical control the network maintained over all aspects of telefilm production, including script development, casting, choice of directors, and the screening of all dailies and rough cuts. One production company executive working with CBS-licensed series told Dodd's panel that "in producing a show for the networks, the producer ... is subject to complete control of the network."[24] Veteran telefilm producer Frederick Ziv later claimed he decided to sell his production company to United Artists in 1959 "because I recognized that the networks were taking command of everything and were permitting independent producers no room at all."[25]

In addition to network television's sensitivity in the early 1960s to charges of program mediocrity, commercial censorship, and unfair business practices, another politically sensitive issue was repeatedly raised by witnesses before the Dodd Subcommittee: the effect on the U.S. image abroad of American television program exports. Indeed, the rapid growth of the international television program market helped fuel the shift from live to film programming that so many television critics had decried. In 1961, for the first time, there were more television sets in operation outside the United States than inside, and the U.S. networks were quick to exploit the new market for action-adventure telefilms, considered more lucrative in foreign markets than were genres held in higher critical esteem. In the case of *The Untouchables,* for example, the series' two-hour ABC pilot and subsequent two-part episodes were distributed as theatrical feature films in foreign markets, under such titles as *The Scarface Mob* and *Alcatraz Express.* Total network profits from both domestic and international syndication increased from $1,947,000 in 1960 to $7,738,000 in 1964, and network revenues from foreign telefilm sales grew from $1,700,000 in 1957 to $15,800,000 in 1964.[26] By 1963 CBS's film sales division had become the world's largest exporter of programming, and for the first time its foreign sales exceeded domestic syndication revenues.[27] Oliver Treyz, program head of ABC, which had led all three networks into the new domestic syndication and export markets, explained the logic of network program control in the emerging international television market to *The Saturday Evening Post* in 1961:

> Television has a great future. ABC is out in front on the international front. . . . *The Untouchables, 77 Sunset Strip, Maverick* are the most popular programs in Australia. In Bangkok they watch *Wyatt Earp.* Half the people in the world are illiterate. Television can penetrate that barrier. . . . Television is a worldwide medium. You have to think globally. If you own a show, you own it worldwide.[28]

But the new global penetration of U.S. programming in the early 1960s engendered domestic anxieties and self consciousness about the image of America abroad—the fear, as CBS Chairman Frank Stanton told a Japanese-American business group in 1961, "that what entertains us at home may embarrass us abroad."[29] As J. Hoberman recently argued, "a dozen years after the end of World War II, the United States was suffering from an new sort of malady, namely an 'image problem,'" as works such as the 1959 novel *The Ugly American* "took this self-doubt global."[30] Many witnesses before Dodd's Subcommittee expressed fear for the effects of violent programs on the allegedly more impressionable audiences abroad. Inevitably, such concerns enlisted Cold War rhetoric. Clara Logan, president of NAFBRAT, the National Association for Better Radio and Television, one of the most active lobbying groups against violent television programming, told Dodd's Subcommittee: "Worst of all, the Communists the world over use gangsterism in American telefilms for their own political ends, propagandizing that this TV gangsterism and violence really is America."[31] Psychiatrist Frederic Wertham explicitly linked his infantilizing view of the international television audience with child audiences in a 1960 *Ladies Home Journal* article which Logan entered into the *Congressional Record* on behalf of NAFBRAT:

> Credulous people in other countries, who get their ideas of Americans only from our exported motion pictures, often believe that we are a nation of gangsters and gun slingers. We would not recommend to a visitor from another nation that he base his estimate of our national character on our violent TV shows and movies. How can we expect our children to learn about "real life" from these programs?[32]

The possible harmful effects of television program exports on the U.S. image abroad thus provoked much debate during the Dodd hearings. The three U.S. networks, which had quickly become the world's largest international sellers of television programs through their control of licensing and syndication rights, were keenly aware of the lucrative foreign program market and fearful of official attempts to restrain program exports. At Edward R. Murrow's confirmation hearings as director of the United States Information Agency, one Senator expressed concern about the harmful effects of American movies and television programs on the U.S. image abroad. Could Murrow "persuade" the industry to stop exporting them? he was asked; Murrow replied that he would try.[33]

anatomy of an investigation

If the conditions within the U.S. television industry were unsettled in 1961 when the Senate's television violence hearings began, Senator Thomas J. Dodd himself represented something of a political loose cannon with an unusual background: a former seminary student, Nuremberg prosecutor, and FBI agent, Dodd was described by the trade magazine *Sponsor* as " an anticommunist zealot ... and a more than casual acquaintance of J. Edgar Hoover," and by columnist Drew Pearson as a "bargain basement McCarthy."[34] In 1961 Dodd received an Americanism Award for anticommunist activities as vice chairman of Internal Security Subcommittee of Senate Judiciary Committee.[35] During the same period, the trade press noted a surge of anti-communist programming in commercial television, riding what one producer called a "wave of conservatism in America." In January 1962, *Broadcasting* magazine wrote that "communism has suddenly emerged as the hottest new program subject in television," with networks and syndicators "building a bandwagon" involving 100 planned programs "from the straight documentary to out-and-out anti-communist preaching." "You don't have to be objective about narcotics, morals, or communism," the magazine quoted one producer.[36] Dodd's anti-communist reputation dovetailed neatly with his moralistic attacks on television sex and violence in the Juvenile Delinquency Subcommittee's hearings.

Dodd's television violence hearings moved fitfully, beginning with a well-publicized round in June and July of 1961 which involved friendly testimony from antiviolence critics and social scientists and more hostile exchanges with network and telefilm executives concerning *The Untouchables* and several other Western and action-adventure programs. The early hearings unearthed the infamous *Untouchables* script memos containing such headline-bait as "I like the idea of sadism ... " from producer Quinn Martin to one scriptwriter, and "not as much action as some, but sufficient to keep the average blood-thirsty viewer fairly happy," from an *Untouchables* script reader.[37] A hastily called one-day round of hearings in January 1962 chiefly concerned a single episode of the ABC anthology drama program, *Bus Stop,* which, ironically, ABC executives had proudly pointed to as a high-prestige departure from its action-adventure programming in the previous year's Subcommittee testimony. The *Bus Stop* episode, directed by Robert Altman, featured the teen idol Fabien as a small-town psycho killer and provoked Senator John Pastore to remark, "I looked at it and I haven't felt clean since. I still have the stench in my nose." ABC president Oliver Treyz's initially unrepentant response to Dodd's hostile questions on the show were viewed in the industry as causing the executive to lose his job a few weeks later.[38]

Some trade observers saw the early rounds of hearings aimed at *The Untouchables* and *Bus Stop* as the high points of Dodd's investigation, though the Subcommittee garnered new headlines during the third round of public hearings in the summer of 1962 when Dodd challenged earlier network disclaimers of responsibility for program violence with testimony from production company executives concerning the degree of program control exercised by the networks. This third round saw Dodd denounce what he called the "Treyz trend," the "Aubrey dictum" and the "Kintner edict," all supposed injunctions to inject sex and violence from the program heads of all three networks. Dodd accused CBS program head James Aubrey of ordering more sex in programs like the quasi-anthology two-men-and-a-Corvette roadside drama *Route 66* with his reported demand for "broads, bosoms, and fun."[39]

After this round of splashy 1962 hearings, Dodd convened a final anticlimactic series of hearings in the summer of 1964, consisting of one day of hearings on some disputed ABC shows, including the science fiction anthology drama *The Outer Limits* and the World War II drama *Combat.* Expressing frustration at the end of what the press by then was calling his "long, drawn-out investigation," Dodd told the assembled network heads before his Subcommittee: "The people won't take it forever. You better mend your ways ... I don't think you care. But unless you do care the American people are going to make you care."[40] Dodd's television violence investigation ended quietly in 1964, without an official final report or recommendations for any specific legislation or regulatory reforms.

Press reaction to and commentary on the Dodd inquiry ranged over the multiyear probe from sympathetic accounts of the opening testimony of social scientists, moral reformers, and production executives to more cynical judgments of Dodd's motives. *New York Herald Tribune* critic Marie Torre was skeptical of the prospects for Dodd's investigation from the start:

> The subject of television violence, which preoccupies publicity-wise Washington investigators almost as much as profit-seeking TV producers, ought to be the talk of the town for a while.... It's unlikely that the committee will turn up with anything we don't already know, that violence on television cannot trigger the normal, well-adjusted child but can have harmful effects on the emotionally disturbed. Seems to us there are better ways to spend the taxpayers' money.[41]

More sympathetic was the *New York Post* television columnist who wrote in July 1961 that the Dodd committee, "which had been written off as a short-lived affair, is continuing," and quoted Senator Dodd:

> This inquiry is not going to die on the vine. It's not just another Senate hearing—and that's the end. We've hit much closer to home than anyone expected. I think we're going to lift the lid on the question of responsibility for all this violence such has never has been done before.... I did not appreciate the network officials avoiding and evading answers to simple questions.[42]

The subsequent 1962 hearings by Dodd's Subcommittee also received mixed press reaction, although now there was growing skepticism about Dodd's motives and behavior. *New York Tribune* television reporter Richard K. Doan wrote that "Sen. Thomas J. Dodd, D. Conn., ran the top officialdom of television through his sex-and-violence mill yesterday and harvested little more than chaff," and the following week complained that network heads "deserved a fairer shake than they got" from Dodd in the 1962 hearings. Doan referred to Dodd's "mysterious purposes," and complained: "He has dragged his inquiry on for more than a year. His knack for erratic, unpredictable interrogations has been shown before." The reporter described the atmosphere at the May 1962 hearings: "The Connecticut Democrat's apparent objective last Monday seemed clear to those on hand: he hoped to play a headlined role as father confessor for the sins he has found television committing in the recent past." Doan said that network executives responded with "remarkable calm" to Dodd's criticism: "Were they repentant enough to suit Mr. Dodd? Not so. He moaned that nobody would accept his juicy charges as true. He seemed to want somebody—anybody—to grovel before him on bended knee and beg forgiveness." Doan argued that it was increasingly clear that if Dodd's juvenile delinquency investigation were serious, the Subcommittee would pursue testimony from expert social scientists, not industry executives:

> There was a semblance of inquiry in this direction last June. Evidently Mr. Dodd soon found TV's minions riper for headline picking.... In any case, the investigation which the Senator announced Monday as closed never got anywhere near an answer on how much TV keeps the kids away from Sunday School and leads them down crimson paths. Somebody, presumably less interested in the limelight, will have to pursue that.[43]

By the time of Dodd's reelection campaign in 1964 the million-dollar cost of his still-ongoing television violence investigation had become a political liability. The multiyear probe had resulted in no legislative action or regulatory reform, and in the closing days of the campaign Dodd hurriedly put together a relatively mild, 73-page interim report that failed to get the endorsement of the entire Subcommittee.[44] Though the *New York Herald Tribune*, in reporting the release of the interim report, called Dodd the "scourge of the TV networks," Dodd had become a much less intimidating threat to the networks by 1964.[45] National Association of Broadcasters executive vice president Vincent Wasilewski promptly denounced Dodd's interim report and repudiated each of its proposed recommendations, indicating how toothless Dodd's once-fearful inquiry had become.[46]

Some of the factors behind the networks' sanguine reaction to Dodd's final saber-rattling in the 1964 hearings were to emerge only after the hearings were concluded and Dodd was reelected. The compromised integrity of the Subcommittee's television violence investigation became a minor strand in the spectacular Senate Ethics Committee investigation of Senator Dodd a few years later. Fueled by charges from close former Senate aides and evidence they smuggled out of Dodd's Senate office and fed to newspaper columnists Drew Pearson and Jack Anderson, Thomas Dodd was eventually censured by the Senate 94–5 in 1967 for converting campaign contributions to private use and double-billing government travel expenses, becoming only the fifth Senator to be censured in U.S. history. The Senate Ethics Committee declined to pursue charges that Dodd took cash from industries under the jurisdiction of his Senate committees, steered government contracts and employment to campaign contributors, and used his Senate staff for private purposes. James Boyd, Dodd's former chief aide and main accuser in the Senate Ethics Committee inquiry, later wrote that early on it became clear to Subcommittee staff members that Dodd's television violence probe had been compromised. While in July 1961 the staff uncovered evidence that NBC program head Robert Kintner was directly involved in network pressure on telefilm producers to increase the level of program violence, NBC officials were able to evade the Subcommittee's subpoenas and in closed executive hearings NBC officials changed their testimony and suffered such incredible lapses of memory that the Subcommittee's staff counsel believed that perjury had been committed. According to Boyd, Dodd responded by refusing to enforce Subcommittee subpoenas and forbade further cross examination. In addition, Dodd rebuked his staff counsel in front of NBC officials for aggressive questioning, later fired him, shut down the entire line of investigation, prevented the release of the incriminating executive testimony, rejected several staff reports, and eventually showed the Subcommittee's watered-down report to NBC officials before its release to his fellow Senators on the Judiciary Committee.[47]

Similar to patterns relating to other industries under Dodd's investigative purview (insurance, firearms, aeronautics, pharmaceuticals, motion pictures), Dodd began to receive contributions and favors from the television industry during his extended television violence investigation. Indeed, when Dodd faced the Senate Ethics Committee's probe of his conduct, he enlisted the elite law firm Cahill, Gordon, Rheindel, and Ohl to defend him with a full-time team of eight lawyers and a private detective to dig up derogatory information about his informants; the expensive legal help was paid for by NBC, belatedly described as a $47,000 loan when columnist Jack Anderson made the contribution public.[48]

The Subcommittee's 1964 interim report, like much of the later phases of Dodd's public hearings, devoted disproportionate attention to ABC; the report spent twice as many pages criticizing the program policies of ABC than the other two networks, and even praised executives at CBS for what the report saw as progress in eliminating screen violence.[49] Similarly, when the Subcommittee staff sought to pursue its probe of violent television programming in the program policies of independent stations, including those of large chain-owner Metromedia, Dodd ordered the probe aborted and placed the son of Metromedia's lobbyist on the Subcommittee's staff. Dodd had received campaign contributions and personal gifts and favors from Metromedia chairman John Kluge since the start of the television violence probe in 1961.[50] James Boyd learned that even Dodd's anticommunism had a professional aspect: Dodd refused to make anticommunist speeches unless he was well paid, receiving over $50,000 over five years for his anticommunist speeches and writings, Boyd estimated.[51]

the legacy of the dodd inquiry

Weighing the effects of the Dodd scandal-tinged inquiry on the U.S. television industry of the early 1960s is less a matter of concrete legislation or regulatory reform than of evaluating the private business decisions of a network-dominated industry with a powerful desire to avoid critical and government scrutiny of any kind. Dodd's hearings had some clear short-term effects on U.S. television programming decisions. In what *Variety* described as an early "reaction to official and public outcries against television violence," in July 1961 ABC's Cleveland affiliate took *The Untouchables* off the air, citing a local newspaper account of the exploits of a teenage gang calling themselves "The Untouchables," including harassing phone calls to Eliot Ness's widow, a Cleveland resident. No other Cleveland station moved to acquire the series, then ranked in television's top five popular programs and reportedly getting a 50 share in the Cleveland market; "Normally, a show as hot as 'Untouchables' would be grabbed before you could say Eliot Ness," *Variety* noted. More broadly, *Variety* reported around the same time the frantic efforts by all three networks to juggle action adventure episodes selected for summer reruns; producers' choices for summer reruns were "given the heave for more placid segments," it reported; one executive told *Variety* that the network had axed ten of his thirteen suggestions for reruns. "Westerns and the ilk of *The Untouchables* are said to be the most vulnerable.... Said a network exec, 'We're being closely watched in Washington and we're starting right now to clean house. We have been told to brake violence in no uncertain terms and there's nothing we can do but conform.'"[52]

The Untouchables was the lightning rod for organized protest against violent television programming, undoubtedly fueled by Dodd's hearings. The program was attacked by Italian American groups protesting ethnic stereotyping in the portrayal of gangsters in the show. Their boycott threats against cosponsor Liggett and Myers tobacco company led the firm to abandon the show. Furthermore, in 1961 the National Bureau of Prisons director James Bennett, a board member of NAFBRAT, filed an official complaint before the FCC after *The Untouchables* presented a two-part episode about an attempted prison-train jailbreak; Bennett insisted that the show's closing billboard crediting Eliot Ness's book gave audiences the mistaken impression that such an escape attempt, involving corrupt prison guards, actually happened. The FCC eventually endorsed Bennett's complaint. These external pressures, in addition to the scrutiny of *The Untouchables* by Dodd's Subcommittee, led to numerous specific changes in the program's content. Memoranda from the show's production company subpoenaed by Dodd's Subcommittee document the producer's efforts to rename gangsters, introduce more law-abiding Italian Americans, tone down explicit violence, and revise the closing billboard.[53]

The effects of the Dodd hearings were felt in other production contexts as well. By the fall of 1961, *Broadcasting* reported that Bill Dozier, West Coast vice president of Screen Gems (producer of *Route 66* and the New York-based police series *Naked City*) was "very mindful" of the new atmosphere, making certain that there would be a "low degree" of violence in programs for the new season.[54] The pilots for the 1962–63 television season unveiled in the spring of 1962 revealed a decisive shift away from sixty-minute action adventure at all three networks; the proportion of action adventure shows among new pilots dropped from 40 percent in 1960 to 20 percent in the 1962–63 season. An article in *Broadcasting* magazine in February 1962 noted that "comedy seems to be the key to TV programming for the 1962–63 season" and observed a sharp increase in the number of situation comedies, prime-time animation (following ABC's success with *The Flintstones*), and medical drama (after the success of *Dr. Kildare* and *Ben Casey*).[55] By August 1962, the trade press was reporting the "complete—if not necessarily permanent collapse" of the suspense-mystery genre, with not one new show scheduled on any of the networks.[56] The 1962–63 season saw a 33 percent decline in action-adventure programs; situation comedy was up 43 percent, including fantasy sitcoms like CBS's *My Favorite Martian*, the success of which triggered a slew of "magic sitcoms" in the mid-1960s.[57]

By 1964 one trade observer called Dodd's television violence hearings "the death knell for action programming," and traced the extraordinary ratings strength of CBS to that network's ability to fill the scheduling hole left by the decline of action adventure shows with hit situation comedies like *The Beverly Hillbillies*.[58] By the time of the 1964 CBS stockholders meeting, Chairman Frank Stanton was able to point to 1963 as the best year in CBS history in sales and profits: CBS maintained an overall television ratings lead of 19 percent over second-place NBC, with nine of the top ten prime-time shows and ratings supremacy on six of seven nights.[59] In April 1964 *Business Week* estimated that CBS captured 75 percent of total network profits.[60] Network head James Aubrey, the architect of CBS's successful programming strategy, in 1964 discussed the lessons he took from both CBS's earlier overcommitment to the high-stakes quiz shows of the 1950s and ABC's later overdependence upon the action adventure format:

What everyone in TV fears, of course, is a debacle similar to the experience of ABC a few years ago. From 1957 to 1961, ABC seemed to have hit on a formula for permanent success with one filmed series after another in the so-called action-adventure format. *77 Sunset Strip* and *The Untouchables* were the prime examples. Then came the congressional hearings on violence in television, and the public's taste shifted. The result: ABC's nighttime ratings lay in ruins.[61]

Aubrey and CBS were able to ride the success of a string of hit sitcoms, often with rural settings, into several years of unprecedented network prosperity, until, ironically, the programs' aging demographics forced a wholesale dumping of the still-popular shows at the end of the 1960s. Aubrey perfected the use of the sitcom spinoff ("this is not wildcatting; it is drilling an offset well," according to Aubrey) and audience flow across adjacent programs ("simply the principle of inertia applied to television," he noted) to cement CBS's program appeal.[62] CBS, long recognized as the most skillful of the networks in political and public relations matters, adroitly rode the political winds of television violence campaigns in the early 1960s to even greater network prosperity and legitimacy. CBS was singled out repeatedly in Dodd's 1964 interim report as the network that had most sanitized its program schedule of violent content.[63]

Despite the booming profits of all three networks in the early 1960s, there were muted but persistent industry fears of the loss of television's light viewers, composed disproportionately of opinion leaders and cultural and economic elites. In March 1961 *Variety* cited "a growing concern among some top TV thinkers that the medium has lost a vital segment of its audience—the professional class of doctors, lawyers, teachers and business leaders. In short, the opinion makers, the people who used to talk up the medium and who used to get excited about its crusades and accomplishments as well as its failings."[64] In 1964 James Aubrey admitted that CBS's program strategy meant that the network was weak in capturing light viewers of television, but argued:

> Most of the people who are senior in government or business are print-oriented. The youngsters—the group with the economic and social potential—are television-oriented. Don't forget, pretty soon, 50 percent of the population will be 25 years old or younger. These people believe in TV. It's the greatest sales medium ever devised.... Criticism is irrelevant. People not interested in TV will be replaced by people whose lives revolve around it. The young, growing families with children are the ones that shoot the viewing up over five hours a day.[65]

Instead of responding to program criticism with new high-brow programming, the networks in the early 1960s continued to fill prime time largely with advertiser-friendly rural sitcoms and other popular fare. While their response to the attacks on action-adventure programming by Dodd and other antiviolence campaigners was financially successful for the networks, it did nothing to reverse the steady erosion of television's cultural capital in the eyes of U.S. intellectuals and opinion leaders.

Other effects of Dodd's television violence investigation on the U.S. television industry are less direct. A 1964 article in *Telefilm* magazine, "The Hearings that Changed Television," admitted that Dodd's probe had been less successful in addressing the purported links between television programs and juvenile delinquency than in "demonstrating that the networks are exercising immense power over the kind of programs that go on the air, and that this concentration of power can be readily abused." The magazine continued: "By digging deep into the industry's most intimate interoffice correspondence, the investigators were able to strip away the platitudes which smother most investigations in Congress or the FCC, and to provide the outside world for the first time with authentic vignettes of the scurrying that occurs in Hollywood and even in the ad agencies when the network bosses swing into action." In an generous assessment of the impact of Dodd's inquiry, *Telefilm* concluded:

> The investigators have not, of course, achieved any revolution in the character of network programming. But they undoubtedly contributed to the dismissal of at least one network head; they supplied valuable ammunition to those who hope to put some curb on the power exercised by network heads, and they strengthened the hands of those in the continuity acceptance branches of the networks and the code authority of the National Association of Broadcasters who must resist the efforts to hypo mediocre programs with injections of material to stir the libido of the 'teenagers, and the depraved imagination of those who crave violence.[66]

The extended investigation lead by Senator Dodd into television and juvenile delinquency also had an important impact on the wider debates about media and youth and the role of social science research in television policy making. As historian Ellen Wartella has argued, disputes about television's influence upon young audiences have often served as stalking-horses for wider debates over the general social role and responsibilities of commercial media, debates which have been muted or considered off-limits for most of American television's history.[67] For many social scientists, Dodd's hearings brought new prominence and legitimacy for their work, and spurred new private and public funding for their behavioral and survey research efforts. In testimony before Dodd's Subcommittee, James Aubrey proudly pointed to CBS's funding for Joseph T. Klapper's *The Effects of Mass Communication* (1960); the network also funded the large scale survey research in Gary A. Steiner's *The People Look at Television* (1963).[68] The NAB's new Television Information Office mobilized a small army of paid journalists and researchers to refute hostile expert witnesses, and a Dodd-supported joint NAB-U.S. Department of Health, Education, and Welfare research project supplied grants to twenty-five researchers into the effects of television upon children.[69] The hearings' spur to the institutionalization of social science research in the 1960s, culminating in the mammoth U.S. Surgeon General's Report, *Television and Growing Up: The Impact of Television Violence,* contributed to a paradigm shift in the regimes of knowledge about children and television, as historian Carmen Luke has argued.[70] The legacies of the Dodd hearings thus include the institutionally-favored behavioral models of media audiences that have dominated U.S. communication research since the 1960s and only recently been the object of reevaluation.[71]

Finally, and most generally, Dodd's investigation marks an instance of the tendency of large television institutions to create what John Hartley calls paedocratic regimes, where the presence of children in the television audience is construed to rule all judgments of programmers and regulators.[72] The early 1960s witnessed a new institutional construction of the U.S. television audience, suggested by the good-parent, bad-parent figures of CBS head James Aubrey and his "broads, bosoms and fun" on the one hand, and the stern "father confessor" ex-seminarian and ex-FBI agent Thomas Dodd on the other.[73] Whether permissive or censorious, both discourses construed the television audience as irresponsible and fundamentally childlike. The easy slippage displayed in the Dodd hearings between visions of the objectified and paedocratic domestic television audience and the equally objectified and infantilized foreign viewers of American program exports reveals the persistent anxieties that underlie institutional discourses about television audiences.[74] The shifts and exchanges in the self-serving scientific and institutional constructions of the television audience which Dodd's Subcommittee both witnessed and advanced may be the longest lasting legacy of his ill-fated inquiry, contributing to the ways in which television viewing continues to be understood in our culture.

Notes

1. U.S. Senate, Committee on the Judiciary, Subcommittee to Investigate Juvenile Delinquency, *Television and Juvenile Delinquency, Interim Report* 88.2 (1964): 12.

2. Jay Lewis, "'Main Event' This Week as DC's TV Probers Go on Location," *Variety* (14 June 1961): 20.

3. Richard K. Doan, "F.C.C. Spectacular Soon," *New York Tribune* (3 December 1961).

4. For a discussion of the Congressional hearings which led to the establishment of the 1952 Television Code of censorship, see Matthew Murray, "Television Wipes Its Feet: The Commercial and Ethical Considerations Behind the Adoption of the Television Code," *Journal of Popular Film and Television* 21: 3 (Fall 1993): 128–38; for an account of the 1954–55 Hendrickson-Kefauver Subcommittee hearings, see James Gilbert, *A Cycle of Outrage: America's Reaction to the Juvenile Delinquent in the 1950s* (New York: Oxford University Press, 1986), chapter 9.

5. For trade reaction to Minow's speech, see "Black Tuesday at the NAB Convention," *Broadcasting* (15 May 1961): 36; Davidson is quoted in Bill Greeley, "Writers Blast Dearth of Quality TV, Blame 'Controls' & 'Cost-Per-M,'" *Variety* (21 June 1961): 45; "DuMont: Created a Frankenstein," *Variety* (21 June 1961): 23; also see Mary Ann Watson, *The Expanding Vista: American Television in the Kennedy Years* (New York: Oxford University Press, 1990).

6. For a discussion of ABC's program strategy, see "ABC-TV's Oliver Treyz: Daring Young Man with a Mission," *Printers' Ink* (20 June 1958): 51; and Christopher Anderson, *Hollywood TV: The Studio System in the Fifties* (Austin: University of Texas Press, 1994).

7. "Strategy for a Program Battle," *Broadcasting* (17 August 1959): 27–30.

8. "NBC-TV Fall Nighttime Plans," *Broadcasting* (11 April 1960): 30; "Anyone Hurt by Sarnoff Blast?," *Broadcasting* (28 November 1960): 27–28.

9. "Treyz Attacks Copy-Cat Tactics of CBS and NBC," *Advertising Age* (17 April 1961): 147; "Are CBS-TV and NBC-TV Copycats?," *Broadcasting* (17 April 1961): 46; for a discussion of ABC's post-1953 programming strategy by Thomas W. Moore, vice president in charge of programming and talent, see U.S. Senate, Committee on the Judiciary, *Juvenile Delinquency Hearings* . . . 87th Cong. 1st and 2d sess., 8 June 1961–14 May 1962, Part 10. *Effects on Young People of Violence and Crime Portrayed on Television,* 1774–91.

10. For a discussion of sponsor censorship of program content, see U. S. Federal Communications Commission, Office of Network Study, *Interim Report: Responsibility for Broadcast Matter,* Docket no. 12782 (1960): 142–43, 170, 149; Mayra Mannes, ed., *The Relation of the Writer to Television* (Santa Barbara: Center for the Study of Democratic Institutions, 1960); Charles Winick, *Taste and the Censor in Television* (New York: Fund for the Republic, 1959); "Sponsors Spell Out Their Do's, Don'ts," *Broadcasting* (9 October 1961): 34; "Two Views on Sponsor Control," *Broadcasting* (2 October 1961): 24; "Who Controls What in TV Films," *Broadcasting* (17 October 1960): 30.

11. "Sponsors Spell," 34; "Two Views," 24.

12. U. S. Federal Communications Commission, Office of Network Study, *Second Interim Report: Responsibility for Broadcast Matter,* Docket no. 12782 (1964): 376–77.

13. FCC, *Interim Report,* 169.

14. "TV Violence is Blamed on Money-Men," *New York Herald Tribune* (17 June 1961).

15. "Disillusion Between the Lines," *Television* (6 June 1961): 92.

16. FCC, *Second Interim Report,* 371.

17. Quoted in Marvin Barett, "TV: Dial Anything for Murder," *Newsweek* (13 October 1958): 67.

18. ABC Continuity Acceptance Report, 16 March 1960, reprinted in *Juvenile Delinquency. Hearings . . . ,* 2358.; see also ABC Continuity Acceptance Report, 30 December 1960: "I don't see how we can do this scene acceptably. It's too gruesome a killing; a woman does it—the man is laughing—it's the end of an act before a commercial and we've got too much violent death in the show as it is. Please kill him another way. Even off camera it's too awful." Reprinted in *Juvenile Delinquency Hearings . . . ,* 2364.

19. "For TV Networks: Long Day in Court," *Television* (March 1962): 72.

20. Albert R. Kroeger, "Dark Days in Syndication," *Television* (October 1961): 36; for discussion of the business of first-run syndication, see FCC, *Second Interim Report*, 16, 19, 762; "First-run Film Series: Its Heyday Is Past," *Broadcasting* (8 May 1961): 84; "Syndicators' New Programming for '59," *Sponsor* (8 November 1958): 44; Arthur D. Little, Inc., *Television Program Production, Procurement and Syndication* (Cambridge: Arthur D. Little, 1966), 82.

21. George Rosen, "TV Practices and Malpractices," *Variety* (19 April 1961): 27.

22. Murray Horowitz, "Webs' equity in Pix Shows," *Variety* (19 April 1961): 31.

23. *Juvenile Delinquency Hearings . . .*, 1850.

24. See the testimony of Oscar Katz, CBS vice president of network programs and that of Frank Reel, ZIV-UA vice president of business affairs, in *Juvenile Delinquency Hearings . . .*, 1837–53.

25. Interview with F.W. Ziv, 16 July 1973, in Morleen Getz Rouse, "A History of the F.W. Ziv Radio and Television Syndication Companies 1930–1960" (Ph.D. dissertation, University of Michigan, 1976), 243.

26. FCC, *Second Interim Report*, 739; Little, *Television Program Production*, 50, 73.

27. Columbia Broadcasting System, *Annual Report* for year ending 28 December 1963 (New York: Columbia Broadcasting System, 1964), 4, 19.

28. Quoted in John Bartlow Martin, "Television USA: Part One; Wasteland or Wonderland?," *The Saturday Evening Post* (21 October 1961): 24.

29. Frank Stanton, Keynote Address, Second United States-Japan Conference on Cultural and Educational Interchange, Washington, D. C., 16 October 1963, 3. Collection of CBS Reference Library.

30. J. Hoberman, "Believe it or Not: J. Hoberman on *The Ugly American*" *Artforum* (April 1991): 27–8.

31. *Juvenile Delinquency, Hearings. . .*, 1883; see also the testimony of Dr. Peter P. Lejins, professor of sociology, University of Maryland on the injuries to the U.S. image abroad from film and television exports, 1678–81; for a discussion of the New Frontier politics and American television's international role see Michael Curtin, "Beyond the Vast Wasteland: The Policy Discourse of Global Television and the Politics of the American Empire," in *Journal of Broadcasting and Electronic Media* (Spring 1993): 127–45, and Michael Curtin, *Redeeming the Wasteland: Television Documentary and Cold War Politics* (New Brunswick: Rutgers University Press, 1995), chapter 3.

32. Frederic Wertham, "How Movie and TV Violence Affects Children," from *Ladies Home Journal*, (February 1960), reprinted in *Juvenile Delinquency, Hearings. . .*, 1963, 1917.

33. See "TV, Movies, Cast as Villains of Delinquency," *Broadcasting* (20 March 1961): 76; James L. Baughman, *Television's Guardians: The FCC and the Politics of Programming 1958–1967* (Knoxville: University of Tennessee Press, 1985), 56. Indeed, one of Murrow's first acts as USIA head was an attempt to pressure the BBC to cancel a scheduled airing of the recent *CBS Reports*, "Harvest of Shame" which he had himself hosted, and to remove the documentary from all USIA programs abroad. See "TV Guessing Game of the Week: What Made Ed Murrow Do It?" *Variety* (29 March 1961): 18; "U.S. Pubaffairs Shows—'Favorable' or Not—A Major Plus in Balancing U.S. Exports, Negating Vidpix Violence," *Variety* (29 March 1961): 23.

34. "Pressure is Hot Problem in Radio-TV," *Sponsor* (10 June 1963): 28–30; the article describes Dodd's harassment of nonprofit licensee Pacifica at the presumed behest of FBI Director Hoover. Pearson is quoted in James Boyd, *Above the Law: The Rise and Fall of Senator Thomas J. Dodd.* (New York: New American Library, 1968), 25; for background on Dodd's political career, see Drew Pearson and Jack Anderson, *The Case Against Congress: A Compelling Indictment of Corruption on Capital Hill* (New York: Simon and Schuster, 1968).

35. "Extremists Scored," *New York Times*, July 8, 1961, np.

36. "Red Threat Liveliest Program Theme," *Broadcasting* (22 January 1962): 27—28; for a discussion of organized pressure to restrict freedom of expression in classrooms and mass media at the time, see Donald E. Strout, "Causes for Concern: Intellectual Freedom Landmarks, 1955—60," Part II *Library Journal* 86 (August 1961): 2575—80.

37. *Juvenile Delinquency. Hearings . . .* , 2331 quotes Quinn Martin memorandum to Retchin 19 July 1960: "I wish we could come up with a different device than running the man down with a car, as we have done this now in three different shows. I like the idea of sadism, but I hope we can come up with another approach for it." See also the 30 September 1959 memorandum from Austin Peterson to Thomas W. Moore: "Not as much action as some, but sufficient to keep the average blood-thirsty viewer fairly happy," 2329.

38. Pastore is quoted in Harry Castleman and Walter J. Podrazik, *Watching TV: Four Decades of American Television* (New York: McGraw Hill, 1982), 151.

39. "Says CBS Switched It to 'Rt. Sexty-Six," *New York Daily News* (1 May 1962): 3; "Networks Offer Definition of Sex," *New York Times* (12 May 1962).

40. Richard K. Doan, "Sen. Dodd Summons Heads of 3 Networks," *New York Tribune* (28 July 1964); "Senators Stirred by Violence on TV," *New York Times* (31 July 1964).

41. Marie Torre, "Senate Violence Probe May be on Wrong Track," *New York Herald Tribune* (15 June 1961): 20.

42. Bob Williams, "On the Air," *New York Post* (19 June 1961): 28.

43. Richard K. Doan, "More on Sex and TV," *New York Tribune* (15 May 1962): 1; Richard K. Doan, "Make a Senator Happy: Confess," *New York Tribune* (20 May 1962): IV, 7.

44. For trade reaction to the interim report, see "At Last, Wraps Taken off the Dodd Report," *Broadcasting* (2 November 1964): 56.

45. *New York Herald Tribune* (28 October 1964): 21.

46. "NAB Lashes Out at Dodd Report," *Broadcasting* (9 November 1964): 48.

47. Jack Anderson, "Dodd's TV Hearings," *New York Post* (22 May 1967): 38; *Above the Law*, 188—93.

48. "Dodd's TV Hearings," 38; *Above the Law*, 159.

49. *Television and Juvenile Delinquency, Interim Report*, 22—36.

50. Drew Pearson, "Washington Merry-Go-Round," *New York Post* (6 September 1966); *Above the Law*, 191—93; *The Case Against Congress*, 85—86.

51. *Above the Law*, 56.

52. "Anti-Violence Binge Begins," *Variety* (5 July 1961): 23, 34; "Ness Bumped Off in Cleveland—WEWS Buries 'Untouchables,'" *Advertising Age* (17 July 1961): 94; one UA executive told *Variety* that some violent episodes were re-edited for or withheld from European markets, see Murray Horowitz, "TV Throughout Europe Screening U.S. Entries for Violence: Rumor," *Variety* (14 June 1961): 25.

53. On the sponsor boycott, see John Crosby, "Committee to Tell the Truth," *New York Herald Tribune* (22 March 1961): 23; Jack Gould, "Disturbing Pact: Compromise on *Untouchables* Holds Dangers for Well-Being of TV," *New York Times* (26 March 1961): II, 17; "Sponsors Line up for 'Untouchables' Despite Italians' Ire," *Advertising Age* (27 March 1961): 12; "'Untouchables': Peace at Last," *Variety* (29 March 1961): 18; "Stockholders, Too," *Broadcasting* (3 April 1961): 49—50; "Boycott Against L&M Called off by FIADO," *Broadcasting* (3 April 1961): 52; on Bennett's complaint, see "FCC Fingers *The Untouchables*," *Broadcasting* (2 October 1961): 68; "FCC Criticizes ABC for 'Untouchables," *Advertising Age* (9 October 1961): 132; for examples of producer and network sensitivity to criticism from Italian-American groups, see memorandum from Quinn Martin to *Untouchables* producer Joe Shattel, reprinted in *Juvenile Delinquency Hearings . . .* , 2361 and ABC Continuity Acceptance Report, 7 December 1960, reprinted in *Juvenile Delinquency Hearings. . .* , 2362.

54. "Let's You and Him Fight—Off Screen," *Broadcasting* (28 August 1961): 74—76.

55. "More Rib-Tickling, Less Rib-Busting," *Broadcasting* (19 February 1962): 110.

56. "Comics Up, Mysteries Down," *Sponsor* (27 August 1962): 39–40.

57. "Next Season? More of the Same for TV," *Broadcasting* (18 February 1963): 96.

58. Albert R. Kroeger, "Iron Fist Less Velvet Glove," *Television* (March 1964): 48.

59. Frank Stanton, Report of the President, Columbia Broadcasting System, Inc. Annual Meeting of Stockholders, Chicago, 15 April 1964, pp. 1–4. CBS Research Library.

60. "Number-One Supplier of TV Viewers," *Business Week* (25 April 1964): 90.

61. *Ibid.*, 93–94.

62. *Ibid.*, 96.

63. *Television and Juvenile Delinquency, Interim Report*, 7, 22, 30–31.

64. Bob Chandler, "Where the TV Elite Don't Meet," *Variety* (29 March 1961): 1.

65. "Number-One Supplier of TV Viewers," 93.

66. "The Hearings that Changed Television," *Telefilm* (July-August 1962): 12–14.

67. Ellen Wartella, "The Public Context of Debates about Television and Children" in Stuart Oskamp, ed., *Television as a Social Issue* (Newbury Park: Sage, 1988), 62.

68. "Treyz Predicts Decline of Action Shows," *Broadcasting* (19 June 1961): 52; for a discussion of the links between broadcast firms and social science researchers at the time, see Willard D. Rowland, *The Politics of TV Violence: Policy Uses of Communication Research* (Beverly Hills: Sage, 1983), 72–75.

69. Memorandum from Roy Danish, Television Information Office, to TIO Sponsors, 11 November 1963, collection of the Television Information Office, Museum of Television and Radio; "More Sex-and-Violence Hearings in '64," *Broadcasting* (23 December 1963): 55.

70. Carmen Luke, *Constructing the Child Viewer: A History of the American Discourse on Television and Children, 1950–1980* (New York: Praeger, 1990).

71. See Rowland, *The Politics of TV Violence;* Ien Ang, *Desperately Seeking the Audience* (New York: Methuen, 1991), 1–42; David Morley, "Changing Paradigms in Audience Studies," in Ellen Seiter, Hans Borchers, Gabriele Kreutzner, and Eva-Marie Warth, eds., *Remote Control: Television, Audiences and Cultural Power* (London: Routledge, 1989), 16–43; David Morley, *Television, Audiences and Cultural Studies* (London: Routledge, 1992), chapter 1.

72. John Hartley, "Invisible Fictions: Television, Audiences, Paedocracy, Pleasure," in Gary Burns and Robert Thompson, eds., *Television Studies: Textual Analysis* (New York: Praeger, 1989), 223–43.

73. "Invisible Fictions," 223–43.

74. Ang, *Desperately Seeking the Audience*, 43–98.

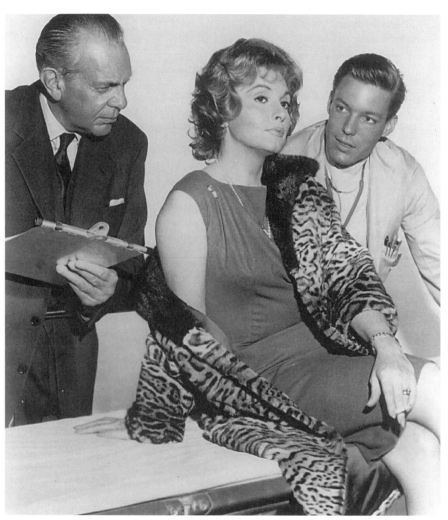

Raymond Massey, Joan Patrick, and Richard Chamberlain in *Dr. Kildare*

james dean in a

surgical gown

making tv's

medical formula

j o s e p h   t u r o w

The first half of the 1960s represents a defining period in the history of television's prime-time medical drama both because of the genre's successes and its failures. Descended from magazine stories, novels, radio shows, and movies of the 1930s and 1940s, the medical drama made a shaky start on television in 1952 with two short-lived series, *City Hospital* and *The Doctor*. Two years later, a series called *Medic* enjoyed moderate success. *King's Row*, another medical drama, failed quickly in 1955. In the fall of 1961, however, the form catapulted to genuine hit status when *Ben Casey* and *Dr. Kildare* appeared. Centering on the experiences of young physicians in big-city hospitals, the two programs and their stars became a phenomena that spilled over to newspapers, magazines, and even toys and records. The faddish success led network executives to believe that the two programs were establishing a formula that subsequent televised efforts about medicine should follow.

The medical genre's formula was developed by producers who combined personal support for the institution of medicine with an understanding of the dictates of the popular-culture industry. Their activities were fine-tuned by physician organizations whose members were concerned about changes in the social position of the medical industry after World War II. Physician organizations were interested in making sure that programs about doctors showed health care settings, characters, and patterns of action that matched the values that organized medicine was fighting to protect.

The result of these influences was that television "doctor shows" were heavily influenced by the interests of organized medicine. The shows took place in the hospital, and portrayed it as a citadel of high-tech healing with unlimited resources. The hospital activities, in turn, were built around characters that doctors considered appropriate—male physicians aided by female nurses. At the same time, the formula as it was developed under these influences ruled out patient care at home or in other nonhospital settings. It kept out alternative healing techniques, and it barred nonphysicians (which also tended to mean women) from roles as central authorities. The forces converging on the doctor show formula, in other words, defined it from the outset both by what it included and excluded. And, as the history sketched in the following pages will reveal, attempts to change those basic features, although first allowed by the television networks, were then severely policed by powerful interests from outside and inside the television industry. The results affected television's approach to the prime-time medical series for decades to come.

converging forces[1]

The interests of individual producers, organized medicine, and the commercial television industry began to come together around prime-time storytelling for the first time with *Medic* in 1954. The idea for the series came from writer James Moser, who had won fame as cocreator of the popular police show *Dragnet*. Moser's best friend was going through his medical residency, and his experiences became a window through which Moser saw a world of high-tech, hospital-based medicine. It was a world quite different from what he called the "soap operatic" world of health care that he noted in movies, radio, and early television. Moser envisioned creating a half hour prime-time drama that would show physicians in realistic life-and-death struggles with the aid of modern technology.

The demands of commercial television came into the picture the moment Moser tried to put together a pilot program to show to potential sponsors. (In the mid-1950s, most programs were aired by a network only if they were fully sponsored by advertisers.) However, because Moser did not have the money to create a hospital set for the pilot program, he set out to persuade the Los Angeles County Hospital to be his pilot's principal stage. With the help of the hospital administration and the Los Angeles County Medical Association (LACMA), he got the actors into a real operating room and filmed an actual childbirth for the final scene.

Although Moser's pilot persuaded Dow Chemical to be a sponsor for the series, it was with the understanding that the budget would remain low—$35,000 an episode. *Medic*, therefore, would continue to need real hospitals for low-cost filming, and Moser knew that LACMA held the key to this access. In addition, he and his producer realized that LACMA's aid would serve as an important sign to Dow that the series had credibility and class. LACMA executives worried, however, that mistakes and controversies relating to the series would be blamed on them if they continued to help *Medic* find places to film. So, in return for their seal of approval and a commitment to help open doors for the show, the physicians required that *Medic*'s creator and executive producer sign a contract that gave the Association control over the medical accuracy of every *Medic* script.

Medical leaders quickly saw LACMA's fortuitous involvement in primetime television as a broader opportunity to guard their institution's public image during a politically sensitive time. The American Medical Association (AMA) and its related groups of physicians (including LACMA) believed that they had to stave off a number of recent challenges to their power. That power had grown tremendously since the turn of the century, when the heads of organized medicine decided to tie medicine closely to the rigors of science in order to create a credible profession. Under the guidance of doctors, who as part of their bid for credibility enforced the overwhelmingly male and white complexion of their profession, the United States built a medical research and clinical establishment that dwarfed anything that had come before it.[2]

By the end of the World War II, penicillin and sulfonamides, better vaccines, and improved hygiene had all but conquered yellow fever, dysentery, typhus, tetanus, pneumonia, and meningitis. The hazards of surgery had been reduced through the increased availability of blood and plasma for transfusions.[3] In 1955, a vaccine for polio was approved. In describing the ecstatic national reaction, one observer wrote that "more than a scientific achievement, the vaccine was a folk victory."[4]

As people were encouraged to hope for more such victories, health care began to take center stage in the nation's budgetary priorities. The AMA and its coalition of medical interest groups guided federal and state legislators toward laws and policies designed to shape medicine's growth in ways that medical leaders wanted it shaped. Underlying their work were values that the AMA and its allies considered irrefutable. Health care was to be led by physicians (typically men), who were to be guided by scientific principles and aided by technologies. Medical aid was to be a private, fee-for-service activity between an individual and that person's physician. Within that relationship, the physician should do all that could be done to help the patient.

By the early 1960s, though, the optimism of physician-leaders about medicine's possibilities existed in counterpoint with concerns that their strong control over the people, settings, and activities involved in health care might be slipping away. They worried about three major developments. The first was their perception that physicians' traditional strong relationship with, and influence over, their patients was waning. Beginning in the 1950s, professional journals continually voiced the sense of antagonism between doctors and the public. The concern was so great that a number of medical organizations hired the famous motivation researcher Ernst Dicter to diagnose the problem and recommend solutions.[5]

The second major concern for leaders of organized medicine was the physician's changing role in the hospital, the most profitable and highly visible setting for medical work. As the hospital became more complicated from an organizational standpoint, a professional administration emerged to challenge the virtually absolute authority that physicians formerly enjoyed. Sociologist Robert N. Wilson noted at the time that the physician was becoming increasingly bound by the dicta of the hospital as an organization. As that happened, the doctor's relationship to the cast of other characters in the hospital changed. No longer did "nurses open doors for him" or "administrators always bemoan his uncontrollability," or trustees "confine themselves to financial surveillance." While the core of the physician's interaction was still the two-person system of doctor and patient, effective treatment of the patient became restricted less often to this framework. Rather, said Wilson, physicians were being forced to change their behaviors in relation to other health care workers and administrators.[6]

The third development, which physicians believed grew out of the public's declining respect for their profession, was Medicare. The Federal program was first introduced in 1958 to cover hospital costs for the aged on Social Security. The proposal was modest compared with earlier attempts to secure national health insurance; coalitions led by the AMA had always managed to defeat those attempts. Yet organized medicine saw even this small step as a dangerous infringement on physicians' established patterns of action. The AMA tried to frame this government interference in the medical marketplace as a threat to the doctor's traditional relationship with patients.[7]

Increasingly, many physicians in the early 1960s were being forced to confront the possibility of becoming players in settings that they could not control, and with characters that might not be totally of their own choosing. The single doctor treating the hospitalized patient with all but total independence was gradually becoming an anachronism in the face of hospital bureaucratization, medical specialization, increasing patient distrust, and impending government involvement. Certainly, these developments were not distributed evenly around the country. Nor did they mean that physicians had lost their ultimate power to define and treat disease. Nevertheless, enduring challenges to this power were emerging from government policymakers and other health care practitioners. It was with the aim of ensuring that this threatened loss of prestige and power was not reflected or encouraged through television's images that organized groups of physicians approached the settings, characters, and patterns of action television's medical dramas.

safeguarding medicine's image[8]

In one sense, the concerns of organized medicine were not new. Physicians had been sensitive about their profession's representation since the turn of the century. From that time until the beginning of the 1960s, organizations of physicians, led by the AMA, had carefully articulated a perspective about health care that had become extraordinarily influential within U.S. society. In addition, doctors had been hired routinely as consultants for "accuracy" in Hollywood movies and on radio as far back as the 1930s.[9] That was, however, an individual affair. Before television, no professional organization of physicians had ever become involved in the creation of high profile entertainment on an ongoing basis.

As it turned out, James Moser's positive attitude toward modern medicine meant that LACMA physicians did not have to worry about *Medic*'s treatment of basic setting, characters, and patterns of action. Nevertheless, at a time of growing anxiety about their power in the larger society, the committee insisted that the physician's image and actions fit organized medicine's ideal vision. They even considered what car a doctor drove and how he spoke. Cars that were too expensive and language with slang or contractions were ruled out.

The most common concerns these medical consultants had were with the relationships among medical professionals and between medical professionals and patients. In one situation, a physician on the review team refused to allow a script's direction that a physician drink coffee while speaking to a colleague about an injured patient. (The censor felt it would signal to viewers the impression that the doctors did not have grave concern for their charge.)

Conflicts between physicians were nonexistent on *Medic* as a result of nervousness by LACMA leaders. And because hospital administrators might be associated with conflict, they didn't exist either. Moser also came to realize that all the specialists on the review team expected him to write about their various bailiwicks. So, he learned to rotate medical areas in order not to get anyone angry.

While LACMA's supervision of *Medic*'s settings, characters, and plot lines sometimes presented problems for James Moser and his writers, network executives appreciated their work because it insulated them from battles with organized medicine. As a result, the idea of an oversight body was adopted when *Ben Casey* and *Dr. Kildare* went into production a few years later, even though those series had enough money for sets and did not need to use actual medical facilities. By this time, however, LACMA physicians, feeling overwhelmed with the work and responsibility for their profession's image, had asked the AMA to take over the monitoring chore. AMA officials agreed and set up a ten-person (all male) Advisory Committee for Television, Radio, and Motion Pictures, and the AMA's public relations council in Los Angeles managed the work on a day-to-day basis.

It made the AMA's work easier that the creators of each show were well-known to Los Angeles medical circles. Ben Casey's originator was James Moser, of *Medic* fame, and *Dr. Kildare*'s executive producer was Norman Felton, who had produced afternoon docudramas on the accomplishments of American medicine for NBC radio during the 1940s. Both men were optimistic about the direction of medical science, and they believed that *Medic* had pointed out the possibility for creating a realistic prime-time television series on medicine. But both had come to believe that *Medic* had not hit it big in the ratings because its patterns of action were too realistic, too "stark" (to quote Felton), in stressing health care techniques and technology.

Felton, who headed MGM's television division, believed that a way to make a medical series compelling was to blend the realism of *Medic* with the standard characteristics of melodrama. He specifically wanted to employ the themes from MGM's highly popular movie and radio series from the 1940s about an intern named Doctor Kildare. Felton had no interest in duplicating the previous Kildare incarnations; he said they were soap operatic adventures that did not focus enough on actual medicine. He did, however, tell his colleagues and the programming executives at NBC that it would useful to exploit the popularity of the Kildare name to create a "slice of life in a hospital." Felton added that it would be interesting for the audience to follow the progress of an attractive young doctor. NBC programmers agreed, especially after seeing the enthusiastic test audience's reaction to the star, Richard Chamberlain.

James Moser had also decided that he had to get closer to a more melodramatic approach to medicine if he were to successfully pitch his next idea for a medical drama to a network. Visiting a friend at L.A. County Hospital to search for story ideas, he decided that the medical area he should focus on was neurosurgery, which, he believed, pulsated with the human drama that television required. He said he also knew that what network television executives wanted was emergency situations ("You know, right away. Red blankets"). Another selling point, he decided, was a central male character with the gruff style he saw in the surgical interns. This character, he believed, could be the perfect medical counterpart to the popular antihero of the late 1950s. He would be James Dean—the "Rebel Without a Cause"—in surgical gown. "It struck me," Moser recalled, "that was a pretty good hook. It was believable, argumentative—you know, challenges his superiors, the whole bit."

Working on the first *Ben Casey* script, Moser decided pragmatically to place less emphasis on realistic hospital activities than on the tried-and-true conventions that he had worked so hard to avoid in *Medic*. He prided himself on knowing all the tricks of the popular culture trade and had become an avid reader of successful medical novels. For example, after first resisting the idea, he decided to employ a younger doctor-older doctor relationship that could add for dramatic tension. "I figured, if it was good enough for A.J. Cronin [author of a classic novel about medicine] and a few other guys, you'd better do it this way." He also put in a sidekick (he said that was necessary for an hour-long show) and a possible love interest (though in a bold break with tradition, he made her a doctor rather than a nurse).

ABC's *Ben Casey* and NBC's *Dr. Kildare* both debuted in 1961. The similarities between the two shows on the screen (each revolved around a young physician mentored by an older physician in a major hospital) mirrored similarities behind the scenes. Both James Moser and Norman Felton were concerned with ensuring the authentic medical "look" of their hospital-based series, as well as the accuracy of the specific information mentioned in them. They hired technical advisors, usually MDs, to check scripts and guide verisimilitude on the set. But the experience with *Medic* had added a new requirement to the medical formula. Remembering the public relations mileage and network satisfaction that *Medic* had gotten out of its formal association with organized medicine, the *Casey* and *Kildare* production companies wanted a continuing seal of approval—this time from the AMA. They received the seal on the condition that the AMA Advisory Committee acquired the right to pass on each script. The Committee members saw themselves as both safeguarding their profession's public image during a stressful period, and reinforcing medicine's role as a teacher of responsible health care behavior. When they talked publicly about their work they emphasized the latter role. For example, they contended that they had encouraged a *Kildare* episode that saw an unwed girl die in childbirth. The lesson, they stressed, was that she died because she had not sought medical care during pregnancy.

Studio personnel recall that AMA demands centered on preserving the traditional godlike image of the physician as the unquestioned ruler of the health care setting. In support of that image, the Advisory Committee would not allow television physicians to smoke cigarettes in front of patients. One producer recalled that a committee member refused to allow a script's instruction that a physician sit on the edge of a patient's bed. It was too informal, he said, and insisted that the physician stand. Similarly, *Ben Casey* reviewers constantly tried to tone down the hero's gruff speech. They particularly cringed when the actor who played Casey adlibbed slang into his dialogue.

Even touchier to the Committee were patterns of action in the programs that reflected the strains that organized medicine was facing in the real world. Both James Moser and Norman Felton noted that the Advisory Committee could be hard-nosed when it perceived that a story line was a direct attack on organized medicine's process of training and accrediting physicians. At least one "bad doctor" plot, a *Ben Casey* script about a quack, was forced out of production by the AMA. The physician-reviewers insisted that the quack's knowledge was so outlandish that he could never have become a physician in the first place.

Moser, Felton, their writers, and their producers said that they had to be pragmatic about their dealings with the medical establishment if they wanted its support. All admitted that such pragmatism resulted in self-censorship. Moser noted specifically that there were stories—about doctors shielding one another from legitimate complaints, and about turf fights between medical specialties—that he and others on *Ben Casey* felt were too sensitive for television. At the same time, the producers were able to get Committee members to compromise now and then. So, for example, the physicians moderated their stance on accuracy to allow for the dramatic telescoping of time and the use of inappropriately large syringes that would look good on camera. The producers even convinced them, though rarely, to approve scripts in which physicians lied, made mistakes, or committed malpractice. Part of the way in which Felton and producer David Victor soothed Advisory Committee concerns was to take the medical establishment's side in a number of plots relating to lawsuits against physicians. Their central characters would always vigorously state the case for high-quality mainstream medicine, and show that organized medicine could police itself.

In general, the producers of *Ben Casey* and *Dr. Kildare* made sure that the continuing doctors of their series and the hospitals in which they worked were above reproach. The central characters in *Kildare* and *Casey* fit a mold that transcended the medical drama. Both had a handsome young man and an older man who acted as his mentor, confidante, and sometime antagonist. As for the plots, there was a definite pattern to follow. Mostly, as James Moser noted, "it was doctor/patient/hospital." The unblemished doctor in the unblemished hospital would establish a relationship with a physically distressed patient. Throughout the action, physicians were clearly positioned as the leaders of the medical ship who were sworn to see health care as an unlimited resource. Patients would get all the attention and technologies they needed, with costs never a concern.

Ideas that fit this form could come from all sorts of places in the popular culture realm. Moser found that he could adapt material from *Medic* very easily to fit *Casey*. He even found it useful to dredge up old scenes from his *Dragnet* police show and transform them for hospital use. Knowing how to put an episode together also meant knowing there had to be guest stars. That was because the primary focus was rarely the continuing physicians. The viewer really learned very little new about them. Instead, they were catalysts. They sparked an exploration of the "visitors" and their concerns.

The exploration often tied into a contemporary social issue—child abuse, greedy funeral directors, marital problems, fear of epileptics—that the visitor represented, even while the visitor was there for a physical problem. The patterns of action reflected the interests of both the medical and television industries. Since a hospital stay was needed, the medical problems tended to be rather complex, and they were almost always physically (rather than mentally) based. Because each episode was generally expected to tell a story that stood alone, the patients' difficulties were typically acute or in their acute stages. That allowed the patients to move towards a cure or (much less often) death that allowed a natural end to the episode.

The two hits of the early 1960s did have their differences. James Kildare matured over time while Ben Casey did not. Casey was gruff while Kildare was kind, even sweet. Overall, though, the two programs illustrated approaches to medicine that were similar enough to one another to constitute a clear program "type." Through it the power of physicians, and of physician-guided high-tech hospital medicine that lay at the core of the U.S. health care system in the early 1960s, was displayed in all its glory.

deviating from the formula[10]

As the popularity of *Kildare* and *Casey* swept the nation, their producers decided to vary the formula to bring new wrinkles to the health care drama. The changes created controversy about the roles and boundaries of physicians in relation other health care workers. They also raised tensions about the role of gender in medical power. The result was controversy in so many quarters that it had the eventual effect of souring program creators and producers on deviating from the physician-centered formula.

Two series that began in 1962, *The Eleventh Hour* and *The Nurses*, stood at the center of the firestorm. *The Eleventh Hour* was Norman Felton's attempt to expand the formula beyond the physician in the high-tech hospital. He persuaded NBC that a show focusing on sicknesses of the mind could work, despite the failure of a 1950s program about psychiatrists called *King's Row*. Felton made his case by building a pilot around a mentally ill wife who murders her husband and is caught through the medical expertise of the central characters. Network executives were intrigued with the notion of bringing overt violence into the health care domain.

But Felton's variation on the Kildare-Casey formula contained two features that angered powerful constituencies in the health care system. The first problem was the association of mental illness with violence. Concerns about portrayals of mental illness in popular culture had received sporadic, but intense, attention throughout the 1950s and early 1960s, particularly in relation to its portrayal in violent comic books and television shows. Many mental health professionals were alarmed not just that *The Eleventh Hour*'s pilot exploited mental illness in the same controversial way, but also that network press releases implied that the link between crime and diseases of the mind would be a common theme for the show. Television critics and health professionals also felt that acute patterns of illness that characterized Kildare and Casey were simply not appropriate for psychiatry. They believed that it was irresponsible to emphasize the acute hour of ultimate crisis (the "eleventh hour") to the neglect of what they felt was the essence of psychiatry: finding the root of chronic, maladjusted behavior in "the first hour," the critical moments of a patient's past.[11]

Even stronger attacks on the show came as a result of the second departure from the formula, the use of a nonphysician in the central older man/younger man duo. Sam Rolfe, Norman Felton's writer of *The Eleventh Hour* pilot, had initially intended that both central characters would be psychiatrists; the two would share an office. But with his discovery that "psychiatrists do not share offices," Rolfe decided to change the younger man's vocation. He would be a clinical psychologist who would do the legwork for the psychiatrist and help him with the testing of patients. Their work together would retain what he felt was the key attraction of the formula's older man/younger man relationship: its father/son, tutorial nature. Sometimes they would argue about appropriate methods. Their professional conflicts would lend drama to the program.

What he didn't know when he first thought of the idea was that a fierce battle was then raging within and between the worlds of psychiatry and psychology as to what role the clinical psychologist ought to play in relation to the psychiatrist. That intelligence came slowly, only as Rolfe relied on a psychiatrist to help him assemble the by now mandatory advisory panel for the show. The psychiatrists who ran the advisory panel for *The Eleventh Hour* were absolutely insistent that the psychiatrist on the show be dominant over the psychologist. Rolfe and Felton accepted the physicians' decree, partly because they knew the network expected them to keep the AMA imprimatur. The American Psychological Association (APA), however, was riled by organized medicine's ability to take control of the program and define the psychologist's position as subservient to the psychiatrist. In a public relations blitz two months after the show's debut, the APA contended that the one psychologist on the advisory panel had not been able to place his imprint on the program.[12] The result, the APA announced, was an entirely unrealistic presentation of the mental health setting, its professionals, and its patterns of activity.[13]

During the same fall 1962 season that NBC's *The Eleventh Hour* came under attack over its portrayal of the relative status of physicians and psychologists, CBS also found itself grappling with issues of medical status. The producers and network executives of its new show *The Nurses* struggled over appropriate ways to depict the status of physicians and nurses in the medical formula. Previously, the only series to center on nurses had been *Janet Dean, R.N.*, a syndicated, nonnetwork program that aired in 1954. Aside from that one (not terribly successful) program, the opportunities for nurses to involve themselves deeply in continuing medical dramas were slim. To the producers of *Medic, Ben Casey, Dr. Kildare* and *The Eleventh Hour*, doctors were central to the formula. As James Moser said of Nurse Wills, a regular on *Ben Casey*, "She was a standby. We got into nurse stuff, but it was peripheral."

In 1961, producer Herbert Brodkin persuaded CBS to allow him to redirect the medical formula by moving the nursing profession to center stage. Despite the gender and vocational differences, he envisioned a series with several of the elements that network programmers had come to associate with successful doctor shows: the tension between neophyte and experienced supervisor, the interplay between scientific progress and human emotion in a modern hospital, and the ultimate tension of life versus death. Carrying a reputation for brashly independent but successful programming, he refused to allow an AMA review committee on the set. He wanted the plots to dwell less on life-and-death cures than the other medical shows did, and instead focus on moral issues of health care. He even commissioned scripts that questioned the medical establishment and cast a critical eye on health-care policies run by doctors.

It quickly became clear, however, that Brodkin had made a mistake in building his show in a way that ignored the power that physicians exercised over nurses. In the medical show formula, physicians tended to be men, nurses tended to be women, and the men—as physicians—were the captains of the medical system. This truism was reflected in doubts that newspaper and magazine commentators expressed about whether a drama series starring two women could survive, especially since the program was scheduled opposite *Dr. Kildare*. And in fact, when ratings did turn out to be dismal, network officials themselves began to worry that the absence of male leads in *The Nurses* was driving both male and female viewers from the show. Herbert Brodkin's agent persuaded Michael Dann, CBS's programming head, to move the program to a different time period, and the ratings improved enough for the network to renew it for the next year.

Nevertheless, the question of whether nurses could be successful at the center of a series continued to haunt network executives as well as the show's producers. The producers began to worry that the subsidiary role that nurses played in hospitals was not allowing for the kind of great life-and-death drama they associated with the doctors, lawyers, and policemen who were showing up increasingly on television. At CBS, executives seemed to feel that the problems of profession and gender in *The Nurses* were linked. Their proposed solution combined both issues, as Michael Dann remembered:

> There was a great feeling about how do you get more masculine
> appeal into *The Nurses*. There were arguments going on with
> Brodkin constantly about how you get masculine appeal. They
> did try. There were always men involved. But Herbert used to
> say, "The name of the show is *The Nurses*." And later we said...
> "Why can't we make it *The Doctors and the Nurses*?"

Network officials forced the solution on Brodkin and his producers as a condition for renewing the show for a third season. Two male doctors who had appeared in earlier episodes, a supervisor and a resident, were made central to the continuing cast. Speaking to the press about the changes, the head of CBS programming conceded that he had not felt "altogether secure" about the show from its start because "it was a completely female-oriented show."[14] Brodkin himself admitted the difficulty of finding good stories for a pair of nurses.

the tyranny of the formula

Despite the changes, *The Doctors and The Nurses* was not renewed for a fourth season.[15] It had lasted a year longer than *The Eleventh Hour*, which had endured for two seasons. Another show about psychiatrists, *The Breaking Point*, which suffered many of the same criticisms hurled at *The Eleventh Hour*, had survived only one year. After that, only *Ben Casey* and *Dr. Kildare* remained. When they were pulled from prime time in 1966, the first doctor show cycle on American television had come to an end. By then, network programming executives had begun to feel that the potential of prime-time "medicos" (as *Variety* called them) had waned.

Nevertheless, the hits and controversies of the early 1960s had established the boundaries for what elements would work in such programs and what would not. Michael Dann at CBS was an opinion leader for the industry. To him being cautious meant the shows had to evolve around male physicians, not nurses or women. It also meant that the dramas had to enact clear, high-emotion issues of life and death, not subtle problems of the mind or the politics of the hospital or the medical system.

It was a perspective that urged the medical show back toward its core approach to setting, characters, and patterns of action. The talk around the networks was that *The Eleventh Hour* and *The Nurses* pointed to the political headaches that could come from straying too far from the traditional core of the formula. Sam Rolfe had found that using psychologists with physicians invited a tumultuous rivalry between the two professions. Similarly, Herbert Brodkin and his associates had learned that centering a medical show around nurses rather than doctors raised thorny questions about the depiction of sexual and professional power. To would-be medical show creators wanting to avoid trouble, the message was that doctoring (rather than nursing, psychology, or any other health care role) was the craft to use.

A male-dominated, physician-centered, high-tech, acute care medical world that typically revolved around the hospital and saw costs as unnecessary obstacles to care: this was a formula—and a message—that would stay with television programmers and producers for many years, with only a few exceptions. The AMA's power to influence television scripts as part of its attempts to shape public opinion diminished in the late 1960s. Nevertheless, the vision that the Association had insisted upon as the public image of doctoring was integrated into the formula. It kept, for example, the guiding proposition that physicians ought to see medicine as an unlimited resource, even as public policies in the real world of health care challenged that basic assumption.

Some features of programs did change beyond the 1960s. Responding to pressures from the society at large, producers and networks did eventually allow some women into their physician pantheon. People of color, who were almost never seen in positions of medical authority, began to make their appearance. Still, most aspects of status and setting—especially the taboo about centering programs on "allied" medical personnel—continued into the 1990s.[16] The doctor show formula, in other words, took on a life of its own and imposed a sort of "tyranny" over prime time's dramatic depiction of the health care world for decades after its development.

notes

1. In addition to published sources cited, materal for this section was based on interviews with the following people: network television executive Michael Dann; AMA Advisory Committee Chair Eugene Hoffman, M.D.; William House, M.D.; writer-producer James Moser; and AMA Advisory Committee Member Clinton Roath, M.D. The interviews were conducted in 1984 and 1985.

2. Paul Starr, *The Social Transformation of American Medicine* (New York: Basic Books, 1983), 335–37.

3. Starr, 336.

4. Starr, 347.

5. Ernst Dichter, "Do Your Patients Really Like You?," *New York State Journal of Medicine* 54: 1 (1 January 1954): 222–26.

6. Robert W. Wilson, "The Physician's Changing Hospital Role," *Human Organization* (1959–60): 182.

7. Newell Philpott, "Doctors and the Present Challenge," *Journal of Medical Education* 34 (October 1959): 1033–34.

8. In addition to published sources cited, material for this section was based on interviews with the following people: George Andros, M.D.; Actor Lew Ayres; TV writer John Bloch; TV writer Calvin Clements; MGM movie producer Joe Cohn; actress Larraine Day; network television executive Michael Dann; actor Vince Edwards; producer Norman Felton; director James Goldstone; talent agent Abby Greshler; AMA Advisory Committee Chair Eugene Hoffman, M.D.; William House, M.D.; actress Betty Ackerman Jaffe; television writer Norman Katkov; ABC TV Standards and Practices Executive Tom Kurzy; writer-producer James Moser; talent agent Marvin Moss, television writer E.J. Neumann; AMA Advisory Committee member Clinton Roath, M.D.; director Elliot Silverstein; producer David Victor; and CBS TV president Robert Wood. The interviews were conducted in 1984 and 1985.

9. See, for example, review of "Young Doctor Kildare," *Time* (7 November 1938): 41.

10. In addition to published sources cited, materal for this section was based on interviews with the following people: producer Buzz Berger; actor Joseph Campanella; programming executive Michael Dann; producer Norman Felton; actor Jack Ging; AMA Advisory Committee Chair Eugene Hoffman, M.D.; producer Joel Katz; producer Arthur Lewis; writer E. J. Newman; writer-producer Sam Rolfe; AMA Advisory Committee member Clinton Roath, M.D.; and producer David Victor. The interviews were conducted during 1984 and 1985.

11. See Robert Lewis Shayon, "For this Freud Labored?" *Saturday Review* (3 November 1962): 30; and Robert Lewis Shayon, *Report from West Point: First Conference on Broadcasting and Mental Health* (Unpublished manuscript, Robert Lewis Shayon Archive, Boston University, 1963).

12. Richard K. Doan, "Psychologists Hit NBC over 11th Hour Program," *New York Herald Tribune* (2 December 1962). (Clipping files, Television Information Office Library, Museum of Television and Radio, New York City.)

13. Emma Harrison, "TV Show Assailed by Psychologists," *New York Times* (2 December 1962): 84.

14. Muriel Davidson, "The 'I Don't Care' Actor Who Cares Too Much," *TV Guide* (22 June 1963): 11.

15. After the program left prime time, ABC executives transformed it and redubbed *The Nurses* into a daytime serial aimed at women viewers. With a different cast and a totally different thematic slant, the program continued for two and a half years.

16. See Joseph Turow, *Playing Doctor: Television, Storytelling and Medical Power* (New York: Oxford University Press, 1989).

Mama Cass and Harry Belafonte in *The Smothers Brothers Comedy Hour*

the smothers

brothers comedy

hour and the

nine youth rebellion

aniko bodroghkozy

On Sunday, October 27, 1968 *The Smothers Brothers Comedy Hour* opened with the following teaser: A collage of newspaper headlines about Mexican students rioting was followed by one of the show's writer-comics Murray Roman dressed as a Mexican police official proclaiming, "The reason that the students of Mexico City are rioting this weekend is because of outside agitators." This was followed by a collage of headlines about the spring uprisings in Prague. Roman, dressed as a Soviet general, stated, "The reason that the students of Prague are rioting this weekend is because of outside agitators." Headlines about the May uprisings in Paris and demonstrations in Japan were followed by Roman in appropriate French and then Japanese military costume blaming outside agitators. The final headlines referred to the uprisings at Columbia University. Roman, as a New York cop, affirmed again, "The reason the students at the universities are rioting this weekend is because of outside agitators." The camera then cut to Tom and Dick Smothers who smiled broadly and, in unison, proclaimed, "Hi! We're the outside agitators!"[1]

The hosts of CBS's highly rated weekend variety show as instigators of youthful revolution? Two clean-cut television comedians aligned with student rioting? The sketch was an absurd joke; however, there had to be some kernel of truth for the sketch to have any meaning and to be at all funny. The Smothers Brothers did attempt to align themselves with the politicized youth movement of the period. In its three years on the air, from early in 1967 to April 1969—during a period of almost unparalleled political and social turmoil in modern American history—the show functioned as a site for generational and ideological battles over the Vietnam war, the psychedelic drug culture, and other aspects of antiestablishment youth dissent.

Much of what has been written about the show and its embattled history has tended to focus largely on questions of taste. The Smothers' sketches, featuring sacreligious sermonettes and other parodies of America's middle-class morality, eventually catapulted the show "over the edge of tastelessness," as Steven Carr has argued, into a showdown with CBS over censorship and free speech issues.[2] While this battle was a key feature of the show's legacy, the issue of "good taste" was only part of a larger process of escalating confrontation that evolved in fits and starts over the program's three year run. Central to this process was the Smothers's attempts to attract a politically and socially disaffected youth audience—a 16-to-24-year-old cohort which had largely abandoned television by the 1960s. In their attempts to gain legitimacy with the era's campus revolutionaries and countercultural dropouts, the Smothers increasingly incorporated oppositional politics into their show. The Smothers's attempts to assert their political allegiances on prime-time television—when some of those positions were highly explosive—resulted in a cultural playing out of contemporary social, political, and generational warfare. The controversies and censorship struggles the show underwent suggest something about how even prime-time television could contribute to the contentious process of change in the 1960s as the brothers, their parent network CBS, and viewers attempted to map the boundaries of acceptable political and cultural representations.

hippies with haircuts

When the Smothers first joined CBS's Sunday lineup on February 5, 1967, there was little inkling that the show would eventually become a battleground. It was scheduled on Sunday night to play opposite NBC's perennially top-rated family western, *Bonanza*, and was supposed to appeal to a younger audience—one that CBS, of all three networks, seemed particularly incapable of capturing.[3] The show was surprisingly successful and, initially at least, it seemed that the Smothers, with their short hair, neat suits, traditional folk music, and whimsical banter over whom "mom liked best," would be able to bridge the growing generation gap and still uphold traditional values. Popular press accounts played this up, calling them "hippies with haircuts."[4] Tom Smothers, whose intelligence and articulateness belied his slow-witted persona, told a *Time* magazine reporter in June, 1967: "We're so college-looking and clean-cut.... The American Legion likes us and so does the left wing." The reporter went on to note, "And so does every wing of the younger generation."[5] Here, it seemed, were two performers who identified with a growing generation of disaffected young people but who would offend nobody.

The show's attempts to encompass the American Legion and the youthful left wing can be seen in its first season. The opening credit sequence had the show's dance ensemble dressed in marching band costumes parading around with trumpets, bass drums, and cymbals while other dancers marched by with placards and sandwich boards bearing the names of the week's guest stars. The John Philip Sousa atmosphere evoked a very traditional sense of small-town celebration, placing the Smothers within a nostalgic, Frank Capra-esque version of Americana.

Sketches from the first season also revealed an ideological balancing act as the show struggled for generational consensus. In an attempt to cater to the youthful portion of their audience, the Smothers invited the rock group Buffalo Springfield to perform its anthem of political and generational division, "For What It's Worth." Lead singer Stephen Stills began: "There's something happening here/What it is ain't exactly clear/There's a man with a gun over there/Telling me I've got to beware."[6] Suddenly, the camera cut to Tom dressed up in wild west gear pulling a six-shooter; then back to Stills, who was shown breaking into a grin. In another verse, Stills sang, "A thousand people in the street/Singing songs and carrying signs/Mostly saying 'Hooray for our side.'" The sequence cut to a shot of Dick holding a sign with that slogan painted on it. The audience broke into laughter.

The sequence's comedic cutaways succeeded in defusing the song's anguished message. Stills's lyrics about police power weighing down on the rebellious young and about the generational gulf created by the war in Vietnam were defused by the comedic illustrations. For those already familiar and aligned with Stills's sentiments, the meanings of the song were still available despite the Smothers' comic intrusions. For audience members who did not know the song and its political implications, the cutaways might have made the material politically meaningless.

Despite this mildly political material, little distinguished the first season of

203

The Smothers Brothers Comedy Hour from other television variety shows. Guests included Jim Nabors, Jack Benny, George Burns, Eddie Albert, Eva Gabor, Bette Davis, Jimmy Durante, and Lana Turner—guests more suited to CBS's traditional audience than to the younger set. Reinforcing the inoffensive, middle-of-the-road quality of much of the first season, Dick Smothers was featured in frequent solo numbers. Seated in an often bucolically designed stage setting and wearing a cardigan sweater, Dick would croon ballads that suggested the singer had more in common with polite pop singers like Perry Como or Andy Williams than with political folk singers like Phil Ochs or Pete Seeger.

The show could be considered a prime example of what Todd Gitlin has identified as "hegemonic ideology . . . domesticating opposition, absorbing it into forms compatible with the core ideological structure."[7] Network television, a cultural institution that typically functions to celebrate ideological consensus, had apparently found a mechanism to absorb portions of the discourse of a growing insurgency movement through comedy and song.

hi(gh)! and glad of it

Nevertheless, this process of hegemonic incorporation sometimes opens the door to oppositional worldviews. Bert Spector has thoughtfully analyzed the intense conflict between the Smothers Brothers and the network regarding the appearance of folksinger and antiwar activist Pete Seeger. What has received far less attention are the many ways the program subtly shifted leftward during the same 1967–1968 season.

The Smothers's attempts to align themselves with dissident youth and appeal to their tastes and lifestyles was particularly evident with the character Goldie O'Keefe, who began appearing regularly in the second season. The creation of comedienne Leigh French, Goldie was both the ultimate "hippie chick" as well as a Gracie Allen figure, harkening to the show's vaudeville/variety format. Playing on both these feminine icons, she bore an infantalized demeanour with her wide eyes, constant giggle, beatific smile, long, girlish braids, and outrageously astute airheadedness. However, French's hippie chick tended to make ridiculous these taken-for-granted sexist assumptions about femininity. Along with that, her comedy revolved around television's taboo subject when it came to depictions of countercultural activity: she affirmed and celebrated mind-altering substances.

Television representations of hippies were frequently sympathetic to counterculture critiques of consumerist, acquisitive, rationalist American life. Perceived hippie values of love, simplicity, communalism, and spiritual search were often held up as social attributes that America had lost and needed to embrace again in order to renew itself. Nevertheless, embedded in many hippie values and activities was the use of LSD, marijuana, and other psychotropic drugs. This presented a problem for CBS because illegal drug use could not be condoned, much less advocated on network television. To uphold hippie values but to condemn pychedelics was a contradictory stance that the networks assumed over and over.[8] The Smothers Brothers show, in its showcasing of Goldie O'Keefe, was perhaps unique in its unconflicted support of the counterculture—drug use and all.

In one of Goldie's first appearances on the show, Tom pulled her out of the audience and brought her up on stage where they discussed the flowers and bag of fertilizer Goldie had given him.[9] Tom explained, "I shared it with my friends and we all grew a lot." Tom then thanked her for coming down from San Francisco. Goldie giggled and responded, "Oh, I never come down." She proceeded to give Tom a set of love beads made out of seeds that she compared to oregano.

Goldie O'Keefe became a regular fixture on the show, appearing in a continuing segment called "Share a little tea with Goldie," a parody of afternoon TV advice shows for housewives. Goldie would open the sketch with salutations such as "Hi! And glad of it" or "Hi—isn't it? It sure is!"[10] In one sketch she mentioned that she had previously given advice on how to get rid of "unsightly roaches." She went on to thank viewers who had sent her theirs.[11] In another sketch she pondered ladies' faces, "which are directly connected to our heads. And we all know how important our heads are. And if you don't, I'm sure all the heads do."[12]

Goldie and her drug-oriented humour created certain potential censorship problems for the show and for the network. Surprisingly, much of the material was cleared for broadcast.[13] A memo from Thomas Downer to head censor W.H. Tankersley emphasized the fact that much of Goldie's material made it to the air. The memo, written shortly after CBS had cancelled the show, was Downer's response to Tankersley's request for a rundown of marijuana references from the 1968–69 season. Downer's itemized list included many examples from Goldie O'Keefe. Item number five was described as follows:

> Show 0217, for air January 26: The "Tea With Goldie" spot included the line "A lot of you ladies have written in asking when I'm on.... Ladies, I'm on as often as possible and I highly recommend it." This was broadcast. The line "You know anything with tea and pot in its name is going to give you a groovy sound" was scripted but omitted from the tape.[14]

How can we explain the relatively easy time Goldie's material had with

CBS censors, who were becoming progressively more and more vigilant and scissor-happy with the show's scripts and review tapes?[15] One answer is the discursive advantage the show's young writers had over the fifty-something Tankersley and his staff. Terms such as "roach," "head," "tea," (and, for that matter, "Goldie" and "Kief") all had drug-oriented meanings within counter-cultural circles. The show's facility with the current slang may have assisted in legitimizing its material with young people and mystifying its meanings to the older generation. Tankersley and company may have realized that many of these terms were drug code words, but seemed incapable of preventing all the "roaches" from sneaking through. The slang and punning use of language became a means to evade the network's policing. Young "heads" could take pleasure from the broadcasting of celebratory references to drugs, supposedly taboo on network television.

The censors may also have been less concerned with Goldie's humour since the the majority of Americans probably did not know all the drug code terms she used, and thus her humor probably resulted in fewer complaints. So too, Goldie's playful ambiguity and appeal to "lifestyle" issues rather than "politics" may have given her comedy more room to operate.

Despite those comic mechanisms of disavowal and defusement, Goldie's construction as a childish, innocent "hippie chick" also functioned as an important site for potentially subversive play. On the one hand, the sketches normalized notions of feminity and domesticity (through the parody of housewife shows in "Share a Little Tea"); but on the other hand, Goldie stretched them into hyperbolic excess, thus deconstructing and denaturalizing them at the same time. By taking the most innocuous and culturally safest genre of "ladies" programming and turning it into a celebration of "dangerous" drugs, Goldie interrogated the menace of pot and LSD, as well as the desirability of being a "lady." In her costuming and performance, Goldie also foregrounded patriarchal constructions of feminine childishness which were so taken for granted in other televisual representations. Her braids, her wide eyes, and her giggling were so exaggerated as to call attention to themselves. One could read them as signs pointing, parodically, to precisely the manufactured ways in which female hippie characters tended to be portrayed in many popular cultural representations.

206

a crisis of authority

As *The Smothers Brothers Comedy Hour* moved into its second and truncated third seasons, the Smothers attempted to slip through more unambiguous and politically charged material. The show's sketches became more overtly confrontational, almost inviting network censorship. The struggles between the brothers and the network, which became more pitched between the fall of 1968 and the spring of 1969, tracked with and mirrored upheavals reverberating throughout the American political terrain during the period.

In the late 1960s, the vision of America as a consensual society in which a variety of voices all had equal status and the opportunity to flourish in a marketplace of ideas was beginning to unravel. Insurgent voices threatened various segments of the status quo, no longer accepting the ground rules set down by those in power. The insurgency of African Americans, for example, had shifted dramatically from Martin Luther King's assimilationist politics. The ascendant Black Power position was far more revolutionary in its rejection of equality with whites based on white definitions of social behaviour and success.[16] Segments of the antiwar movement had also shifted to a more confrontational position, as orderly picket lines and marches on Washington did not appear to be halting the war. The march on the Pentagon in October 1967 marked a turning point from the "politics of protest" to the "politics of confrontation." Thousands of mostly young protesters swarmed onto the grounds of the Pentagon to "confront the warmakers" and "obstruct the war machine," as the demonstrators put it.[17] Protests on campuses were also becoming far more militant, leading occasionally to pitched battles between students and police. The militant directions into which these insurgent movements were heading struck at the heart of the dominant social and political order, questioning its legitimacy and revealing as myth many previously held tenets of what America was all about.

Perhaps nothing revealed the revolutionary possibilities residing with these mostly youth-oriented insurgent movements better than the series of crises in 1968. Beginning with the Tet Offensive in January and the public's growing realization that the President and the nation's military men had lied about the progress of the war and its winnability, one section of the social structure after another began to be called into doubt. The assassinations of Martin Luther King and Democratic presidential hopeful Robert Kennedy shattered hopes for many that any progressive leaders would be allowed to live long enough to promote change peacefully through approved channels. The pent-up rage King's murder unleashed in the nation's cities led to riots, burnings, and countless casualties, causing concern among many whites that America's black population was perhaps finally on the verge of outright insurrection. The police clubs and blackjacks that rained down on the heads of protesting Columbia University students led to questions about whether higher education in America could function at all anymore. How could colleges and universities continue reproducing the social order through their production of professionals when educational assembly lines appeared to be grinding to a halt all over the country? The televised agonies of the profoundly divided Democratic Party at its Chicago convention called into question whether the political process could continue to function. National Guard troops with barbed wire stretched across their vehicles mediated between the disintegrating Party and youthful demonstrators, who seemed far more unified and purposeful than those who were supposed to be their representatives in political office.

Thus 1968 was the epitome of a "crisis of authority."[18] A whole range of social institutions seemed to be coming undone, no longer able to legitimate themselves ideologically and resorting to coercion to maintain power. Television was intricately bound up with the unmasking of power at the Chicago Democratic Convention as protesters used the medium to reveal the brutal power that hid behind American liberal democracy. Network news coverage carried live broadcasts of Chicago police indiscriminately beating and bloodying antiwar protesters, bystanders, even journalists trying to cover the story. The crisis of authority wreaked havoc throughout the universities, the cities, the military complex, and the political process itself. This crisis was also playing out within the popular culture industry. What happened on Chicago's Michigan Avenue in August was happening metaphorically on *The Smothers Brothers Comedy Hour* in September.

don't stop the carnival

The opening segment of the Smothers's third season premiere, aired September 29, 1968, attempted to illustrate the social transformations and political upheavals that the late 1960s had witnessed. The brothers appeared standing behind a podium looking noticeably different from their clean-cut, short-haired, burgundy-suited previous selves. They now both wore longer hair, mustaches, and mod nehru jackets.[19] After Tom banged a gavel, Dick announced: "The first order of business will be to vote on the subject of the physical appearance of Tom and Dick Smothers." Tom asked, "All those in favour of the Smothers Brothers *having* mustaches say 'aye.'" Someone in the studio audience gave a small, unenthusiastic "aye." Tom then asked, "All those in favour of the Smothers *not* having mustaches say 'no.'" This elicited a huge response of audience members shouting "no!" In consternation, Tom gavelled the podium and announced, "In the true American democratic, conventional, spirit, the 'ayes' have it. The mustaches stay!" The camera panned the audience as members began booing, jumping up and down, waving arms, giving the thumbs down, and launching into "We Shall Overcome." Tom gavelled away, shouting "Drown them out, bring in the band!" The audience continued to boo as the familiar marching band credit sequence commenced. As the show's dancers went through their routine, there were cuts back to Tom and Dick at the podium and cuts of the audience booing.[20]

The politically confrontational stance continued with the Smothers's opening duet that included lyrics such as: "The weekly grind is stretching out before us/The bleeping censors lurking in the wings/CBS would like to give us notice/And some of you don't like the things we say/But we're still here/We're still here/You may not think we're funny/But we're here."

The brothers metaphorically gave the finger to CBS and to critics and viewers who complained that the comics were no longer funny. The song seemed targeted to viewers like Paul McCalib in St. Cloud, Minnesota, who wrote to *TV Guide* observing:

> *The Smothers Brothers Comedy Hour* was once fresh, original, and true satire because it was impartial in choice of targets. By the end of the season the brothers seemed to have been converted to hippyism, the so-called new politics, and similar "causes." Having lost objectivity, they, their cast, and guests have become propagandists—and propagandists are rarely funny; they take themselves too seriously and consign all who disagree, even slightly, to limbo.[21]

As perceived propagandists for the New Left, the Smothers in this third season premiere took every opportunity to emphasize where their political allegiances lay. While the episode was rife with allusions to Chicago, next to the opening sketch, none was so pointed as guest star Harry Belafonte's number "Don't Stop the Carnival." Lyrics to the calypso piece included the following:

> Oh Lord, I feel so low
> About the toddlin' town
> Of old Chicago
> Humphrey, Muskie, McGovern and McCarthy
> Split the party
> Now nobody be happy
> Tell all the population
> We're havin' a confrontation
> Let it be known freedom's gone
> And the country's not our own
> Lord, don't stop the carnival
> Carnival's American bacchanal[22]

Belafonte and the Smothers wanted to use footage from the Chicago convention and demonstrations to illustrate the song. CBS initially agreed, with two provisos: the footage could not show closeups that could identify anyone, and the footage could contain no violence.[23] The second demand was rather ludicrous, since the police beatings both on the streets and on the convention floor defined what the phenomenon of Chicago was all about. The network's concern about allowing the Smothers use of the material is instructive. News footage and photos of the event had been widely disseminated. Viewers were probably familiar with the material. CBS News had carried extensive live coverage. Its news reporter Dan Rather had been unceremoniously clubbed by police inside the convention hall. Walter Cronkite, on the air, referred to the officers as thugs.[24] The news division encountered a barrage of complaints about the supposed bias towards the demonstrators of its coverage. Clearly, representations of Chicago carried politically charged meanings, meanings that network executives were afraid could not be contained. Even within a news context where strategies of journalistic distance and objectivity should dampen politically explosive materials, the imagery from Chicago could not be controlled. The explosiveness and threatening nature of that material was indicated yet again when CBS demanded that the Smothers use that imagery only in ways that would have effectively defanged the number.

The "Carnival" number went through various different run-throughs as network representatives and the Smothers negotiated allowable footage. However, shortly before broadcast, the whole sketch was summarily censored. The Smothers refused to insert new material to fill the five minute gap. The network in turn sold the time to the Republican Party, which ran an advertisement for the Nixon/Agnew presidential ticket in the last five minutes of the Smothers Brothers Sunday night time slot.

smothering dissent

On October 13, 1968, the Smothers's opening teaser tracked down a line of men in suits (all played by the show's writers, including the still-unknown Steve Martin). Each in turn looked down at the show's script, laughed uproariously at what he read, then tore out those pages and handed the script to the next in line who did the same thing. The script with one page left got down to the last man on line who read it without laughing. He then turned to Tom and Dick and handed them the page saying, "Nothing funny in this. Here you are boys, we're through censoring your show."

While the Smothers and their supporters recognized only political repressiveness as the network's motivation, CBS faced a clear economic dilemma that cannot be ignored or dismissed. There was a certain amount of protest from advertisers about the show's material. By the third season, however, much of the advertising on the Smothers' show was clearly targeted to a youth market. Volkswagen became a participating sponsor.[25] For the car manufacturer, this was astute marketing; VW Beetles and Microbuses had become synonymous with youth culture. While sponsorship concerns seemingly abated, opposition from network affiliates grew more intense. The head of a group of stations in Michigan and Nebraska wrote CBS's head of affiliate relations complaining about how "sick" the show was, "especially from its political orientation and religious standpoint."[26] The letter strongly suggested that CBS not renew the show and warned that if the network was "unable to temper the show, there is a serious question as to whether we will be able to clear it next year, especially in prime time." The station manager of another affiliate in Topeka, Kansas, even took to the airwaves in an editorial denouncing the show's "filth," proclaiming that "we've had enough."[27] The network, even if it wanted to, could not totally ignore such sentiments.

Also of concern were the show's ratings. The show started the season as the seventh most popular show with a 37 share of the audience. Archrival *Bonanza* stood right behind in eighth place.[28] By the end of the year, the Smothers had dipped slightly, to twelfth place.[29] By March 1969, the Smothers were down to twenty-fourth place, while *Bonanza* had staged a robust recovery, grabbing third place in the Nielsen ratings.[30] The ratings may have fallen because the Smothers were no longer giving more than the appearance of wanting a diverse audience. They almost exclusively targetted young people, experimenting with ways to bring them into the Smothers' tiny and ever-under-attack, semiliberated zone of prime time. The Beatles, for instance, were featured a number of times in taped segments. Jefferson Airplane appeared, with lead singer Grace Slick in bizarre blackface and gloved fist clenched in a Black Power salute as she sang the group's paean to dissident youth, "Crown of Creation." The Doors did a decidedly strange number called "Wild Child." If these were all attempts to appeal to the cultural side of the movement, the show also included material with which insurgent young people could identify in other ways. The opening sketch on December 15, 1968, had Tom fiddling with a helmet, gas mask, and leather gloves as he complained to Dick about what a drag it was that 18,000 people had to go through with this. "A group of certain people make you do this," he added as he put the helmet on. Dick asked him what he was doing. With helmet and gas mask in place, Tom replied, "I'm getting ready to go to college."

Perhaps the clearest overture to youth was the Smothers's attempts to depart entirely from their show's conventional TV variety setup. The Smothers experimented with a number of concert-in-the-round programs that broke the proscenium arch performance environment and thus brought the audience into the scene. This kind of performance space suggested the folk music/coffee house roots of the Smothers and the nonhierarchical, participatory ideals of that entertainment form. Spectators could be seen in every shot and from every camera angle. The most notable characteristic of these spectators was that they were almost uniformly young and "hip" looking. This set design provided the Smothers a tangible way to point out to television viewers exactly who they thought their audience really was and exactly who they wanted to address.

The appearance of folk singer Joan Baez in a concert-in-the-round episode led to one of the Smothers' final showdowns with CBS censors before the network removed the brothers from the air entirely. Baez had been closely associated with both the civil rights and antiwar movements. When she appeared on the Smothers' show, her husband David Harris was facing a lengthy prison sentence. She dedicated a song to him and explained why he was going to jail: "He refused to have anything to do with the draft or Selective Service or whatever you want to call it. Militarism in general. If you do that and you do it up front, overground, then you're going to get busted. Especially if you organize—which he did."[31] CBS not only censored the Baez segment, but pulled the entire episode from its March 9, 1969, scheduled airdate. The network relented, to a degree, broadcasting the show a few weeks later; however, Baez's explanation of why her husband was going to prison was cut.[32] The network's rationale, according to a *Saturday Review* article, was that Baez's "remarks on the Smothers Brothers show were 'editorial' and not suitable for entertainment programs."[33]

Despite their desire to cater to politically committed youth with guests like Baez, the Smothers continued to feature middle-of-the-road entertainers more likely to appeal to the older set. The strategy appeared to be to use guests such as Kate Smith, not so much to bring in a general audience (as in the early seasons), but to legitimize the politics of the young. Smith, who appeared in the same episode as the Jefferson Airplane, was featured in a sketch about the Bill of Rights. She and Pat Paulsen played a married couple sitting in their living room with Smith doing a crossword puzzle. The segment involved Smith asking Paulsen for a series of seven-letter words:

Smith: A seven letter word that means "United States."
Paulsen: America.
Smith: A seven letter word that means "difference of opinion."
Paulsen: Dissent.
Smith: One who loves his country.
Paulsen: Patriot.
Smith: Objection made to official of the government.
Paulsen: Protest.
Smith: Word that means all those things.
Paulsen: Freedom.[34]

The sketch was as much an example of "editorialization" as opposed to "entertainment" as the Baez segment (neither had a comic punchline). Smith was not publicly aligned with an insurgent protest movement, however, thus making the political sentiments she spoke seem less threatening. Nobody could question the patriotism of Kate Smith.

Segments like this came to the attention of readers of the underground press through rave notices from Harlan Ellison, science fiction writer and television critic for the youth movement underground newspaper *Los Angeles Free Press*. Ellison described the segment for his readers and then declared that it was their "unholy chore" to support the Smothers:

> Dig, this is somewhere near where it's at, I think.... So, inexorably, they will kill a show like *The Smothers Brothers Comedy Hour*. They have to. It threatens them [the entrenched forces who rule the mass media] too much. Courage and honesty such as Smothers II show us each week must be protected. And if a couple of hundred dingdongs can get something like *Star Trek* renewed, it would seem to behoove all of us who *care*, to start writing letters to CBS to counteract the potency of those assassin diatribes from Mashed Potato Falls, Wyoming.[35]

Ellison affirmed that "the hip folk are watching the show religiously (or antireligiously, depending on where your Valhalla is located)...."[36] Ellison's review also pointed out that the very fact that the show was "somewhere near where it's at" was terribly threatening to network forces. CBS could not really tolerate the dissemination of counterculture sentiments that were attracting socially and politically uncontrollable "hip folk." Something had to give.

Inevitably, the network acted. On April 3, 1969, Robert D. Wood, president of the network, informed Tom Smothers by wire that since he had not sent in an acceptable broadcast tape in time for preview by the Program Practices Department and affiliated stations, the contract between the brothers and the network was officially terminated.[37]

the smothers brothers and the underground press

The cancellation of *The Smothers Brothers Comedy Hour* became a media cause célèbre. Most of the print press was sympathetic, constructing the situation as an infringement of First Amendment free speech rights.[38] Sentiments constructed by those writing for the various organs of the youth movement's underground press were more complicated, befitting the movement's oppositional relationship to the dominant order. The fact that the underground press paid as much attention to the show as it did signals that the Smothers were at least somewhat successful in their bid to align themselves with youth dissent.

The *Los Angeles Free Press*, one of the most widely read underground papers, covered the show in Harlan Ellison's column and in news articles on the program's censorship woes. Chicago's counterculture-oriented *Seed* also began paying attention as censorship and cancellation threats loomed: "Middle America has been sending nasty letters to CBS about the Smothers Brothers Show. Whether you see the show as an agent of radicalization or just laugh a lot, it might help to send a letter of support...."[39] Ellison's column also urged *Free Press* readers to write the network to counteract the "moral indignation and raw-throated outrage from the neatsy-clean and tickytacky types out there in the Great American Heartland. The scuttlefish."[40]

It should come as no surprise that the underground press began taking an active interest in the Smothers as soon as the show became the target of repressive institutional practices. The show gained legitimacy as an expression of oppositional, antiestablishment politics by the amount of metaphorical billy-clubbing the Smothers endured. Movement papers could embrace the Smothers because they saw the state power that menaced insurgent youth mirrored in the Smothers's situation. Thus Allan Katzman in New York's hippie-oriented *East Village Other* described Tom and Dick as "the men who took the 'New Left' teachings and made it [sic] entertainable."[41]

The *Free Press* campaign to support the Smothers went into full gear in the aftermath of the show's cancellation. The paper launched a letter-writing drive to try to force the network to relent and reinstate the show. Printed in its classified section was an ad reading: "CENSORSHIP SUCKS. Black-out Columbia Bullshit System, Sundays 9 p.m. Viva Tom and Dick & their right to speak. If you agree, cut out this ad & mail to Program Practices Dept., 7800 Beverly Blvd L.A. 90036."[42] A few weeks later, the *Free Press* again used its classified pages to run a half page petition in support of the Smothers.

Much of the ire and wrath evident in underground press articles was directed at CBS as unjust authority attempting to exert its domination upon a public resource. A column in the *East Village Other* characterized CBS and its action this way:

> The precise control device of television was being pushed and too much information was getting to the people. CBS's action against the popular Smothers Brothers Show was unprecedented and has established a repressive trend by the power structure to stomp out all alternative information. The Smothers' presentations were certainly not radical but CBS still felt them a threat to honky culture.[43]

Even if the show was not radical, the article implied that there was something effectively subversive about the Smothers show, something that needed to be repressed. Alice Embree, writing for New York's other major underground paper, the *Rat*, also was at pains to point out that the Smothers were not radical. That was not the point—at issue was the network and its actions: "The question is not whether CBS made a mistake, but why CBS is permitted to exist. The question is one the movement must resolve (having never mounted a successful media campaign)...."[44]

While movement circles showed clear support for the Smothers, they also expressed a certain amount of ambivalence. Distrust for all dominant institutions was so great that anyone connected to its various organs, even in the underdog position of the Smothers, was bound to raise some doubts. Embree, in her interview with Tom Smothers, was initially concerned about his neatly groomed appearance. She observed that he seemed "the type who would have gone through all the Proper Channels."[45] While the article was supportive of Tom Smothers and the show, Embree apparently felt a need to put forth another view: "Most radicals would argue that the show was a perfect co-optive device, diverting youth energy away from anything destructive, giving kids a sense of representation."[46]

This theme was put forth far more forcefully by the *Free Press*'s perpetually wrathful columnist Lawrence Lipton. Adopting an apocalyptic vision of impending revolution which allowed for no mediation between "US" and "THEM," Lipton had nothing but contempt for the Smothers and their ilk. "Mort Sahl and the Smothers Brothers are weeping and wailing, NOT because they were DROPPED out by the Top Rats of the television Rats Nest, but because they are not being invited back again in/on acceptable sell-out terms."[47]

Another *Free Press* article, written before the cancellation and detailing the Joan Baez controversy, also chided the Smothers. The article pointed out that by collaborating in any way with the network's censorship system, the Smothers were acting as accomplices to the stifling of free expression over the airwaves. The article observed that "[s]ince CBS has already indicated that it wants the Smothers back next year, they are obviously in a position to bargain for their own artistic manumission. Otherwise, why should it matter if there is no Smothers Brothers Show next season?"[48]

These harsher views represent the confrontational direction the insurgent movements were adopting in the later part of the decade. The appeal to use "proper channels" for the address of grievances had long since proven ineffective. Working within the system would not bring the war to an end, would not bring economic and social justice to African Americans, would not change the established order of power relations. Many in the movement saw the Smothers Brothers incident as another marker of that very fact—the Smothers could not negotiate proper channels in order to bring even sanitized antiestablishment youth culture to television. Those who condemned the Smothers for even trying were responding from their own rage and despair. The desire for fundamental change was so deep and the pitfalls to achieving it were so numerous. The strategies of co-optation used by power elites raised legitimate fears among members of a movement. For these commentators, the *Smothers Brothers*, regardless of the censorship it faced, was just another example of popular culture's ability to absorb and defuse any form of political opposition.

While the criticism that the Smothers Brothers were part of a mass culture co-optive process was part of movement discourse, it was never the majority perspective among underground writers. The brothers were able to use evidence of the coercive power imposed upon them as their ultimate validation. Thus, the shadow of the censor's scissors—the imprint of hegemonic force—was an enabling device for the brothers. By displaying the markings of political repression evident on their youth-based material, they gained legitimacy from a disaffected social segment that was disinclined to view anything coming from the "boob tube" as politically subversive. Had the Smothers not encountered such heavy handed censorship, they might never have achieved support from the movement (albeit, support that was conflicted and at times ambivalent).

The Smothers Brothers Comedy Hour was enormously significant in the cultural context of the late 1960s because it shows concretely how popular culture became a battlefield or a "terrain of struggle" at a historical moment when almost every institution and facet of the social order was a potential site of conflict. The Smothers show developed into a crisis of authority in entertainment television at the very moment that crises of authority were threatening other institutions of social, political, and cultural power. The turmoil and controversy surrounding the show were thus symptomatic of the fissures and cleavages menacing the social order both internally and externally. The show, in its contested production and conflicted reception, revealed that more was at stake on Sunday nights at 9 p.m. than whether two folk singer/comedians would be allowed to entertain the households of America with material of questionable taste. At stake was a new political and social common sense. The question posed by the Smothers's ill-fated show was what kinds of negotiations and struggles would be necessary to bring this new common sense into the living rooms of a desperately torn nation.

notes

I would like to thank the Smothers Brothers for allowing me access to their papers. I am particularly grateful to Cathy Bruegger, who runs the Smothers's office, for her kind assistance. I would also like to thank the staff of the UCLA Film and Television Archive for making viewing copies available of all seventy-some episodes of *The Smothers Brothers Comedy Hour*.

1. All episodes of *The Smothers Brothers Comedy Hour* have been deposited by the Smothers at the UCLA Film and Television Archive. Final draft scripts for all episodes are also available at the UCLA Theater Arts Library. My description of the "Outside Agitators" sequence is drawn from both a reading of the script and a viewing of the episode.

2. Steven Allen Carr, "On the Edge of Tastelessness: CBS, the Smothers Brothers, and the Struggle for Control," *Cinema Journal* 31:4 (Summer 1992), 3–24. See also Bert Spector, "A Clash of Cultures: The Smothers Brothers vs. CBS Television, *American History/American Television*, ed. John e. Occonnor (New York: Frederick Ungar, 1983), 159–83.

3. CBS began worrying more and more about the preponderance of older and more rural viewers its programming tended to draw. In 1970–71 the network launched a campaign to lure younger, urban audiences by dumping its "hayseed" shows and gambling with "socially revelant" programming like *All in the Family*, *M*A*S*H*, and *The Mary Tyler Moore Show*. For a producer's oriented view of that campaign, see Todd Gitlin's chapter, "The Turn to Relevance" in *Inside Prime Time* (New York: Pantheon Books, 1983).

4. "Snippers v. Snipers," *Time* (2 February 1968): 57.

5. "Mothers Brothers," *Time* (30 June 1967): 41.

6. This verse apparently refers to a police assault against hippies congregated on the Sunset Strip in Los Angeles.

7. Todd Gitlin, "Prime Time Ideology: The Hegemonic Process in Television Entertainment." In *Television: The Critical View*, 4th Ed., ed. Horace Newcomb (New York: Oxford University Press, 1987), 526.

8. This issue is discussed in detail in my chapter "Plastic Hippies: Popular Culture and Counterculture," in *Groove Tube and Reel Revolution: The Youth Rebellions of the 1960s and Popular Culture* (Ph.D. dissertation, University of Wisconsin/Madison, 1994).

9. Episode aired 27 September 1967.

10. Episodes broadcast, respectively, 22 December 1968 and 2 February 1969.

11. Episode broadcast 3 November 1968.

12. Episode broadcast 2 February 1969.

13. William Kloman, in his in-depth article on the Smothers-CBS controversy, "The Transmogrification of the Smothers Brothers," *Esquire* (October 1969), noted that the segments were "never cut or drastically censored ... in spite of the drug-oriented nature of her act. The reason was that nobody at CBS could figure out what she was talking about. For a period of two months, the Smothers writers called Miss French "Goldie Kief"—both words are marijuana references—on the air and nobody at CBS batted a corporate eyeball," 148.

14. CBS memo, 2 May 1969, uncatalogued Smothers Brothers papers, Los Angeles.

15. According to Tom Smothers, 75 percent of the show's episodes were subject to censorship in the second and third seasons.

16. See Claybourne Carson, *In Struggle: SNCC and the Black Awakening of the 1960s* (Cambridge, MA & London: Harvard University Press, 1981) for an analysis of the shift from integrationist civil rights to Black Power.

17. See Charles DeBendetti with Charles Chatfield, *An American Ordeal: The Antiwar Movement of the Vietnam Era* (Syracuse: Syracuse University Press, 1990).

18. This is Antonio Gramsci's term for a period in which the ruling classes are no longer able to naturalize their power and are no longer able to lead. During such a crisis hegemonic forces can only dominate, using coercive means rather than

consensual methods attributable to a smoothly functioning hegemonic order. Subordinated groups no longer participate in validating the ruling classes in their positions as rulers. Dominant ideology is no longer accepted as common sense. See Antonio Gramsci, *Selections From the Prison Notebooks*, eds. and trans. Quintin Hoare and Geoffrey Nowell Smith (New York: International Publishers, 1971).

19. Dick Smothers would keep his mustache, which he wears to this day. Tom shaved his off after a couple of episodes.

20. Episode broadcast 29 September 1968. Final draft script, UCLA Theatre Arts Library.

21. *TV Guide* (31 August 1968): A—2. The magazine printed numerous letters with this theme in its letters section.

22. The number is included in the tape "Smothered Sketches," UCLA Film and Television Archives. The lyrics for the entire song are in the final draft script for air date 29 September 1968, UCLA Theatre Arts Library.

23. CBS memo from Sam Taylor, Jr. to "File," 23 September 1968, uncatalogued Smothers Brothers papers, Los Angeles.

24. For an insider's view of the coverage of the Chicago demonstrations, see the account by head of CBS News in New York, William Small, *To Kill a Messenger: Television News and the Real World* (New York: Hastings House, Publishers, 1970).

25. The episodes of *The Smothers Brothers Comedy Hour* collected in the UCLA Film and Television Archives all contain at least some commercial spots.

26. Letter from Carl E. Lee, Fetzer Broadcasting Company to William B. Lodge, Vice President of Affiliate Relations, CBS, 8 March 1968, uncatalogued Smothers Brothers papers, Los Angeles.

27. "Smothers & Others Rub 'Main St.' TV Wrong Way; Topeka's WIBW Among Stations in Midwest Beefing to CBS," *Variety* (26 March 1969): 63.

28. "Video Top 20. 2nd Round," *Variety* (16 October 1968): 35.

29. *Variety* (15 January 1969): 43.

30. "Top 50 Primetime Shows," *Variety* (2 April 1969): 42. The Smothers' variety show rival, *Laugh-In*, was firmly entrenched as the number one show in the country.

31. The tapes deposited by the Smothers at UCLA contain two versions of Baez's introduction. In the other one she says, "And the reason he's going to jail is because he refused to have anything to do with the Armed Forces or Selective Service. As a gift to him, I made this album." See episode scheduled for air 9 March 1969, broadcast 30 March 1969.

32. According to Robert Metz in his examination of the Smothers' censorship problems, "Tommy was sure viewers would figure Harris was guilty of grand larceny or worse." Metz, *CBS: Reflections in a Bloodshot Eye*, 301.

33. Robert Lewis Shayon, "Smothering the Brothers," *Saturday Review* (5 April 1969): 48.

34. Episode broadcast 27 October 1968.

35. Harlan Ellison, *The Glass Teat: Essays of Opinion on the Subject of Television* (New York: Ace Books, 1983 [1970]), 113—14. The book reprints all of Ellison's columns from the *Los Angeles Free Press*. This one ran in the *Free Press* 21 February 1969. It is worth noting that Ellison wrote one of the most celebrated *Star Trek* episodes, "City on the Edge of Forever."

36. Ellison, *The Glass Teat*, 111.

37. CBS press release, 4 April 1969, uncatalogued Smothers Brothers papers, Los Angeles. The press release reprinted the text of three wires from Wood to Smothers, 3 April, 25 March, and 27 March.

38. See, for instance, *Look* magazine's cover story, "The Smothers Brothers: Who Controls TV?" (24 June 1969). The article was written by First Amendment champion Nat Hentoff.

39. See regular feature of news blurbs, "Roaches," *Seed* 3: 8 (*n.d.*): 18.

40. Ellison, *The Glass Teat*, 111.

41. Allan Katzman, "Poor Paranoid," *East Village Other* (10 September 1969): 6. Katzman was a regular contributor to *EVO*, and this was his featured column.

42. "Classifieds," *Los Angeles Free Press* (18 April 1969): 49. *Free Press* classifieds were infamous for their sexually explicit personal ads, a feature pioneered by the paper and taken up by many other underground papers. The practice, along with the publication of ads for pornographic films, became one rallying site for movement women, who pointed out the sexist and misogynist nature of these ads.

43. Rudnick/Frawley, "Kokaine Karma," *East Village Other* (23 April 1969): 16.

44. Alice Embree, "Pollution Smothers: Tom Smothers vs. Smog of CBS," *Rat* (24 September 1969): 14.

45. Alice Embree, 14.

46. Alice Embree, 14.

47. Lawrence Lipton, "Radio Free America," *Los Angeles Free Press* (23 May 1969): 4.

48. Leonard Brown, "Censorship Hits Smothers Brothers: Show Will Run Without Joan Baez Segments," *Los Angeles Free Press* (21 March 1969): 21.

aniko bodroghkozy

Early Seventies telecommunications promotion in *Channels*

blue skies

and strange

bedfellows

the discourse

of cable television

t h o m a s   s t r e e t e r

[T]he stage is being set for a communications revolution ... audio, video, and fascimile transmissions ... will provide newspapers, mail service, banking and shopping facilities, data from libraries and other storage centers, school curricula and other forms of information too numerous to specify. In short, every home and office will contain a communications center of a breadth and flexibility to influence every aspect of private and community life.[1]

The preceding passage was published in *The Nation*, not in the last few years, but in 1970. The wondrous new technology that was supposed to bring about this communications revolution was not the information superhighway, but cable television. The author went on to argue that government should make a "commitment for an electronic highway system to facilitate the exchange of information and ideas."[2]

This chapter looks at what I will call "the discourse of the new technologies," a pattern of talk common in the policymaking arena in the late 1960s and early 1970s and remarkably similar to much of the recent talk about the information superhighway. This discourse flowed from an odd alliance of groups: 1960s media activists, traditional liberal groups, industry lobbyists, and Republican technocrats all made their contributions. As a result, government television policy was subtly transformed, and beginning in 1970, the Federal Communications Commission (FCC) reversed its attitude towards cable, turning the industry from a regulatory outcast into a protected element of the media system.

"Discourse," it should be pointed out, is not debate. The talk about cable, this chapter will show, was characterized by a systematic *avoidance* of central issues and assumptions, and by a pattern of unequal power in the discussion and its outcomes; the discourse of the new technologies was shaped not so much by full fledged debate as by a lack of it. By the same token, the argument here is not simply that debate was suppressed by a conspiracy, or that the policy process was captured by an interest group. The discourse of the new technologies was what Michel Foucault might call a collective habit of talk, action, and interpretation embedded in an historical context that establishes and enacts relations of power and resistance. The discourse had a kind of life of its own; it was not only shaped by but also itself shaped economic and social forces.

In particular, the discourse had the specific effect of systematically drawing attention away from political differences and creating a terrain for collective action that masked underlying conflicts. The form of the discourse—its particular mixture of themes, blind spots, and gaps—made possible an odd alliance between the Community Antenna Television (CATV) industry, certain professional groups, and some liberal progressive organizations. The discourse of the new technologies thus made possible some major actions in the policy arena, actions that simple self interest would not warrant. Diverse and often antagonistic viewpoints were united around a shared sense of awe and excitement; maybe the new technologies were good, maybe they were bad, but in any case they inspired a sense of optimism and opportunity.

The goals, interests, and philosophies of the many people who spoke of new technologies were widely varied, sometimes to the point of being mutually antagonistic. At the time, the people did not understand this as a compromise between groups with competing but overlapping interests; rather, they saw it as a consensus of opinion among objective experts. The new discursive field thus helped create a *sense* of expert consensus, of unity and coherence, where in fact there was a variety of conflicting motivations, attitudes, and opinions.

"an ever expanding chorus of expert opinion"

Cable began around 1950 as CATV, a service providing improved television signal reception in remote areas. Over the years, CATV helped fill in the gaps in the ragged periphery of a system dominated at the center by the three television networks, which distributed their signals nationwide via coaxial cable and microwave relay to broadcast transmitters in local communities. When the tiny but growing CATV industry set off a squabble in the broadcast system's periphery by threatening the profits of small local broadcasters, the broadcasters used their inordinate importance with the FCC to generate a set of regulations that effectively halted CATV's growth. By the mid-1960s, CATV was thus locked out of television's economic motherlode, the top 100 markets. CATV operators conducted a strident campaign to remove the restrictions, but to no avail, largely because they had little support outside their own ranks. The struggle between CATV operators and local broadcasters, for the most part, was seen as a minor affair, of interest only to industry insiders—until the late 1960s, when the climate of opinion began to change.

In what one contemporary writer described as "an ever expanding chorus of expert opinion," a new, hopeful view of cable television echoed throughout the policy arena in the late 1960s and early 1970s, appearing in numerous articles, studies, hearings, and journalistic publications.[3] One important galvanizing force in this development was the Rand Corporation, which began research on "cable television issues" in 1969 with support from (among others) the Ford Foundation. Rand published more than a dozen reports on the topic over the next three years. The Alfred P. Sloan Foundation established a Commission on Cable Communications in the spring of 1970, which solicited over fifteen studies and produced a book length report.[4] The fever went beyond the foundations, however. Articles appeared in *The New York Times* and *Saturday Review*. The influential British weekly *The Economist* became a regular advocate of the new vision. And a major article appeared in *The Nation* in the spring of 1970, later to be published in expanded form as a book called *The Wired Nation*.[5] Numerous progressive groups such as the Americans for Democratic Action (ADA) and the American Civil Liberties Union (ACLU) also became interested and began making contributions to cable policy proceedings. While there are important differences in many of these texts, they all share a sense of urgency, a sense of activism, and a sense of working against stifling and powerful conservative forces. Cable had captured the imagination, not just of those traditionally concerned with television regulation, but of what seemed to be an entire cross-section of the U.S. policymaking community.

Significantly, however, the sense of "an ever expanding chorus of expert opinion" was not based on any explicit, thoroughly worked-out theory that can be located in a single statement or document. Rather, these sentiments were typically invoked in passing, as introductory or concluding passages to otherwise more concrete and specific arguments, policy recommendations, and research reports. For example, in 1968 an Advisory Task Force on CATV and Telecommunications for the city of New York published a report that was, for the most part, relatively brief and pragmatic. It recommended the introduction of state-of-the-art cable systems for each borough of the city, with rates and programming regulated, but not absolutely determined, by guidelines established by the city council. Most of its fifty pages referred to the specific details of the situation in New York. But the report concluded with the following passage:

> The promise of cable television remains a glittering one.... Those who own these electronic circuits will one day be the ones who will bring to the public much of its entertainment and news and information, and will supply the communications link for much of the city's banking, merchandising, and other commercial activities. With a proper master plan these conduits can at the same time be made to serve the City's social, cultural, and educational needs.[6]

It was this kind of utopian language that filtered most widely into policy debates at large—not the report's data, analyses, and recommendations. The references to the "next generation" of high-capacity, two-way cable systems, to satellites, to systems that combined voice, computer, and television signals all on the same wire, to the generally "glittering promise" of this new dazzling technology—these were the particulars of the New York City Report that found their way into discussions in the FCC, the Rand Corporation, and the elite popular press. The concrete, detailed recommendations of the Report, on the other hand, were in the long run probably less important; they served more to provide an aura of expertise and professional legitimacy than they did to actually influence concrete policy decisions. Paradoxically, therefore, the specific details of the New York Report served largely as window dressing, while its vague utopian speculations had a very concrete impact that went far beyond the borders of New York City. This pattern was repeated in numerous other studies, books, and reports of the period. The frequent incantation of such "gee whiz" themes in policy debates created a feeling of consensus, a "common sense" of the day, without that sensibility ever being worked out in detail.

The key themes and gaps of this discourse, however, can be reconstructed.

In general, it was an example of what James Carey and John Quirk call "the rhetoric of the electrical sublime," which has resurfaced at regular intervals throughout American history ever since the development of the telegraph, and which expresses a quasi-religious faith in the power of new technologies to overcome social and material constraints.[7] In the late 1960s, the theme of technological revolution frequently took the form of a claim that "[n]ew technology is transforming the realm of communication."[8] Almost as frequently, however, it was also suggested that the revolution would embrace not just the realm of communications technology, but all of society. A report filed with the FCC in 1969, for example, stated that the "mushrooming growth in available information is bringing about a revolution in communications which will produce a profound change in the way society is structured and in the way we live."[9] The idea was that the growing use of communications satellites, the increasing involvement of computers in data transmission, and the expanding capacity of broadband coaxial cable were not isolated developments or mere continuations in the technological evolution of communications systems, but were all part of a revolutionary development comparable to that brought about by print or by the industrial revolution.

The theme of autonomous technology is clearly evident in these passages. For example, the report of the influential Sloan Commission on Cable Communications, published in 1971, opens with this typical passage: "Spreading quietly into every corner of the United States—slowly and unevenly and yet with its own air of inevitability—is a new communications technology."[10] Cable television was something that could have an important impact upon society, and it thus called for a response on the part of society; it was something to which society could respond and act upon, but that was itself *outside* society, an autonomous entity that had simply appeared on the scene as the result of scientific and technical research. As Raymond Williams has shown, this assumption of autonomous technology is characteristic of much thought about television and society, and constitutes a false abstraction of technologies out of their social and cultural context.[11]

The terminological shift from "CATV" to "cable" that occurred during this period usefully indicates the discursive tendency to abstract complex issues into a simple, autonomous "technology." Before the late 1960s, the term "community antenna television," or CATV, was dominant. The industry's trade magazine, for example, was titled *CATV*. This reflected an understanding of CATV as a service, an alternative method of program delivery. The coaxial cables, signal amplifiers, and other bits of equipment used by the CATV operators were just variations on the technologies used throughout the television industry. CATV was thus generally thought of as simply an alternate route, a slightly different combination of wires and transmitters for delivering television signals. But by 1970 all reference to the service began to be dropped and to be replaced by the name of a piece of hardware. "CATV" became "cable."[12] FCC reports, Congressional hearings, and the like were peppered with references to the "new technology of cable."

Cable, however, was neither "new" nor best described as a "technology." For one, "cable" had been in existence since the late 1940s under the name of CATV. Furthermore, the practice of distributing television signals by wire grew up alongside television itself, and has actually been central to what we call "broadcast" television all along: The lifeblood of American television, the network programs, were distributed on a coaxial cable network owned by AT&T in the 1950s and 1960s.[13] At the time when cable was most consistently interpreted as a "new technology" by the policy community, therefore, it was arguably no more "new" than it had been since the beginning of television in the late 1940s.

The trait most often invoked as justification for the description of cable as "revolutionary" was similar to the arguments made today on behalf of the information superhighway: an increase in maximum channel carrying capacity. It was frequently pointed out that recent developments had expanded the carrying capacity of coaxial cable to twenty and more television channels, substantially more than could be carried over the air (given the existing allocations). Based on this increased capacity, former CBS news president Fred Friendly claimed that the coaxial cable was "a true turnpike, as geometrically enlarged in capacity as a sixty-lane thruway would be over the old unpaved Boston Post Road."[14] Similarly, FCC Commissioner Nicholas Johnson argued that comparing coaxial cable to a telephone wire was like "comparing Niagara Falls to a garden hose."[15]

The increase in channel capacity obviously did represent a technological development. However, it was arguably only an *evolutionary* development, not revolutionary. It had been going on throughout the period when people were content with the word "CATV." Why not speak of a cable revolution when the channel capacity more than doubled from three to eight in the 1950s, or from three to twelve in the first half of the 1960s? And why focus on the particular piece of hardware called cable, rather than one of the many other, equally necessary kinds of hardware, such as microwave relay? After all, antennas and cables were necessary to the operation of *both* "broadcast" and "community antenna" television. Why draw so much attention to the different ways that individual television sets were linked to the broadcasting system—in one case radio waves, in the other, wires—when in both cases, the links to individual television sets were themselves connected to another set of links, the network web? The network system made television what it was, and it was constructed out of a massive, complex framework of coaxial cable and microwave relay that connected both the local wires and the local radio waves into the sources of national program distribution. But this fact was brushed aside, and the shift from radio waves to wires on the local level came to stand for a transformation of the system itself.

The argument tended to be that the system suffered from a clogged bottleneck on the local level, and the high channel capacity of broadband coaxial cable was a means to remove that obstacle. This was a dubious claim. The most telling evidence against the "local bottleneck" argument was the fact that in the late 1960s nearly two thirds of the allocated UHF broadcast frequencies across the country were left unused (a situation that continues to this day). At the time, Richard Posner argued that, since broadcasting over the air costs roughly the same as "cablecasting," the unused UHF airspace suggested that the problem of broadcasting was that the market was thin, not that access was limited.[16] The larger point, however, is not that a technical mistake was made or that the evidence was not carefully considered. In the overall pattern of events, it becomes clear that careful consideration of such detailed arguments was obviously not the issue; the gaps and contradictions in the scenario of a cable television revolution were easily brushed aside by all the talk about the utopian possibilities for progress through new technology.

This complex set of historical and economic circumstances, however, was thoroughly obscured as CATV was abstracted into a simple "new technology," something that was outside society. Precisely because of that abstraction, moreover, it became possible to speak of cable, not as an embodiment of social contradictions and dilemmas, but as a *solution* to them. Cable came to be associated with the utopian vision of a "wired nation." Cable, it was frequently intoned, was the next step toward a "single, unified system of electronic communications."[17] This theme had many variations: it was also described as the "wired city scenario" or associated with talk of "a nationwide integrated telecommunications grid."

The utopian strain in the discourse is evident in frequent suggestions that problems of the present could be transcended with the help of new communications technologies, particularly insofar as they embodied the utopian dream of the wired nation. One of the key themes was a belief that telecommunications "can play a . . . fundamental role in achieving understanding and harmonizing conflict among modern societies dominated by diversity, mobility, and the claims of social justice."[18] Such speculations naively assumed that telecommunications could magically resolve the power relations among people that caused racism, poverty, and international strife. Although "humanistic," these statements reversed the relationship between people and tools like communication technologies, assuming that technology could solve problems humans created rather than the other way around. Don Le Duc suggested that in a cabled society

> members of the audience would no longer be simply the passive recipients of mass communications messages but would participate actively in their selection and dissemination. ... Thus, direct feedback could well result in the reversal of the traditional roles of mass communications, making the communicator little more than a common carrier in a communications process controlled by each individual subscriber. In such a humanized atmosphere broad governmental control may no longer be necessary, except perhaps for the type of supervision of rates and service exercised over other private communications carriers.[19]

Cable, in other words, had the potential to rehumanize a dehumanized society, to eliminate the existing bureaucratic restrictions of government regulation common to the industrial world, and to empower the currently powerless public. Thus, on the level of discourse, not only were the historic complexities and dilemmas of the situation masked and abstracted by technology, but technology in turn came to be represented as the solution to those dilemmas.

origins of the discourse

At first glance, the enthusiasm for the discourse of the new technologies seemed to spring from a cross-section of the political spectrum. It was not, however, a true cross-section. While on its fringes this group may have bled off in either direction, at its core it encompassed neither the openly revolutionary parts of the then-active New Left, nor the mainstream of the Republican Party. Rather, it was in some ways a New Deal coalition, made up of professional groups, corporations and their intellectual allies, and progressive political groups seeking ways to foster social change by working "within the system." It is possible to locate five key centers of enthusiasm for the discourse of the new technologies: a collection of progressives interested in fostering more democratic forms of communication, the cable operators themselves, a group of economists concerned with regulatory problems, liberal elites interested in fostering alternatives to the existing commercial television system, and a group of influential policymakers centered around Eugene Rostow, who were interested in centralizing the management of the telecommunications system within a government agency.

A faith in new technology has been a recurring theme on the American left at various points throughout this century. In the 1930s, for example, some of Roosevelt's New Dealers rallied around the Tenessee Valley Authority and other big engineering projects as harbingers of a harmonious, equitable future achieved through science and technology. By the 1960s, however, the association between big science and utopian futures had largely disappeared on the left. Much of the 1960s counterculture was in various ways altogether antitechnological, being formed around what Andrew Ross has called the "technology of folklore," an amalgam of preindustrialist, agrarianist, and related values.[20] But there was a strain that saw in technology neither a utopian harmony nor a demonized uniformity, but the promise of an anarchic excess. One source of this vision was the musical avant garde. Composer John Cage, for example, associated technology not with impersonality, regularity, efficiency, and uniformity, but with "heterogeneity, randomness, and plenitude."[21] Another source, of course, was Marshall McLuhan, with his mixture of iconoclastic and euphorically utopian treatments of electronic technologies. These trends, combined with notions of grassroots political organizing current among the 1960s counterculture, fed into the alternative video movement, which advocated for and experimented with new, inexpensive, and portable video technologies as a democratic alternative to big, corporate media.[22]

Few, if any, of the alternative video activists had any direct influence on the policymaking processes of the late 1960s and early 1970s.[23] But some of the spirit and a few of the ideas (especially "cable access") probably informed the efforts of those who did contribute. Certainly the progressive spirit of many of those who gave voice to the discourse of the new technologies is evident on close readings of some of the most influential texts of the era. While introductory paragraphs and chapters were often filled with unadulterated examples of the discourse of the new technologies, long passages were often devoted to cautionary warnings about the coming new media. "Cable television offers vast potential for social good," the message seemed to be, "but that potential will be realized only if we act now." These were not mere apologists for special business interests, nor were they blind technology enthusiasts. They were groups that, for various reasons, wanted to "work within the system" to accomplish democratic social change within the framework of the dominant power structures of society. The new interest in cable television seemed to provide a grand opportunity for such change.

Ralph Lee Smith's _The Wired Nation_ (1972) is the most important example of this pattern. Originally published in the left magazine _The Nation_, Smith's tract, while full of glowing rhetoric about cable's promise, was also a polemic for certain political goals. Smith warned against economic concentration, cross-ownership, and local monopolies in the cable industry. He foresaw the possibility of mediocre, network-style programming patterns being repeated instead of the diverse and community-oriented programming for which he hoped. He warned against the narrow and purely economic industry interests that were already beginning to define the future structure of cable television.[25] These negative possibilities, however, did not dampen his enthusiasm. Instead, they led to his call for a combination of grassroots community action and a state-controlled regulatory structure that would limit rates and prohibit cable operators from controlling program content.

Smith's sentiments were shared by other liberal groups such as ADA and the ACLU, both of which he drew on for support. The arguments of the ADA in favor of congressional intervention in cable television are illustrative. The ADA saw the cable issue as an opportunity for us "to regain our constitutional heritage of freedoms of communication."[25] The ADA urged immediate action to prevent "special economic interests" from taking control of cable TV:

> Our growth, urbanization, and industrialization have now substituted mass circulation, advertising-supported, print and electronic media for the community media of person-to-person speech, assembly, and print. Personal two-way dialogue has been supplanted by one-way "broadcasting" to mass "audiences." Active participation in communications has become passive reception.[26]

The ADA, as this passage shows, obviously did not suffer from a naive faith in technology. The cable issue, for the ADA, was an opportunity to pursue non-technological legislative goals, not a chance to celebrate technology as a value in and of itself. And yet, the contribution of the ADA probably had effects quite different from those intended. The ADA's concrete legislative goals—a rewrite of the 1934 Communications Act that would foster a unified, national common carrier broadband network including television—were never given much serious attention. However, the fact that the ADA had lent its voice to the debate resonated, thus lending weight to the overall momentum of the growing utopianism around new technologies.

cable operators: the discourse as a competitive strategy

One driving force behind the discourse of the new technologies came from a very different perspective: cable operators invoked it in their struggle with broadcasters, particularly during appearances before the FCC. By describing their businesses not as a mere ancillary community service but as new technology, the cable operators were in a position to gain new leverage against their commercial opposition, the broadcasters. In 1966, one of the earliest attempts to shift the terminology from "CATV" to "cable television" came when some cable operators, eager to establish themselves as program providers, moved to change the name of the National Community Antenna Association to the National Cable Television Association.[27]

But it was not until two or three years later that the industry began to regularly draw on the discourse of the new technologies to promote their designs. A classic example can be found in the 1969 Congressional testimony of Irving B. Kahn, the president of the country's then-largest cable operator (who, within months of this testimony, would be sentenced to prison for bribing city officials during a cable franchise negotiation).[28] Kahn's testimony was for the most part standard salesmanship on behalf of removing the regulatory restrictions on CATV—cable provided a needed service, it did not threaten the broadcasters, cable had been mistreated by the FCC, and so on. All this was accompanied by a wealth of anecdotal evidence and some skillful rhetoric designed to portray cable as a misunderstood underdog. He concluded his prepared remarks, however, with a new twist:

> There is one thing that cannot be ignored. And that is the great and growing body of competent, impartial opinion—from scientists, writers and journalists, members of the government, businessmen, economists, and others—that stresses the great potential of CATV if it is permitted to test its wings in an open, competitive, climate.[29]

From Kahn's perspective, his appeal to expert authority was, perhaps, just one more rhetorical device. But it would not have been an effective one a few years earlier. His reference to a "great and growing body of impartial opinion" only made sense because of the recent talk of new technologies. By the early 1970s, when this particular way of speaking about new technologies would reach a fevered pitch, it was familiar enough to the industry to have earned a label in the trade jargon: the "blue sky scenario."

The invocation of this scenario by cable operators, however, is not enough to account for the intensity and pervasiveness that came to characterize talk about the "wired nation" by the early 1970s. The glib, pragmatic style characteristic of business people does not lend itself to the abstract flights of utopian fantasy. The blue sky scenario, as it appeared in the trade press, usually seemed to have a slightly sarcastic inflection to it, and in any case seemed more to connote astounding profits than astounding social transformations. Whether "CATV" or "cable," the basic point was to make money. The cable operators may have set the ball rolling, but the impulses that really gave the discursive transformation its decisive momentum had to come from somewhere else.

economists and liberal elites

One pattern common to most of the various streams of thought that fed the fuels of utopian speculation was that they interpreted the strains, struggles, and problems of the existing American television system to be the product, not of growing pains, but of fundamental structural flaws. In several different elite circles, television was no longer seen as an infant institution, and its problems were no longer interpreted as temporary foibles, amenable to correction within the existing overall structure. People in positions of authority and power were beginning to seek solutions to television's failings not in adjustments to the existing system, but in alternatives to the system itself.

One of these calls for an alternative came from the groups that sponsored the Carnegie Commission on Educational Television. While the Carnegie Commission did not address the issue of CATV or invoke the discourse of the new technologies in any direct way, it did help introduce the idea of considering a fundamentally different kind of television, structured in a radically new way and conceived at the national level. "[T]his is a proposal," the Commission argued, "not for small adjustments or patchwork changes, but for a comprehensive system that . . . will become a new and fundamental institution in American culture . . . different from any now in existence."[30] The important contribution of the Carnegie Commission to the discourse, therefore, was a shift in emphasis from "small adjustments and changes" to the creation of "a comprehensive system" through relatively radical restructuring.

At roughly the same time, another call for alternatives appeared in a very different environment. This was the work of several economists who argued that the existing television structure "unnaturally" restricted economic competition and program diversity. A completely different system, they went on to say, might eliminate the problem. Probably the earliest comprehensive published example of this argument, titled "A Proposal for Wired City Television," by Harold Barnett and Edward Greenberg, appeared in the winter of 1968. However, as the authors suggest, the argument had been current among members of the RAND corporation, certain FCC commissioners, and others of the policymaking elite for some time before that.[31] The article takes as given the inadequacies of the existing television system, such as lack of diversity. The reason for the inadequacy, however, was that there are too few television signals being delivered to homes.... If more channels were available and the expense for transmitting and network connection of programs were less, and correspondingly more dollars were available for creating programs, then the number of programs and their diversity and range would be greater.[32]

The solution to this channel bottleneck, the article went on to say, was "wired city television" (WCTV for short), a system of television signal distribution based on high-capacity wires instead of radio transmission.

the flowering of the discourse: the release of the rostow report

In May of 1969, less than six months after "A Proposal for Wired City Television" was published, one of its coauthors, Harold Barnett, testified before a House subcommittee. Barnett, after arguing in favor of CATV, said:

> Far more exciting than the actual accomplishments of infant CATV is the promise and potential of the wired city and Nation. The promise has significance of the order of magnitude of the Nation's two, already existing wire grids—telephone and electricity—or of the automobile highway grid.[33]

Barnett had tapped into the technological utopianism that was sweeping cable policy at the time. He argued not just for a "wired city" (a relatively specific alternative to local broadcast transmitters) but for a Wired Nation—a vision of and about the future. He elevated his proposal from a relatively concrete and technical argument to a visionary one.

Barnett, however, was just following in the footsteps of others who had testified at the same hearings—most notably, Eugene Rostow—and of many of his colleagues in the policymaking community. The disparate streams of thought fed by the CATV operators, economists like Barnett, and by the liberal groups who had created the Carnegie Commission were all coming together in a complex unity. The repeated incantations of the Wired Nation vision, coupled to vague but grand gestures towards a portentous future, were fusing the mixed bag of interests, visions, and concepts behind cable in such a way as to give the impression of "a rising chorus of expert opinion."

In this context, a series of seminal blue ribbon reports began to surface that crystallized the discourse of the new technologies, giving it a level of legitimacy and respectability rare in broadcast policy debates. One of these was the New York City Report mentioned above. Another, conducted more or less contemporaneously, was the report of the President's Task Force on Communications Policy, headed by Eugene Rostow. This report recommended the creation of a new government agency to coordinate telecommunications technologies because of their awe-inspiring strategic and social importance to the nation as a whole.[34]

The argument advanced by the Report was essentially identical to Barnett and Greenberg's: the problems of television—lack of diversity, network dominance, lack of socially responsible programming—could be resolved by the high channel capacity of cable television technology, which would overcome the bottleneck supposedly inherent in over-the-air television. The Report went beyond Barnett and Greenberg, however, in a few areas. It vaguely but enthusiastically suggested that cable television, by allowing minorities and disaffected groups an outlet to express themselves and to communicate with the nation, might reduce their feelings of alienation and thus help solve the "problem" of the social unrest that was sweeping American society in 1968, particularly the unrest in black ghettoes. The Report also argued for an enhanced role for the federal government as a coordinator of the introduction of cable as a nationwide medium.

the discourse's contradictory unity

On close inspection, the goals of the Rand Corporation, Irving Kahn, the ADA, and Ralph Lee Smith were all quite distinct from one another. Yet at the time, these differences were often obscured by a sense of unity. As one book put it,

> An almost religious faith in cable television has sprung up in the United States. It has been taken up by organizations of blacks, of consumers and of educational broadcasters, by the Rand Corporation, the Ford Foundation, the American Civil Liberties Union, the electronics industry, the Americans for Democratic Action, the government of New York City, and—a tentative convert—the Federal Communications Commission. The faith is religious in that it begins with something that was once despised—a crude makeshift way of bringing television to remote areas—and sees it transformed over the opposition of powerful enemies into the cure for the ills of modern urban American society.[35]

What motivated these diverse groups to respond at all? The cable industry's motivations were obvious, as were those of the electronics industry, which stood to benefit from a growing cable industry. But the link between cable and many of the rest of the participants' interests were less obvious. Why was cable a "challenge" for so many rather than simply another new commercial enterprise? In particular, why did the limitations in the situation generate passion in the progressive groups rather than pessimism?

The answer lies in part in the structure of the discourse itself. One of its most important themes was the transcendence of individual needs and differences through a rational process of society-wide linking and coordination, driven by a neutral, autonomous technology. The notion of a transcendant, utopian unification, coupled to the strategic ambiguities about politics and economics discussed above, resulted in a Janus-faced discursive structure, capable of being interpreted in several different ways while at the same time concealing those differences. Each group could interpret the discourse as embodying their own interests, while at the same time ignoring the substantial differences between themselves and the others who gave voice to the same sentiments.

Thus, in spite of major differences in political and economic goals, taken together, the chorus of voices did create the impression of the religious faith Maddox was describing. Few individual texts or voices produced statements about new technologies in a pure, unadulterated form; few did not qualify it with their own particular concerns. The discourse, however, provided the ground on which the different groups stood, the frame within which their individual enunciations resonated and had an effect. Each group, in pursuing its own goals, sought strength in associating itself with the growing chorus in favor of change. The discourse thus served as a binding, unifying force.

The way that these various voices and the forces that motivated them merged in the policy arena cannot be fully understood in terms of mutual advantage. The interests of participants in the policy process frequently were *not* served, particularly over the long term. This is especially true of progressive groups, but many businesses—such as many financial interests who invested in cable in the early 1970s—also lost money in their overenthusiasm for the idea of "new" technologies. While the discourse of the new technologies by no means eliminated the powers of the various interest groups involved, it did have its own specific conditions and effects; once set in motion, it took on a life of its own. It worked to refract the goals of many of those that originally contributed to it, leading to effects quite other than those envisioned.

This paradox of unintended effects is most evident in the case of the progressive groups. On the one hand, they were not blinded by the discourse in a simple way. The ADA, the ACLU, Fred Friendly, and Ralph Lee Smith, for example, were all quite aware of the narrow-minded commercial interests that were behind the current expansion of cable, of the many factors that could inhibit the hoped-for rosy future of the "new technology." To a large degree, it was precisely those factors to which these progressive liberals were reacting. They hoped to fend off these negative possibilities by influencing cable television policy. The irony of the situation, however, was that it was in part their efforts that set loose the very commercial forces they were trying to resist; their enthusiastic participation in the policy proceedings lent a great deal of legitimacy to the general sense of an expert, impartial, bipartisan, apolitical, and disinterested opinion in favor of cable liberation.

reregulation and the cable disappointment

In the context of the discourse of the new technologies, the FCC eventually changed its policy towards CATV from one of restriction to one of encouragement. By 1971, the reconceptualization of "CATV" as "cable" had made it increasingly difficult to speak of cable as merely a marginal enterprise that concerned the FCC only insofar as it threatened local broadcasters. This reconceptualization, combined with unrelenting pressure from lobbying by the cable industry, made it only a matter of time before new rules were drawn up. The watershed development in the FCC's reversal was the 1972 Third Report and Order, which allowed cable operators access to major markets.

The Third Report and Order alone, as it turned out, was not enough to ensure cable's success. Throughout the rest of the 1970s the FCC and the courts entered a period best called "reregulation," during which they frequently revised, relaxed, rescinded, and otherwise altered the set of regulations governing cable television. The logic governing the rule changes of the 1970s was one that classified the growth and expansion of cable as a natural and valuable element of "progress." Cable's dramatic expansion, when it finally did occur, would not have been possible without that logic.

Cable has brought change. The roughly 60 percent of the public that subscribes has more channels, and channel surfers can now easily hop between the right-wing social conservatism of the Family Channel and the sexual liberalism of a Dr. Ruth Westheimer—perhaps not the best that has been thought and said in either camp, but at least a range of values much broader than was ever common on the politically timid big three networks. But if the discourse of the new technologies had any meaning at all, it was that the hoped-for changes would mark a dramatic departure from the existing system, and that the changes would be technology-driven; neither of these assertions adequately describes what happened. Cable has not revolutionized the basic corporate structure of television. It has been integrated within it.

The discourse of the new technologies suggested that cable could empower the currently passive audience and eliminate the "one way" quality of television, principally through public access channels and "interactive" cable. Yet the only serious effort to develop two-way cable (Warner-Amex's QUBE), was abandoned in 1984, and the numerous promises of interactive systems in franchise agreements were all dropped in renegotiation.[36] Public access channels have been more successful, but suffer from lack of funding, inadequate equipment, and cable company resistance. Certainly, the dream of a cable system in which "members of the audience would no longer be simply the passive recipients of mass communications messages but would participate actively in their selection and dissemination" is hardly less a fantasy now than it was in 1972.

Whatever new diversity in video content exists, furthermore, is less the product of technology than of the fact that, by the mid-1970s, the library of available commercial film and videotaped programs, including old movies and reruns, had grown dramatically. With the increase in supply came a predictable decrease in price. Filling a schedule with material became a much less expensive proposition than it had been in the early days of television.[37] Hence, the overwhelming bulk of the programming available is programming that has been or would be available elsewhere: almost all of the old and new films that make up so much of cable's programming have already played in theaters, and much of the remaining programming consists of reruns of network television programs. Even the more original cable services, such as CNN or MTV, tend to program for the same mass audiences that the broadcast networks have traditionally sought, and minority tastes are once again underrepresented. The discourse's predictions of abundant, diverse programming for all have not been fully realized.

Finally, the industry has hardly shifted from a condition of closed monopoly to one of wide-open competition. Today, most of the pre-1972 companies in the cable industry are gone or absorbed (e.g., Teleprompter), and the key players in recent years bear names familiar from other media contexts (Time, Hearst, CBS, Paramount, Warner, Westinghouse). The few new names that did emerge have gradually shed their entrepreneurial roots and have become increasingly corporate in their approach.[38] The Cable Communications Policy Act of 1984 gave cable operators a legal monopoly on the local level and prohibited cities from regulating content and subscription fees.[39] Concurrently, dominance of the industry by a shrinking number of large corporations has steadily increased for the last twenty years.[40] The industry is now an oligopoly dominated by five, six, or seven conglomerates replacing the previous oligopoly of the three major networks. Perhaps this is an improvement, but it is clearly not the dramatic sort of improvement predicted by the discourse of the new technologies.

237

conclusion: a word to the wired

Today, we are in the midst of another wave of technological utopianism, this time associated with the so-called "information superhighway." Cable has been redefined as just another despised old technology, supposedly due for replacement by some mix of desktop computers, digital video, and fiber optic cables. Interactivity is again a popular buzzword. George Gilder, a "futurist," recently wrote that, with the help of "interactive" television, "the human spirit—emancipated and thus allowed to reach its rarest talents and aspirations—will continue to amaze the world with heroic surprises."[41] The Clinton Administration's "Information Infrastructure Task Force" enthuses:

> The National Information Infrastructure promises to extend the power of the human imagination to new frontiers.... Through the NII the arts and the humanities will play a vital role in creating a new sense of citizenship and community, in strengthening our schools and offering exciting challenges to our children, and in creating new industries and works of art and scholarship yet unimagined.... The NII will bring new opportunities and resources to our nation's disadvantaged youth, allowing them to share their ideas, thoughts and creative energies, and to make new links with other young people throughout the nation.... The NII can give all Americans, of all races, ages and locations, their cultural birthright: access to the highest quality thought and art of this and prior generations.[42]

High hopes of interactivity, technological plenitude, and the transcendance of social problems via new technologies once again abound.

Of course, there are plenty of cautionary warnings, and doubts about the direction of developments in the current environment. The cable industry's recent promise of "500 channel" systems is probably more often criticized than lauded. The business press is peppered with worries about thin consumer interest and exorbitant costs. And a loud chorus of computer professionals and enthusiasts associated with organizations like Computer Professionals for Social Responsibility, the libertarian Electronic Frontier Foundation (EFF), and *Wired* magazine have sounded warnings about privacy, industry concentration, advertising, and the likely limitation of the new technologies to passive entertainment purposes.

But almost identical warnings were sounded during cable's blue sky era, particularly by individuals like Ralph Lee Smith and organizations like the ADA and the ACLU. The problem is not that no one sees difficulties this time around, but that so many approach those difficulties by way of a discourse of inevitable technological progress, technology-driven revolution, and technological transcendance of economic, social, and political constraints.

For example, in an oft-cited essay, EFF cofounder Mitchell Kapor wrote that the "true promise of this technology" will be a

> National Information Infrastructure that promotes grassroots democracy, diversity of users and manufacturers, true communications among the people, and all the dazzling goodies of home shopping, movies on demand, teleconferencing, and cheap, instant databases.[43]

Video, for example, will "at last become a people's medium" because desktop video will spark "a revolution . . . enabling the creators of video content to produce high-quality professional video for a fraction of the cost just a decade ago." The development of much of this, he argues, is inevitable. Of course, Kapor is quick to note that

> crucial doubts remain. . . . Users may have indirect, or limited control over when, what, why, and from whom they get information and to whom they send it. That's the broadcast model today, and it seems to breed consumerism, passivity, crassness, and mediocrity.[44]

He goes on to propose a "Jeffersonian" policy emphasis on openness of access, distribution, and structure, and cautions against many of the plans being hyped by today's corporations. The technology is coming and its potential is enormous, the argument goes, so we must act to take advantage of the opportunities now or all will be lost.

Kapor is a thoughtful and interesting contributor to the contemporary debate with proposals that are worth considering seriously. The point is, however, that technology doesn't promise anything; technological developments do not just happen without someone choosing them, and today's technologies are not revolutionary. They are simply part of the same gradual, evolutionary development of technologies that has marked the last several centuries. (Why is desktop video any more "revolutionary" than super eight cameras, videotape, the original reel-to-reel video portapaks, video cassettes, and the numerous other improvements in low-cost visual media of the last forty years?) Kapor, by lending his sincere and authoritative voice to the generally awestruck sense of inevitable technological revolution, may simply be helping to create the conditions for strategic government intervention and industry realignments on behalf of exactly those centralized, advertising-dominated, media systems he cautions us against.

The problems of privacy, equitable access, freedom of expression, of centralization, and so on that are raised in the context of information superhighways are part of the larger problems of social justice that face our society as a whole. The economic, social, and political constraints that have limited democracy and freedom in the past are exactly that. The constraints were not caused by old technological limits, nor can they be eliminated by new technologies; they were caused by relations between people and can be overcome only by changing relations between people.

At a minimum, the early history of cable provides a cautionary tale about the dangers and blind spots of the concepts of autonomous technology and technological determinism. On the level of public debate, the cable fable is a story of repeated utopian high hopes followed by repeated disappointments. Cable was to be interactive; instead it is just as one-way as its predecessors. Cable was to end television oligopoly; instead it has merely provided an arena for the formation of a new oligopoly. Cable was to cure social ills; instead it at best distracts us from those ills. And so on.

On the level of the media industries, however, the pattern was not a roller coaster of high hopes and disappointments, but a process of gradual, if occasionally halting, growth and integration of cable into the American corporate system of electronic media and communications technologies. The back-and-forth motion between high hopes and disappointments served the industry well; it loosened the regulatory framework at strategic moments, allowing cable to be gradually ratcheted into its place between the usually calcified, tightly joined elements of the corporate industrial system.

It is important to note that the industry which benefited from the policy debate did not simply manipulate the debate toward its own ends; it was not just a case of the public interest being overwhelmed by the power of big business. Cable was brought into the regulatory fold in the early 1970s not simply because an industrial elite demanded it, but because a coalition of groups, some with goals quite at odds with those of corporate management, cajoled the FCC into action through a collective public argument that coalesced around the discourse of the new technologies. The hopes for diversity and democracy may have been naive, but they were rarely cynical; they were largely fueled by genuine social and political concerns.

So the danger today is not only that short-term corporate interests will dominate over the hopes of the visionaries. The danger is also that the visionaries' efforts will ultimately contribute to the reproduction of the limiting social structures that they dream of overthrowing. Clearly, the policy debate of the late 1960s served large corporations much more effectively than it did the social and democratic ambitions that helped generate the debate. If the lessons of the past are not heeded, this time might not be different.

notes

Most of this chapter is derived from Thomas Streeter, "The Cable Fable Revisited: Discourse, Policy, and the Making of Cable Television," *Critical Studies in Mass Communication* (June 1987) : 174–200. Many parts have been reorganized, updated, and expanded, and some parts of the original have been omitted.

1. Ralph Lee Smith, "The Wired Nation," *The Nation* (18 May 1970): 582.
2. Smith, "The Wired Nation," 602.
3. Don R. Le Duc, *Cable Television and the FCC: A Crisis in Media Control* (Philadelphia: Temple University Press, 1973), 5.
4. Sloan Foundation, *On the Cable: The Television of Abundance* (New York: McGraw Hill, 1971), vii.
5. Smith, "The Wired Nation," 582–606; Ralph Lee Smith, *The Wired Nation—Cable TV: The Electronic Communications Highway* (New York: Harper & Row, 1972).
6. New York City, Mayor's Task Force on Communications Policy, *Final Report* (Washington, D.C.: U.S. Government Printing Office, 1967), v–vi.
7. James W. Carey and and James J. Quirk, "The Mythos of the Electronic Revolution," *American Scholar* Part I, 39: 1 (1970): 219–41; Part II, 39: 2 (1970): 395–424.
8. President's Task Force on Communications Policy, *Final Report* (Washington D.C.: U.S. Government Printing Office, 1968), 4.
9. Electronic Industries Association, *The Future of Broadband Communication*, F.C.C. Docket 18397, October, 1969, Part 5, 23, quoted in Le Duc, 1973, 37.
10. Sloan Foundation, 1
11. Raymond Williams, *Television: Technology and Cultural Form* (New York: Schocken, 1977), 10–14.
12. The *Reader's Guide to Periodical Literature* of 1969 lists eight articles under the subject heading CATV, two with references in their title to "cable," six with references to "CATV." In 1970, there were four articles with titles referring to "CATV," and three with "cable." By 1971, the balance had reversed: only five article titles referred to "CATV," while ten referred to "cable." It wasn't until the late 1970s that *Reader's Guide* reversed the priority of its subject headings, listing "see cable television" under CATV rather than the other way around. By that time, the vast majority of the articles listed under CATV referred to "cable." The trade journal *CATV* changed its name to *Vue* at the end of 1976.
13. Over the years, AT&T gradually replaced its national coaxial system with microwave relays, and then began to use satellites to distribute programs to affiliates.
14. Fred Friendly, "Asleep at the Switch of the Wired City," *Saturday Review* (10 October 1970): 58.
15. Friendly, 58.
16. Richard Posner, "The Appropriate Scope of Regulation in the Cable Television Industry," *Bell Journal of Economics and Management Science* 3 (1972): 102–3.
17. Smith, 9.
18. President's Task Force, 5.
19. Le Duc, 14–16.
20. Andrew Ross, *Strange Weather: Culture, Science, and Technology in the Age of Limits* (New York: Verso, 1991), 88.
21. Kathleen Woodward, "Art and Technics: John Cage, Electronics, and World Improvement," in Kathleen Woodward, ed. *The Myths of Information: Technology and Postindustrial Culture* (Madison, WI: Coda Press, 1980), 176.
22. The classic statement of the alternative video ethos is Michael Shamberg, *Guerrilla Television* (New York: Holt, Rinehart and Winston, 1971).
23. Barry Orton, e-mail message to author, October 24, 1994.
24. Smith, 90–94.
25. U.S. House of Representatives, *Regulation of Community Antenna Television Systems—*

1969 (Washington, D.C.: U.S. Government Printing Office, 1971), 388. (Hereinafter cited as U.S. House of Representatives.)

26. U.S. House of Representatives, 383–84, original emphasis.

27. Patrick R. Parsons, "Defining Cable Television: Structuration and Public Policy," *Journal of Communication* 39: 2 (Spring 1989):10–26, 23.

28. Peter W. Bernstein, "The Rise, Fall, and Rise of Irving Kahn," *Fortune*, (28 July 1980): 58.

29. U.S. House of Representatives, 44.

30. Carnegie Commission for Educational Television, *Public TV: A Program for Action* (New York: Harper & Row, 1967), 75.

31. Harold Barnett and Edward Greenberg, "On the Economics of Wired City Television," *American Economic Review* 50 (June 1968): 238–75.

32. Barnett and Greenberg, 217–18.

33. U.S. House of Representatives, 211.

34. President's Task Force, 183.

35. Brenda Maddox, *Beyond Babel: New Directions in Communications* (Boston: Beacon Press, 1974), 145.

36. Les Brown, ed., *Channels of Communications: The Essential 1985 Field Guide to the Electronic Media* (1985) 24.

37. Don R. Le Duc, "Deregulation and the Dream of Diversity." *Journal of Communication* 32: 4 (Autumn 1982): 164–78.

38. For example, in the mid-1980s, Ted Turner, who had been heavily mythologized in the press for his swashbuckling, entrepreneurial approach, sought to vertically integrate his operations by buying the MGM/United Artists library of films; in turn, the high cost of the purchase forced him to sell a large portion of his company's stock to a coalition of fourteen of the nation's largest cable operators, further integrating the industry as a whole while reducing his individual control. Al Delugach, "Turner to Keep Control of Firm with $550-Million Bailout Deal," *Los Angeles Times* (23 January 1987), Business Section, Part 4, 1.

39. Title VI of the Amended Communications Act of 1934, 47 U.S.C. §601 (1984).

40. The six largest MSOs (Tele-Communications Inc., Liberty Media, Time Warner, Viacom, Cablevision Systems, and Comcast) together serve almost half of all cable subscribers and are also heavily involved in programming. TCI, for example, has a stake in Turner and Discovery. Turner, in turn, controls Turner Network, CNN, Headline News, and Superstation TBS. Viacom has substantial interests in MTV, Nickelodeon, VH-1, Showtime, The Movie Channel, and Lifetime. Many of these relations are sealed with corporate interlocks: John D. Malone, for example, doubles as TCI president and Liberty Media chairman, and six of the fifteen directors of Turner Broadcasting System represent part-owners Time Warner and TCI. And predictably, cable has become increasingly intertwined with media interests in general: Capital Cities/ABC Inc. has dominant interests in ESPN and shares Lifetime with Viacom and Hearst Corp., Kathryn Harris, "Reordering the Cable Universe," *Los Angeles Times* (25 July 1993): D1.

41. "What If They're Right?" *The Economist* (12 February 1994): 3.

42. Committee on Applications and Technology of the Information Infrastructure Task Force, draft report: *The Information Infrastructure: Reaching Society's Goals*, NIST Special Publication 868, 7 September 1994, 196.

43. Mitchell Kapor, "Where is the Digital Highway Really Heading?: The Case for a Jeffersonian Information Policy," *Wired* 1: 3 (July/August, 1993): 53–59, 94.

44. Kapor, 53–54.

nation

and

citizenship

part three

Lorne Greene in *Bonanza*

Columbian children greet the visiting President

eleven   **dynasty in drag**

imagining global tv

michael curtin

On July 10, 1962 the world's first commercial communications satellite tri-
umphantly soared into the skies above Cape Canaveral, thereby opening the
door to an era of almost instantaneous television transmissions around the
globe. Excitement about the new medium grew throughout the decade as
rapidly expanding audiences seemed to promise a shared cultural context
that might bring citizens of the world closer together. One of the best known
contributors to this crescendo of popular enthusiasm was literary scholar
Marshall McLuhan, who published *The Gutenberg Galaxy* in 1962, a book that
began his meteoric rise to popular fame. Referred to by *Life* magazine as the
"oracle of the electric age," McLuhan popularized the notion of a "global village" knit together by televisual communication.[1] Drawing his inspiration
from fellow Canadian scholar Harold Innis, McLuhan contended that the
shift from print to electronic media was an important transition in human
history. For too long, according to McLuhan, the printed word had domi-

nated Western consciousness, fostering an overly rational, linear, and individualistic mindset. While the pre-Gutenberg era relied on oral discourse that
stimulated affective bonds between communicators, the development of the
printing press facilitated the rise of the modern bureaucracies that could
organize and manipulate entire nations.[2] For McLuhan, television promised a
departure from the linear and the rational by feeding the senses a multimedia
flood of imagery that increased one's involvement with the communication
process. Moreover, it promised to restore affective bonds by fostering a shared
sense of proximity among people around the world. "Electromagnetic discoveries have recreated the simultaneous 'field' in all human affairs so that
the human family now exists under conditions of a 'global village,'" he wrote.
"We live in a single constricted space resonant with tribal drums."[3] McLuhan
contended that this shared space made possible a collective unconscious that
might transcend national boundaries and transform human relations.

McLuhan's ability to coin controversial, hyperbolic, and quotable phrases
initially endeared him to news reporters and critics, who by the mid-1960s
elevated him to the status of a pop icon. And in 1967, at the peak of his fame,
McLuhan and illustrator Quentin Fiore published *The Medium Is the Message*, a
visual/verbal collage that sought to evoke the new sensibility of the electronic
age. The book is at once playful and probing. Toward the end, in one of the
most provocative moments of the text, the authors reproduce a black-and-
white photo of the fiery self-immolation of a Buddhist monk protesting the
Vietnam War. Superimposed over the picture is a quote from the Chinese
philosopher Laotze, and then the following commentary:

> Electric circuitry is Orientalizing the West. The contained, the
> distinct, the separate—our Western legacy—are being replaced
> by the flowing, the unified, the fused.[4]

Such notions of global communion probably attracted so much attention not
only because they seemed prophetic, but because they acknowledged the tensions engendered by an era of technological innovation, changing social relations, and increasing U.S. involvement in global politics and economy. If the
first two trends encouraged utopian imaginings, the latter one reminded
Americans that global unity was far more easily imagined than attained.

This tension is central to understanding both the social climate of the
1960s and the implementation of U.S. policy regarding global television. Even
though the Telstar launch promised a future of global communion, the
implementation of communications policy by the cold warriors of the New
Frontier harkened back to an imperial mode of thinking reminiscent of the

preceding century. Close analysis of this policy discourse can show how the U.S. government married strategic concerns to popular utopian imaginings, and how policy rhetoric, in turn, helped to define the boundaries of possibility regarding international television. New Frontier policy rhetoric, full of both optimism and dramatic apprehensiveness, set the parameters for development of the new technology and laid the groundwork for future government policy regarding international television flows.[5]

Numerous scholars have shown that utopian rhetoric inevitably accompanies the introduction of new communications technologies, and that this rhetoric often influences the ways in which these technologies are adapted for social use.[6] Historically, a recurrent theme among these utopian imaginings has been the prospect of a new communications technology bringing citizens of the nation closer together. As we shall see, what makes the early 1960s distinctive is that, with the new technology of satellite television, government policymakers were not simply imagining a more cohesive national community; for the first time they were imagining an *international* community of the so called Free World. Even though preceding technologies like Hollywood film and comic books circulated widely around the globe, television seemed to promise a shared sense of political and cultural proximity among peoples of the world. Not simply a form of commercial entertainment nor primarily an instrument of government propaganda, global TV would bring citizens together to share specific moments, emotions, and events.

Yet one of the most striking aspects of this discourse was its profoundly contradictory nature. Global television seemed to offer the prospect of enhancing both global community and superpower struggle. The new medium was characterized as a technology that would encourage mutual understanding, but also as a means of strategic persuasion. It was envisioned as a collective undertaking that would lead to a free exchange of ideas, and yet it was also a technology developed with proprietary corporate interests in mind. In these contradictions, we find important links between television policy and the foreign policy of the New Frontier. For the discourse that emerged with the new technology did not simply produce statements about the national agenda for television, the land of the vast wasteland, it also generated discussions about forging a Free World alliance under the leadership of the United States.

the most exciting part of the new frontier

Globally speaking, the early 1960s was an era of *two* new communications technologies. Although satellite transmissions clearly captured the attention of North Americans, the technology of television itself was still new to most parts of the world, a fact suggested by the dramatic rise in overseas sales of receivers during this period. The U.S. Information Agency estimated that in 1960 alone the number of sets grew by twenty percent.[7] And in 1962, the revenues from foreign syndication of U.S. telefilm programming exceeded domestic revenues for the very first time.[8] Leaders in the U.S. television industry closely followed these developments and became actively involved in these growing markets. Like McLuhan, many industry commentators, such as RCA chairman David Sarnoff, believed that television was ushering in a new historical epoch. In a 1961 speech at the University of Detroit, Sarnoff predicted:

> Ten years hence—if vigorous foreign growth continues—there will be TV stations in virtually every nation on earth telecasting to some two hundred million receivers. An audience of a billion people might then be watching the same program at the same time, with simultaneous translation techniques making it understandable to all. In a world where nearly half of the population is illiterate, no other means of mass communication could equal television's reach and impact on the human mind.[9]

Prominent government policy makers apparently agreed with the RCA executive. After reading newspaper accounts of Sarnoff's speech, Newton Minow, President Kennedy's recent appointee as chairman of the Federal Communications Commission, dashed off a note to Sarnoff. "I was much intrigued with the accounts in the press the other day of your speech about international television," wrote Minow. "I agree that international television is probably the most exciting part of the New Frontier, and I would very much like to talk with you about it sometime."[10]

No record exists of when, or if, this conversation took place. However, there is extensive evidence that during his tenure as chairman of the FCC, Newton Minow paid considerable attention to the issue of international television, and this marked a significant shift in government communications policy.[11] In his first speech to broadcast executives, Minow remarked, "No one knows how long it will be until a broadcast from a studio in New York will be viewed in India as well as in Indiana, will be seen in the Congo as well as Chicago. But surely as we are meeting here today, that day will come—and once again our world will shrink."[12] Global television promised not only to speed communication and expand the range of diffusion, but it would also foster the spread of democratic and dialogic politics. Just as postwar regional trading pacts such as the European Common Market enhanced the free flow of goods, television would make possible, according to Minow, an "uncommon market for the free exchange of ideas."[13] Such an exchange was important because of its utopian appeal and because policy makers contended that better communication would lead to better understanding—not simply among nations, but among peoples of the world. Discussion, compromise, and democratic process were at the core of this vision.

Yet this rhetoric also was shaped by liberal notions of *noblesse oblige*. It was not simply a matter of dialogue among equals, but also a matter of educating the poor and the ignorant in distant parts of the globe and of opening their eyes to the possibilities of the modern world, for the dawning of the age of global television also was the time when the Kennedy administration founded the Peace Corps and rapidly escalated development aid to Third World countries. Shortly after the Telstar launch, Dr. Gerald F. Winfield, chief of communications resources for the U.S. Agency for International Development (USAID), proposed a pilot project that would install television sets in five remote villages of Asia, Africa, and Latin America. Eventually, Winfield hoped to place 200,000 sets in one thousand villages of the so-called Third World. In places where electricity was still uncommon, television would be the first modern appliance, powered by batteries and viewed collectively. Reporting on the proposal, one journalist dryly commented, "We are not informed whether canned beer and TV dinners will be supplied as well."[14] Nevertheless, Winfield was quite serious about the scheme, his enthusiasm no doubt was spurred by a widespread public fascination with television's ability to attract huge audiences at home and abroad.

Among foreign aid policymakers, the reason to enhance communications was both to deliver information and to alter the worldview of people in premodern societies. According to communications researcher Daniel Lerner, social and economic development could only take place if individuals could envision themselves as part of a larger national and global community.[15] Consequently, television was a crucial medium that would help illiterate populations see beyond the boundaries of tribe, custom, and tradition. Moreover, it was suggested that television could cultivate the aspirations and expectations of modernity. Deputy Assistant Secretary of State Richard N. Gardner, who at the time was deeply involved in planning the United Nations satellite program, argued that global television could forge "new bonds of mutual knowledge and understanding between nations" because it would foster a shared symbolic system throughout the world.[16] Furthermore, he projected that someday satellite radio and television signals might be broadcast directly into homes around the globe. And when such a day arrived, the boundaries of superstition, ignorance, and nation would be breached. Satellite broadcasting would bring together the "family of man."[17]

the imagined community of the free world

Such seemingly benevolent enthusiasm for the utopian potential of global television among corporate and political leaders needs to be placed more specifically in the context of the Cold War. The late 1950s and early 1960s were also a time of growing unease among these leaders regarding political changes in the Third World. Particularly worrisome was the fact that independence movements in postcolonial locales often coupled nationalist sentiment with socialist reforms and a nonaligned foreign policy. Countries such as Ghana emerged as sovereign states that vigorously proclaimed their independence from both superpowers, leading some U.S. politicians to fret about pro-Soviet sympathies in West Africa. By the end of the 1950s a consensus emerged among the foreign policy establishment that such independence movements posed a threat to U.S. interests, and therefore necessitated a military buildup and an activist policy of social and economic intervention abroad. It was argued that the United States needed to play a more active role in fostering the integration of the Free World behind American leadership. This consensus was embodied in the Kennedy campaign platform and in the policies of the new administration. In fact, the substance of Kennedy's entire inaugural address was devoted to foreign policy issues and U.S. global leadership.

The cultural dimension of this campaign deserves careful attention as well, for leaders such as John Kennedy, David Sarnoff, and ABC network chieftain Leonard Goldenson believed that television would play a significant role in this global struggle. Yet their ideas about the powerful potential of television were largely based on hunches and assumptions of the era. Recent scholarship has more systematically begun to analyze the role that mass media play in the construction of political affinities across vast expanses of space. By turning our attention to some of this work, we can begin to understand why U.S. leaders felt that television was an important tool for securing the boundaries of the Free World.

Numerous scholars have shown that nation-states are a fairly recent phenomenon designed to integrate economic, political, and cultural activities within clearly marked geographical boundaries. Prior to the late eighteenth century, states were defined around centers; borders between states were porous and indistinct; and the exercise of geopolitical power involved a series of alliances between military and aristocratic leaders. This began to change with the American and French revolutions.[18] Not only was divine rule displaced, but these revolutionary states were envisioned as voluntary political associations in which sovereignty ultimately resided with the people. Yet these new nations did not emerge from a "natural" association of individuals who shared a single language, culture, or ethnic identity. At the time of the

French Revolution, for example, less than half of the population spoke what would come to be characterized as "proper" French. Thus, one of the significant characteristics of these revolutions was that they sought to integrate various cultural and linguistic groups who were geographically dispersed into a voluntary political association. It was argued at the time that one should surrender one's local cultural identity in order to benefit from the political and economic advantages of the modern nation-state, thereby suggesting a link between the processes of industrialization, modernization, and geographical integration.[19]

Benedict Anderson contends that these revolutions were accompanied by a change in consciousness as well. Previously, the average person's loyalties were mostly local, whereas loyalty to the modern nation-state was not so much a matter of face-to-face affinity as it was an imagined relationship. "It is imagined," writes Anderson, "because the members of even the smallest nation will never know most of their fellow members, meet them, or even hear of them, yet in the minds of each lives the image of their communion."[20] Such popular imaginings were made possible by the rapid expansion of print capitalism during the eighteenth and nineteenth century, and especially by the growth of the newspaper industry. Newspapers were important because they standardized language and implied a community of address among individuals who were otherwise anonymous to one another. Furthermore, with the development of telegraphy and news wire services, information throughout the nation was standardized and prioritized according to what were presumed to be the shared interests of the readers.

On the other hand, some modern nation-states evolved not as the product of popular will but as an elite reaction *against* popular agitation by regional groups within the borders of existing empires. Here, ruling aristocratic or dynastic elements tapped one variant of the many different nationalisms within their realm of influence, and promoted it throughout the empire as serving the collective good. Hugh Seton-Watson has characterized this policy as "official nationalism," and nineteenth-century Russia provides one example of this strategy at work. In response to emerging popular movements in the Ukraine, Finland, Russia, and the Baltic states, Czar Alexander III took a number of steps to shore up his regime and integrate his empire. First, he enforced Russian as the official language throughout his realm for the purposes of education and administration. Secondly, the czar sought to integrate administrative functions of the government. Thirdly, he nurtured education, modernization, and mass communications. And finally, his regime promoted symbols of Russian nationalism in an attempt to win popular allegiance to a unified nation-state. All this was done as a way to head off regional forms of nationalism within the empire.[21] Benedict Anderson has characterized these developments as a sleight of hand that was necessary so as to enable the czarist dynasty "to appear attractive in national drag."[22] The Russian empire was thus made to appear as a manifestation of popular will, when in fact it was little more than a dynasty in drag.

During the early 1960s, the foreign policy of the New Frontier can best be understood as somewhat analogous to this policy of Russification. Just as the Russian czar reacted to popular uprisings within his geographical sphere of influence, so did the U.S. foreign policy establishment react to what were then referred to as the growing number of "brushfire wars" in the Third World. Of key concern was the prospect that these struggles might ultimately lead to the establishment of governments that might position themselves outside the realm of U.S. leadership, outside the Free World alliance.

Like the nineteenth-century czarist policy of Russification, one of the major objectives of the New Frontier was to contain political unrest across a vast geographical expanse and to project the image of the American nation as serving the collective welfare within the community of the Free World. Just as the Russian leadership sought to coopt local nationalisms that arose in Georgia, the Ukraine, and the Baltic states during the nineteenth century, so too, did U.S. policymakers envision a response to "unrest" in Southeast Asia, Latin America, and the Middle East that would position these emerging nationalisms within the fold of an American-led Free World.

Yet unlike the imperial regime in Russia or the colonial project of Great Britain, the United States needed to promote the image of a popular, nonauthoritarian leadership within its geographical realm of influence. Ever since the administration of Franklin D. Roosevelt, U.S. policy had been explicitly committed to the decolonization of Asia and Africa, and this commitment restrained the U.S. government from pursuing geographical integration through the exercise of raw imperial power. Instead, the postwar empire of the United States had to be predicated on a respect for popular and national sovereignty. Rather than official nationalism, this policy might best be characterized as a form of official internationalism. And unlike earlier empires that had been bound together by strategic forms of point-to-point communications (e.g., telegraphy and wireless) and by the cooperation (or subjugation) of local elites, this American empire would require a form of communication that could win the "hearts and minds" of average citizens throughout the Free World.

In essence, the challenge confronting the modern state is to contain diversity by promoting a broadly popular narrative of progress—one that promotes a sense of collective movement forward through secular, chronological time. The tensions among and between groups must be submerged in favor of a shared destiny. Yet such attempts at incorporation are never fully successful. Some groups not only resist assimilation, they defiantly identify themselves as separate nations in search of their own territory and government structure. Indeed, within the United States during the 1960s the Nation of Islam and numerous Native American tribes agitated for sovereign political status, seeing their destinies as distinct from those advocated by the federal government. Meanwhile, many nations abroad, like Cambodia, Ghana, and Brazil, proudly proclaimed their independent national destinies outside the master narrative of the Free World. Thus, for the New Frontier, the challenge at home was not unlike the challenge abroad, and in both cases television seemed an important means of promoting a collective commitment to the principles of a U.S.-led Free World. Just as the newspaper made the modern nation-state a viable (if discordant) unit, television promised to solidify U.S. influence via its direct appeal for the allegiance of viewers throughout the Free World. As Marshall McLuhan suggested, the new medium might foster a simultaneous field in human affairs, one in which the mythology of a shared destiny might be promoted. It is in this context that we can begin to understand why the utopian discourse of global television seemed particularly attractive to government officials, corporate leaders, and broadcasting executives.

There are at least four reasons why the technology of global television may have appeared so promising. First of all, television—as a means of visual communication—promised to mobilize support among both literate and nonliterate citizens. Such widespread popular appeal seemed important in the postcolonial world because alliances with local elites no longer were sufficient, owing to the fact that most nationalist movements in the Third World had been predicated on the concept of democratic sovereignty rather than elite rule.

Secondly, global television fostered the image of democratic dialogue, and this was an important feature of U.S. efforts to distinguish Communism from the Free World. That is, the supposed *difference* between East and West rested on the free flow of information and ideas. Therefore, it was not appropriate for the United States simply to exercise raw imperial power as the European states had done during the colonial era; rather, the U.S. had to promote images of informed democratic choice and popular consent.

Thirdly, global television, like the newspaper of the nineteenth century, implied a community of address and a clocked consumption of information and images. It would foster both temporal and spatial integration of populations throughout the Free World. But television promised to do something the newspaper could not. It promised to bring people together across boundaries of the modern nation-state on a regular basis. People around the globe would witness important events on the same day, be they Olympic athletic contests or presidential inaugurations.

Finally, international television promised to bring a regular flow of information about the outside world into the United States. The medium might help American citizens to see themselves as part of a global community and as playing a leadership role in the Free World. Such a sense of communal obligation was crucial, since the U.S. government was then embarking on a massive increase in military and foreign aid programs. In each of these ways television seemed to make it possible for the United States to build a postcolonial empire that extended across the oceans and around the globe.

the global chess game

Within the inner circle of the Kennedy White House, this fascination with television's strategic potential stemmed in part from JFK's successful presidential campaign. Once he was in office, it was further stimulated by the surprisingly strong ratings of the president's live press conferences. Indeed, Kennedy himself became fond of referring to television as his favorite propaganda weapon.[23] Moreover, the promise of *international* television further enhanced the stature of the medium in the eyes of the administration. In February 1962 Jacqueline Kennedy's television tour of the White House proved to be the highest-rated program of the season; more important, it was estimated that global syndication of the program—facilitated by the networks and the United States Information Agency—brought the total audience to several hundred million.[24] The president therefore was quite conscious of television's power to project images across national boundaries, and of the administration's power to influence those images.[25]

Nor was the president alone in making this assessment. In the spring of 1962, Tedson Meyers, administrative assistant to FCC chairman Newton Minow, penned a report that was the product of consultations with top officials at the White House, State Department, Central Intelligence Agency, U.S. Information Agency, U.S. Aid for International Development, National Association of Broadcasters, Ford Foundation, and European Broadcasting Union. The report introduces itself by noting, "The Kennedy Administration holds office at the precise moment when the United States can begin to exploit the potential power of international television and radio broadcasting in our national interest."[26] It then goes on to advocate a centralized body within the State Department or White House that would coordinate international broadcasting policy in order to (1) assist in the development of foreign broadcast systems so all countries of the Free World could be linked into the U.S.

global communications network; (2) encourage American investment in communications projects overseas; (3) ensure access to foreign markets for U.S. programming; (4) stimulate the production of American programming that served foreign policy objectives; and (5) establish government criteria for the content of programs targeted for international distribution.

Shortly after the report reached the White House, it was leaked to the press. Whether it was leaked as a trial balloon is unclear, but it generated swift and impassioned protest from network executives concerned about such intensive government involvement in program production and distribution.[27] Already sensitive to existing pressures for programming reform, broadcasters expressed disfavor for the possibilities of explicit government censorship. Even though most industry leaders shared the administration's enthusiasm for global TV, they jealously guarded their status as the final arbiter of all programming decisions. As a result, the White House publicly distanced itself from Meyers's recommendations. Nevertheless, the report seems to provide a summary of the administration's strategic interest in global television.[28] As correspondent Robert Lewis Shayon noted a year before the Meyers report was drafted, "In the global chess game that we and the Russians are playing there are many pieces, and international TV is clearly one of them."[29]

On one level, this chess game involved candid use of global broadcasting for propaganda purposes. This was largely the domain of Radio Free Europe, the Voice of America, and the USIA.[30] Such overseas information activities had increased only incrementally during the Eisenhower years. When JFK took office, however, he not only named a prominent television newscaster to head the USIA—CBS correspondent Edward R. Murrow—but he increased the budget dramatically, almost doubling it within two years, to $217 million.[31] Despite the increase, USIA resources were still reportedly stretched to the limit given the agency's broad mandate to promote U.S. ideology throughout the globe. Indeed, one high-level analysis of world opinion contended that the challenge was especially daunting because the Cold War concerns of the administration were not shared by many citizens of the Free World. "People in developing areas do not express deep concern for democracy and such abstractions as free speech and personal independence. Avoiding Communism usually is considered of little importance in underdeveloped nations, in comparison with the great importance attributed to it in the United States," concluded the report.[32]

Such findings led USIA director Murrow to arrange a meeting between the president and leaders of the three networks, hoping he could encourage closer cooperation between broadcasters and government. Murrow was particularly interested in network documentaries about Cold War issues, and in a

255

memo to the president he wrote, "This Agency does not have the capability in terms of money or manpower to produce a significant number of television documentaries. This means we must follow the route of acquisition, adaptation, and distribution, and this, in turn, means we must acquire secondary rights to the maximum number of features and documentaries prepared and produced by the three American television networks."[33] At the White House meeting that ensued, Murrow sought, and received, permission from the networks to distribute documentaries that promoted American interests in countries where the networks were unlikely to sell them in syndication. In this way, network executives explicitly cooperated with government efforts to use television to promote a vision of the Free World that was consonant with the foreign policy of the New Frontier.

On another level, however, television's role in the global chess game with the Soviet Union involved the private, commercial activities of broadcasters as they moved into overseas markets. Despite the fact that the administration officially distanced itself from the intrusive recommendations of the Meyers Report, government regulators such as Newton Minow continued to prod industry leaders to be sensitive to the political implications of their television exports. In a speech to broadcast executives Minow remarked:

> Your country will look to you to exercise your trust with responsibility. We will look to you to be concerned not only with commercial check and balance sheets, but also with democratic checks and balances; not only with avoiding red ink, but also with preventing red dictatorship.
>
> Your government will not and cannot monitor or censor your world programs—either the programs you send or the programs you receive and show to America. That's going to be the job of your conscience and your character. The penalty for irresponsibility will be more serious for the nation than the revocation of a station license. If this is too much responsibility for you, you should not be involved in international television.[34]

Besides such explicit public entreaties, Minow also used more informal channels to convince industry people that they were our national image custodians, responsible for spreading a positive view of America overseas. In correspondence and conversation with network executives, he emphasized that television would play a key role in combating Communist propaganda. In part, Minow suggested that broadcasters should help to project a positive image of the American nation as a land of prosperity and of model democracy that operated through enlightened reflection and debate. He also indicated that broadcasters should take it upon themselves to project a negative image of the outsider, the monolithic Communist threat, and finally, that television programming should portray the important struggles taking place along the boundaries of the Free World. Minow's appeal did not fall on deaf ears. Many agreed with him, including ABC chairman Leonard Goldenson, who wrote in an appeal to fellow broadcasters, "We must get our message of democracy to the uncommitted countries as soon as possible, then let them see us as we are, not as the Russians paint us to be."[35]

Finally, in the global chess game with the Soviet Union, U.S. leaders carried on their struggle at the level of emerging media technologies. During the drafting and adoption of the Satellite Communications Act, for example, the Kennedy administration angled for an international system that would be dominated by U.S. corporate and political interests. Despite a professed allegiance to "free market" principles, the negotiations leading up to the legislation took place behind closed doors and involved collusive pie-sharing among some of America's biggest corporations, such as AT&T and RCA.[36] According to the *Wall Street Journal*, Minow—who orchestrated the collaboration—defended the arrangement because "a wide-open approach, the FCC fears, might in effect force the U.S. to offer ownership to foreign manufacturers as well, so splintering ownership that control of the combine could pass out of U.S. hands altogether."[37] Nor was there any consultation with the United Nations during this early planning stage.[38] Rather—as Brian Winston, Herbert I. Schiller, and Anthony Smith have argued—the COMSAT corporation emerged as an exclusive product of U.S. government and private enterprise which firmly consolidated control of satellite communications in American hands.[39]

For his part, Minow justified this closed process not only because it would provide a competitive advantage to American firms, but also because it would maintain an edge over the Soviets, who were supposedly ready to launch a competing system.[40] During an address to the Third National Conference on the Peaceful Uses of Space, Minow remarked, "As citizens, each of us has a staggering stake in the issues. A basic question of our time is whether a free society or a totalitarian dictatorship can make the best use of the technological revolution."[41] Thus, Minow contended that the "national interest" superseded free market principles in this instance, and he cited Senator Hubert Humphrey as articulating "our national purpose" when Humphrey said, "I wish to afford the world an example of what can happen in this country when the Government works with the private sector of our economy and when Government and industry walk arm-in-arm toward a common purpose and with a common goal."[42] That common goal was to defeat the Soviets economically, technologically, and militarily. Global television was but one more way in which the United States pursued geopolitical supremacy at the height of the Cold War.

On all three levels, then, policy discourse about the new medium married utopian aspirations to strategic concerns. This union was not love at first sight, of course. There was nothing inevitable about the connection of one with the other. Leaders of the New Frontier worked actively, if sometimes unconsciously, to articulate linkages between popular visions of the future and strategic concerns of the present. Their attempts to shape the debates over global television required tenacious and coordinated effort; otherwise the technology might have taken a different turn. As some suggested at the time, global television might have been developed as a truly collaborative international effort, sponsored perhaps by the United Nations; or it might have been promoted solely as commercial entertainment medium; or it might *not* have been funded and developed at all. It was the rhetorical efforts of the Kennedy administration that consolidated the alliances necessary to create a specific system of global television. As linguist V.N. Volosinov suggested, such attempts to shape language are not unusual, for the contest over meaning is intimately connected to the struggle for power in society. Therefore, the meaning of global TV, its very definition, played an important role in the technology's development. What was envisioned as a utopian step toward global communion by thinkers like Marshall McLuhan was transformed into a policy discourse of Cold War competition by leaders like Newton Minow. Government officials therefore did not exercise their influence through explicit rules or economic sanctions. Rather, it was the policy discourse of global television that suggested the parameters for corporate behavior and technological development, parameters that made it difficult for broadcasters to focus on profitability while ignoring the ideological implications of the new medium.

the potentate of the global village

This is the political context that shaped the emergence of global television during the early 1960s. At the time, the Kennedy administration faced a challenge that was very much like the one that confronted leaders of dynastic regimes during the nation-building era of the nineteenth century. And like the leaders of that earlier time, the administration sought to use new communication technologies to integrate its sphere of political influence. Yet the Cold War era also posed distinctive challenges of its own. Changes in the U.S. economy and in foreign policy during the 1950s, along with the continuing decolonization of the Third World, generated a crisis for American leaders. By the end of the decade, the United States was at the zenith of its postwar power, but it was also struggling to integrate and defend a vast geographical area of influence. Rather than simply exert raw imperial power, the United

States had to respect the sovereignty of newly independent states and curry the favor of diverse peoples throughout the Free World. This attempt to integrate, solidify, and mobilize popular support across international boundaries can best be understood by placing it in a wider historical context that pays attention to the relationship between mass communications and the construction of "imagined communities." Global television was therefore considered important because of its ability to entertain, enlighten, and inform. It would not only counter Soviet propaganda, but would also foster an imagined comradeship among citizens of the Free World. It would offer an explicit vision of the values, attitudes, and ideals that motivated the New Frontier. Many powerful officials believed that television—a medium most often disparaged by cultural critics and public opinion leaders—would play an important role in the eventual outcome of the Cold War.

These tensions between the utopian promise of global television and the strategic interests of the U.S. government shaped communications policy throughout the 1960s and continue to shape our lives even today. While the first decade of satellite communications was explicitly controlled by the U.S. government, it has been followed by an era of privatization in which U.S. corporations continue to dominate. Even though a global system by its nature requires that others participate, the United States nevertheless retains a dominant voice in satellite policy and technological development. Therefore what has emerged does indeed resemble a "global village," but it is one ruled by a powerful potentate who parades in drag under a banner promoting the "free flow" of communication. Free flow now, as in the early 1960s, primarily means the movement of images and ideas from a few cosmopolitan centers out to the margins of the international system, and it has come to be equated ironically with the export of Hollywood programs like *Dallas* and *Dynasty*; shows that are interpreted in many parts of the world as representing the very sorts of ruthless power that earned the United States its position of prominence in the age of global television.

notes

Variations of my analysis in this chapter are also to be found in *Redeeming the Wasteland: Television Documentary and Cold War Politics* (New Brunswick, NJ: Rutgers University Press, 1995) and "Beyond the Vast Wasteland: The Policy Discourse of Global Television and the Politics of American Empire," *Journal of Broadcasting and Electronic Media* 37: 2 (Spring 1993): 127–45.

1. Marshall McLuhan, *The Gutenberg Galaxy: The Making of Typographic Man* (New York: Signet, 1962). McLuhan elaborated on his ideas about the electronic age in *Understanding Media: The Extensions of Man* (New York: Signet, 1964).

2. Harold Innis's work had a powerful influence on McLuhan's ideas about the distinction between oral and print cultures. Innis's historical research pays painstaking attention to the economic and institutional changes that occurred

with the introduction of the written and then printed word. See Innis, *The Bias of Communication* (Toronto: University of Toronto Press, 1951) and *Empire and Communications* (Toronto: University of Toronto Press, 1950).

3. McLuhan, *The Gutenberg Galaxy*, 43.

4. Marshall McLuhan and Quentin Fiore, *The Medium Is the Message: An Inventory of Effects* (New York: Bantam, 1967), 144–45.

5. For example, consider the relationship between the discourse of global television during the early 1960s and Roach's discussion of the U.S. position on the New World Information and Communication Order. Colleen Roach, "The U.S. Position on the New World Information and Communication Order," *Journal of Communication* 37 (1987): 36–51.

6. James Carey, *Communication as Culture: Essays on Media and Society* (Boston: Unwin Hyman, 1989); Daniel Czitrom, *Media and the American Mind: From Morse to McLuhan* (Chapel Hill: University of North Carolina Press, 1982); Susan Douglas, *Inventing American Broadcasting* (Baltimore: Johns Hopkins University Press, 1989); Carolyn Marvin, *When Old Technologies Were New: Thinking About Electrical Communication in the Late Nineteenth Century* (New York: Oxford, 1988); Lynn Spigel, *Make Room for TV: Television and the Family Ideal in Postwar America* (Chicago: University of Chicago Press, 1992); Warren Susman, *Culture as History: The Transformation of American Society in the Twentieth Century* (New York: Pantheon, 1984).

7. "TV gains throughout the world—USIA," *Broadcasting*, (14 May 1962): 146.

8. Wilson Dizard, "American Television in Foreign Markets" *Television Quarterly* (Summer 1964): 57–73 and "Foreign Syndie Biz: 50 % Mark," *Variety* (21 November 1962): 23.

9. News release, Radio Corporation of America, 5 April 1961, Box 35, Newton Minow Papers (hereafter NMP), State Historical Society of Wisconsin, Madison.

10. Newton Minow to General David Sarnoff 10 April 1961, Box 18, NMP.

11. For example, Minow said that when he was being briefed by his fellow commissioners soon after he took the job, they went over all the key policy issues confronting the FCC. Significantly, Minow recalls that nothing was mentioned about satellite policy or international television (personal communication, January 10, 1989). It is also interesting to note that prior to Minow's arrival at the Commission, the FCC's most recent action regarding programming makes no mention of the international implications of television programming. See Federal Communications Commission, "Report and Statement of Policy re: Commission en banc Programming Inquiry," 29 July 1960, 25 Fed. Reg. 7291; 44 FCC 2303.

12. Newton Minow, "Vast Wasteland," address by Newton N. Minow to the National Association of Broadcasters in Washington, D.C., 9 May 1961, in Frank J. Kahn, ed., *Documents of American Broadcasting,* 4th ed. (Englewood Cliffs, NJ: Prentice Hall, 1984), 215.

13. Newton Minow, Address to the International Radio and Television Society, 27 September 1962, in Minow, *Equal Time: The Private Broadcaster and the Public Interest* (New York: Athenaeum, 1964), 212.

14. Clipping, *Chicago Tribune* (28 August 1962): Box 56, NMP.

15. Daniel Lerner, *The Passing of Traditional Society: Modernizing the Middle East* (New York: Free Press, 1958), 43–75.

16. Richard N. Gardner, "Countdown at the UN," *Saturday Review* (17 March 1962): 105.

17. These notions of global community and mutual knowledge also are interesting in light of popular notions regarding "the family of man" during this period, for not only does development theory suggest that all societies progress through similar stages of economic development, but it also suggests that underneath their racial and cultural exteriors, all humans are essentially the same. See Edward Steichen, *The Family of Man* (New York: Simon and Schuster, 1955), a coffee table picture book that was popular during the 1950s and early 1960s. This book

grew out of a museum show that traveled the globe during the 1950s courtesy of the USIA.

18. Here I use the term *American* to refer to revolutions throughout the Western Hemisphere during the eighteenth and nineteenth centuries. As Benedict Anderson points out, revolutions in Latin America were some of the first to base their legitimacy on popular sovereignty. Benedict Anderson, *Imagined Communities: Reflections on the Origins and Spread of Nationalism* (New York: Verso, 1983).

19. This historical trajectory has been sketched by numerous scholars from a variety of perspectives. See Anderson, *Imagined Communities*; Anthony Giddens, *The Nation-State and Violence* (Cambridge, England: Polity Press, 1985); E. J. Hobsbawm, *Nations and Nationalism since 1780: Programme, Myth, Reality* (Cambridge: Cambridge University Press, 1991); Hugh Seton-Watson, *Nations and States: An Enquiry into the Origins of Nations and the Politics of Nationalism* (Boulder, CO: Westview Press, 1977).

20. Anderson, 15.

21. Seton-Watson, 77–87.

22. Anderson, 83.

23. *Variety* (7 March 1962): 1.

24. Minow, memo to the president, 26 June 1962, Box 24, NMP and memo from Donald Wilson, acting director of the U.S. Information Agency, to Pierre Salinger, presidential press secretary, 21 June 1962, president's office files, Box 91, John F. Kennedy Presidential Library, Boston, MA (hereafter JFK).

25. Watson, *Expanding Vista* pays particular attention to the media savvy of the Kennedy administration.

26. Tedson Meyers to Ralph Dungan, special assistant to the president, with attached report, 24 May 1962, Box 18, NMP.

27. *Variety* (29 August 1962): 24.

28. K. R. Hansen, assistant director of the Bureau of the Budget, makes this point in an internal memo to McGeorge Bundy, special assistant to the president for National Security Affairs, undated, Central Subject File, Box 992, JFK.

29. Robert Lewis Shayon, "Breakthrough in International TV," *Saturday Review* (14 January 1961): 35.

30. Holly Shulman, *The Voice of America: Propaganda and Democracy, 1941–1945* (Madison: University of Wisconsin Press, 1990).

31. Regarding USIA funding during the 1950s and 1960s, see "Annual Budget Message to Congress," *Public Papers of the Presidents of the United States: Dwight D. Eisenhower* (Washington, D.C.: Government Printing Office, 1959–1961), and *Budget of the United States Government* (Washington, D.C.: Government Printing Office, 1960–1963).

32. During the late 1950s and early 1960s, the USIA began actively to track public opinion in countries around the globe. USIA Report, "A Review of USIA Research," 4 March 1963, President's Office Files, Box 91, JFK. In this same box there are numerous other opinion surveys; see especially "Public Opinion in Italy prior to the Elections," 9 May 1963; "First Effort to Measure World Opinion," 10 July 1963; and "Foreign Reaction to Diem Repression and U.S. Foreign Policy," 28 August 1963.

33. Memo from Edward R. Murrow, USIA director, to the president, 24 July 1961 President's Office Files, Box 91, JFK. The meeting with network heads took place on October 5. On a related front, Minow was urging the president to meet with the heads of the twenty-five corporations that spent the most on television advertising in order to encourage their support for public affairs programming. Memo from Frederick G. Dutton to the president, 6 November 1961, central name file, "Newton Minow," JFK. Regarding both Minow's and Murrow's interest in documentary see Curtin, *Redeeming the Wasteland*.

34. Minow, Address to the International Radio and Television Society, 27 September 1962, in Minow, *Equal Time*, 211.

35. *Variety* (1 March 1961): 27

36. These corporations saw satellite communications as vital to their future growth. For example, in 1951, RCA derived 80 percent of its revenues from entertainment-related business. One decade later, over half of its sales volume came from industrial, government, and space-related communications. See *Broadcasting* (18 December 1961): 105. Among other corporations with strong interest in this area were AT&T, GE, GTE, ITT, and Western Union.

   It is also important to note that existing transoceanic cable systems were not an outmoded technology. Numerous scholars have pointed out, however, that British interests controlled much of the traffic by cable, and therefore one of the reasons for U.S. government and corporate support of satellite development had to do with a desire for a global communications system which the U.S. controlled. See Herbert I. Schiller, *Communication and Cultural Domination* (Armonk, NY: M.E. Sharp, 1976), 24–45; Anthony Smith, *The Geopolitics of Information: How Western Culture Dominates the World* (New York: Oxford, 1980), 41–67; and Brian Winston, *Misunderstanding Media* (Cambridge: Harvard University Press, 1986), 256–61.

   Finally, the monopolistic tendencies of American communications firms did not go unnoticed by antitrust lawyers in the Justice Department. While they acknowledged the importance of speedy development of a satellite system, they cautioned that monopoly behavior would undermine the U.S. position on free trade and free enterprise. Statement of the Department of Justice before the FCC, 5 May 1961, President's Office Files, Box 78, JFK.

37. *Wall Street Journal* (12 September 1961): 14; see also *New York Times* (1 June 1961): 34; and *Christian Science Monitor* (6 June 1961): 2.

38. *New York Times* (1 June 1961): 34.

39. Herbert I. Schiller, *Mass Communications and American Empire* (Boston: Beacon Press, 1971); Smith; and Winston.

40. *Wall Street Journal* (12 September 1961): 14. Although this is an oft-repeated concern during this period, there was no tangible evidence at the time to support the claim that the Soviets were ready to launch a competing system.

41. "Address before the Third National Conference on the Peaceful Uses of Space," in Minow, *Equal Time*, 274.

42. Minow, *Equal Time*, 274.

The Lawrence Welk Show

twelve   **citizen welk**

bubbles, blue hair,

and middle america

victoria e. johnson

In an installment of the 1994 summer series *TV Nation*, Michael Moore sent twentysomething and former MTV icon Karen Duffy to investigate "North Dakota: The Least Visited State." The segment ironically defends the state's tourist industry by uncovering its significance for fellow Americans. At the state capitol, Duffy is told that the first person inducted into the North Dakota Hall of Fame was Lawrence Welk, although the tour guide cannot think of a single reason why he was chosen. In rural Strasburg, Duffy sees the Welk Homestead, where its director cannot recall the name of any tune made famous by the bandleader's orchestra.

If Welk seems like an obvious target for the young liberal Moore, we might remember that Republican President George Bush also attacked Lawrence Welk's legacy in his 1992 State of the Union Address. In light of an uproar over Congressional funding for a German-Russian Pioneer and Home-steading museum—planned to celebrate the state's centennial and to boost tourism in Welk's hometown—Bush attacked "the annual ritual of filling the budget with pork-barrel appropriations" such as "a Lawrence Welk Museum."[1] Bush's reference was most effective, in part because Peggy Noonan and her staff omitted the not so subtle distinction made by the museum's planners between a "German-Russian Interpretive History Center" and a Lawrence Welk Museum. As Bush would have it, the nation's funds were not to be whittled away for a "Graceland on the prairie," in honor of the "Liberace of the accordion."[2] This common use of Lawrence Welk as shorthand for a cultural void is most provocative—especially as it is used similarly by the young "populist" Moore *and* the old guard, conservative Bush. Inherent to both references is the awareness that a majority of the audience will *get* this joke, will know who Welk was, what his program was like, and therefore why his image conjures up such loaded presumptions about American identity, place, and cultural worth.

In 1955, Lawrence Welk made a successful transition from local television to ABC's prime-time schedule concurrent with television's standardization as a newly national medium. The concluding years of the 1950s saw *The Lawrence Welk Show* acquire top ratings in ABC's Saturday night line-up, which suggests its broad national viewership and market acceptance. Welk's ratings increased throughout the 1960s (defined here as the years between 1958 and 1973). Yet after its 1971 network cancellation, when the program moved into first-run syndication, Welk embraced an older demographic and altered his production style to suit that more narrowly defined niche audience.

During these years, broadcast industry commentary, popular press criticism, and Welk's program questioned what type of television programming was nationally valid or culturally "worthy," and who constituted its audience. Network and popular press discussions about Lawrence Welk's show particularly express assumptions and concerns about the "Midwest," as both a place that was imagined as singularly sparse and rural (loosely defined as that American territory that fell between the coastal hubs of New York and Los Angeles), and as an audience with conservative tastes and ideals (generally portrayed as middle-aged to senior citizens). While most depictions use a hypothesized "Midwest" pejoratively against an enlightened nation, Welk appropriated and claimed these same assumptions to positively define his program's "family" organization, appeal, and audience "community."

live from the aragon...

The Lawrence Welk orchestra began hosting weekly "dance parties" on television after twenty-six years of entertaining on the road, on radio, and in the ballrooms of Pittsburgh and Chicago. In August, 1951, after Welk had spent about a month at Santa Monica's Aragon Ballroom in Pacific Ocean Park, KTLA Los Angeles agreed to telecast one of his appearances. According to Welk scholar William Schweinher, "Viewers began to call before the show was over," requesting more appearances of the orchestra. KTLA aired Welk's program for the next four years.[3]

The key to this incarnation of Welk's television success would seem to have been a combination of the orchestra's rapid-fire musical transitions (from waltzes to swing tunes to polka, etc.), and the bandleader's rather awkward but sincere persona. Welk's producer Don Fedderson has characterized this appeal as "genuineness . . . credibility and actuality . . . which enables people to relate."[4] Mark Williams's detailed study of KTLA quotes station manager Klaus Landsberg as determined to promote such sentiments, through programming that

> needn't be elaborate. The people look at those lavish furnishings and they feel betrayed. They don't belong to them . . . they'd much rather find a warm, friendly personality on the air that's considered one of them—one they would welcome in their homes . . . there's far greater appeal in that than in all the lavishness.[5]

According to his sponsors, the Dodge Dealers of Southern California, Welk's unlavish appeal instilled

> confidence in his viewers by projecting an image of sincerity and honesty [so] that they buy the product he recommends. We know of actual instances of people buying Dodge automobiles who couldn't even drive, just because Lawrence Welk recommended them.[6]

Locally, then, KTLA presented Welk as an ordinary personality and familiar presence—qualities enhanced by the fact that his orchestra played arrangements of folk music and dances that were common to many viewers' family or community heritage. Welk's phenomenal sales success for Dodge brought his program to national network attention in 1955. While Welk's success in the Los Angeles area recommended him for a national prime-time trial, network executives saw his unglamorous persona and thick accent as risks to widespread audience attraction and to the networks' promotion of television as "a means with which to overcome the unequal distribution of cultural capital within the nation" in the "creation of an all-people elite."[7]

Throughout the 1950s and into the 1960s, NBC argued for television's role as a national medium and cultural authority that might override "local" interests and unite the nation as a community of shared "common cultural experience," transcending geographic boundaries. As Matthew Murray's study of NBC's files notes, "the classless nation was, by implication, the 'placeless' nation."[8] Overall, the network strategy of moving television programming away from locally marked production in the interest of a national televisual culture, and the Welk plan of exposing a national audience to geographically characteristic folksy attributes, are rooted in similar attitudes about the power of television technology to simultaneously unite a viewing community. Where the two approaches differ is in their respective definitions of television's national purpose and its role in the promotion of social change.

While network rhetoric implied that a unified market/community of viewer/consumers would raise the cultural literacy (and commercial fluency) of the nation, Welk assumed that television could promote communal gatherings and activities evocative of shared ideals that had *historically* informed American traditional behavior (celebrations or ritual festivals, courtship and marriage, family, etc). If the "nationalizing trends" of the networks promoted America's technological future as one nation under shared consumer ideals, Welk embraced television's ability to celebrate his audience's shared connections to the *past*, underscoring the benefits of citizenship and free enterprise.

Benedict Anderson's definition of the "nation" as an imagined community suggests the possibility of a unified United States—imagined through its citizens' perceived ties to a shared past and their understood, if unspoken, communal sense of progress.[9] According to Anderson, "the bases for national consciousness" were first enabled through media such as the novel and the newspaper, which were printed in the language of everyday life rather than Latin, the language of the Church hierarchy and educated elite. Such properties of contemporary media also allow for their meanings to travel across diverse communities or fragmented territories within a nation. This helps to create the sense that the nation itself "is interestless," departicularized, and unified.[10] Language, in this regard, allows

> a special kind of contemporaneous community.... Take national anthems.... No matter how banal the words and mediocre the tunes, there is in this singing an experience of simultaneity.... The image: unisonance.[11]

In the American context, this sense of unisonance has historically been related to the frontier myth and theorized most famously by Frederick Jackson Turner in the late 1800s.

Originally presented to the World's Congress of Historians in 1893, Turner's "frontier thesis" remained, through the 1960s, the reigning paradigm for defining what was unique or particular to American history and development. As envisioned by Turner, the frontier thesis was a route to uncovering a "useful past, a version of American history ... that would propel America onto the road to a desirable culture" in the face of a worldwide transportation and communications revolution. Turner's frontier thesis allowed its proponents to explain "almost all that was desirable in American life and character" as emanating from the pioneer experience and westward expansion.[12] Turner proposed that "this perennial rebirth ... with its new opportunities, its continuous touch with the simplicity of primitive society," were the "forces dominating the American character."[13]

Others, however, challenged the admirability of this mythology, pointing to the pioneer's "social conformity" and "naive" politics.[14] Criticism of Turner's thesis was crucially tied to *place*. As historian Warren Susman argued, by the 1920s:

> The frontier thesis in effect had made the contemporary Middle West "the apotheosis of American civilization," and that was exactly the problem...the significant point here is that the kind of character produced by the pioneering experience was no longer valued in any way by an important body of American intellectuals.... The revolt against this particular 'useless past' was part of a larger revolt against what was considered to be the Midwestern domination of American life and values.... It admitted that American development had been the creation of the frontier process. Yet it insisted that the consequences of that process had been detrimental to the creation of a valuable political and cultural life.[15]

The frontier thesis was the first to outline "a composite nationality for the American people." But even while Turner spoke of the nation, he proposed the possibility of national conflicts among regions rooted in different economies and geographies. He also proposed a model of shifting *sectional* significance within the national framework (e.g., the Old Northwest, the Middle West, etc.).[16] As Turner noted, "the US means much more than a single country ... it is too large and various to be seen as an entity."[17] While notions of expansion and progress which implied a shared vision of the future might periodically engender a national sense of identity and purpose, the American community could be examined best as an ongoing dynamic within which notions of national progress and local tradition, the intellectual elite and the common person, the urban ideal and rural retreat struggle to capture dominant roles in the national imagination. According to Turner, such conflicting ideals coexist and are perhaps magnified at critical points in U.S. history. In this sense, even while Turner sought to explain a national "common sense," his thesis is not incompatible with more recent theories of culture and nation that emphasize the uneven developments and tensions between the past and the future, the national and the local.

As Raymond Williams argues, at every stage of cultural development there remain "residual" tendencies, or cultural elements that have been "effectively formed in the past, but (are) still active in the cultural process, not only . . . as an element of the past, but as an effective element of the present."[18] Residual cultural elements may be active in the dominant/prevailing cultural order, or take their place on national television screens, but they are understood as having been formed in the past. According to the above paradigms, residual elements are, potentially, symbols of a useless past, and yet especially in times of social upheaval, "there is a reaching back to those meanings and values which were created . . . in the past, and which still seem to have significance because they represent areas of human experience, aspiration, and achievement which the dominant culture neglects, undervalues."[19]

In these terms, *The Lawrence Welk Show* is suggestive of residual cultural ideals in the post-World War II American consumer landscape, as it often features a single set and uses only two studio cameras, while its content features familiar folk tunes, historic dance steps, and promotes a family atmosphere with rural, Midwestern, and church-going ties. As Williams notes, at this historical juncture "the idea of rural community is predominantly residual . . . in some limited respects alternative or oppositional to urban industrial capitalism," and Welk's program was promoted and often reportedly received as evoking such a community within the nation's airwaves. For Welk, this acknowledged "reaching back" to historically tried and true values evoked tradition in the name of a continued or contemporary recognition of the significance of place and community.

FCC Chairman Newton Minow's famous "Vast Wasteland" address to the National Association of Broadcasters in 1961 envisioned a striking contrast to such Welkian ideals. Here, Minow challenged local broadcasters to blaze the New Frontier by promoting a national agenda via local programming. Inherent to this call for cultural refinement was the recognition that the local citizen/constituent deserved a more national—and increasingly, *international*—vision from her/his programming.[20] President Kennedy's administration thus positively engaged the image of the frontier to support America's position as leader of the Free World, which was soon to be extended into outer space. In this context, the notion of a residual American past identified with the Midwest suggested a vision that was literally not up to speed with the interests and identity of the larger nation, and might in fact hold America back.[21] Thus, Kennedy's New Frontier was not just new in its expansive embrace of outer space, but in its internationalist, cosmopolitan outlook that promoted the United States as a youthful, sophisticated world leader rather than maturing, old-fashioned, and inwardly isolationist.

By comparison, Welk not only achieved his first television popularity by appealing to imagined Midwestern ideals, but he did so in the context of immediate postwar Los Angeles, whose boom of this era was largely attributable to its affordable housing, new industries, and sunny climate that attracted a mass of G.I. family migrants from Midwestern states. Rather than change his program content and strategy, Welk interpreted his position in the network schedule as affirmation that his local approach and production style were right on target with the desires of the American television audience. Echoing Landsberg's comments above, early Welk interviews and essays point to his strategy of attributing his orchestra's popularity to his knowledge of "the people." Here, Welk combines his awkward, amateurish, immigrant, farmboy persona with an expert awareness of the public's musical zeitgeist. According to Welk, the national community of viewers was not an "ultra-sophisticated" intellectual elite but "essentially an audience of simple people." Therefore he and his orchestra "are more content than ever to remain exactly what we always were, and always will be—a group of musicians dedicated to entertaining the great millions with the danceable, bouncing beat of Champagne Music which they tell us they understand, and like."[22]

locating the midwest

At the crux of much of the debate about *The Lawrence Welk Show*'s cultural worth is the association of his audience and its pleasures as regionally territorialized and resistant to an erasure of regional identity. Welk's audience is consistently particularized as "Midwesterners." The imagined, shared vernacular attributes and communal bond of this group are those of the culturally ill-equipped provincial viewer (especially the senior citizen, and particularly older women) of the Midwest and of the rural plains states—a portrayal that remains surprisingly consistent in both academic and popular press criticism. In David Marc's book-length analysis of television comedy, for example, is a passage regarding the popular cultural fluency of the rural viewer:

> though it baffles the imagination, the ratings coolly substantiate an image of a lone TV antenna standing against the stark Nebraska prairie pulling down a snowy black-and-white image of Sid Caesar performing in a spoof of Japanese art films, written by Carl Reiner and Mel Brooks.[23]

Marc purposefully locates a hypothesized rural spectator in order to illustrate television's educational value for even the most marginal of American viewers. Should it equally "baffle the imagination" that Lawrence Welk's 1950s ratings as a national program on ABC were strongest in Boston and Philadelphia? Significantly here, Cincinnati, on the cusp of the Midwest, handed Welk his lowest ratings during the 1950s. Notably, Welk attracted his largest nationwide audience after ten years on the air, from 1965–1968,[24] the time when the networks were increasingly attentive to counterculture interests and demographic appeals.

During Welk's network run, his approach to musical selection, production numbers, and "family" assignments contributed to the program's apparent concern with specificity of "place" and an address to imagined midwestern sympathies—those residual elements of the pioneering experience that the Frontier Thesis found to be *positive*, "square" ideals. Considering this approach and the above critical conventions, it appears logical that much of the popular criticism and network apprehension about *The Lawrence Welk Show* stemmed from concerns that the program, its star, and its audience were not in tune with the national ideals of progress. The program was considered to be irrevocably associated with the past, and not indicative of the latest available techniques in television production.[25] These concerns are primarily manifest in responses to Welk's persona, the series' production values, and his orchestra's musical style. Welk and his music are alternately criticized and praised according to the different weight given to his North Dakota homestead pioneer past or his Horatio-Algeresque rise to fulfillment of the American dream; his image as an amateur-performer or expert-entrepreneur with regard to the television and music industries; and finally, his role as a "moral" celebrity who prioritizes ideals of "citizenship" and character over those of consumerism and personality.

In the network premiere, which was broadcast July 2, 1955, to serve as a summer replacement for *The Danny Thomas Show*, it is clear that the "amateur" television performer is uncomfortable with the camera, as Welk fastidiously fidgets with his hands and baton when he is not conducting the orchestra. At this early stage in the series' tenure, remarks from the bandleader such as "Well, now we have the opening out of the way," and "Thank you kindly. Now, on with the show," underscore Welk's intent to just get on with the music and dancing. There are two primary camera setups in this episode: one focuses on the bandstand and moves in for medium closeups of Welk, while another hovers over the field of dancers on the floor. As the dancers are all dressed in similar formal attire and are primarily shot in high-angle, they are not particularly distinguishable. Apart from the unique trademark bubble machine, which makes for a lively backdrop, there is no visual standout in the program's organization and presentation. As a *Newsweek* review stated: "For all there is to be seen, as Welk himself admits, 'you can turn your TV set upside down while we're on the air.'"[26]

In the face of industry experts who were poised to redeem America's broadcast future from past midwestern "domination" of the nation's life and values, Welk's persona clearly emphasized his North Dakota farmer upbringing, complete with the unmistakable German accent that led to malapropisms and verbal tics (e.g., "babbling" for bubbling, and "Wunnerful, wunnerful"). This grated upon critics who read this "unsophisticated" presentation as unsuited to a new technology with so many possibilities. As Hal Humphrey remarked in 1955 in the *Detroit Free Press*, "I doubt that even his most fervent fans would credit him with being the Heifetz of the Accordion ... his personality holds a sort of shy, clodhopper charm."[27] In 1963, *The Charlotte News* agreed, and attached place to these qualities, stating: "Welk is good in his own way. Whatever it is about him that is unique is one-hundred percent Midwest American, red, white, and blue, though lacking in musical taste."[28]

While these assessments envision Welk's audience as tasteless, graceless clutzes, Welk's production staff, whose perception was that they were already on "the fringe area of show business," encouraged portrayals of the orchestra leader as a "farm boy" in contrast to the "television experts."[29] For his proponents, Welk embodied an Horatio Alger novel come to life. As historian Warren Susman observes, Alger's novels were directed to an ostensibly rural population, and they provided "an easy and terror-free way of making possible rural adaptation to urban life."[30] While *The Lawrence Welk Show* did not serve this same function, it did position Welk as a rural "common man" navigator of modern technological airwaves, surrounded by a schedule of programming that contrasted with his show's "environment" and appeal (e.g., *The Outer Limits*, *Shindig*, and *The Dating Game*).

This notion of Welk as an amateur in an expert's business appealed to positive conceptions of the American frontier past that were foundational to both Turner and Alger's myths of the country's successful entrepreneurial future. A wistful 1980 interview in *The Saturday Evening Post*, for example, recalls that Lawrence Welk was "one of us—the farm boy who made good ... he seems to personify all that is best in the American character, a man who made good by being good" and who "reflects almost exactly the musical tastes of the average American."[31] There is an exuberance here, in the idea of Welk and his audience's uniquely shared cultural fluency through a homesteading, rural past. Welk's "making good" is closely tied to value-laden ideals of honesty, faith, and bootstrap entrepreneurism—what Welk has called the "'underlying toughness about Americans that comes from our farming experience.'"[32]

Welk's amateur, ordinary farmer persona also inflects his field of expertise.

When asked about his accordion playing in interviews, Welk repeatedly stated his inadequacy. In a *Life* photoessay from 1957, he underscores orchestra member (and lead accordionist) Myron Floren's proficiency by downplaying his own, stating, "'I make no claim to being a great musician.... Even as an accordion player I just don't rate."[33] Critical responses to this amateurishness frequently zeroed in on both the aforementioned lack of musical "taste" and the "non-televisual" aspects of Welk's program. While network officials in New York and Chrysler executives in Detroit had wanted Welk's transition to prime time to include "some improvements in his traditional musical variety format including the suggestion of a chorus line, a recurring comedian, and featured guest stars,"[34] Welk resisted any changes in favor of a series of musical numbers of different genres presented in rapid succession. Significantly, while New York network executives' rhetoric of the time suggested that the ideal television program would have no sense of place apart from an amorphous national character, Welk's program stubbornly called attention to the importance of regional and local places in the history of particular musical numbers, especially with regard to the origination of his orchestra members, known as his "musical family."

During the 1955 premiere, for example, Welk clearly introduces each of the members of his orchestra and feature singers between musical numbers, such as "our little Champagne Lady, Alice from Dallas," and tenor Jim Roberts, "a typical young American from Madisonville, Kentucky." Even though the cast's hometowns range from New York City to Escondido, California, Welk and his orchestra highlight the importance of the Midwest as centrally defining the Welk community. Myron Floren—"a very talented young man from South Dakota"—speaks for the entire orchestra, as a preface to his accordion solo, stating, "It's really wonderful to go coast to coast and to see all of our friends way back in the Midwest and the Mideast.... We hope to do it for a long, long time." Welk's efficiency in moving from number to number, though very prompt—often breathtakingly so for the musicians—never precludes the performers' introductions according to heritage and place. This was attached, throughout the years, to Welk's theory that each of his musical family should be perceived as familiar and next door neighbor-like. Rather than viewed as untouchable celebrities, the "family" was to be seen as hometown friends or nonprofessionals who happened to have some musical talent. This amateur appeal, which was overtly localized in an unstylized way, ostensibly underscored Welk's fluency with the desires of "the people."

Welk's impression of folksy amateurishness is in no small part attributable to his musical style, featuring instrumental arrangements known as "Champagne Music." While only a few of the musical numbers in each show feature champagne arrangements, this is the characteristic Welk sound. The champagne style emphasizes woodwinds over brasses, which is further accentuated as the brass instruments are muted. Clipped sixteenth notes establish these arrangements' dominant beat, moving the music along and giving it what Welk calls a "bubbly" character. In terms of tone quality, the reedy and quickly paced champagne music evokes Welk's favorite instrument, the accordion, and its home genre of the polka, but these arrangements are conceived as a mélange of big band, folk music, and upbeat popular dance tunes.

For Welk's detractors, Champagne Music most clearly epitomized the presumed "uncultivated taste" of his audience.[35] For example, in 1975 reviewer John Bull of the *Philadelphia Inquirer* proclaimed:

> If sugar could kill, I'd be dead by now for listening to Lawrence and his Musical Family. Saturday night was a saccharine venture into a world that no longer exists.... Music seems fizzingly artificial.... Welk insinuates that life really is free and easy and we can merely dance our troubles away.... There are sure a lot of people who like to pretend that's the way things still are.[36]

Mentioned in these discussions of a "world that no longer exists" and "resistance to innovation," is the "nostalgia that is Welk's stock in trade."[37] If there is nostalgia at play in the loyalty of Welk's audiences, it is focused around his persona's fusion of the "amateur" and the successful entrepreneur in the name of "vernacular" history—a shared language of place, tradition, and "pioneering" bootstrap values. Welk's celebrity evokes legacies of the past (e.g., community festivals and celebrations at which the polka would be danced) in order to manipulate the technology of the present in a meaningful way for his audience.

In this context, while the network "experts" may appear crassly material in their designs for retooling Welk's program to have more zip and flair, Welk appears to be a staunch man of the people, playing for "the public" rather than himself. *Life* magazine's interview with Welk in 1956 supports this assessment, arguing that his farmboy values have influenced every phase of his life in Hollywood, including the fact that he has no swimming pool, and therefore no worries. If Welk rejected the swimming pool, that ultimate 1950s object of Hollywood's conspicuous consumption, how could he with good conscience not only sell Dodge automobiles, but become the most successful pitchman in Dodge automobile history?

the citizen consumer and the car you've been dreaming of

Contemporary cultural critics have theorized that the ascendency of the market over vernacular economies occurred during the same period as the emergence and critique of the frontier thesis. Historically parallel to this development, the concepts of character and personality began competing as routes to "solve the problem of self in a changed social structure."[38] Susman notes that by 1800 the concept of character had come to define the individual felt to be essential for the maintenance of the social order—that is, the ideal citizen, the self defined through adherence to community ideals, obedience, and law. This ideal type of individual for the community was historically associated with an older culture that stressed moral qualities and the self's fulfillment through sacrifice as opposed to personal gratification. By the mid-1910s, however, there was a new attention to individual needs and interests, self-mastery through consumption, and the more intangible qualities of personality such as "magnetism," charm, and "the quality of being Somebody."[39]

Sharon Zukin has argued that post-World War II era America represents the apex of such contemporary consumer and consuming ideals. In this period, she notes, local communities have become archaic (that is, the community as a center of vernacular economies or economies that are contingent on indigenous agricultural, artisanal, or industrial production, rather than finance or investment capital).[40] In this context, it has been argued that American television was conceived and developed as a transportation and transmission technology for delivering products and information. Television encourages and positions its audience to be consumers rather than citizen-producers who inhabit places which are tied to a natural cycle of production and consumption.[41] Arguably, in postwar American culture, both general market shifts and television's address to its audiences have emphasized consumership over citizenship.

Here, Lawrence Welk's residual emphasis on the importance and inscription of place, as well as his program and persona's valuation of the qualities of character outlined above, again suggest his position as a mediator between vernacular ideals—the older community-biased culture definitions assumed to be common to his viewing audience—and the consumer realities of a postwar America in which he had risen as a show-business personality and individual entrepreneur. Sponsored by the Dodge division of Chrysler throughout his network run, Welk was positioned as a citizen spokesperson who "evoked the experiences of the past to lend legitimacy to the dominant ideology of the present."[42]

George Lipsitz has meticulously outlined this task with regard to the 1950s subgenre of working class ethnic sitcoms, which disappeared by the 1960s in favor of suburban family sitcoms. As Lipsitz states:

> television's most important economic function came from its
> role as an instrument of legitimation for transformations in

values initiated by the new economic imperatives of postwar America. For Americans to accept the new world of…consumerism they had to make a break with the past.[43]

One route to ease this break "consisted of identifying new products and styles of consumption with traditional, historically sanctioned practices and behavior,"[44] thus merging traditional ideals of adherence to the values of character and community while also anchoring them to the contemporary reality of consumerism. By this strategy, Lipsitz argues, "morally sanctioned traditions of hearth and home could be put to the service of products that revolutionized those very traditions."[45]

Welk's "citizen" stature as a man of tradition, community, and character was essentially defined by his denial of conspicuous personal gain in favor of a rigorous code of moral and behavioral standards. If Welk refused to play Las Vegas because it might offend some of his staunchly religious fans, must it not be the moral thing to do to drive a Dodge? Characterized as "one of the shrewdest citizens on Main Street and in Middletown,"[46] Welk's moral reliability was illustrated by a constancy to that imagined Midwest community which was characterized by political fixity and ideological stasis: "In practicing his art, Mr. Welk shoots away from the hippie—and other current distractions—straight to the heartland."[47] He is also seen, in the 1960s, as the only musical series star to counter the medium's "current kick of exalting teenage beat music and the weirdos who play it."[48] It is important to note that Welk's supposedly moral, family, citizen ideals—rooted as they were in a residual stability—were contrasted with images of urban affiliated youth and Left political activist movements that suggested a "rejection of American values" and "straight American society."[49]

Significantly, as with many other TV variety hosts, Welk's spokespersonship for his sponsor is an implicit one. He does not appear in print ads for Dodge, and family members and on-air Dodge announcer Lou Crosby did all voice-overs and testimonials on the automobile's behalf. Advertising copy, however, was closely affiliated with the same values promoted by Welk and his musical family. Each weekly installment of the program was nationally sponsored in the name of local Dodge dealers, and Crosby's introduction offered "best wishes from the friendly Dodge dealer in *your* community." The automobiles were portrayed as offering "traditional reliability" and "champagne glamour." Themes and values emphasized in each advertisement include corporate trust, product accountability, and consumer safety. Above all, however, Dodge is associated with a solid return on one's hard-earned money. Offering a series of models to fit different budgets, Dodge promises that small amount of glamour acceptable to the good citizen, but at a traditionally cost-effective price.

In the premiere episode of *The Lawrence Welk Show*, driving is associated with healthy social activities or community gatherings. Here a Dodge Lancer floats playfully to the front of the credits in a Welkian bubble, which bursts as announcer Lou Crosby says "Dodge: the car that says 'Let's go!' brings you the music that says 'Let's dance!'" A 1964 episode clinches the idea that Dodge can be a communal joy, no matter how large or limited the budget. Crosby shows the television audience the Lawrence Welk Orchestra parking lot lined with every model of new Dodge available on the market. Trusting that a loyal viewing audience is in some sense sympathetic to Welk's claims that his musical family is an extension of the viewing family, this is a powerful testimonial.

blue-haired ladies and the rural welk masses

The Welk program's home-spun, community, and family-oriented advertising was successful on cross-class and cross-geographical lines, as is evidenced by its sixteen-year successful national run. What seems to consistently mark the program and its popularity according to an imagined place and shared community is its focus on tradition over "progress" (e.g., Dodge value over a new sports car for the sake of keeping up with the Joneses), and family over "theatrical types" (that is, "ordinary people" populate the musical family). In Welk's world, these valued attributes give the word "square" a positive meaning. Embracing one of the most consistent terms in Welk criticism, the bandleader notes,

> When I was growing up, 'square' was a compliment. You gave a
> man a square deal, looked him square in the eye, stood four
> square on your principles.... I grew up in a community of
> squares ... squares as a group ... enjoy clean fun, understand-
> able music, pretty and wholesome girls....[50]

During the 1950s and through the mid-to-late 1960s, Welk's program may have intended its message for a shared community of "squares," but it was very concerned to attract squares of all ages. The bulk of Welk's audience in the first ten years or so of his success formed an inverted curve, attracting children and mid-teen teenagers, and then viewers who were twenty-five years and older. In 1956, the most loyal Welk audience was somewhere between the ages of twenty-five and sixty-eight. A 1960 special from Welk's live, weekly dance party at the Aragon, for example, took advantage of remote filming possibilities to promote his program's cross-generational appeal. Cuts are made between the adults' enjoyment of the fox trot dance contest to children in the viewing audience being serenaded by the Lennon Sisters and the comic bass voice of Rocky Rockwell. The teen audience is addressed in couples' duets and male-group songs that take place at attractions and on exotic rides throughout the park.

Even in the last episodes of Welk's national network run, Bobby and Cissy continued to attempt to attract an audience of younger viewers interested in a variety of dances. Aided by "upbeat" music, vividly bright lighting, and Welk's jarring combinations of costume colors, the pair took advantage of extant color and soundstage technology. One example is their tribute to the history of rock dances in which they demonstrate such steps as the pony, mashed potato, and alligator, in rapid succession. Aesthetically, this segment is very different from the black and white period of shows and remains distinct from the syndicated series. Not only are the colors splashy, with clashing contrasts, but the television technology is revved up in floor camera transitions that simulate rapidly animated movement—a departure for Welk, but characteristic of shows marked by counter-culture appeal such as *The Smothers Brothers Comedy Hour* or *Laugh-in*.

In spite of Welk's cross-place, cross-generational ratings appeal, the popular representations of his fans continued to recall the imaginary uncultivated middle of America, a middle that was further marginalized and ridiculed according to generational and gender stereotypes. In 1964, Thomas Murphy of the *Hartford* (Connecticut) *Courant* perfectly encapsulated the most popular strategy for the quick critical dismissal of Welk's program and its significant ratings:

> In both Welk and Liberace the design is to make little old ladies like them. And both succeed beyond the fondest dreams of man.... There must be some solution to the enigma, for ... [Welk], like Liberace, is not what anyone would say conforms to the standards of masculine beauty. Both share ... cornball music and fantastic success.[51]

After the critic appropriately distances himself from the object of adoration, he evokes the image of old women enamored with a television celebrity. At Welk's live local performances the appearance of older women "out of control" with pleasure and desire is apparently so threatening that the object of adoration must be in some way desexualized.

In a 1964 *Jack Benny* episode, the guest Welk is portrayed as a much bigger star than Benny himself.[52] Two featured Welk fans are portrayed as stereotypical "little old ladies" who have changed their passionate allegiance and club booster support from Benny to the orchestra leader. The fan club officers are dressed in predictably frumpy hats and dresses and joke about their weight gain, respective attractiveness, and their desire to stand in for the accordion Welk is squeezing. From these women, who herald from Glendale—that midwestern enclave in Southern California—to the "wig flippers" in Milwaukee,[53] Welk fans are not only marked by gender and generation, but again by place.

On the surface, the joke here seems to be a jab at any amount of loyal devotion to Welk, an unlikely celebrity with "clodhopper charm." Fundamentally, however, the notion of a midwestern housewife or farm woman as desirous or sexually active outside of the sphere of motherhood "down on the farm," evokes a cultural threat based on notions of proper place and what is nationally seemly or tasteful regarding older women, desire, and the Midwesterner. Finally, such discomfort would also seem to signal a fear of the threat of regional difference, and what is assumed to be concomitant cultural regression, from urbanity and progressive ideals; the threat that televised exposure to "unenlightened," residual cultural artifacts might literally hold the nation back from its future promise.

Such perceptions of Welk's audience were, in part, perpetuated by Welk's own attitude toward each program as a potential musical journey and education to different types of instrumentation, tempo, timbre, and orchestration. The "ethnic other" in these journeys was defined as non-Anglo and generally non-Agrarian. The most frequently performed and implicitly natural or shared ethnicity on *The Lawrence Welk Show* was the German polka-culture showcased by Myron Floren's accordion solos. Welk emphasized that each member of his cast came from a place with specific characteristics and that each element of his family was part of a "mini democracy." Along these lines, Welk wrote of his program:

> Whenever I feel truly downcast, I look at our orchestra ... a little 'America' ... democracy all its own. And if a German bandleader and a Jewish musical director can become such pals, that's a very positive sign! We are Gentile and Jew in our band, and Catholic and Protestant, and black and white, and old and young, Republican and Democrat ... but we're alike in our devotion to what's best for all of us....[54]

In practice, however, ethnically or racially distinctive family members were asked to, literally, perform their ethnicity in stereotypical ways, and under Welk's scrutiny, as symbolic white patriarch.

During the show's early years such ethnic and folk numbers are the domain of Irish tenor Joe Feeney, and "Aladdin" (no last name is given) the violinist. "Aladdin's" unidentified ethnicity allows him to assume various identities in these set pieces, from a "Gypsy Violinist" to a German beer cellar proprietor. By the early 1970s, Anacani (again, no last name is given), a Mexican American woman, assumes this multipurpose ethnic character role. According to Anacani, "Mr. Welk always liked [for her] to sing Spanish songs on the show," (referring to the language), and she generally sang songs that were already familiar to a predominantly non-Mexican audience or novelty songs that were translated to Spanish, such as "Feliz Navidad" and "Happy Farm."

However, Welk's program generally featured the cheerful Anglo couple, Bobby and Cissy, doing a "dance like Carmen Miranda," rather than Anacani. In production numbers which featured whites "doing" ethnicity—as in Bobby and Cissy's case, or when a white country singer performs "Jambalaya," or the orchestra joins in unison for that "favorite folk song" "Jimmy Crack Corn"—the dance or song was thus "demonstrated," for the audience's education. Severed from any autobiographical connection with the Welk Family cast, such performances are able to remain generalizable community property.

calling all revolutionaries: the welk community comes to pbs

Once Welk was cancelled by ABC in 1972, he jumped into syndication under a new sponsor banner—Geritol. The change in television markets and sponsors mirrors a conscious shift on Welk's part to retool his program to a very particular demographic. After years of reading *Billboard* and planning programs around teenage dance parties, Welk wholeheartedly embraced an older audience, stating, "Some people ridicule us for playing what they call 'mom and dad music.' We think it would be wrong to pace the show for the teenage audience that isn't home on a Saturday night."[55] Welk was taking an ideological and political stance which he had previously, if very thinly, disguised in the name of a national network audience. Now, his "squares" were rhetorically positioned as the silent majority who "pay their bills … keep their children clothed and fed, send them to Sunday school, raise them to believe in God and this country."[56] Now his tunes were played as the alternative to musical "extremes" in the contemporary environment.

According to Welk's son, Lawrence Welk, Jr., his father's career was marked by an attempt to mediate "the tensions between an old-world culture from rules and tradition and a new-world culture of curiosity, independence, and diverse values … Few men and women of his generation integrated these two worlds so successfully into their lives and work."[57] Historian Alan Nevins has written that "unity in American life and political thought certainly does not stem from general agreement on any body of doctrines … It is not the look backward but the look forward that gives us cohesion. The great sentiment of America is hope for the future."[58] The look backward, however, was where Welk saw his mediation skills, his hope was for the young members of his cast-family to learn rules from this old-world culture that they might apply to the present day.

In the first years of syndication, Welk began doing theme shows for holidays (Christmas and New Year's Eve only) that examined "Americana," such as a tribute to the Rose Parade at New Year's or a tribute to "the Ladies." In 1972, fresh off the sting of network cancellation, Welk did a Country and Western show in which the family performed the Roy Clark song, "Music Revolution." Welk himself does not seem to know what to make of Clark's intent in penning the lyrics, but states, "even if you're only kidding, I'm flattered." With wholehearted family gusto, the cast sings:

> We're goin through a music revolution
> The hippies say they'll overcome us all.
> But while they're blowin' smoke in air pollution,
> we're hangin' on with the help of Geritol.
> They're roundin' up the squares in California
> They're pickin' off our heroes in New York
> But they'll never take away our champagne music
> as long as Lawrence Welk can pop his cork.
> They still do the polka in Milwaukee
> Still do the waltz in Tennessee
> Still singin' bluegrass in Kentucky
> with old-fashioned country harmony.
> So give me some good ol' champagne music
> And play that double-eagle march for me
> For they still do the polka in Milwaukee
> So let me hear that one-ah-two-ah-three.

This production number seems hyperbolically poised to reterritorialize the Welk audience's geographical and ideological space within the nation, to reinstate the vernacular within the market, to insist that folk traditions are part of a usable past that is rapidly threatened, here, by a diffuse hippie-led deterritorialization or assertion of a common national culture. While claiming square bastions in New York and California, the revolutionaries are firmly ensconced in the frontier community behavioral traditions of the Welkian Middlewest.

This example of "family values" being threatened from all angles insists upon attaching those values to places within the nation that share common goals and ideas from the (frontier) past. The Welk program, in general, attempts to affix "traditional community" to the Midwest by imagining it as a stable center against which the nation is defined as following any new whim that comes its way. By 1975, Welk began taking these political implications seriously, in an eerily Perot-ian fashion. One of his fans began a drive to nominate him for President of the United States, and Welk wrote three books outlining his "system" and his "plan" for the restoration of the strength of the country through family, morality, and free-enterprise.

In his *My America, Your America,* Welk suggested that successful television production could serve as a model, stating that "what we had been able to do in our Musical Family on a limited scale could be done for our great American family." When George Bush distanced himself from Welk—levelling criticisms at the farmboy as a wasteful cultural icon—he was also implicating Welk's following, ostensibly part of the President's own peer constituency, as part of a useless past. If *The Lawrence Welk Show* seemed already part of the residual past when it first came to television in 1956, its continued popularity in the 1990s certainly merits more detailed analysis. Much like the *Miss America Pageant* and other perennially successful "bad TV objects," Lawrence Welk inhabits a voluminous televisual past and present through which communities and their "place" have been imagined—if diffusely defined.

victoria e. johnson

Notes

1. Joe Queenan, "The Pork Barrel Polka," *Washington Post* (12 September 1991): A21.
2. *People Weekly* (19 November 1990): 68, and Steven Stark, "A Wunnerful, Wunnerful Idea." *Washington Post* (23 June 1991): B5.
3. William K. Schweinher, *Lawrence Welk: An American Institution* (Chicago: Nelson-Hall, 1980), 53.
4. Schweinher, 15.
5. Mark Williams, "Televising Postwar Los Angeles: 'Remote' Possibilities in a 'City at Night.'" *Velvet Light Trap* 33 (Spring 1994): 27.
6. Schweinher quoting producer Don Fedderson, 16.
7. Matthew Murray, "NBC Program Clearance Policies During the 1950s: Nationalizing Trends and Regional Resistance," *Velvet Light Trap* 33 (Spring 1994): 37, 38.
8. Murray, 39. Ironically, however, both class and place were inescapably inscribed in this approach to cultural enlightenment, defined as it was according to urban-eastern U.S. "cosmopolitan" productions and assumed taste standards.
9. Benedict Anderson, *Imagined Communities: Reflections on the Origin and Spread of Nationalism* (London: Verso, 1991).
10. Anderson, 144.
11. Anderson, 145.
12. Warren Susman, *Culture as History: The Transformation of American Society in the Twentieth Century* (New York: Pantheon Books, 1984), 29, 31.
13. James D. Bennett, *Frederick Jackson Turner* (Boston: Twayne, 1975), 44.
14. Susman, 31, 35.
15. Susman, 31, 33, 36–7.
16. Bennett, 47, 62.
17. Bennett, 64.
18. Raymond Williams, *Marxism and Literature* (New York: Oxford University Press, 1977), 122.
19. Williams, *Marxism,* 124.
20. Newton Minow, "The Vast Wasteland: Address to the 39th Annual Convention of

the National Association of Broadcasters, Washington, D.C., May 9, 1961," *Equal Time: The Private Broadcaster and Public Interest*, ed. Lawrence Laurent (New York: Atheneum, 1964), 44–69.

21. I am indebted to Michael Curtin for his insightful observations regarding political establishment and network appeals to the Midwest and its role in America's "global" outlook at this time.

22. Lawrence Welk, "Television Places Unique Burden on Bands," *Downbeat* (18 April 1956): 71.

23. David Marc, *Comic Visions: Television Comedy and American Culture* (Boston: Unwin Hyman, 1989), 43.

24. Schweinher, 151.

25. I would qualify that these assertions and all which follow are based upon screenings of four to five episodes of *The Lawrence Welk Show* (including *The Dodge Dancing Party*) from each decade of its run—approximately sixteen episodes in all, plus "reunion" specials packaged in the 1980s, and a guest appearance Welk made on *The Jack Benny Program* in 1964.

26. "Champagne With Welk," *Newsweek* (21 May 1956): 75.

27. Quoted in Schweinher, 163.

28. Quoted in Schweinher, 164.

29. Schweinher, 111, x.

30. Susman, 244.

31. Bernice McGeehan, "Champagne and Grace Notes," *The Saturday Evening Post* (March 1980): 52.

32. Lawrence Welk, "The American Spirit—As Lawrence Welk Sees It," *US News and World Report* (24 January 1977): 69.

33. "Some Champagne for the Folks," *Life* (6 May 1957): 127.

34. Schweinher, 56, 73.

35. Schweinher, 175.

36. Quoted in Schweinher, 178.

37. Jay Joslyn, "Now They're Screaming for Welk," *Milwaukee Setinel* (31 August 1970): TV 7.

38. Susman, 277–8.

39. Susman, 277–8.

40. Sharon Zukin, *Landscapes of Power* (Berkeley: University of California Press, 1991), 12.

41. Graham Murdock, "Citizens, Consumers and Public Culture," *Media Cultures: Reappraising Transnational Media*, eds. Michael Skovmand and Kim Christian Schroder (New York: Routledge, 1992), 17–41.

42. George Lipsitz, "The Meaning of Memory: Family, Class, and Ethnicity in Early Network Television Programs," *Camera Obscura* 16 (January 1988): 80–81.

43. Lipsitz, 83.

44. Lipsitz, 85.

45. Lipsitz, 108.

46. Elting Morrison, "Wunnerful, Wunnerful: A Wooden Baton and an Iron Rod," *The New York Times Book Review* (17 October 1971): 39.

47. Morrison, 39.

48. Pete Rahn, "Red, White and Blue 'Special': Welk's 'Thank You America'" *St. Louis Globe-Democrat* (20 November 1970): 13C.

49. A sentiment clearly expressed in television documentary coverage, including *CBS Reports: The New Left* (1968).

50. Lawrence Welk, *My America, Your America* (Englewood Cliffs, N.J.: Prentice-Hall, Inc., 1976), 133, 135.

51. Quoted in Schweinher, 170–171.

52. This program illustrates Denise Mann's analysis of Benny's program as one of

several in the 1950s and 1960s which "reworked the middle-class housewife's relationship" to celebrities "by foregrounding the position of the female fan." Uniquely here, however, "Benny undermined his own status as a star by pitting himself against" a broadcast television star rather than a "glamorous movie" star. See Denise Mann, "The Spectacularization of Everyday Life: Recycling Hollywood Stars and Fans in Early Television Variety Shows," in *Private Screenings: Television and the Female Consumer*, eds. Lynn Spigel and Denise Mann (Minneapolis: University of Minnesota Press, 1992), 41–70.

53. Joslyn, 1.

54. Lawrence Welk with Bernice McGeehan, *My America, Your America* (Englewood Cliffs, N.J.: Prentice-Hall, Inc., 1976), 109.

55. Quoted by Rahn.

56. Welk, *My America . . .* , 133.

57. Michael Miller, "Polkas, Waltzes, and Champagne Music," *North Dakota Horizons* (Winter, 1994), 28.

58. Cited in James W. Carey, *Communication as Culture: Essays on Media and Society* (New York: Routledge, 1992), 179.

James Arness in *Gunsmoke*

from old frontier

to new frontier

horace newcomb

Between the ages of four and twelve I lived with my mother, father, and sister in a small town in north Mississippi. For much of this time my father owned a little cafe on Main Street. Two doors away was the local movie theater, a third and fourth run establishment. From my sixth year on I saw almost every movie that came to that theater with the exception of *Duel in the Sun*, censored to adult level by the owner for its miscegenistic content. It was a great loss. westerns were important to me and to most boys of my generation. Almost every Saturday I sat through a double feature in which one element was a western, usually a B-level program produced in a fashion that would later inform the television industry. Occasionally, however, a truly marvelous moment would occur. A *Shane* or a *Red River* or a *Broken Arrow* would appear. We knew the difference and for days afterward we would adopt the roles as we "played cowboy," recognizing the richer characterization in these fine features, often enacting the moral dilemmas presented to us in popular fashion.

In 1954, when I was twelve, my family moved back to Jackson, the largest city in the state, where we lived in a new suburb. We had already owned a television set for two years, reaching out to Memphis for a snowy signal. Now we had, if memory serves, two channels, and soon a third. It was important to have this thing in the home. My parents did not go out to movies except on rare occasions (*The Ten Commandments, Battleground*), and for me, seeing movies now meant a ride on a rattling, smoking commuter bus. The Saturday afternoon sessions became increasingly rare, and movies dropped out of my experience until the first driver's license appeared among my friends.

Cheyenne was a favorite in my home, as was *Gunsmoke*. I remember no discussions, just involvement in the narrative, figuring out what would happen. But I also remember complex characterizations, revelations of interior conflict. And I remember my father waiting for the comic moments of Chester Goode or Festus Hagen in *Gunsmoke*, or the wry sensibility of Cheyenne Bodie. He delighted in their ever-predictable, utterly sincere commentary on the world of Dodge City or some other back lot frontier community.

Here there was a kind of moral certitude, a degree of political simplicity, an implicit nationalist fervor. These elements were easily, perhaps too easily, accepted by a generation of men and women who had survived both the Depression and World War II—and by many of their children. (In those days my father, and many of his friends, still flinched at the explosion of unexpected firecrackers.)

These memories are, of course, personal. While I suspect they are shared by some of my generation, the television medium and the genres it produced were experienced differently by different segments of the population. For example, while I remember Jackson, Mississippi as the place of my boyhood encounters with television, many adults in Jackson at the time were attuned to the fact that Jackson was the site of the era's precedent setting WLBT Case, a suit filed by black residents of Jackson (with the United Church of Christ) against the city's NBC/ABC affiliate station that systematically barred blacks from representation on the air. Students of American broadcast history will recall that after over a decade of deliberation with the FCC, the station's license was, by order of a Circuit Court of Appeals, finally revoked at the end of the 1960s. Moreover, as Steven Classen's oral history project in this volume demonstrates, many of the black community leaders remember this period in broadcast history as a time of struggle against segregation in Jackson—both at WLBT and in Jackson's "whites-only" theaters. Most notably, for my purposes, these African American memories of struggle are especially tied to the most popular western of the time, Bonanza. In fact, Classen shows, black community leaders successfully agitated against WLBT and whites-only theaters by getting the much revered cast of Bonanza to speak and act out against the segregationist entertainment venues in Jackson. In this regard, both the television medium in general, and the western genre in particular, were directly affected by the Civil Rights protest that redefined our sense of nation and citizenship in the 1960s. This historical drama took place off screen, among TV audiences, and was most likely not anticipated by the producers of the shows or the network. Understanding the way the TV western itself dramatized issues of race, nationalism, and citizenship, and understanding how such dramatizations related to social and cultural changes of the 1960s, are other matters—ones that I want to address here.

Since James Fennimore Cooper first offered us *The Pioneers* in 1823, the western genre has been one of the central American forms through which a sense of public experience—of nationalism and citizenship—has been represented and re-represented. Its appearance on television in the late 1950s coincided with numerous cultural transitions through which notions of the Old Frontier were again being rechanneled into something new. Indeed, quite literally, those notions were being reapplied in what President Kennedy called the "New Frontier," a sense of progress through international expansion (which was connected to policies of racial desegregation at home), through a renewed emphasis on the arts and sciences, and through particular attention to personal and public style as a cultural symbol for change—all of which can be seen to emerge in the television western during this period. Here, I am interested in how this genre provided a public space through which audiences could contemplate the transition from old to new frontiers, and how that transition might affect their own lives. To those ends, I want in particular to consider the genre in relation to its own textual structures, its institutional context (especially the schedule), and its individual texts which, while following certain overall structures and formats, did vary in content and in form.

Perhaps like the history of the American West itself, the broad historical outline of the television "adult western" is generally well known. With antecedents in film, radio, and television's own juvenile programming, the genre's beginnings are usually marked in 1955 with the appearance of *Cheyenne, Gunsmoke, Frontier, The Life and Legend of Wyatt Earp* and a handful of other programs. From that point the surge of popularity surrounding westerns was rather phenomenal. By 1959, 31 different versions were appearing on primetime, network television. Seven of those were among the ten top-rated programs on the air. Yet the decline in prominence was as precipitous as the rise. In the 1964–65 season only seven westerns remained on the schedule. The trend then narrowed even more acutely; it dwindled, tapered, and faded. *Bonanza* ended in 1973, *Gunsmoke* in 1975. With the exception of a few mini-series such as *Lonesome Dove* and some instances of "domestic westerns" such as *The Guns of Paradise* and *Doctor Quinn Medicine Woman*, the form has drawn little attention from television audiences or producers since the mid-1960s.

Equally as familiar as this history is the reckoning of significance attached to it. Early in the general cultural critique of television the western was lumped with other genres as a point on the map of the "vast wasteland," Newton Minow's still widely accepted, often cited, and rarely examined assessment of the medium's offerings. Similarly, in one standard history of television, Erik Barnouw's *Tube of Plenty*, the form is burdened with collusion in two aspects of television's swift opening decade of degeneration. First, westerns are presented as indicative of the shift from the art of television, live drama, to the business of television, telefilm. Second, they become exemplars of telefilm's crude reduction of all narrative complexity to a single solution.

> Although many fine films throughout film history have dealt with internal character conflicts, such conflicts were seldom important in telefilms. Telefilms rarely invited the viewer to look for problems within himself. Problems came from the evil of other people and were solved—the telefilm seemed to imply—by confronting or killing them.... There seemed to be an unspoken premise that evil men must always, in the end, be forcefully subdued by a hero; that the normal processes of justice were inadequate, needing supplementary individual heroism.[1]

These evaluations are commonplace, familiar changes rung upon the usual chimes denouncing the medium's tilt to Hollywood.

But unlike some other forms of '60s television, the western has also received far more serious attention than this, more careful and close analysis. J. Fred MacDonald's *Who Shot the Sheriff? The Rise and Fall of the Television western*[2] is a thoughtful and detailed examination of his title question. In that book MacDonald outlines the economic and industrial history of the genre, exploring the juvenile and adult versions of the form, charting the numbers of network and syndicated programs produced and their prominence in the television schedule during the 1950s and 1960s. He surveys and examines the attitudes of producers, actors, and critics. He cites specific episodes of individual western series, pushing analysis beyond generalized "genre study."

Contrary to the simplistic generalizations regarding westerns, for example, MacDonald acknowledges the potential for complex story telling found in the form; its "accent was upon personality under stress and the human condition examined in the mythic past."[3] Moreover, he delineates shifts far more subtle than simple notions of decline and disappearance. His account of the trend toward "domesticity" in the western, linking it to cultural change as well as to the rising popularity of other domestic forms on television, is exceptionally insightful, as is his placement of the western in the larger debates concerning television violence. In general, MacDonald's account of the unusual history of this genre offers a welcome alternative to the vague descriptions offered by historians of the medium.

In spite of this greater precision, however, MacDonald produces generalizations of his own, especially with regard to his explanation for the demise of the western. He relies on a particular way of understanding the relationship of expressive culture (television in this case) to society and culture at large that is finally circular in its logic.

MacDonald's assumptions are explained in this manner:

> As with other entertainment genres, the success of the video western was based on a synchronization between qualities inherent within the genre and values relevant to American life at the time. In an era characterized by East-West confrontation and new national and international initiatives for the United States, the western stories and symbols fit the temper of the time. Their political, military, social, economic, and spiritual implications were most appropriate. For a people seeking direction and justification, the western offered purposeful explanations. Its overwhelming popularity was neither a fad nor a function of cyclical patterns of cultural taste. In an unprecedented manner the video western captured the national imagination because many Americans understood themselves and their civilization in terms of the genre. Always a militaristic art form, the western spoke especially well the language of Cold War America.[4]

Given this approach to interactions among audiences and artifacts, an explanation for the decline in popularity and the disappearance of a genre is one step away. MacDonald claims, "If it [the western] is no longer viable, the reasons for its fall must be related to fundamental sociopolitical changes that render the genre obsolete. The roots of these basic shifts are found in the reevaluations in popular thinking that began in the 1960s."[5]

Thus, according to MacDonald, the western comes to fail as "legal drama" because "[t]he formulaic framework of western legality no longer fit the litigious world emerging by the end of the 1960s."[6] It failed as "moral drama" because "[t]he generalized reformism of the past 20 years has created a moral ambivalence unanticipated by the genre.... [I]f good can change, and good equates to moral, where is the universal morality so crucial to the western?"[7] The genre failed as "political drama" because "Where once it meshed perfectly with the fearful yet crusade-like temper of the Cold War era, the western now must fit into a society of conflicting, articulated, and relatively informed political awareness."[8] And finally, MacDonald argues the genre failed because its myth of a coherent "nationalism" could not account for a society riven with racial, gender, and ideological conflict.

From the lesson of this generic extinction, MacDonald draws a fortunate conclusion:

> The demise of the TV western signifies a new level of national awareness. As it flourished on television, the western was for a less complicated and less informed era. It was the pastime of a people who trusted more and understood less. If the promise of TV was in part the enlightenment of society through the dissemination of information, the withering of the western signals a partial achievement of that pledge.
>
> A vestige of an earlier time, the western has become incompatible with a civilization where the flow of events—especially when exposed through popular television—forced a reevaluation of the innocence and satisfaction with which most Americans had accepted the functioning of their society.[9]

According to this logic, then, the western declines at a time when a version of American society is unraveling, when contradictions, conflicts, and fissures are more frequently exposed. The newer versions of American society do not "fit" some aspects of the genre. Thus, we read the western in particular ways to show how it fails the new attitudes.

The parallel is striking, but the relationship remains tenuous. Social change, cultural expression, and personal experience rarely match so neatly or in such monolithic and structured ways. We do well in such instances to remember Raymond Williams's fundamental observation that we engage with and apply residual and emergent ideas, representations, and ideologies even as dominant perspectives seek to inform our general understanding of them.[10] Or, as George Lipsitz has put it with special attention to the role of television in the formation of collective memory in its earliest period, "...television did not so much secure the supremacy of new values as it transformed the terms of social contestation. As mass culture gained importance as an instrument of legitimation, oppositional meanings filtered into even hierarchically controlled media constructions like network television programs."[11] Recognizing these overlapping and intertwined aspects of culture and society may make our work more difficult, but they should also make it more precise. Certainly this is true of the western, in which the topics MacDonald finds shifting beneath the cultural feet are in fact primary issues

within the genre, concerns that motivate plot, subject matter, and characterization.

It is not my intention here, however, to construct a counter-explanation
for the demise of the genre. Rather, my concern is with other, additional
ways of understanding the western. It may be true, though I have some
doubts, that the era of the flourishing western was less informed. But I am
sure it was no less complicated. And while westerns may have been the pas-
time of a people who trusted more, I am not convinced they understood less.
This essay, then, is an attempt to examine what the genre offered large numbers of viewers and, in so doing, perhaps to clarify how and what it in fact
contributed to the increase in "awareness," the cultural shift, noted by Mac-
Donald.

In television, perhaps more than in most media, these layered and inter-
acting meanings are evident at many sites, even in the 1960s. First, there was
the schedule itself, a selection and ordering of television programs which suggests a range of choices, not all of which shared the same set of cultural
norms and values that the western presented and encouraged audiences to
assume. Despite the large number of westerns on that schedule, audiences
watched many other things. That seven westerns were among the top ten
television programs in 1959 is indeed startling when compared to our contemporary television experience.[12] But when we realize that these programs
accounted for four-and-a-half hours of the schedule, the astonishment
diminishes. Even when we add the five other westerns among the top twenty-
five programs we come to a total of eight hours, barely over ten percent of the
schedule. Popularity alone neither describes nor explains experience.

In that year, for example, *Cheyenne* was programmed by ABC at 7:30 on
Monday nights. It ranked at number seventeen for the year. On CBS at 8:30
came *Father Knows Best*, tied for thirteen, followed by *The Danny Thomas Show* at
9:00, ranked at number five, ahead of many westerns. *Wagon Train*, the number
two show, was followed on Wednesday nights by *The Price is Right* (8:30) at
number eleven, both on NBC. But *I've Got a Secret*, at 9:30 on CBS ranked at
number nine. Also among the top twenty-five shows of that season were *The
Red Skelton Show*, *Peter Gunn*, *Perry Mason*, *The Ann Sothern Show*, *Name That Tune*, *Alfred
Hitchcock Presents*, and *General Electric Theatre*.[13]

I do not think it can be said that the scope of programs offered viewers by
the television schedule was ideologically monolithic. The schedule for 1959
demonstrates a mixture of genres and programming strategies, narrative
styles and star personae, all presumably somehow "able to relate significantly
to the values, fantasies, aspirations, anxieties, self-conceptualizations and
other prevailing attitudes shared by the audience/customer."[14] But not, I suggest, in the same manner or with the same results. Expressive culture is first

encountered imaginatively (except, perhaps by critics and professors, though even they were once ordinary citizens), and the range of imaginative possibility indicated by these offerings is broad. Indeed, one of television's great contributions to American society in this and earlier periods was its presentation of variation, the battering of boundaries, within the relatively closed, distinctive regions and communities of the larger "nation." (In this sense the medium, in both fictional and informational programming, did aid greatly in contributing to a better informed citizenry.)

More to the point, if we remain at the level of the schedule, it is unlikely that, with the demise of the western, television programming immediately "reflected" or "presented" a shift in ideological significance that can parallel MacDonald's confident suggestion that America was now more informed, less trusting, or somehow otherwise enlightened. As indicated in his account, by 1962 only three westerns remained in the top ten rankings, and only one additional example appeared in the top twenty-five. And even though the three in the top ten, *Wagon Train, Bonanza,* and *Gunsmoke* (in order), were the *top* three of all programs, it hardly seems plausible that numbers four and five, *Hazel* and *Perry Mason,* indicated an enormous growth in the ideological or cultural sophistication of the audience or an increasing sense of social complexity in general. Indeed, the argument more commonly made is that shows such as *Car 54, Where Are You?* or *The Andy Griffith Show,* or *Candid Camera,* or *The Flintstones,* or *The Perry Como Show* were, in fact, *retreats* from the social issues of the day. And so, it is often said, television continued throughout the decade until the arrival of Norman Lear and other strong-voiced producers at the beginning of the next.

But the schedule offers us another way to examine the overlapping cultural shifts that were doubtless occurring in this period. Two years after the examples just cited, in the 1961 schedule, the arrangements, juxtapositions, and resonance are even more striking. On Saturday nights, for example, CBS began the evening with *Perry Mason,* followed that with *The Defenders,* then offered the 30-minute *Have Gun—Will Travel,* and ended the evening with the hour-long *Gunsmoke.* Given the social problem emphasis of the last three of these programs, and the subtextual challenge to conventional justice in the first, it is unlikely that social, cultural, or ideological coherence marked this lineup. Similarly, on CBS's Friday nights, *Route 66* followed *Rawhide,* presenting two versions, two centuries, two narratives of wandering, searching young men confronting the American landscape, physical and social. But *66* was then followed by *Father of the Bride* before *Twilight Zone* appeared, and the evening ended with *Eyewitness to History,* a news program hosted at the time by Charles Kuralt and devoted to analysis of major news events.

The fact of the matter is that neither television nor social history has ever been "neat." Put another way, the western contributed, as did many of these other forms, to the very shifts described by MacDonald. The western, and the other genres, were frequently less ideologically coherent than his overview suggests. Moreover, to leave ideology at the level of content, manifest or subtextual, is to miss and mistake the issues crucial to understanding the role of television in the 1960s.

Watching television in the late 1950s and early 1960s required no special analytical talent to be made aware of shift and change, of trouble on the horizon and at the dinner table. That the world was coming apart was no secret then, certainly not in the Deep South, where I grew up, and most likely nowhere else. More than anything at that time we were—in all generations—involved with making difficult, at times extreme choices. Television heroes and personalities fit well with other presentations of alienated, dark, nonfamilial, sometimes even paranoid masculinity then being represented in the literary scene—most notably by the Beat Generation's Jack Kerouac or by J.D. Salinger. In *Have Gun—Will Travel* Paladin's darkness-under-control epitomized these influences. And the echo of Rod Serling's eccentric narration was always present on *Have Gun*. For these figures the overly meticulous pronunciation, the baroque diction, the quiet, against-the-grain postures made clear that every motive, every structure, every institution was open to question. Tod and Buz from *Route 66* presented nonprofessional, nongeneric versions of a similar mentality, and perhaps Paladin was even more akin to Maynard Krebs, caricatured beatnik in *The Many Loves of Dobie Gillis*, or to private detective Peter Gunn, than to some cowboys or gunfighters.

All of these characters were possessed and defined by an oxymoronic quality. Theirs was a detached engagement, a distant connectedness. David Janssen's Richard Kimball in *The Fugitive* could have, perhaps in a script by Serling, stepped off a stagecoach in an episode of *Have Gun*, and my friends and I would simply have nodded quietly, knowingly, satisfied with the connection.

These television figures, and others like them in films, in literature, increasingly in music, offered an attitude, a role. The stories in which they appeared either attempted to capture or to rewrite, in submerged form, in admitted generic rigidity, the world in which we actually lived. It was not always a conscious, programmatic, discursive ideology of television that we took up. As often it was the stance that mattered.

Indeed, stance was crucial to television at this time, and to the western particularly for at least two reasons. First, in the system of factory production of routinized, generic cultural artifacts, character variation served as a form of distinction. It was part of the regulated difference, the familiar novelty designed to attract audiences with something noticeable while not overloading them with radically alternative representations. But stance and style were also important because of another feature of the television western often overlooked in cultural analysis. This characteristic, the western's anthological aspect, contributed to the rise of the form as industrial product and was central to the production economy of the genre. Focus on a single, strong central character meant that long-term budgets need not account for regular casts with their demands for ever-increasing salaries. Populated primarily by guest actors, occasionally by guest stars, the anthological western moved the central figure into and out of varied crises. That the frontier towns and remote ranches usually had an evident familiarity, a back-lot commonality, made little difference here, for as MacDonald rightly indicates, it was the inner turmoil of the characters that counted for drama. In other words, both the narrative and moral economies of these series paralleled the production economy.

In most cases the turmoil focused on the guests, for the regular character, the western "hero" was already defined. While we might discover a few more facts about these characters over the course of a series run, they were for the most part, stable and predictable. Their stalwart positions—physical, moral, ethical, at times political—were the rocks against which outlandish and troubled individuals crashed. Similarly, those central characters offered a safe haven for those needing protection, the compendia of wisdom for those needing instruction, the strong, sometimes violently capable arms for those needing action. They stood against the unruly, irrational, immoral, excessively and illegally violent villains, outlaws, and psychotics who threatened life on the fictional frontier—and the social structures in the America of television viewers in the 1950s and 60s.

Like the live anthology dramas they replaced, then, and similar to the anthological filmed drama found in series as distinctive as *Route 66*, *Twilight Zone*, *The Defenders*, or *The Fugitive*, the television western as narrative was open to a huge range of topics and plot configurations. Civil rights, gender issues, corporate greed, environmental degradation, educational inequality—all these were treated by westerns as well as in more contemporary dramas that appeared in both live and filmed versions at other times on the schedule.

The point is better illustrated when we move away from the level of genre, or the level of the schedule, to that of the specific episode. In this case consider one 1958 installment of CBS's *Trackdown*. The episode is entitled "The Chinese Cowboy," already indicating a racial problematic. It opens in Wong's stereotypical Chinese laundry as Wong, played by Keye Luke, steps out to deliver the day's wash. Quickly he is pushed off the sidewalk by a gang of toughs. The laundry spills, the toughs wipe their boots on it, and their leader, Les Morgan, ridicules the "Chinaboy." Hoby Gilman (Robert Culp), Texas Ranger stationed in this town, breaks up the ruckus. Wong refuses to lodge a complaint, and Gilman's assistant explains that Les is "just a wild kid" who "knows how to handle that gun."

Following the title sequence, Gilman speaks with Wong in the laundry. Wong says he has no desire to cause trouble; Morgan may tire of these antics. Still, he is puzzled. "Why does he do these evil things? Others laugh. I want to work, have people like me. I've seen how they respect Les Morgan." Gilman retorts that the townspeople respect Morgan's gun, and Wong expresses a sentiment that probes the core of the western as conventionally understood. "I do not understand this respect for a man who is skilled with a gun, a man capable of killing."

Later, in the local newspaper office, Gilman continues the discussion with the editor, Henrietta (Ellen Corby). She suggests Wong is at fault. It's just teasing and he ought to get used to it.

> Gilman: "You keep using the word tease. I call it abuse."
> Henrietta: "Look at it from the other side. It takes time for a town like this to get used to Wong. He's different. He's a foreigner."
> Gilman: "People of this town ought to look at the law books, even take a glance at the Constitution. I don't remember anything there about special rules to take care of certain people just because they happen to be different. It says everybody's equal. And it was made up by a group of men in 1776. [sic] You could have called any of them foreigners."
> Henrietta: "I feel like a darned fool."
> Gilman: "I guess everybody feels that way once in a while."

Lesson concluded. Not only is the episode going to deal with violence, but with race and race relations as well. It's all there on the surface, but the next turns are slightly more surprising. Gilman leaves town to testify in a trial in Austin. During his absence the local toughs abuse Wong even more severely. Wong goes to the general store and buys a gun. (He is shocked at the price of the shiny new weapon and ends up buying a battered, used six-shooter for two dollars, oiled and cleaned for 50 cents extra. "It'll work fine when you get it cleaned up," the store keeper tells Wong.)

Gilman returns, and while still outside of town, he hears gunfire. He tops a ridge and finds Wong, practicing with his pistol. "It is permissible for someone like me to own a gun. . .?" he asks. "No law against it," Gilman says, "let's see how you handle it." He's then surprised at Wong's facility. When he shoots several cans off a log, Wong is disappointed because he hit them all on his last attempt. He explains to Gilman that he practices his fast draw at night, when his work is done. Gilman asks why. Wong replies, "People here respect a man with a gun. I thought if I did this they would respect me, too. I want people here to like me, respect me."

Gilman explains that Les Morgan also knows about guns and tells Wong that he, the lawman, should stop trouble.

> **Wong:** "I did not learn to use a gun for purposes of killing. I'm not capable of violence."
>
> **Gilman:** "A gun *is* violence, Wong. It's hard to tell what a man's going to do if he's pushed hard enough."
>
> **Wong:** "Les Morgan's abuse does not hurt me as much as the others who laugh at his abuse, laugh at me. I don't believe in violence. I only wish to find respect with this [the gun]."

The next steps are predictable. Morgan pushes harder, more viciously. Wong steps into the saloon wearing his gun, calls Morgan out and kills him. When Gilman arrives the bartender declares, "It was a fair fight." Wong explains to the astonished onlookers: "I only wanted you to accept me, like me, respect me. Now you grant all this to me, but only because I've killed, because I've shown violence. But I do not see acceptance and respect on your faces. I only see fear. This I do not want from these people, Mr. Gilman."

In the end, predictably, the townspeople have a change of heart and try to persuade Wong to stay with them. But he leaves.

"Stop him," Henrietta says to Gilman, "tell him these people mean well."

"He knows it," Gilman replies, "but their good intentions come a little bit late. Don't they always."

I summarize this episode not because it is in any way superior or distinctive. It is, in fact, very ordinary. But it does illustrate the range of topics, the social and cultural allusions, that could be accommodated in the anthological western. In this conjunction of race and violence the gun itself becomes a charged object. I have little doubt that the episode was intended primarily as a lesson regarding race and violence, but re-examined today it is also about gun control. The sense of social texture, in other words, is dense, even in a version so overtly didactic. When Gilman discovers Wong at target practice in the hills, for example, he tells him that a man can find respect in other ways than through violence. "Even a man like me?" Wong asks. As the camera shows him in his black ethnic costume, his hair braided—a gunbelt strapped tightly around his waist—he appears for all the world like a parody of the black-clad gunfighter. Nevertheless, his skill with the weapon prevails at one level. And at another the same skill opens questions implicit in all other westerns.

Those questions were often treated in more sophisticated ways in *Have Gun—Will Travel*, perennial favorite for those of us interested in the television western. I will examine the same episode ("The Misguided Father," February 27, 1960) cited by MacDonald in his discussion of the series.

Paladin is called away from one of his elegant dinners (including a special preparation of zucchini blossoms), when Hey Boy finds a man sleeping on Paladin's sofa. It's an old friend, Charlie Blackburn, and he's not sleeping— he's dead. In the next scene Paladin delivers Blackburn's body to his home town and there finds an inept Sheriff who seems to know more than he says, and a town driven into submission by Keith Loring, a pathological killer and son of a local timber baron. The father, Ben Loring, has assigned "keepers" to watch his son, but some of them, along with citizens of the town, have been murdered. Still, the townspeople support Loring, who provides all the available labor and thus "owns" the town. In fact, when Paladin tries to find out more about the situation, a group of timber workers beat him severely.

Nevertheless, Paladin returns to the Loring mansion and in a long scene we explore the conflicts heaped upon Ben Loring. He promised his dying wife he would let no harm come to their son. He provides for the town. All the pressure is on him. Keith Loring, meanwhile, manages to murder again, this time killing his current "keeper" as they unload Charlie Blackburn's casket. When Paladin challenges the young man, the father attacks, and during a long fist-fight Keith escapes. Paladin trails him into town, confronts, admonishes, and kills him. When the distraught father rushes onto the scene, Paladin acknowledges their joint responsibility for the young man's death: "My bullet, your mistakes."

Paladin's suavity, his capability for violence, his stereotypical masculinity, all highlighted in this episode, are central to the series, as were similar qualities to the genre as a whole. But to mark these qualities without qualification, to see them as the primary salient features of this series or episode, overlooks too much. As suggested above, the styles of masculinity, even of violence, had much to do with variations among westerns and, I suspect, variations in popularity among series. Paladin was always able to contextualize his violence— with historical allusion, poetic quotation, cultural comparison. It was his erudition as much as his demeanor that attracted some of us. And that erudition always called his own behavior into question. His comment to the father of the young man he has just killed comes only after significant narrative contextualization. It is ironic and introspective. And it is not, in fact, the final word in the episode.

As for context, a key scene in this episode occurs between father and son, Ben and Keith Loring. While Paladin lies unconscious on the floor of the Loring mansion, Ben finally confronts his son and his responsibility.

> **Ben:** "Don't you realize you're only able to stay in this house, to stay alive because of my power to protect you?"

Keith: "That's a father's duty, isn't it?"

Ben: "You can't count on it any more. Because if I ever see you use a gun to commit murder again, I'm going to close my eyes to any pity, any fatherly love I have for you. And I'll only open them again to see you swing at the end of a rope."

Keith: "You don't mean that."

Ben: "Oh, yes I do. You're right, son, there was a time when I didn't. But this time I do. I'll break any promise I ever made to your mother, God forgive me, but if you're gonna use the gun, use it on me. Then whatever happens afterwards, I won't know about it. Let me have [the gun]."

Keith refuses both the command and the offer of patricide, then runs out of the house. Paladin regains consciousness and engages in the fist fight with Ben and defeats him, then goes on to his tragic encounter with Keith. It is at that point that he admonishes Ben with "My bullet, your mistakes." But after this comment, Ben once again asks for punishment—and relief.

Ben: "All right, Paladin, use the gun again. This time on me. The right man. I had Blackburn killed. I admit it. Use the gun."

Paladin: "Murder shrieks out in the voice of the murderer. You'll be heard Mr. Loring—if you shriek loud enough."

The emotional power of this exchange, highlighted by the very violence so abhorred by critics, shaded by Boone's persona, elaborated by Hampton Fancher's portrayal of the psychotic Keith Loring, a portrayal immediately reminiscent of James Dean's or the young Dennis Hopper's exaggerated and strained exhibitionist performances—all this combined to make such an episode at once outstanding and ordinary. It was ordinary because it was part of the schedule, part of television, a predictable rendition of the character we expected. In fact, the confirmation of our expectations, the realization of Paladin's complex consistency, was much a part of the pleasure of the experience. One waited for his summations as one anticipates an aria, an improvisation of any sort. In a jazz club or at the Met his "moments" would have been applauded.

But the issues were never diminished by such bravado. The unusual aspects of the episode had to do with the extremity of the violence, the pathology. Few sons among the viewing audience were psychotic killers, but families knew stress and strain at the time of this episode. And they were about to know more as the 1960s progressed. Greed and abuse of power were well known phenomena, but rarely at the level of murderous rampage and hired-gun protection. But greed and abuse of power were increasingly to become touchstones for cultural conflict in the near future.

Television was part of, presenter of, all these cultural and social processes and negotiations, not an evasion of them, and the western, for a time, was central to television. Most commentary on these programs focuses on the formulaic, the predictable, the given in the genre. The gunfight endings are taken as emblematic and conclusive, singular definition of the western's significance—easy answers presented as solutions to hard problems.

But I argue that the endings were no more than a stylized, artificial motif. The gunfights solved nothing. Unlike the western novel, or even the movie, in which endings open gateways to new worlds, new lives, the television western offers no such sense of conclusive renewal. It must—for purely industrial reasons—return with the same character the following week, a character who must once again confront the issues of the day—our day.

What I wish to suggest finally is that this combination of genre, schedule, issue, and character made the western into a locus of public display. It was the platform on which many of the intertwined and conflicting aspects of the 1960s (and the inseparable years leading to them) were put forward. In these narratives the problems were far more believable than the solutions. There was almost always one more dramatic beat following a gunfight or other violent confrontation. Indeed, the actual endings were often exclamation points on insoluble dilemmas. *After* the gunfights in their particular episodes: Wong walks out of a town bewildered by his refusal of newfound community spirit. Loring is left alive with the horror of his son's ruined life, his own tragic legacy. A frontier minister, worn weary by his bloody participation in the Civil War has vowed never to kill again, but must take up arms to protect family and wife; when done he prays for forgiveness. A sheriff and a lawyer find themselves entangled with Native Americans who have left their reservation and taken to the mountains—and in the end watch them fade into the forests knowing they are the last of their tribe.

Many more instances could be brought forward, and doubtless as many conventional, unproblematic endings could be found. I have no stake in redeeming every western ever broadcast. But I do want to argue that the television western is as conflicted as more long-lived genres, that its ability to engage audiences involved more than simplistic narratives of male power and dominance, glorifications of violence, or celebrations of national ego. Doubtless, all these factors are always potential in the western, in any form or medium. As often as not, however, in American television from the mid-1950s until the mid-1960s, these very elements were subject to self-reflexive exploration. When this exploration was combined with fictional, dramatic presentations of specific social problems, the genre and the programs became arenas for cultural conflict made visible. That these arenas were synonymous with some of television's most popular, most widely shared programs is a fact that should not be lost on today's increasingly narrowed and fragmented audiences.

notes

1. Erik Barnouw, *Tube of Plenty* (New York: Oxford University Press, 1982), 214–215.
2. J. Fred MacDonald, *Who Shot the Sheriff? The Rise and Fall of the Television Western* (New York: Praeger, 1987).
3. MacDonald, 62.
4. MacDonald, 1.
5. MacDonald, 101.
6. MacDonald, 104.
7. MacDonald, 106.
8. MacDonald, 109.
9. MacDonald, 109.
10. Raymond Williams, *The Long Revolution* (London: Penguin, 1965).
11. George Lipsitz, "The Meaning of Memory: Family, Class and Ethnicity in Early Network Television," in *Time Passages* (Minneapolis:University of Minnesota Press, 1990), 73–74.
12. MacDonald, 56–57.
13 Tim Brooks and Earle Marsh, *The Complete Directory to Prime Time Network TV Shows 1946–Present, Fifth Edition* (New York: Ballantine, 1992).
14. MacDonald, 87.

Mayor Is Hot

NOBODY'S Coming

No Horn For 4000 — Too White

Ben, Lil Joe Follow Hoss

Al Hirt, "America's greatest trumpet showman, joined the "Bonanza" stars in refusing to appear before a segregated audience.

The New Orleans trumpeter and his jazz group cancelled their engagement at the Mississippi Coliseum l a s t Saturday night just a few minutes before show time.

Since Hirt was the featured attraction of the evening, his cancellation left an audience of over 4,000 with little reason for sitting in the Coliseum. Gradually people picked up their belongings and filed out, and by nine o'clock on Saturday night the Coliseum was empty and dark.

Hirt's refusal marks the third protest against Mississippi's "way of life" by out-of-state entertainers in less than a month. Just one week ago, Dan Blocker, star of "Bonanza," cancelled his engagement at the Mississippi I n d u s t r i a l Exposition. He was later joined by the two other top s t a r s of the television show.

Together with Blocker, who plays "Hoss"; Mike Landon, known as "Little Joe"; and Lorne Green, who plays the father "Ben Cartright"; the stars submitted a joint statement to radio

(Continued on Page 8)

Mississippi

FREE PRESS

"The Truth Shall Make You Free"

Vol 3 No 8   38   Jackson, Mississippi — February 1, 1964   10c Per Copy

The Mississippi Free Press

southern

discomforts

the racial struggle

over popular tv

s t e v e n   c l a s s e n

The assassination of NAACP field secretary Medgar Evers during the early hours of June 12, 1963 delivered a severe blow to the "Jackson movement"—a local insurgency dedicated to direct action and racial desegregation in the Mississippi capitol.[1] In the days following the murder and Evers's funeral, "go slow" forces within the NAACP and the Kennedy administration employed successful strategies to curtail the movement's sustained confrontation campaigns. Still, the deeply felt dissatisfaction of black Mississippians regarding segregation and its implications could not be quickly or strategically allayed. And in the months following Evers's death, African American frustration with the segregationist status quo motivated further direct action attacks on the terrain of consumerism, popular culture, and entertainment in the Jackson area.[2]

This essay analyzes what was called the "cultural and artistic agitation" campaign carried out by student activists in Jackson, Mississippi during the winter of 1963—64, involving popular television programs such as *Hootenany USA* and *Bonanza*. Although televised entertainment and fiction, then as now, was often dismissed as at best peripheral to the prominent issues of the day, during the early 1960s many Jackson area residents regarded the viewing of certain television shows and patronage of program sponsors as important social markers. Examination of the activism surrounding *Bonanza*, as well as other televised and local entertainment, reveals how student agitators, employing tactics often invisible to those in power, brought the artificiality and corruption of segregation into the light of public scrutiny, and in the process, disrupted the hegemonic dynamics of coercion and consent necessary to continue such practices.

Theoretically, this account and analysis makes use of Gramsci's insights regarding hegemony, coercion, and consent. Hegemony is conceptualized as the "process whereby the subordinate are led to consent to the system that subordinates them. This is achieved when they 'consent' to view the social system and its everyday embodiments as 'common sense,' [or as] self-evidently natural."[3] Attempting to understand how and why such consent occurs, contemporary theorists have pointed to an important connection— the link between coercive power and hegemonic consensus. An argument prominent in African American scholarship is that consensus is only naturalized or deemed "common sense" when it denies its dialectical relationship to coercion.[4] What is examined here, through the lens of a particular historical moment, is how activism, even with limited resources, exposed the coercive racist practices of segregation in Jackson, and in doing so temporarily disabled the creation of consensus necessary to white power.

The white community's failed segregationist responses to the black student agitation campaign also show how difficult it was for white city officials to unify and police cultural consumption, even among whites. While the reception or consumption of any product may be deemed impolitic, dangerous, unpatriotic, or immoral, this history provides another example of how officially sanctioned proclamations about the "evils" of popular culture may be publicly acknowledged yet privately ignored.

306   **cultural agitators**

A sense of glee, if not gloating, permeated the February 1, 1964, issue of Jackson's alternative civil rights newspaper, the *Mississippi Free Press*. The periodical described trumpeter Al Hirt's last minute cancellation of a local concert as yet another blow to Mississippi's segregationist status quo. The two-inch headline announced: "Nobody's Coming: No Horn for 400—Too White." The *Free Press* described the Hirt cancellation as part of several recent attacks on segregated entertainment initiated by Tougaloo College students and staff devoted to "cultural and artistic agitation."[5] Over the course of approximately six months, the small but dedicated Tougaloo "Culture and Arts Committee" had prompted cancellations of scheduled Jackson visits by cast members of popular television shows, world-class musicians, and other prominent personalities. About a half dozen activists, primarily college undergraduates, had severely disrupted the cultural and popular entertainment calendar for a large number of white residents in the Jackson area. In response, an infuriated mayor of Jackson and thousands of Mississippians called for white reciprocation. The seemingly solid walls of segregated entertainment became a site of pitched battle.

The intensity of white backlash to these cancellations was surprising, even to the most enthusiastic activists. Public responses by Jackson Mayor Allen Thompson and other segregationists manifested deeply held convictions regarding the power and importance of popular entertainment in the maintenance of particular social formations. In fact, the mayor went so far as to define the segregationist response to this agitation campaign as "one of the most important efforts" to date. Defending the traditional, yet fragile, racial barriers of segregation alongside the mayor were the vast majority of Mississippi's political, cultural, and economic institutions. Still, even while enjoying this dominance, many white Mississippians were inconvenienced and deprived of long anticipated cultural events by a small number of activists. The cancellations came unexpectedly, since most white Mississippians, and some of the state's African Americans, believed strict segregation of entertainment was necessary and natural.

For Austin C. Moore III, a newly arrived student from Chicago, such segregation seemed anything but necessary and natural. Although segregationist practices were widespread in Chicago, racial integration was more common in a limited number of social settings. And as Moore traveled to Tougaloo from Illinois in the autumn of 1962, he was immediately overwhelmed by the oppressive character of southern segregation. Dingy, poorly maintained "Negro" waiting rooms along the railway had welcomed him to Mississippi. As he was driven into Jackson, his "Aunt Sugar" pointed to a prominent downtown movie theater and remarked, "That's a white theater—I'll never be able to go in. . . ." Since Moore had worked as an usher at an integrated Chicago theater, he was surprised by his Aunt's statement and silently pledged to change things in Jackson.[6]

Approximately a year later, Moore became the coordinator of "cultural and artistic agitation" within the small group of Tougaloo staff and students calling themselves the "Nonviolent Agitation Association of College Pupils," a group affiliated with the national Student Nonviolent Coordinating

Committee (SNCC). At a November 11 meeting at the campus home of Ed
and Jeanette King, the Association decided to "work intensively to open
entertainment in Jackson." With regard to segregated events and venues, they
resolved that "if we can't go . . . nobody should be able to attend."[7]

The most recent catalyst for this meeting was the early November arrest
of Tougaloo student Robert Honeysucker and Nicolas Bosanquet, a visiting
Cambridge graduate, as they attempted, with tickets in hand, to attend a concert of London's Royal Philharmonic Orchestra in downtown Jackson.[8] Eventually the city police dropped all charges, aware of their precarious legal
position, yet unaware that their racial zealotry would have widespread consequences. Meanwhile, on the campus at Tougaloo, the "cultural and artistic
agitators" began correspondence with major motion picture producers and
NBC, specifically asking the television network to cancel the Jackson appearances of the *Bonanza* stars, scheduled for early February.[9]

Of more immediate concern to the student group was the appearance of
the cast of ABC-TV's *Original Hootenany USA* at the Jackson City Auditorium
on November 15. The network television show, hosted by Jack Linkletter,
took the form of "a traveling musical jamboree," and was taped at a variety of
college campuses. Pop-folk musicians such as the Limeliters, the Chad
Mitchell trio and the Smothers Brothers were featured on the program,
while the producers routinely "blacklisted" artists thought to be leftist, such
as Pete Seeger and the Weavers. In response to these McCartheyesqué practices, some prominent musicians refused to appear on the show.[10]

Nevertheless, the *Hootenany* cast set to appear in Jackson were folk performers riding a wave of popularity—including Glenn Yarbrough of the
Limeliters, the Journeymen, and Jo Mapes. In Mississippi, *Hootenany* fever had
been spreading. Shopping malls held "Hoot-teen-nany" promotionals to
attract adolescent shoppers and the town's drive-ins offered films such as *Hootenany Hoot*.

While the pre-concert excitement mounted, the Tougaloo students tele-
phoned the *Hootenany* cast at their Memphis hotel and arranged an informal
meeting at the Jackson airport on the day of the concert. Three Tougaloo
undergraduates—Austin Moore, Calvin Brown, and Steven Rutledge—met
the entertainers upon their arrival in Jackson to explain their position as well
as their intention to force a confrontation, if necessary, by attempting to seat
Tougaloo students at the *Hootenany* concert. After intensive negotiations
involving talent agents and long-distance phone calls, the group cancelled
the downtown show, just three hours before the scheduled start. The cast
relinquished their appearance fee and volunteered a free and integrated
concert that same evening on the campus of Tougaloo. The downtown audi-

torium box office provided refunds for 1,500 ticketholders, many of whom were already dressed for the event.[11]

Yarbrough, speaking for the folk singers, told the local paper, "We're not here to raise moral issues. We didn't want it to happen ourselves, but it was a decision we had to reach."[12] Given the conservative history and management of the *Hootenany* program, it was an especially surprising decision that testified to the persuasiveness and power of the students' tactics. A few days after the incident, Steven Rutledge, who also served as president of Tougaloo's student government, sent the *Hootenany* cast a letter of appreciation for their "courageous and difficult sacrifice," adding that "our evening together with laughter and song did much to reinforce our conviction that we are not alone in the great struggle for human dignity and high principle."[13]

Many white residents and officials in Jackson were embarrassed by the *Hootenany* debacle, but said little publicly, hoping a calm and measured response might be the best strategy. This changed three months later, however, when similar pressure was mobilized regarding upcoming visits from trumpeter Al Hirt and the stars of *Bonanza*, one of television's most popular shows.

Advertisements for the Mississippi Commerce and Industry Exposition promised "Five Big Shows" by the "Three Great Stars of Bonanza—Little Joe, Ben Cartwright, and Hoss," to be held at the Jackson state fairgrounds during the first two days of February. What the local show promoters did not know was that the agitation committee had written letters to NBC and each of the *Bonanza* stars regarding the scheduled appearances. As Moore stated in his appeal to the network:

> The American Negro is now struggling for … basic freedom.…
> You can play a tremendously important part in this venture. We
> understand that NBC is sending a group from *Bonanza* to Jackson
> in February. Two weeks ago a promising young musician,
> Robert Honeysucker, a Tougaloo music major was arrested. He
> walked to the same door the white people of Jackson will be
> entering to see the *Bonanza* cast.…
>
> We cannot risk another arrest—or possible violence. There-
> fore, we hope that the Bonanza cast will be willing to take their
> stand on the issue. We are asking that you refuse to perform
> before a segregated audience.…[14]

In response to the Tougaloo appeal, the *Bonanza* cast contacted NAACP field secretary Charles Evers in his Jackson office to discuss the local conditions of segregation and subsequently offer their statements of cancellation. Dan Blocker ("Hoss") sent a telegram that was reprinted in the *Jackson Daily News*: "I have long been in sympathy with the Negro struggle for total citizenship, therefore I would find an appearance of any sort before a segregated house completely incompatible with my moral concepts—indeed repugnant."[15] Later the same day, January 22, Lorne Green ("Ben Cartwright") and Michael Landon ("Little Joe") joined Blocker in withdrawing from the appearance. As a last minute replacement, promoters scrambled to arrange an appearance by Donna Douglas —"Ellie Mae" of the *Beverly Hillbillies*—only to have her state that she would be unable to perform. Ironically, as the *Bonanza* cast announced its disgust with the sanctioned practices of Jackson and the South, the *Beverly Hillbillies* and *Bonanza* were among the region's most popular TV programs. Many Mississippians came to feel that the television stars, influenced by a liberal Hollywood, had snubbed their most faithful fans.

The frustration and anger of white Jackson only intensified when Al Hirt cancelled a March of Dimes benefit concert three days later. Austin Moore attempted to contact Hirt before his arrival in Jackson via a friendly columnist for the *Chicago Sun-Times*, Irv Kupcinet. In his column on January 22, Kupcinet wrote, "A long distance call from Jackson, Mississippi, informed us that Al Hirt ... is scheduled for a concert in the municipal auditorium down there. Audiences in the auditorium are segregated. And the caller wants us to so inform Hirt. Which we hereby do."[16] When the trumpeter still traveled to Jackson for the January 25 concert, Moore sent a telegram to him. It read in part:

> Your performance this evening at the Mississippi Coliseum will serve the purpose of perpetuating the vicious system of segregation in Jackson. We speak in behalf of many Negro citizens who would like to attend your performance in dignity but are prevented from doing so by the city's racial policies. Other groups, including *Hootenany USA* and *Bonanza*, have cancelled their scheduled performances for this reason. We urgently request you to cancel also....[17]

Approximately three hours prior to curtain time, Hirt asked to talk with Moore face-to-face. Accompanied by friends, Moore gained access to the musician's room at a whites-only motel by borrowing a jacket and disguising himself as a room service waiter. Hearing that African Americans would attempt to attend the concert and that violence and arrests might ensue, Hirt finally decided to cancel. The time was 8:40, forty minutes after the scheduled performance was to start. Four thousand concert-goers sat in place as a sponsor reluctantly came onto the stage and read Moore's telegram to Hirt, adding that the program was cancelled. Before he had finished, he was drowned out by shouting voices and obscenities. Jackson's *Clarion Ledger*, after contacting Hirt, claimed that the musician reneged out of concern for the safety of his crew and the audience. It went on to quote Hirt as telling Moore, "I think you're kind of using me, and so are the March of Dimes people."[18] Another local newspaper account stated Hirt's agent "had been worked on by Negro groups."[19]

However the incident was portrayed, it was the talk of Jackson, a story told with considerable resentment and anger by many white Mississippians. Not only had they been snubbed by Hollywood, but now literally "stood up" by a white Southerner of considerable fame. Further, the *Hootenany*, Hirt, and *Bonanza* incidents had established a threatening precedent. A few days later, a top administrator of the National Aeronautics and Space Agency (NASA), James Webb, cancelled an appearance sponsored by the Jackson Chamber of Commerce, citing the problem of segregation. In February and April, pianist Gary Graffman and soprano Birgit Nilsson both refused to perform before all-white Jackson audiences. The musicians, each internationally renowned, had been contacted by Moore, as the Culture and Arts Committee targeted all visiting artists associated with the Jackson Music Association community concert series.

Reacting to these events, the *Mississippi Free Press* editorialized in a column titled, "Now It's Beginning to Hurt Both Ways":

> It appears as though a precedent has been established that any-body that is anybody in the entertainment field does not per-form in Jackson to segregated audiences. . . . So now, some of the white folks know what it is like to have the right to enjoy some-thing kept from them. Under the circumstances, we bet that they do not like the system any better than we do. Let's get together and do something about it.[20]

The cancellations in Jackson also had implications outside the city, as they articulated a successful strategy for drawing national attention to the prac-tices of various entertainers and southern communities. Prominent newspa-pers such as *The New York Times* began to carry articles highlighting the debates between performers, agents, and talent organizations regarding appearances before segregated audiences. During the winter months, the national SNCC leadership, the Congress of Racial Equality (CORE), and the NAACP joined in the protest against segregated entertainment in Mississippi. In March, the NAACP appealed to about sixty prominent musicians to form a committee to help make cultural events accessible to both black and white citizens in southern cities, using musician boycotts when necessary.[21]

Although the NAACP, CORE, and other civil rights groups had made pro-gressive strides through legislation, law, and direct negotiation with various industries, the tactics of Tougaloo's Culture and Arts Committee were noticeable for their relative informality, immediacy, and lack of official sanction. Frustrated by the gradualist gains of the national NAACP, the student committee and the Jackson movement chose to engage in direct action strategies that were often outside the purview and control of larger official institutions. Rather than enter into a protracted process of negotiation and compromise, the students moved quickly and decisively to achieve their goals. When various performers such as Hirt and the *Hootenany* cast initially resisted Committee appeals to cancel local segregated appearances, the group countered by threatening to appear at performances, risking violent confrontations with local patrons and police. These tactics were agreed upon without consultation from those outside the campus or within the college administration, as students knew that while Tougaloo was a "safe haven" for black Mississippians, a majority of campus residents and employees, as well as many outside the college gates, were uncomfortable with or opposed to such activism. The Committee's attacks on segregationist culture displayed a quality of spontaneity, coming from a small group that was only loosely organized, yet filled with enthusiasm, ideas, and frustration.

So while white constituents of legitimated culture planned and promoted events, Austin Moore and others quietly mounted a counterattack, using quasi-invisible practices—actions that were visible only as they disrupted public activities and consumption.[22] Operating on the terrain of dominant culture, the student agitators looked for, and found, points of vulnerability in a superficially stable social practice. This was, as the theoretical work of Michel de Certeau suggests, a tactical struggle in which the creativity of the subordinated was revealed and artfully practiced in hostile territory. As de Certeau theorizes:

> The space of the tactic is the space of the other. Thus it must play on and with a terrain imposed on it and organized by the law of a foreign power.... It must vigilantly make use of the cracks that particular conjunctions open in the surveillance of the proprietary powers. It poaches in them. It creates surprises in them....[23]

312

While there was little the Tougaloo group could do with regard to the production of network television shows or popular music, it intervened tactically on "foreign territory" where segregation was most pronounced and also most vulnerable—in the local conditions of performance and reception. These conditions represented a momentary window of opportunity for the students and were the point of productive struggle.

Given the size and resources of the Tougaloo group, there were relatively few opportunities for such an effective public resistance to the status quo.

And the students' activism, more than merely "making do" within an oppressive social system, bolstered other efforts to boycott or disrupt segregationist white commerce, both in Jackson and elsewhere. The students also effectively publicized the continuing African American fight to change racial segregation.

White Mississippians were nothing if not surprised by the exposed vulnerability and instability of the segregationist tradition. Most of the state's citizens had known nothing other than a racially segregated society. Suddenly, this routine and tradition was under attack, as was the foundational myth of the happy Negro living in a world shut off from white experience and privilege. While the Evers murder, funeral, and ensuing mass marches publicized black dissatisfaction, the Tougaloo students demonstrated that this discontent was not anomalous or short-lived, but enduring and deeply rooted in the segregationist past. Recognizing this as a moment that threatened segregation, some of Mississippi's dominant institutions responded with appeals to consolidate white power and further police popular tastes and practices.

blacking out bonanza

Leading the charge to rescue Jackson's "way of life" and cultural reputation was Allen Thompson, the city's mayor. He initiated the segregationist counterattack with a lengthy speech to the city's department heads, the day after *Bonanza* stayed away:

> ... this "Bonanza" thing to my mind is one of the greatest insults to the intelligence and to the activities and the good works that the people of Jackson and Mississippi are doing that I have ever heard.... But let me tell you something. We want industries, we want business, we want people to come to Jackson *only* if they like what they see—only if they like what we are doing, and only if they see the potential booming future of this City.[24]

The civic leader went on to read letters that Moore had sent him, outlining the Cultural and Artistic Committee's concerns and correspondence with NBC-TV regarding the *Bonanza* appearance. The mayor had underestimated the student activists, and admitted as much, with marked condescension: "Feature that—a student writing a letter like this and having more influence than all of the other conservative White people, good Colored people—one little pupil."[25]

Thompson concluded his attack on the Tougaloo students and "Bonanza" cast by calling for a "countermovement" that reemployed the selective buying strategy already used with great success by black Mississippians against white businesses. During the 1963 "Black Christmas" campaign, the Jackson nonviolent movement, including students and staff from Tougaloo, conducted a sustained, successful boycott of downtown merchants by discouraging the holiday purchase of decorations and gifts. The economic impact was severe, and several white businesses eventually closed or moved. Still hurting from this experience, with another embarrassment fresh on his mind, Thompson called for reciprocation, echoing a local newspaper columnist who suggested, "Why not fight them with their own weapon?"[26] Selective buying of goods advertised on television was to be accompanied by what he termed "selective looking" at television programming. Under such scrutiny, he was convinced programs such as *Bonanza* would fade away:

> Jackson, a typical Mississippi city, and Mississippi will be here a long time after "Bonanza" is gone, a long time after "Hoss" and the others have galloped away—because TV programs come, and they go. You look at some of the wonderful people who have been stars in the past. Look at the TV programs that you wouldn't have missed a year or so ago—you won't even sit down and look at them today. "Bonanza" will be gone unless it is a great exception, and it seems to me the great exceptions are people who don't get to meddling with other people's local business....[27]

The daily newspapers of Jackson immediately picked up and retransmitted the mayor's remarks, as did the Jackson Citizens' Council's February newsletter. Thompson admitted that he had enjoyed *Bonanza*—in fact, had "thought it was a wonderful program," but vowed that it would never come into his home again. A few days later, the *Jackson Daily News* pictured him sitting in front of a desk covered with "approximately 2,500 cards and letters ... calling for a blackout of the *Bonanza* television show."[28] Heartened by this "favorable response," Mayor Thompson announced he would expand his efforts to destroy *Bonanza* across the state. In an accompanying article, the Mayor was quoted as saying:

314

> [The blackout] will lead to the cancellation of the Bonanzas.... It will renew our courage to do what is right and necessary. Hundreds of thousands of people in at least several southern states will go along with us—and other millions all over the U.S. will later on regret they did not.... If we prevail in this— one of our most important efforts—your public officials in Mississippi and all over the South will be tremendously encouraged....[29]

The Jackson Citizens' Council, a chapter of the segregationist white Citizens' Council, used Thompson's statements to warn Mississippians against watching "TV programs which feature ... integrationist entertainers, or any other program which favors race-mixing." The Council's newsletter also reiterated the mayor's selective buying scheme.[30]

Thus, a turn of events that some might have considered trivial, or at worst, slightly frustrating, became the focus of public discourse. Concert cancellations and white boycott plans were regular front page news in Jackson's two notoriously racist dailies, the *Daily News* and *Clarion Ledger*. Going beyond expected statements of white denunciation, the mayor forced the issue: Watch *Bonanza* and further imperil southern culture and traditions, or "black out *Bonanza*," and bring honor to the state of Mississippi as well as the segregationist fight. In bringing this battle to the fore, Thompson and institutions of dominant culture called attention to the centrality of coercion in racial crises. They had, perhaps unwittingly, recirculated the knowledge that at least some, if not many, African Americans both desired and were forcibly denied cultural opportunities. The racist myth of the happy, content Negro was being eroded. Rather than ignoring, trivializing, or downplaying the Tougaloo interventions, segregationist leaders marked them as a point of primary identification, and opted for a response that only encouraged wider scrutiny and discussion of entertainment, popular culture, and their relationship to nonconsensual domination.

Letters to the editors of the Jackson dailies reflected some of the issues converging at this point in time. A majority of the letters printed in the *Clarion Ledger* and *Daily News* repeated the mayor's call for a "Bonanza blackout," while asserting that such programs were unneeded and unwanted. One letter, written by a resident of Vicksburg, Mississippi, and reprinted in different forms by both Jackson papers, epitomized much of the published correspondence:

> When the Hollywood stars of *Bonanza* refused to appear in Jackson recently, I immediately cut that show off my list. I am sure most of my fellow Mississippians feel as I do. Who gives a tinker's damn about Hollywood stars, or that rat race in Hollywood anyway, and who needs some Hollywood actor or actress in Mississippi to be happy, or to put over any show in Mississippi when we have Mississippi people with the best talent in the U.S.A., and our Mississippi girls are the most beautiful in the world. . . . I predict television won't last, just as the movies didn't. Some of the TV shows are terrible and the singing commercials and other stupid commercials get on an adult's nerves as well as children and sometimes they feel like busting the TV up, and it probably

would be a good idea.... If the actors from Hollywood do not want to come to our wonderful state, I say good riddance. Let Al Hirt blow his trumpet in the French Quarter in New Orleans or on Ed Sullivan's show.[31]

Along the same lines, a Jackson citizen wrote a letter combining the common "who needs them" theme, with an inflection of Christianity that was also standard to segregationist arguments, juxtaposing the purity of white Bible belters with the heathens outside:

> Speaking of the Cartwright family of the *Bonanza* Chevrolet show, we got along fine before we ever heard of them, and we can get along fine without them or the products they advertise, as long as they feel the way they do. They should stay away from Mississippi, or some good, kind, warmhearted Christian may get to them and convert them to a real clean way of living and loving. I feel sorry for them because they need some teaching on God's Word, because they do not practice what they preach. I watch their show mainly because I haven't seen any Negroes on it. But from now on my TV set will be turned off during this and Ed Sullivan's shows—and neither will I buy their sponsor's products.[32]

Throughout the newspaper coverage and official comments on the cancellations, as well as letters to the editor, were condemnations of "promises broken" by the stars that failed to appear. In connection with the broken promises theme, several letters aimed at Hirt claimed he had abandoned sick children by failing to appear at the March of Dimes fundraiser. For example, one Jackson resident opined:

> It has been really amusing to watch the NAACP frighten the Ol Hoss mules and Hootenany goats into tucking their tails and littering the air with heel dust.... But the amusement was turned into "Hirt" horror to find that there exists, anywhere in the civilized world, a group or any kind of being capable of striking such a low blow to little sick and helpless, crippled children, in need of medical aid, as Al Hirt did here.... Civilized people should not tolerate an entertainer with that kind of a heart.[33]

Throughout the letters, mayoral statements, and periodicals of the white Citizens' Council, there were similar characterizations of Al Hirt, the *Bonanza* cast, and other artists as immoral, unethical, untrustworthy, un-Christian, and liberal or "communistic." Tremendously popular personalities were transformed into dishonest cowardly villains, virtually overnight. As *Clarion Ledger* columnist Tom Ethridge wrote with regard to *Bonanza*:

> These famous "Cartwrights" portray he-men of courage and honor on television every Sunday night—heroes who brave all manner of dangers and threats in routine manner. But now, they stampede when the NAACP whispers "Boo" off camera. It is well known to all "Bonanza" fans that the word of a "Cartwright" is as good as his written bond. On the screen, that is. But in real life, it now develops that the "Cartwright" word can't be trusted any further than a Ponderosa bull can be tossed by the tail.[34]

A few days later, the *Clarion Ledger* took the unusual step of publishing a response to Ethridge from Charles Evers, the state's NAACP field secretary. Evers directly challenged the hero/villain theme advanced by Ethridge and others. Speaking of Dan Blocker, Lorne Green, and Michael Landon, Evers argued:

> That these three men have indicated that they will not aid or abet "age old customs in Mississippi" is not astonishing. It is astonishing, however, that the people of Mississippi continue to believe that they can expect to be treated with respect while they treat nearly 50 percent of their native Mississippians with disrespect. Sorry, Mr. Ethridge, any way you read this incident, Mississippi can't be made the hero.[35]

Although the published letters of support for the "Bonanza blackout" far outnumbered correspondents critical or skeptical of the crusade, a few letters provided unusual perspectives on the cancellations. For example, after folksinger Joan Baez had made a successful concert appearance at integrated Tougaloo College, a Biloxi resident concluded his letter with tongue firmly in cheek: "If many more renowned artists cancel Jackson performances, we may all have to go to Tougaloo for our cultural and aesthetic pleasures. But, of course we could always watch TV—or could we?" Weeks earlier, this same writer had penned:

317

> Another drab week has passed without *Bonanza*. Tell me again, now, just what is the difference between white and Negro boy-cotts? Of course, this dilemma would never have arisen if we pure white Christians had been attending our segregated worship services on Sunday evenings.
>
> P.S. Rumor has it that some Jackson citizens have lowered their shades and watched *Bonanza* anyway....[36]

Finally, after weeks of angry letters to the editor decrying the actions of Hirt, *Hootenany*, and the Ponderosa gang, one reader said "enough":

> Quit sending in those letters concerning "fat old Hoss Cart-wright." Don't you realize that this is just what that communis-tic NAACP wants you to do? Nothing could make them happier than to see all you learned sociologists, politicians, and philoso-phers out there in prejudice land squirming. All this outraged uproar is just what Mr. [Medgar] Evers would have wanted—had he not been murdered in cold blood. If you had just ignored the whole situation and acted as if you didn't care, you would have defeated the NAACP.[37]

This reader's assessment was largely correct. Although the Jackson move-ment and Tougaloo students would not have been simply stopped by white apathy and silence, aggressive white reaction called attention to the opera-tions of white power and domination. These previously naturalized opera-tions of power were put into public debate, discussed on the streets of Jackson, and detailed in popular media accounts both outside and within Mis-sissippi.

Earlier Jackson activism, such as Tougaloo student sit-ins, had received lit-tle, if any, local media attention, and the agitation group expected more of the same in the *Bonanza* incident—unofficial censorship and nonrecognition. In fact, nonrecognition had long been at the heart of segregationist strategy, in reaction to individual African Americans as well as the larger black free-dom fight. White supremacist violence against rights activists was certainly a constant threat and reality, but publicly both it and the voices of dissent were either ignored or explained away. The Jackson police had an informal agree-ment with the local broadcast media that any scenes of racial confrontation or violence were not to be aired, in order to maintain "public safety." The local censorship of any broadcast materials deemed communist, integra-tionist, or otherwise unsettling to the status quo was commonly justified by the seemingly ambiguous, yet quite revealing, call to "maintain the public order." At Jackson's powerful ABC and NBC affiliate, WLBT-TV, the news policy was that controversial or confrontational news footage would not be broadcast, nor would any programs discussing issues of "segregation or inte-gration."[38] So it was to the students' considerable delight that the mayor and local media loudly articulated the counterattack in the case of *Bonanza*—con-firming the importance of entertainment and the struggle for its control. What was usually dismissed as "just entertainment" now became a vital social concern.

While dozens of Mississippi residents spoke of their disdain for *Bonanza*, Al Hirt, and others, they took the time and energy to write letters to publications for months after the initial incidents. The issue had incredible salience and resonance within the white community. For at least two years after the cancellations, letters were being received by the newspapers, denouncing the performers and advising boycotts. Moore received letters from detractors outside Mississippi that obviously had heard of the agitation campaign and had taken the time to rebuke his "dangerous" activities. For all the language about not "giving a damn," many people did care, and some admitted they were forgoing their favorite shows. Others said nothing, or perhaps publicly toed the segregationist line, but kept the TV on and the shades down.

watching out of sight

While claiming a dedication to segregation and a "southern way of life," many Jacksonians were loath to give up Sunday evenings with the Cartwrights. In Jackson, and around the nation, the popularity of *Bonanza* had grown with its move in 1961 to the nine o'clock Sunday evening slot. In fact, shortly before the cast cancelled in Jackson, a local newspaper described the program as Jackson's top-rated television show.[39] Even those most committed to killing integrationist efforts, such as the mayor, admitted that the program was a personal favorite.

It is understandable, then, that the rumors regarding secretive viewing of *Bonanza* behind closed doors had considerable substance. Despite the mayor's plea, invoking all things good and southern, and perhaps feelings of guilt, the pleasures of the Ponderosa often privately won out. Watching the program was nothing to announce in church or to talk about with friends in restaurants, but people still enjoyed it outside the surveillance of institutionalized segregationism. The show's local ratings remained strong, in the midst of a publicly well-supported campaign against it.

Even as fallen segregationists watched in privacy behind drawn shades, Jackson's WLBT-TV refused to disrupt airing of the weekly program, and local businesses continued to air advertising alongside the show. This is somewhat surprising, as the station was a well-established foe to all integration and civil rights efforts, and eventually lost its license after investigations into accusations of racial discrimination. The station's manager, Fred Beard, was a prominent member of the Jackson Citizens' Council, and had publicly gloated about interrupting or blocking network television programs featuring African Americans. But in this instance, WLBT, as well as thousands of viewers, had only a deaf ear for the mayor's appeal. The station's programming director, Hewett Griffin, recalled that the show continued to be a strong performer for the local broadcaster. In short, people continued to watch, and businesses persisted in their pursuit of profit.

By repeating widespread calls for boycotts of *Bonanza* and network sponsors, Jackson's mayor and many white Mississippians hoped to "boycott the boycotters"—to wound the civil rights movement with one of its own weapons. Hundreds, if not thousands, of Mississippians publicly vowed in newspapers and meetings to undercut integrationist interests through the power of white dollars. Published letters carried promises not to purchase Chevrolet cars or other products advertised on *Bonanza*. Writers argued that a unified white Mississippi would be a crushing economic force opposing civil rights activity.

However, despite the best efforts of Mayor Thompson and the pleas of the supremacist press and prominent Jackson citizens, the white counter-boycott never achieved its goal—*Bonanza* was never "blacked out." In practice, the "southern way of life" was quite at odds with its romantic and politicized abstraction. WLBT continued to air *Bonanza*, with local advertising support, and thousands of Mississippians remained at least privately loyal to a publicly discredited practice, despite the fact that published segregationist voices spoke out against those who failed to fully support Thompson's boycott call. As the various factions of Mississippi's white establishment argued among themselves and failed to form strategic alliances, the fissures in racial segregation grew large and more vulnerable to attack.

In terms of economic interests, Jackson commerce and industry followed a pattern common throughout the South. Businesses at first reacted to local activism with shock and resentment, followed by a period of silence (allowing extremists to fill the vacuum), and finally took back a degree of civic leadership through opposition to extremist activities that threatened economic progress.[40] As one historian has argued, while southern businesses previously believed that economic progress and southern racial practices could be simultaneously supported, civil rights activism forced a choice, and in the "new ordering of their values and priorities," economic imperatives were placed above those of race.[41] In Jackson, for example, the Chamber of Commerce publicly urged compliance with the 1964 Civil Rights Act following its Congressional codification, and the white Citizens' Council grew resentful of what it called the "surrender" by prominent city businesses.[42] Even while Mayor Thompson urged wide-scale boycotting of *Bonanza* and its sponsors, many conservative state politicians remained mum. Behind such actions, or inaction, was an abiding fear that in the absence of legal obedience and order, new capital investments would be discouraged and/or economic stability and progress would be imperiled.

320

In this instance, the contradictory impulses of capitalism, though fraught with their own histories of racism and oppression, prompted Mississippi business interests to prioritize the pursuit of profit over adherence to a particular white supremacist agenda. To pursue a hard segregationist line was to risk the appearance of political and racial extremism, jeopardizing cooperative efforts with interests outside the state as well as long-term development and growth. Eventually, southern business people began to further acknowledge and appreciate the economic power of African American patronage. And gradually, a desire to gain a larger share in the national economic prosperity of the 1950s and 1960s diluted southern segregationist zeal.[43]

conclusion

When considered within the larger context of the '60s civil rights movement, the Tougaloo students' "cultural and artistic agitation" bears similarities to integrationist campaigns waged elsewhere. As in other parts of the South, many of the agitators that called for change and risked segregationist retaliation were youths and college students that had grown impatient with gradualist agendas that looked to law and official governmental institutions. In Mississippi and elsewhere, these direct action and confrontation campaigns signaled the rise of SNCC and altered the course of the black freedom fight.

The activism and reactionism in Jackson put the lie to the notion that popular culture, its productions, or pleasures could be perfectly disciplined or managed by a particular social formation. Integration activists intervened in cultural productions they neither owned nor permanently controlled. Popular entertainment, such as *Hootenany*, *Bonanza*, and Al Hirt, were both sites of and resources for racial struggle, appreciated and employed by both oppressor and oppressed.

Somewhat ironically, it was the voice and communicative power of white Mississippians that aided the disruption of segregationist practices. As one letter writer in the *Clarion Ledger* noted, white reaction worked to the advantage of the activists, calling wider attention both to the segregationist position and the reality of coercion. In doing so, it forced a veiled contradiction into public view. Contrary to the fundamental tenets of segregationism and the "southern way of life," African Americans were not satisfied with limited cultural opportunities and resources, but were forced to adapt under the threats of police violence and jail. For decades consent had been enabled and encouraged through the coerced segregation of popular entertainment, a system that came to be widely regarded as natural and inevitable. But as knowledge regarding the coercive nature of segregated entertainment gained wider circulation and attention, consent and cooperation with segregation began to

321

fragment. The struggle over entertainment revealed that which the system had worked so hard to conceal.

Although Austin Moore left Tougaloo College shortly after the agitation campaign, he stayed in touch with family and friends, including his Aunt Sugar, and heard regular reports about the changes slowly occurring in Jackson. One such report was a memorable telephone call he received from his aunt several years later. Something she had thought impossible in 1963 had occurred: She had attended a movie at one of the previously white, segregated theaters in downtown Jackson. Gradually—too gradually for many—the ideas and beliefs that undergirded racial oppression were being more fully revealed and challenged. While Moore and the other "cultural and artistic agitators" had not brought an immediate halt to segregationist practices or racist policies, they had prompted progressive change by further eroding what one "agitator" termed "the self-serving segregationist myth of Mississippi black satisfaction."[44] Calling attention to the nonconsensual domination that accompanied such mythology was but one part of the larger, ongoing struggle against white supremacy and its institutions.

notes

For their generousity, help and encouragement, I wish to thank the staff of the L. Zenobia Coleman Library at Tougaloo College, Austin C. Moore III, Jeanette King, and Rev. R. Edwin King, Jr. Reverend King graciously offered his own unpublished manuscript describing this activism, in addition to the wealth of archival holdings in his name. An earlier version of this paper was presented at the 1994 conference of the International Communication Association.

1. Before he was shot in the back in his own driveway, Medgar Evers was one of a handful of civil rights activists that dared challenge the powerful cultural institutions of segregationist, white supremacist Mississippi. During the late 1950s, as "Mississippi stood still," Myrlie Evers remembers that her husband worked tirelessly with the press, "literally dragged reporters to the scenes of crimes," issued press releases that challenged segregationist narratives, and in a challenge to one of the state's most powerful broadcast stations, WLBT-TV in Jackson, filed official complaints with the FCC. These memories are recorded in Myrlie Evers' *For Us, the Living* (New York: Ace, 1970) 176–94.

    In John Salter's primary account of the Jackson movement, *Jackson, Mississippi: An American Chronicle of Struggle and Schism* (Malabar, Florida: Kreiger, 1987), civil rights activist and Tougaloo chaplain Reverend R. Edwin King, Jr. recalls the Evers assassination and defines the early '60s as "times of madness" in Mississippi and elsewhere (xvii). In his recent history, *Local People: The Struggle for Civil Rights in Mississippi* (Urbana: University of Illinois Press, 1994), former Tougaloo College professor John Dittmer provides an excellent overview of the battle against white supremacy in the Magnolia state. He notes that the perceived failures of the legally "respectable" white Citizens' Council during the late 1950s and early 1960s provided racist rationales for increasing violence and intimidation. The prospect of federal civil rights legislation, promises of additional integrationist activism within the state, and expectations regarding the enforced desegregation of local schools all exacerbated white supremacist fears and frustration (217). The Mississippi chapter of the Ku Klux Klan, officially inactive since the 1930s, was revived in late 1963. And in ensuing months, while white business leaders and state government officials rhetorically opposed Klan revival, murder and white supremacist violence swept largely unchecked through the state (215–18).

2. In addition to the activities discussed in this chapter, the Jackson movement engaged in extensive boycott campaigns, aimed primarily at downtown merchants, that provided strong financial and political support for segregationist practices and policies. Among the demands made by the movement were calls for respect of, and courtesy toward, African American consumers.

3. John Fiske, *Television Culture* (London: Methuen, 1987), 40. Also see Antonio Gramsci's *The Prison Notebooks*, portions of which have been published in English, edited by Geoffrey Nowell-Smith and Quintin Hoare, under the title *Selections from the Prison Notebooks* (New York: International, 1971).

4. For an excellent discussion of these theoretical points, see Kimberlee Crenshaw, "Race, Reform, and Retrenchment: Transformation and Legitimation in Antidiscrimination Law," *Harvard Law Review* 101 (1988): 1331–87.

5. Tougaloo College is a small liberal arts institution located in Tougaloo, Mississippi, just outside the city limits of Jackson. It was founded in 1869 by the American Missionary Association "to respond to the needs of emancipated blacks immediately following the end of the civil war," and in the twentieth century has operated as a private, integrated, majority black institution. See Clarice Campbell and Oscar Rogers, Jr., *Mississippi: The View from Tougaloo* (Jackson: University of Mississippi Press, 1979), xi.

6. Austin C. Moore III, interview with the author, 21 July 1993.

7. See papers of R. Edwin King, Jr., Box 2: Folder 69, Lillian Pierce Benbow Room of Special Collections, Coleman Library, Tougaloo College, Tougaloo, Mississippi.

8. Dittmer, 226.

9. Paramount, Desilu, MGM, Buena Vista, and Twentieth Century were among the major motion picture producers contacted by Moore in November of 1963. His letter to the studios stated, in part, "We are asking all the major film producers to withhold their films from segregated theaters in the Jackson area. This would be what is needed to enlarge the audiences of our theaters to include Negroes. Please help us. We cannot risk arrest again—or possible violence. We can't do it alone. The key is yours." See papers of R. Edwin King, Jr., Box 2: Folder 68. Moore does not remember receiving any response from any of the motion picture producers, and there are no documents in the Tougaloo archives to suggest otherwise.

10. Tim Brooks and Earle Marsh, *The Complete Directory to Prime Time Network Shows, 1946-Present* (New York, Ballantine, 1979), 409–10.

11. This description of the Hootenany cancellation, as well as the situations surrounding the cast of *Bonanza* and the Al Hirt show, come from a combination of primary sources. Jackson's daily newspapers, the *Daily News* and *Clarion Ledger*, as well as a local civil rights publication, the *Mississippi Free Press*, were relied upon heavily. In addition, materials from the papers of R. Edwin King, Jr. at Tougaloo College provided key insights regarding Tougaloo activism.

12. "Hootenany Called Off in Jackson," *Clarion Ledger* (16 November 1963) 2.

13. Letter of Stephen Rutledge, 19 November 1963, in papers of R. Edwin King, Jr., Box 2: Folder 68.

14. Letter of Austin Moore, 11 November 1963, in papers of R. Edwin King, Jr., Box 2: Folder 68.

15. "Bonanza Family Won't Come Here," *Clarion Ledger* (23 January 1964): 6.

16. Irv Kupcinet, "Kup's Column," *Chicago Sun-Times* (22 January 1964): 44.

17. Copy of telegram sent to Al Hirt, 25 January 1964, Box 9: Folder 450, Papers of R. Edwin King, Jr.

18. "Furor Grows Hotter Over Hirt's Pullout," *Clarion Ledger* (27 January 1964): 8.

19. "Another Performer Cancels Show Here," *Jackson Daily News* (26 January 1964): 1.

20. "Now It's Beginning to Hurt Both Ways," *Mississippi Free Press* (1 February 1964): 2.

21. "Nonviolent Agitation Association of College Pupils," *Voice of the Movement Newsletter* (27 March 1964): 5–6.

22. I borrow these terms and ideas from *The Practice of Everyday Life* (Berkeley: University of California Press, 1984), in which Michel de Certeau offers an analysis of the ways in which the marginalized make use of that which is imposed upon them.

23. de Certeau, 37.

24. Press release of Mayor Allen Thompson in papers of Reverend R.L.T. Smith, Box 6: Folder 117, Lillian Pierce Benbow Room of Special Collections, Coleman Library, Tougaloo College, Tougaloo, Mississippi.

25. Press release of Mayor Allen Thompson, Papers of Reverend R.L.T. Smith.

26. Tom Ethridge, "Mississippi Notebook," *Clarion Ledger* (6 February 1964): 8.

27. Press release of Mayor Allen Thompson, Box 6: Folder 117, Papers of Reverend R.L.T. Smith.

28. "Ask Bonanza Blackout," *Jackson Daily News* (31 January 1964): 1.

29. "Ask Bonanza Blackout."

30. Jackson Citizens' Council, *Aspect*, February 1964, 1.

31. "Hollywood Stars Not Needed Here," *Jackson Daily News* (28 January 1964): 6. As Edwin King has noted in his unpublished account, "For about ten years some white Mississippians had refused to watch the Ed Sullivan show because Negro entertainers appeared frequently (and were frequently blocked out by the local station claiming cable trouble)." King recalls some whites called the show the "N.L. Sullivan" show—the N.L. meaning "nigger lover." See R. Edwin King, Jr., "1964 Concerts," unpublished manuscript, 31.

32. "Dislikes Sullivan and the Cartwrights," *Jackson Daily News* (28 January 1964): 6.

33. "Hirt Hurts Sick Children by Runout," *Jackson Daily News* (28 January 1964): 6. Although the reader nominates the NAACP as the activist force behind the cancellations, the NAACP had little to do with these interventions, at least in their initial stages. This attack on the organization was typical, as distinct integration efforts or civil rights organizations were frequently conflated by white Mississippians.

34. Tom Ethridge, "Mississippi Notebook," *Clarion Ledger* (24 January 1964): 8.

35. "Voice of the People," *Clarion Ledger* (28 January 1964): 6.

36. "Voice of the People," *Clarion Ledger* (10 April 1964): 12; "Voice of the People," *Clarion Ledger* (20 February 1964): 10.

37. "Voice of the People," *Clarion Ledger* (24 February 1964): 13.

38. Testimony of Robert L. McRaney, Jr., general manager of WLBT-TV, in Federal Communications Commission Records, 27 July 1971, Docket 18845, Box 24, Volume 22, Folder 56, 6514–16, U.S. National Archives, Suitland, Maryland Branch.

39. "Bonanza Family Will Appear Here," *Clarion Ledger* (9 January 1964): 2.

40. Elizabeth Jacoway, "An Introduction," *Southern Businessmen and Desegregation*, ed. Elizabeth Jacoway and David Coburn (Baton Rouge, Louisiana State University Press, 1982), 8–9.

41. Jacoway, 6.

42. Charles Sallis and John Quincy Adams, "Desegregation in Jackson, Mississippi," *Southern Businessmen and Desegregation*, 242–44.

43. Jacoway, 12–14.

44. Salter, *Jackson, Mississippi*, xxiv.

Wayne Maunder in *Custer*

white network/

fifteen red power

abc's *custer* series

roberta e. pearson

In the fall of 1967, ABC premiered the 20th Century Fox Television production *Custer*, a Western somewhat loosely based upon the life of the famous Civil War general and "Indian fighter" who met an early and violent death in the 1876 Battle of the Little Big Horn. After seventeen badly rated episodes, ABC replaced *Custer* at mid-season with the British import *The Avengers*, but not before Dell had issued its tie-in comic *The Legend of Custer*. On the cover of the first volume, ABC's Custer, played by actor Wayne Maunder, wears the black hat, red cravat, buckskin jacket, and long curly hair of his historical counterpart, his upraised hand signalling the charge. The accompanying text reads: "George Armstrong Custer. The Man who became a Legend in His Own Time. Explosive Tales of a Daring Man of Destiny." The first panel shows Custer, his saber raised and pistol blazing, charging at an Indian opponent, Crazy Horse, who has his bare back to the reader and his lance poised. Custer shouts to his troops, "Leave Crazy Horse to Me!!" while the Indian yells "EEEEIIII! KILL YELLOWHAIR!" A text box reads:

> Crazy Horse, war chief of the mighty Sioux, led the screaming
> warriors at the famed 7th cavalry regiment ... at whose head
> rode George Armstrong Custer, a legend in his own lifetime ...
> beloved by his tough troopers, bedeviled by his superior officers
> ... a fighting man who packed more excitement, heroism, and
> controversy into his brief lifetime than most men who live twice
> as long![1]

The image of the dashing, gallant, cavalryman on the comic's front page
and first panel clashes radically with other 1960s representations of the
famous (or infamous) Indian fighter. For example, P. M. Clepper's *TV Guide*
article "He's Our George," published shortly before the *Custer* series' debut,
mocks the general and sympathizes with his Indian foes, more characteristic
of the period's attitude toward Custer than the comic book's and television
show's glorification.[2] Clepper also debunked the myth that the Lakota and
Cheyenne refrained from scalping Custer out of respect.

> To the Sioux he was 'the chief of thieves'.... To the Cheyenne,
> he was a squaw-killer. In a surprise attack on a peaceful village in
> Oklahoma in 1867 it's said that he and his troopers killed (and
> scalped) more women and children than braves.[3]

An article in that bastion of middle-American sentiment, *The Saturday Evening
Post*, also reveals that Custer's stock had slipped badly by the second half of
the twentieth century. Titled "Bad Day Ahead for the Army's Greatest Loser,"
the article claimed: "Ninety years ago Gen. George Armstrong Custer rode
out to fight Sitting Bull—and lost everything but one horse. Now he tries
again every year, but the Indians are still writing the script." *The Post* article
reported on the annual re-enactment of the Little Big Horn Battle in Hardin,
Montana, extensively quoting the native American organizer of the event.[4]

If broadcast half a century earlier, ABC's image of Custer as dashing *beau
sabreur* would have been perfectly consistent with other popular and even historical representations.[5] But as early as 1934, when Frederick Van de Water
published his influential biography *Glory Hunter*, Custer's status as hero was
undermined. That biography portrayed Custer as ambitious, selfish, reckless
and a rather bad tactician. Although Custer continued to figure as the hero
of some popular texts, such as the 1941 film *They Died With Their Boots On*, *Glory
Hunter*'s interpretation shaped many subsequent historical works, as well as
fictional accounts such as Thomas Berger's 1964 novel *Little Big Man* and the
1970 film of the same name. By 1967, the ridiculing and condemnation of
Custer by middle-brow venues such as *TV Guide* and *The Saturday Evening Post*
attested to the shift of opinion among the white majority, while Native

Americans continued to loath the man who for them apotheosized the worst excesses of their Euro-American conquerors.[6]

The National Congress of American Indians and other Native-American organizations, outraged at the prospect of a series glorifying a man they considered a mass murderer, unsuccessfully tried to persuade ABC not to air *Custer*. A memo from the director of the Washington office stated, "The name Custer connotes a serious and basic threat to the image of all American Indians."[7] Indeed, for key figures within the newly emerging but not yet media-prominent red power movement, the name "Custer" served as a reminder of their people's long mistreatment at the hand of the white man.

Given the circumstances, ABC's decision to broadcast the *Custer* series in the first place is far more surprising than the series' poor ratings and eventual cancellation. This essay poses two central questions: 1) Why, in 1967, when George Armstrong Custer might have seemed a most unlikely candidate for a television series' hero, did 20th Century-Fox produce and ABC Television air the *Custer* series and generally ignore Native American protests? and, 2) Why did the series fail with the television audience? Seeking to answer these questions, I first examine the historical record concerning protests against the show lodged by the National Congress of American Indians and other Indian activist groups, briefly contrasting their tactics and results with those of other minority groups. I look at dominant perceptions of historical and contemporary Native Americans in order to place the producers' probable attitudes and the program's episodes themselves within their historical and cultural frameworks. Finally, I analyze several episodes of the *Custer* series. These strategies provide a route for interrogating the connection between 1960s television and cultural history.

native american protests

By 1967, ethnic interest groups had successfully pressured television producers and the networks for more positive representations, making it particularly curious that 20th Century-Fox Television and ABC did not pay greater attention than they did to Native American complaints about the new *Custer* series. In 1961, for example, efforts to persuade ABC to modify *The Untouchables'* portrayal of Italian Americans as gangsters yielded detailed coverage in *The New York Times* and concessions from the show's producers. Italian American organizations, often led by prominent public officials, picketed ABC and threatened boycotts of sponsor products. After meeting with representatives of the National Italian American League to Combat Defamation, Desi Arnaz, president of *The Untouchables'* production company, Desilu, agreed not to use "fictional characters as hoodlums with Italian names" and to give more prominence to the Italian American member of the Untouchables, Nick Rossi.[8]

A 1964 U.S. Court of Appeals ruling provided more direct economic leverage against a television industry that had previously been subject only to moral suasion and threatened boycotts. In that year a coalition of civil rights groups filed a petition asking the Federal Communications Commission to deny Jackson, Mississippi station WLBT's license renewal, claiming that the station failed to serve the local black population, ran programming discriminating against blacks, and was biased with regard to racial issues. The FCC failed to respond, but the Washington, D.C. Court of Appeals ruled that the protesting groups be granted a hearing on the grounds that the petitioners had legal standing as consumers of broadcast material. During the course of complicated and protracted legal proceedings the FCC twice renewed the station's license on a short term basis, but in 1969 the Court of Appeals revoked it permanently. The granting of legal standing to viewers together with WLBT's punishment for racist policies served as a lesson to network affiliates and hence the networks themselves, making them more responsive to the myriad media watchdog groups that arose in the wake of the ruling.[9]

Despite the precedents established by *The Untouchables*' negotiations and the Court of Appeals' ruling, neither the national press, nor 20th Century-Fox Television nor ABC, paid serious attention to Native American concerns about *Custer*, a disparity for which the relative public profiles and political connections of the respective organizations—Italian Americans and African Americans versus Native Americans—might partially account. Strong commitments to tribal rather than "racial" identity, and to traditional ways rather than to direct involvement in the white man's government, had mitigated against a unified national political presence and also produced a reluctance to follow the activist tactics of other "minority" groups attempting to ameliorate their screen images.

The National Congress of American Indians, established in 1944 and composed of representatives from more than one-third of tribal governments,[10] while committed to the improvement of the Native American's status in the United States, at first avoided involvement in the well-publicized civil rights struggles of the late 1950s and early 1960s.[11] *The New York Times*, reporting on the NCAI's twentieth annual meeting in 1963, said: "Indian tribes ... made it clear that their aims did not match those of Negroes struggling for integration. ... Indians want to remain a group apart, to preserve their ancient culture." A comment from the group's executive director perhaps spoke more directly to the possible political motivations behind Native Americans' disinclination to follow the confrontational tactics of African Americans. Robert

Burnett asserted that Native Americans would not engage in protest demonstrations because "we want to give no aid to communist propaganda about dissension."[12] By the mid-to-late 1960s, however, some Indians were considering a more activist stance. At the 1966 NCAI convention, Vine Deloria stated that, "Red Power means we want power over our own lives. . . ."[13] Deloria's phrase, perhaps the first utterance of the slogan and clearly an adaptation of the civil rights rallying cry, had ironic overtones in light of Burnett's fears, but this did not dissuade other Indians from taking the civil rights movement as a tactical model. In 1967, *Ebony* magazine reported that a group of Native Americans—Washington State Indians fighting to maintain their traditional fishing rights—were considering a more activist stance as they engaged in "an agonized re-appraisal of organized social protest."[14] The group hired NAACP attorney Jack E. Tanner, and was "following a plan of resistance closely resembling the civil rights movement." Attorney Tanner, pointing to the rationale behind such an alliance, said, "By and large, the same folks who hate Indians hate Negroes."[15]

When ABC announced the inclusion of the *Custer* series in its fall line-up, the National Congress of American Indians, although counseled otherwise, was prepared to employ the same persuasive tools used by other racial and ethnic organizations to keep the show from airing. A group of Indian tribal leaders, representing Kiowas, Comanches, Cheyennes, Arapahos, Chickasaws, Choctaws, Seminoles, and Creeks, met in Oklahoma City to discuss possible responses. Ben West, the general manager of local ABC affiliate KOCO-TV, and a member of ABC's Board of Directors, promised to arrange a preview of the show's first two or three episodes, as well as to propose that ABC produce and air a thirty minute documentary on Native Americans.[16] West continued to recommend conventional, nonconfrontational tactics, suggesting that rather than simply condemning *Custer* the NCAI might create a group to monitor film and television images or begin a program of public education. While promising to arrange a meeting between an NCAI representative and ABC and 20th Century-Fox executives, West cautioned, "If you demand and protest then this will only close the doors."[17]

John Belindo, director of the NCAI's Washington office, was inclined, however, to emulate the approach that Italian American organizations had employed in wresting concessions from ABC regarding *The Untouchables*. Belindo wrote to a supporter:

> I am enclosing a list of sponsors of the *Custer* series for your information. I would advise your writing these sponsors asking them to halt advertisements on the grounds that the series glorifies Custer's animal atrocities against Indian people and presents American Indians in a derogatory manner.[18]

Whether as a result of West's contacts or of the NCAI's pressure on sponsors, two NCAI representatives did in fact meet with William Self, head of 20th Century-Fox's television division, and Frank Glicksman, the show's producer. Self apparently tried to soothe his visitors fear concerning the show, promising to correct technical errors and pointing "out how we've done everything possible to make Chief Crazy Horse the hero he was."[19]

Lacking the NCAI's contacts with the industry, other Native American organizations did not attempt to achieve a rapprochement with ABC, but lodged protests and complained vociferously to the press, perhaps in the hope of gaining public support. Activities in Minnesota, original home of the Sioux as well as the present-day location of many Native American tribes, received coverage in local newspapers and *Variety*. *Daily Variety*, saying that other organizations were following in "the National Congress of Indian's footsteps," quoted an archdeacon of the South Dakota Episcopal Church as saying,

> The series must not go on TV. It would cause irreparable damage
> to the image of the Indians as human beings and as people trying
> to join the modern technological world. All the old hatreds
> would come to the surface.

The Right Reverend W. W. Horstick of Minneapolis responded to this appeal, urging his diocese to join him in protesting against the show.[20] The Red Lake Tribal Council and the Consolidated Minnesota Chippewa Tribe also spoke out against ABC's new show. Roger Jourdain, chairmen of the Council stated, "The Custer series will stir up old animosities and revive Indian and cowboy fallacies we have been trying to live down." Picking up on the issue, Twin Cities newspapers ran editorials condemning the series.[21]

None of the actions of the NCAI or its allies persuaded ABC to cut the program from its fall schedule, and the concessions made by *Custer*'s producers to Native Americans were relatively minor compared to those made by *The Untouchables'* producers to Italian Americans. In addition, while *The New York Times* had featured several articles on the Italian American protests, only the most impassioned denunciation of Custer and the new series received more than passing mention in the national press. On July 21, preceding the NCAI meetings with Ben West, A. Hopkins-Duke, the Kiowa director of The Tribal Indian Land Rights Association, held a press conference at which he said:

> General Custer was the Indian's worst enemy. Glamorizing
> Custer is like glamorizing Billy the Kid. The Tribal Land Rights
> Association is planning to petition the federal courts for an
> injunction restraining the series. We are lodging a complaint to

ABC, petitioning sponsors of the series to boycott [sic] it. We hope the nation's 600,000 Indians and all persons interested in the welfare of Indians will protest the Custer series. General Custer endorsed a policy of genocide and massacred village after village of Indians. We think it's about time a true picture of the American Indian be portrayed on the American film and TV screen. The industry continues to build its unrealistic image of my people because of the phenomenal success of cowboy versus Indian films. This Custer is the last straw.[22]

Hopkins-Duke's facility for soundbites, coupled with threats of legal and economic reprisals, resulted in articles in both *Newsweek* and *The Los Angeles Times*, neither of which had heeded the NCAI's complaints. The *Times'* jocularity typifies the tone of much mainstream reporting on Native American concerns about screen representation: "Wants TV Series' Scalp," states a smaller headline above a main headline, "Indian Chieftain Still on Custer Warpath."[23] An editorialist at the *Pittsburgh Post-Gazette*, also discussing Hopkins-Dukes' press conference, reveled even further in anachronistic humor.

We should be relieved ... that the Indian groups are resorting to the courts rather than to the tomahawk. But somehow we can't conceive of Cochise slapping an injunction on a television network. Neither can we imagine Geronimo consulting his mouthpiece. We hate to say it, but we think red man talks with forked tongue."[24]

These journalists' deployment of historical metaphors paradoxically dehistoricized Native Americans by portraying them as primitive savages rather than as twentieth-century human beings—a strategy which Edward Said characterizes as typically "orientalist." In his classic study of the Western representation of Arabic culture, Said argues that westerners have consistently perceived Arabs as the backwards, primitive, and irrational "other," this subhuman characterization justifying their domination by the more enlightened Euro-American world.[25] Conceiving of Native Americans in twentieth-century terms such as "mouthpieces" and "injunctions" made them more like Euro-Americans, potentially destabilizing hierarchies of domination; conceiving of them in nineteenth-century terms such as "scalps," "warpaths," "tomahawks," and "forked tongues" kept Native Americans in their place as the justifiably dominated "other." The disparity between the jocular treatment of the Native Americans protesting against *Custer* and the respect accorded Italian Americans protesting against *The Untouchables* seems typical of the "orientalization" of the former. A 1960s journalist simply could not have "orientalized" Italian Americans by lamenting that they were resorting to boycotts rather than tommy guns since this particular group no longer occupied the bottom of the ethnic hierarchy.

dominant perceptions of native americans

As outlined above, obvious structural factors, such as political organization and connections, partially explain the relative impact of "minority" protests upon screen images; but I would argue that we must also account for a rather less tangible factor, the dominant culture's generalized perception of the "minority" group.[26] The dominant perceptions of the 1960s, as expressed in contemporary cinema, historical fiction, and journalism, exhibited certain continuities with the preceding centuries of Euro-American depictions of Native Americans. Since the moment of first encounter between the indigenous tribes of the Americas and their European conquerors, the representation of Native Americans has alternated between that of "noble savage" and "savage savage," the choice of trope primarily dependent upon the Native American's degree of proximity and threatening potential. As we have seen, the journalistic "orientalization" of Native Americans involved the retention, in parodic form, of the "savage savage," but the relegation of most Native Americans to invisible status on the reservations had, by the second half of the twentieth century, made the "noble savage" most prominent. And the vast majority of these noble savages, at least as they were represented in popular fictions such as the movies and the other mass media, were members of the nineteenth-century plains tribes—the Lakota (Sioux), Cheyenne, Kiowa—who had proved such a powerful impediment to westward expansion, but became admirable mainly through their suppression once that expansion was accomplished.

The United States cinema had portrayed whites mistreating noble savages since the days of D. W. Griffith, but in the 1950s such films became a minor genre, including, among others, *Devil's Doorway* (1950), *Broken Arrow* (1950), and *White Feather* (1955). Hollywood went so far as to make sympathetic biopics very loosely based upon the lives of Custer's chief opponents—*Sitting Bull* (1954) and *Crazy Horse* (1955). And even John Ford, the director most celebrated for his celebration of the United States cavalry and its heroic exploits against the Indian foe, first expressed doubt in *The Searchers* (1956) and then all but recanted in *Cheyenne Autumn* (1964).

Historical fiction kept pace with the cinema's portrayal of the long-suffering redman. For example, *The Dauntless and the Dreamers* and *The Fighting Cheyenne*, two 1960s novels dealing in part with Custer and the Little Big Horn from the Native American perspective, rendered their Indian heroes decidedly superior to their white foes.[27] In his forward to *The Fighting Cheyenne*, Will Henry asserted the myriad virtues of the tribe:

> The Cheyenne was in many ways the most admirable of Indians; indeed, of men. Kind to the old and the afflicted, gentle with the lost of mind, loyal to friend, devoted to all children, honoring the given word, punishing the broken vow, he was a man who did not understand the forked tongue of the white brother until far too late."[28]

In the years of the civil rights struggle, cultural relativism in an historical fiction that may have reached a fairly small audience is not particularly surprising, but it is startling to see a culturally relativist viewpoint represented in that compendium of middle-American knowledge, *The Reader's Digest*. In an article on the famous portraitist of the mid-nineteenth century plains Indians, George Catlin, the author approvingly quoted the artist's comparison between his own culture and that of his subjects:

> I love a people who have always made me welcome to the best they had, who were honest without laws, who have no jails and no poorhouse, who never fought a battle with the white men except on their own ground, and oh! how I love a people who don't live for the love of money.[29]

The novels and the *Digest's* article were part of the revival of interest in Native Americans, at least those safely in the past, that Robert Berkhofer tells us occurred in the late 1960s and early 1970s (and which many of us probably remember or even participated in):

> Real and imitation Indian jewelry festooned the arms and necks of White American men and women, while bedspreads, towels, and tablecloths decorated with supposed Indian motifs adorned their homes. Books by and about Indians made the best-seller lists, and Indian heroes appeared upon movie and television screens. Authentic and fake Indians emerged in mass-media advertisements to sell everything from breakfast cereals to ecology.[30]

Given dominant perceptions of historical "noble savages" and the potential profit in all things native American in the late 1960s, ABC's decision to air *Custer* (a program that inevitably cast Indians as villains opposite the series' hero rather than creating a series around an Indian hero) seems strange as does the network's relative insensitivity to Native American protests concerning the program.[31] But an examination of the dominant perceptions of contemporary rather than historical Native Americans makes ABC's decisions more understandable. Despite the prominence of the nineteenth-century plains Indians in film and television westerns, present-day Native Americans remained largely absent from these media during the postwar years.[32] Then, in the first part of the 1960s, articles in the print media tended to contrast African Americans' civil rights activism with Native Americans' regard for tradition and nonconfrontational attitude, as we have seen in the *New York Times* article quoted above. The advent of President Johnson's New Society caused journalists to pay greater attention to these "forgotten" Americans, article after article chronicling the poverty and disease-ridden conditions on the reservations.[33]

These exposés, while sympathetic, for the most part denied Native Americans any agency, portraying them simply as victims dependent upon the white man's good will for improvement of their misery-ridden existences. Indeed, "orientalization" occurred not only through a concentration on the past, as seen in film and television westerns and the journalists' deployment of nineteenth century stereotypes, but also through representing contemporary Native Americans as helpless and passive or, as Said says of the Arabs, "supine." Small wonder, then, that ABC executives felt no need to make the same concessions to the National Congress of American Indians that they had made earlier to the National Italian American League to Combat Defamation.

the *custer* series: textual analysis

While not overly sensitive to Native American protests, the program's producer, Frank Glicksman, seemed well aware of his central character's public relations problems, saying that Custer was a "much maligned man" and leading *Newsweek* to conclude that ABC planned to "spruce up his image with a sympathetic weekly series."[34] This sprucing-up made virtues of the historical character's supposed faults: while many contemporary texts, emulating Van de Water's revisionist biography, portrayed Custer as a reckless, selfish commander who needlessly led his men to their deaths at the Little Big Horn, the *Custer* series made its hero a long-haired rebel determined to pursue his own course and succeeding where his superiors would have failed, apparently in the hope that such a character would appeal to younger viewers.[35]

Each week the series' credit sequence reminded viewers of Custer's rebel status, a "voice-of-God" narrator authoritatively intoning: "At 24 he had been the youngest general in the Civil War. Within five years he had been reduced in rank and sent West to be forgotten. But he was not the kind of man to let the world forget. His name, George Armstrong Custer." The historical record offers a competing construction of these events: 1) After the Civil War, every officer holding a brevet (or temporary) field-appointed rank in the wartime army had been "demoted" to a rank consistent with the needs of the peacetime, regular army; and 2) Custer himself had requested a frontier posting in the hopes of advancing his career through achieving a reputation as an "Indian fighter." The premiere episode furthers the impression that Custer's demotion resulted from his own actions rather than army policy, as Custer tells his troops, "My name is George Armstrong Custer. Rank, Lt. Colonel, U.S. Cavalry, formerly brevet major general. Found guilty of dereliction of duty and suspended for one year. I was courtmartialed for being absent from my post without official leave." Once again this fictional representation simplifies and even revises historical events. As punishment for an unauthorized visit to his wife Elizabeth, who was suffering from an outbreak of cholera, as well as for numerous other infractions including summarily executing deserters, a courtmartial did suspend Custer from duty for a year but did not reduce him in rank. The program's reconstruction of these events, however, makes Custer a more acceptable action-adventure hero by fitting him to popular formulas. The omission of his wife from the series, as well as the introduction of a potential love interest in the premiere episode, provides both the absence of entanglement and the potential for romantic involvement typical for television heroes. Making the character a disgraced but potentially innocent man fighting to clear his name, like the heroes of the successful *Branded* or *Fugitive* series, enhances his outsider status and creates dramatic potential. *Variety*'s review of the premiere episode pointed out:

> The yarn effectively sketched Custer's character and straits as a
> sort of man-on-the-lam type (busted from general) out to re-
> establish his credentials. It's clear enough the producers intend
> for Custer's situation to springboard the bulk of the action.[36]

In 1960s "televisionland" where young cops, young doctors, and even young secret agents continually contested their elders' authority, Custer's relationship with his commanding officer further contributes to the outsider characterization. While the historical Custer had enjoyed sole command of the 7th Cavalry, the series places both Custer and the 7th under the direct command of General Alfred Terry, a crusty, irascible but ultimately understanding character in the mold of Dr. Kildare's Dr. Gillespie or Napoleon Solo's Mr. Waverly. In the premiere episode, Custer first meets Terry when he saves him and his cavalry column from an Indian ambush. Rather than thanking Custer, Terry gruffly orders him to be in his office first thing in the morning. At this meeting Terry sets up the narrative tension between the two characters: "For the record, Custer, I don't like you. You're too sure of yourself, too much your own man." Nonetheless, says Terry, he has supported Sheridan's campaign to give Custer another chance because he thinks that the younger man is a good soldier.

Custer is such a good soldier that professional behavior overrides all other considerations. At General Terry's dinner party, Captain Reno declares that after the discovery of gold there will not be troopers enough to keep prospectors out of the Black Hills (sacred to the Lakota). Terry agrees, saying that "the whiskey traders and the land speculators" will follow the miners. Custer says this will cause a major Indian attack but that "as professional soldiers, we best leave the question of morality to those whose job it is. Our job is to fight." The statement, which might well have issued from General William Westmoreland rather than General George Armstrong Custer, seems at odds with the program's effort to characterize its hero as a long-haired rebel, but does provide the necessary ambivalence to negotiate ideological contradictions and thus appeal to a mass audience.

Custer's statement further testifies to the strength of narrative formula: in the *Custer* program the 7th's job *is* to fight. It is also the job of their Indian foes, for the show's scriptwriters would quickly have run out of ideas had they not continually cast the Indians as the bad guys: of the series' seventeen episodes only two do not revolve entirely around the conflict between the red man and the white.[37] This narrative demand may provide another explanation for why ABC executives did not respond to protests against *Custer* by significantly altering the representation of Native Americans. Elliot Ness and his Untouchables can almost as creditably fight gangsters with Anglo names as with Italian names, but Custer and his 7th Cavalry have to fight Indians.

This narrative formula demanded abstract, conventionalized treatment of Native Americans, whom the *Custer* series most often represented simply as the nameless moving targets that had previously been featured in so many film and television Westerns. The first Indians seen in the premiere episode skulk in the bushes waiting to ambush General Terry's column, but Custer quickly defuses the threat, together with one other soldier charging the Indians from the rear, scattering them and breaking through to ride toward the cavalry column, their foes in vain pursuit. The next Indian scene sets up the episode's story: again, as in so many previous film and television Westerns, a renegade white man sells guns to the Indians. The nighttime setting, replete with eerie lighting from a blazing campfire and ominous "Indian" music, intensifies the sense of danger from these "savages," whom the white man tells to get money to pay for the guns. The program then shows a series of Indian assaults upon helpless whites. In one scene, Indians attack two miners, first shooting flaming arrows into their tent and then riding them down as they flee. As they surround one hapless miner, a low angle point of view shot from his perspective shows the Indians on horseback waving their tomahawks, the editing putting the viewer in the place of the terrified man as he awaits his death. In another scene, a band of whooping, yelling Indians circles a burning home as the camera singles out a fallen "Home Sweet Home" sign and a broken-open cash box, these signifiers of the white man's violated domestic and public spheres again positioning the viewer against the Indians. One certainly gets the impression that the program's writers and directors have watched many a John Ford film.

Narrative formula demanded that the Indians play the bad guys, but the period's "noble savage" imagery does emerge in the *Custer* episodes, which to some extent address the issue that has always been at the center of white/ Indian conflict—the expropriation of the latter's land. The program permits the Crazy Horse character to articulate the Native American critique of the white man's expansionist policies. In the first episode Crazy Horse asks the white gun runner what payment he requires. "What is it you want? Our land? Our women? What do we have left that the white man hasn't already taken from us?" In another episode, "War Lance and Saber," Custer and Crazy Horse forge a momentary alliance as they flee from their mutual enemy, the Blackfeet. In one scene a rattlesnake threatens to strike the helpless Custer, and Crazy Horse takes the opportunity to taunt his enemy. "There are others that claim this land, Yellowhair. Tell him about the white man's might. Tell [the snake] how you will conquer his land. Go on, Yellowhair, tell him about the white man's ways." Later, the two men come upon water dripping from a rock wall. Custer tastes the water and spits it out, telling Crazy Horse that it has arsenic in it. Crazy Horse drinks nonetheless, saying, "My people have learned to drink bitter water. The white man made it necessary."

Many other Custer texts and many other film and television Westerns acknowledge Indian land rights and the white man's injustice in similar fashion, presumably because these are no longer controversial issues in the second half of the twentieth century (except to Native Americans); but the *Custer* program also addresses a more contemporary and more contentious civil rights debate. In the episode "Suspicion," Captain Merino, the first Indian West Point graduate now serving with the 7th, is suspected of collaborating with the enemy. A young lieutenant newly arrived on the frontier asks Custer how Merino ever became an officer since "he seems foreign." Custer responds, "We live in a country made up of many different kinds of people. A man's looks, his speech, make no difference if he does his job well." In another episode entitled "Spirit Woman," Agnes Moorehead is rather improbably cast as a Lakota holy woman trying to arrange a peace between her people and the white men. In the final scene she assists Custer in burying the Indians who fought against the treaty. Custer moralizes, "Someday this will all be one country where men can live in peace together regardless of the color of their skin." The spirit woman responds, "That day will not be soon, Yellowhair, but will be." In such episodes, notwithstanding the reluctance of Native American organizations to ally themselves with the African American civil rights activists, the rhetoric of the civil rights movement characterizes white/Indian relations and forecasts not a multicultural but a melting-pot future.

While the *Custer* series acknowledges the white man's mistreatment of the Indian, and even makes obeisance to racial equality, the episodes remain relatively unmarked by the cultural relativism seen in many period texts ranging from historical novels to *Reader's Digest* articles. In the "War Lance and Sabre" episode in which Custer and Crazy Horse flee from the pursuing Blackfeet, Custer says he is hungry. Crazy Horse turns over a fallen tree, uncovers a mass of wriggling grubs, scoops them up, and eats them with relish. Then he offers some to Custer, who reacts with disgust. Crazy Horse points out that Custer is behaving irrationally. "White man eat raw oyster. Cook frogs but grow pale about eating worms. You have strange ways, Yellowhair." Custer tries his best, saying, "From your point of view I agree. On the other hand. . . ." He eats a grub and then spits it out as Crazy Horse laughs. While Crazy Horse relativizes the culinary habits of white civilization versus those of his own, viewers likely to react with visceral repulsion to the eating of insects (undoubtedly a majority) most probably remained unconvinced. Worse yet, the scene may in fact have reinforced conceptions of Native Americans as primitive savages.

For the most part representing Native American culture as clearly inferior to the white man's, the program poses the usual alternatives of assimilation or extermination to the Indian "problem." In the "Suspicion" episode in which the Indian officer is suspected of giving information to the enemy, Custer discusses the matter with his scout, California Joe, asking whether the army has given Merino a reason to betray his oath of loyalty to the United States.

> **Joe:** I don't think we had to give him no reason. I think he was born with one.
>
> **Custer:** Then blood's stronger than duty, honor, and friendship?
>
> **Joe:** I've always's said that blood's stronger than water and I reckon it's stronger than a uniform.
>
> **Custer:** I don't think so, because if that's true then there won't be an end to this fighting, this war or any other. A man can change, learn, and be something better.

Custer here articulates the assimilationist policy that led to the establishment of Indian boarding schools that took children away from the reservations and their parents, cut their hair, and punished them for speaking their native language, and led to the banning of dances and other religious rituals among those remaining on the reservations. Later Merino complains that the white man thinks of the Indian as "not quite human." Custer responds, "Remember one thing. It's men like you who can make the word Indian mean something more than a creature not quite human." In other words, only if an Indian becomes a white man, even to the extent of taking up arms against his own people, can he become a human being.

And if assimilation fails, there is always the threat of extermination. The "War Lance and Sabre" episode includes a fascinating conversation between Custer and Crazy Horse that seemingly attempts to resolve the ideological contradiction resulting between the demands of the narrative formula and the period's emerging valorization of Native American culture. Crazy Horse begins by asserting the right of his people to maintain their ancient ways. "[The white men] try to take from us everything that we have known. They try to make us over in the image of themselves. Is your way of life so fine, so great that no other should exist?" Custer mounts a social Darwinist argument:

> If I were a philosopher I might have an answer for you but I haven't. But this I do know. Our country will be great someday, but only if it has a chance to grow. Time always brings changes. No people can stand still. Without progress they die as many ancient civilizations have died before us.... The Arikara, Crow, Cree, even the mighty Cheyenne, bow to the great force of the Sioux nation and now it's the turn of the Sioux to feel the might of a stronger people and if they chose to resist through means of war they will be destroyed.

Of course, the Sioux's capitulation, at least within the diegetic world of the *Custer* series, would have posed a serious problem for the scriptwriters.

conclusion

Let us now return to the two central questions of this essay: 1) Why, in 1967, when other popular culture texts exhibited strong sympathy for the "noble savage" and contempt for Custer, did 20th Century-Fox produce and ABC Television air the *Custer* series and, 2) Why did the series fail with the television audience?

Perhaps 20th Century-Fox and ABC Television were gambling that the viewing public would simply embrace yet another Western, since in the 1960s many shows in the genre succeeded in prime time television. In the fall of 1967, seven new westerns, in addition to *Custer*, and five continuing westerns, the highly popular *Gunsmoke* and *Bonanza* among them, began the new television season. It was not, given the circumstances, entirely unreasonable for ABC executives to hope that *Custer* might garner good ratings from a viewing public already favorably inclined toward the "horse opera." Even the *Variety* reviewer believed the program might be a hit if it only toned down the violence, which had become an issue of public debate as early as *The Untouchables*. "If it gives the brush to its more primitive nature, Custer stands to pick up a scalp or two for ABC this campaign."[38]

The hope of a successful new Western series would have provided strong incentives for 20th-Century Fox and ABC to air the program, while Native American protestors were not yet well positioned to provide strong disincentives. Unlike Italian Americans or African Americans, Native Americans had neither prominently placed politicians to plead their cause with television producers nor high-profile organizations capable of garnering media publicity. The "red power" movement had just begun: the American Indian Movement was not founded until 1968 and did not draw national attention until the early 1970s with its much publicized takeover of the Washington, D.C. headquarters of the Bureau of Indian Affairs and the subsequent siege at Wounded Knee, South Dakota. And, as we have seen, much media coverage of contemporary Native Americans prior to 1967 stressed their passivity and dependence upon the white man's charity. Hence, *Custer*'s producers may have felt that they had little to fear from Native Americans in terms of negative publicity, boycotts of sponsors' products or challenges to affiliates' licenses.

The answer to our second question concerning the series' cancellation must remain even more speculative than the above, dealing as it does with the vagaries of the mass audience's preferences. *The New York Times*' reviewer Jack Gould disagreed with his colleague at *Variety* concerning the *Custer* pilot's merits, his assessment of the program's deficiencies presciently speaking for the larger audience:

> The National Congress of American Indians demanded in advance equal time to reply to the American Broadcasting Company's series "Custer."... The plea was misguided; the white man and the red man are entitled to an equal rebate for wasted electricity in turning on the receiver.... The Indians may find their organized protest will be superfluous; probably they can put their faith in A.C. Nielsen, Inc., when the research company announces its ratings of the season's new shows.[39]

Although the *Custer* series constituted part of a successful (if waning) television genre, it remained utterly formulaic, conforming George Armstrong Custer to the action-adventure hero mold and adopting other standard narrative tropes such as the tension between the rebellious young protagonist and his older, more cautious superior. Perhaps this adherence to formula was made in an attempt to get the audience simply to enjoy another prime-time western rather than relating the program directly to the historical Custer, of whose bad reputation the series' producers seem to have been cognizant. The series may have failed precisely because it was so formulaic as to be "bad television," offering its audience nothing innovative enough to sustain their attention.

It may also have offended an audience no longer accustomed to the representation of Indians as "savage savages," suitable only for target practice, or to the representation of George Armstrong Custer as a dashing and gallant hero. As journalist Hal Humphrey argued, "General Custer might have gone over as a hero 20 or 30 years ago, but too many historians began to expose him as bull-headed, arrogant, and ignorant. When that word got around, the public scratched him off its list."[40]

More recent television history does provide some additional confirmation of the hypothesis that successful westerns must to some extent accord with a period's dominant perceptions. In May, 1995 both the CBS series *Dr. Quinn, Medicine Woman* and the United Paramount Network series *Legend* featured "guest appearances" by George Armstrong Custer. *Dr. Quinn's* Custer believed that "the only good Indian is a dead Indian" and massacred helpless women and children. *Legend's* much more sympathetic Custer exposed corrupt officials profiteering from army supplies. *Dr. Quinn* currently ranks among the highest rated television shows, while *Legend* will not appear in UPN's fall line-up. Although factors other than its relatively favorable portrayal of George Armstrong Custer undoubtedly contributed to *Legend's* cancellation, television producers contemplating resurrecting this particular historical character might take heed.

notes

I would like to thank Laura Jenkins of 20th Century-Fox Television for facilitating my access to episodes of the *Custer* series; Janet Kennelly of the National Museum of Natural History; the Smithsonian Institution, for sending me copies of materials in the National Congress of American Indians collection; my research assistants, Mika Emori and Andrea MacDonald, for their invaluable help; the University of Pennsylvania Research Foundation for financial support; and this volume's editors, Lynn Spigel and Michael Curtin, for their perceptive and useful suggestions.

1. *The Legend of Custer*, no. 1, 1968, Dell, Copyright 20th Century-Fox Television, 1967.
2. P.M. Clepper, "He's Our George," *TV Guide* (23 September 1967): 33.

3. Clepper, 34.

4. Anne Chamberlain, "Bad Day Ahead For The Army's Greatest Loser," *Saturday Evening Post* (27 August 1966): 7073.

5. See, for example, my discussion of Custer's heroic image in silent films in "'The Revenge of Rain-in-the-Face'? or, Custers and Indians on the Silent Screen," in Daniel Bernardi, ed., *The Birth of Whiteness: Race and the Emergence of United States Cinema* (New Brunswick, NJ: Rutgers University Press, 1996).

6. Despite initial controversy immediately after the Little Big Horn battle, Custer's wife Elizabeth, together with dime novel author Frederick Whittaker, succeeded in constructing an image of the dead cavalryman as a shining sacrifice on the altar of his country's manifest destiny. Frederic F. Van De Water's revisionist biography, *Glory Hunter*, appeared in 1934, a year after Elizabeth Custer's death. Paul Andrew Hutton argues that Van de Water's "glory hunter interpretation became the standard portrayal of Custer," influencing such novels as Harry Sinclair Drago's *Montana Road* (1935), Ernest Haycox's *Bugles in the Afternoon* (1944), Will Henry's *No Survivors* (1950), Clay Fisher's *Yellow Hair* (1953), and Frank Gruber's *Bugles West* (1954), films such as *Fort Apache* (1948), *Sitting Bull* (1954), *Tonka* (1958), *The Great Sioux Massacre* (1965), and *Custer of the West* (1968), as well as the accounts of academic and popular historians (Paul Andrew Hutton, "Introduction" in Frederic F. Van De Water, *Glory-Hunter: A Life of General Custer* (Lincoln: University of Nebraska Press, 1988, first published 1934), 11–12.

7. John Belindo, Director, Washington Office, Memorandum to the Record, Aug. 30, 1967, Records of the National Congress of the American Indians, Chronological Correspondence, National Museum of Natural History, Smithsonian Institution (hereafter NCAI Records).

8. From *New York Times*, "Italians to Protest," 18 January 1961, 67; "'Untouchables' Yields," 2 February 1961, 59; "Nixon Terms TV Infant in Politics," 10 March 1961, 55; "Against 'Untouchables'," 13 March 1961, 59; "2 Bouts Tonight," 15 March 1961, 29; "TV Show Agrees on Italian Names," 18 March 1961, 47; Jack Gould, "Disturbing Pact," 26 March 1961, 17.

9. For more on the WLBT case, see Fred W. Friendly, *The Good Guys, The Bad Guys and the First Amendment: Fair Speech vs. Fairness in Broadcasting* (New York: Vintage, 1975), Kathryn C. Montgomery, *Target: Prime Time—Advocacy Groups and the Struggle over Entertainment Television* (New York: Oxford, 1989) and Steven Douglas Classen, "Standing on Unstable Grounds: A Reexamination of the WLBT-TV Case," *Critical Studies in Mass Communication* 11 (1994):73–91.

10. Brian W. Dippie, *The Vanishing American: White Attitudes and U.S. Indian Policy* (Lawrence: University Press of Kansas, 1982), 340.

11. Vine Deloria Jr. and Clifford Lytle, *The Nations Within: The Past and Future of American Indian Sovereignty* (New York: Pantheon, 1984), 206.

12. "US Indians Seek to Remain Apart," *New York Times,* 15 September 1963, 74.

13. Robert C. Day, "The Emergence of Activism as a Social Movement," in Howard M. Bahr, Bruce A. Chadwick and Robert C. Day, *Native Americans Today: Sociological Perspectives* (New York: Harper and Row, 1972), 507.

14. Hamilton Bims, "Indian Uprising For Civil Rights," *Ebony*, February 1967, 64.

15. Bims, 65.

16. Memorandum to the Record From John Belindo, Director, Washington Office, 30 August 1967, NCAI Records. As far as I have been able to ascertain, no such program was produced. But *The New York Times* reported that the NCAI had demanded reply time even in advance of the series' premiere (Jack Gould, "TV: A Western Drama," 7 September 1967, 90).

17. John Belindo, Director, Washington Office, Memoranda to the Record, September 6 and September 7, 1967, NCAI Records.

18. Letter from John Belindo to John Dunwoodie, September 21, 1967, NCAI Records.

19. Hal Humphrey, "'Custer' Rating is as Bad as at the Little Big Horn; Apparently

Even His Descendants Aren't Watching," *The Courier-Journal & Times* (Louisville, KY), 15 October 1967 (*Custer* clipping file, New York Public Library for the Performing Arts, New York, NY hereafter NYPLPA).

20. "Indians Take Stand Vs. 'Custer'", *Daily Variety* (28 August 1967) (NYPLPA).

21. "Chippewas Join With Old Enemy Sioux on Kill-'Custer' Trail," *Variety* (11 September 1967) (NYPLPA).

22. Ralph E. Friars and Natasha A. Friars, *The Only Good Indian... The Hollywood Gospel* (New York: Drama Book Specialists Publishers, 1972), 274–75.

23. "Custer at Bay Again," *Newsweek* (7 August 1967): 51; Charles Hillinger, "Indian Chieftain Still on Custer Warpath," *Los Angeles Times*, (22 July 1967) (NYPLPA).

24. Editorial in the *Pittsburgh Post-Gazette* (6 August 1967): 275, quoted in Friars.

25. Edward W. Said, *Orientalism* (New York: Vintage, 1979).

26. In this regard, it is interesting to note that things might have been different a mere decade later. The United States Commission on Civil Rights reported that: "ABC has since noted that [*Custer*] was broadcast in an era when standards were considerably different than they are today. Last year, for example, ABC broadcast 'I Will Fight No More Forever,' a highly acclaimed saga about Chief Joseph and the Nez Pierce Indians told primarily from the Indians' point of view" (Telephone interview with Richard P. Gitter, Director, East Coast Dept. of Broadcast Standards and Practices, ABC, 10 February 1977; *Window Dressing on the Set: Women and Minorities in Television*, A Report of the United States Commission on Civil Rights, August 1977 (Washington, D.C.: US Govt. Printing Office), 7, ft. 2028.

27. Frederick and Frank Goshe, *The Dauntless and the Dreamers: A Historical Novel* (New York: Thomas Yoseloff, 1963) and Will Henry, *The Last Warpath: The Saga of the Fighting Cheyenne* (New York: Random House, 1966).

28. Henry, Forward, n.p.

29. Louise Redfield Peattie, "He Caught the Splendor of the First Americans," *Reader's Digest* (October 1964): 260.

30. Robert F. Berkhofer, Jr., *The White Man's Indian: Images of the American Indian From Columbus to the Present* (New York: Alfred A. Knopf, 1978), xiii.

31. In fact, 20th Century-Fox, responsible for *Custer*, also produced the television series *Broken Arrow*, based on the film of the same name, whose Cochise, Michael Ansara, went on to play a Harvard-educated Indian U.S marshall in the 1959 series *Law of the Plainsman*. See J. Fred MacDonald, *Who Shot the Sheriff? The Rise and Fall of the Television Western* (New York: Praeger, 1987) 49, 60. Of course, both these characters, as well as perhaps the most famous of television Indians, *The Lone Ranger's* Tonto, were "good" Indians, firmly on the side of the white man and the white man's "civilization."

32. A documentary broadcast by NBC in November, 1958, *The American Stranger*, was the first television program to represent the lives of present-day Native Americans, focusing on the poverty occurring as a result of the government's policy of "termination," that is, cutting reservation Indians off from the government aid previously assured them by treaties. Pamela Wilson, a doctoral candidate in the Department of Communication Arts at the University of Wisconsin, Madison, is writing a dissertation on the program's production and reception.

33. See, for example, "The American Indian Today: Out in the Cold?", *Senior Scholastic* (17 February 1967): 3–6+; "Equal Rights for This American Too," *Christian Century* (5 April 1967): 49, Calvin Kentfield, "Dispatch from Wounded Knee," *New York Times Magazine* (15 October 1967): 29; and James Ridgeway, "More Lost Indians: A Trip to the Sioux Country," *New Republic* (11 December 1965): n.p.

34. "Custer at Bay Again," 51.

35. Based upon the program guide faxed to me by Laura Jenkins of 20th Century-Fox Television's Legal Department, I chose to look at the five episodes that seemed potentially most interesting in terms of the representation of Native Americans: "Sabers in the Sun" (aired 6 September 1967); "War Lance and Saber"

(aired 11 October 1967); "Suspicion" (aired 18 October 1967); "Desperate Mission," (aired 8 November 1967); and "Spirit Woman" (aired 13 December 1967).

36. Pit, *Variety* (13 September 1967): n.p.
37. These figures are based on 20th Century-Fox Television's program guide.
38. Pit, n.p.
39. Gould.
40. Humphrey, n.p.

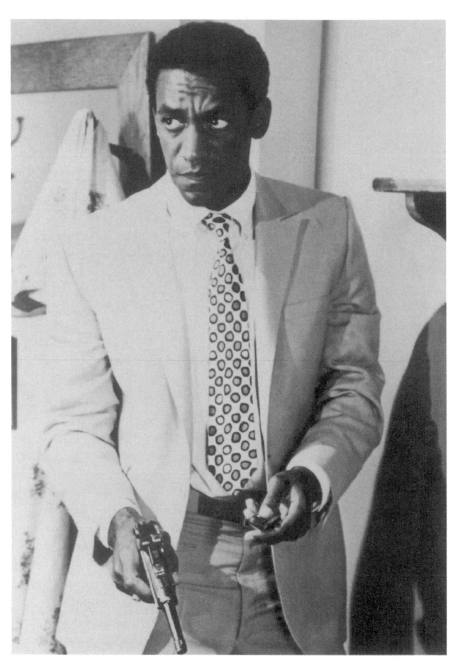

Bill Cosby in *I Spy*

remembering

civil rights

television, memory,

and the 1960s

herman gray

Glance backward for a moment to the decades of the modern civil rights era. Then as now, media—especially television—operated as an important arena of cultural struggle. Television was at once the object of criticism by the leaders of the civil rights and black power movements and yet, because of television many of the aims and struggles of those movements became widely known. For example, the Southern Christian Leadership Council and the Student Nonviolent Coordinating Committee used the media—mainly television news—as an important resource to mobilize moral and financial support for their causes and to focus national attention on various protest campaigns. And even though organizations like the Black Panther Party and the Nation of Islam received largely negative coverage, these organizations nevertheless tried to use press and media coverage to illustrate the complex strategies and machinations at work to contain and neutralize their efforts.

On the other hand, as Richard Lentz points out in his study of weekly news magazine coverage of the civil rights movement, news organizations themselves had clear moral commitments, political positions, and financial stakes in how they constructed their stories.[1] Press demonization, containment, and marginalization of the Black Panther Party, the Black Power Movement, The Nation of Islam, Malcolm X, and Angela Davis are the obvious examples. Nevertheless, the news media were strategic in generating moral outrage and public commitment to the causes of black protesters in the South and, in the case of more radical organizations and causes, for heightening contradictions of race and class in the United States. Almost in spite of themselves, then, the media, especially television, played a crucial role in representing, and in some instances constructing, black subjects who would eventually inhabit the modern American popular imagination.[2] Black people portrayed in news coverage of the civil rights and black power movements appeared either as decent but aggrieved blacks who simply wanted to become a part of the American dream, or as threats to the very notion of citizenship and nation.

As for fictional television, even the most cursory examination of commercial network programming in the 1950s and 1960s reveals the relative absence of blacks, never mind attention to civil rights issues. As illustrated by *Julia*, *Room 222*, *The Bill Cosby Show*, *The Leslie Uggams Show*, and *The Flip Wilson Show*, the imaginary world presented by fictional television in the middle decades of the twentieth century was one of black invisibility structured by the logic of color blindness and driven by the discourse of assimilation.[3]

Even so, as Marlon Riggs's critically acclaimed documentary *Color Adjustment* makes clear, there were enormous pressures that the social transformations in the 1950s and 1960s brought to bear on television itself, especially fictional television.[4] In the areas of fiction and entertainment this impact was not directly felt or at least expressed in television representations of blacks until well into the 1970s (beginning in 1972) with the explosion of Norman Lear-influenced shows about social relevance and black urban life. However small, the civil rights and black power movements indirectly helped to reconfigure television and in the process, created limited but significant "adjustments" that eventually resulted in the proliferation of black representations on television in the mid 1970s and again in the late 1980s.

350

representations of the past

For an entire generation now, feature films, fictional television, documentaries, and popular representations of blacks in contemporary visual culture (including advertising and music television) are the chief means by which memory, history, and experience of the past become part of the common sense understanding in the present. A wide range of examples come to mind including (but not limited to): television series like *I'll Fly Away* and *In the Heat of the Night*; documentary films and television series such as *Berkeley in the Sixties, Freedom on My Mind, Eyes on the Prize*; feature length motion pictures like *X, Do the Right Thing, Mississippi Burning,* and *Boyz n'the Hood*; a host of music videos by Arrested Development, Public Enemy, and Boogie Down Productions, among others; the annual display of documentary films and news footage about Martin Luther King (notably his "I Have a Dream" speech); and finally, in what can only be termed the commercialization and marketing of the 1960s, an endless parade of consumer goods emblazoned with icons and images of Malcolm X, Martin Luther King, the Black Panther Party, and Angela Davis.

Despite their differences, contemporary media representations of black life and struggle in the 1950s and 1960s circulate and signify within a contemporary media environment driven by profit and organized by aesthetic conventions that insist on spectacle, "heroes," immediacy, and drama (rather than different narrative styles and modes of representation which depend on interruption, repetition, and allegory). Clearly, media representations of significant personalities, organizations, movements, and events in the 1950s and 1960s help to reconstruct those events as history. But what, we might ask, are the contemporary political and cultural hopes and longings at work in these wide ranging and complex representations of the recent past? For example, in the scene from *Boyz n' the Hood* (set in a rapidly changing and racially diverse Los Angeles) where Lawrence Fishburne's character Furious Styles comments on the loss of economic control of black neighborhoods by blacks, perhaps the desire is for a return to an economic project of black capitalism. Spike Lee's *X* might well be read as a plea for a politics that recuperates many of the central ideas of Malcolm X. And appearing as it did in the midst of heightened racial antagonism of the late 1980s, a television series like *I'll Fly Away* (a dramatic story about a black woman who works as a domestic for a white widower in the South of the 1950s) may well be driven by the desire to return to a historic period of interracial etiquette of the deep South of the 1950s by showing the dignity of black women domestics and the decency of liberal Southerners who employed them.[5]

Whether or not one agrees with these readings, the social desires at work in these and other representations of the 1960s, and what they mean to us *now*, are serious questions that beg for our attention. Given television's economic imperative, which results in the drive to transform the recent past into televised "history" of the moment, these representations increasingly constitute the major point of access to that past for an entire generation of young people. What, then, are the social and cultural implications of having our collective and individual memory of the recent past meet at sites of electronic mediation like film, television, and advertising? What does it mean for a sense of history to have such events transformed into television spectacles, advertising hooks and, in the not too distant future, theme parks?[6]

a televisual moment

In a memorable closing scene in an episode of *The Cosby Show*, the members of the Huxtable family are assembled in their comfortable living room, their attention fixed on the television set. Although the television image is not visible to the viewing audience, it is clearly discernible by way of the audio track. On the family television (both the Huxtable's and ours) is the Reverend Dr. Martin Luther King, Jr. delivering his historic "I Have a Dream" speech at the 1963 March on Washington. The members of the Huxtable family look and listen, collectively relishing the moment. The adults instruct the children on the significance of the event and in the process recount (for their children and the viewing audience) their own experiences and memories of this momentous occasion. Part of the signifying work that this amazing scene performs is to reaffirm the importance and success of the civil rights movement, especially what it means for a new generation. Like so many of us, the Huxtables—and the real life Cosbys—are the beneficiaries of hard won victories of the civil rights and black power movements.

If this is indeed a rare and moving television moment, for me it is also a curious one. It is a moment filled with political, historical, and social implications about the past and present condition of life for blacks in modern America. For one brief instant the past and the present are collapsed into the same electronic time and space; recognition, celebration, and possibility all condensed into this one television scene.

So, by way of America's surrogate family of the 1980s, we watched television's transformation and translation of this significant social phenomena into collective electronic memory—a televisual moment. But what are the implications, lessons even, of this translation, this transformation of black life and struggle into a televisual moment? From the vantage point of the 1990s (especially the promises realized and unrealized from the civil rights movement), how are we to understand such representations of black life and struggle from our recent racial past? And, following Henry Hampton and Richard Lentz's cautions about the implicit biases of press and television which are embedded in editorial decisions, camera angles, reportorial perspective, and editing, what safeguards can we count on to insure that television will tell our stories from the multicultural and diverse perspectives of what George Lipsitz calls the people's history?[7]

I want to propose that one way of understanding this important scene from *The Cosby Show* is to regard it as exemplary, even emblematic, of the way that television operates as a conduit, a transit point for organizing, representing, and transmitting public knowledge.[8] And since television's own signifying practices increasingly demand that the past and the present, the real and the fictional, progressive and reactionary, be organized according to the same storytelling conventions, I want to ponder just how we come to encounter, remember, construct, represent, and pass on knowledge/memory of key and historic events such as the civil rights movements. I want to argue that contemporary television is constantly engaged in a kind of recuperative work, a kind of retrospective production of raced and gendered subjects who fit the requirements of contemporary circumstance. I believe that television accomplishes this production discursively by reading history backward.

the civil rights subject

Rather than searching for black subjects in television solely by way of an inventory of original programming from the 1960s, I want to pursue this argument by examining contemporary television's representation of the past by interrogating its reconstruction and deployment of a particular kind of black subject—i.e., the civil rights subject, the contemporary black figure to whom television turns again and again to rewrite and readjust the dominant cultural story of black presence in post–World War II America. In this familiar narrative of black presence, America sometimes appears as a beacon of racial enlightenment and tolerance—e.g., annual celebrations of the MLK Holiday; at other times America appears besieged by "excessive balkanization" and identity-based demands on its limited resources—e.g., immigration, affirmative action, welfare, and crime.

The civil rights subject produced in television (as a discourse) and by television (as an industrial apparatus) is an especially interesting and, it seems to me necessary, cultural trope. By civil rights subject, I mean representations of those black, largely middle-class benefactors who gained the most visibility as well as material and status rewards from the struggles and opportunities generated by the civil rights movement. This cultural figure embodies complex codes of behavior and propriety that make it an exemplar of citizenship and responsibility—success, mobility, hard work, sacrifice, individualism. In dominant media presentations, this figure of the model black citizen is often juxtaposed against poor and disenfranchised members of the black community, where it works to reinforce and reaffirm the openness and equality of contemporary American society.

Given the persistent and growing social inequities, the particularly vexed discourses of race and diversity in America (multiculturalism, affirmative action, and immigration), and in light of the contemporary cultural struggles over sexuality, gender, class, and color casting within the black communities, this figure of the contemporary product of the civil rights movement is necessary because it catalyzes and crystallizes the cultural and political terms of these increasingly difficult and troubling issues. The civil rights subject, which is the representation found in many post-*Cosby Show* television representations, works culturally to construct, frame, and advance shifting views and positions on questions of race in America.[9]

Paradoxically, it is this very civil rights subject (embodied by the television Huxtables) that so many contemporary black self representations in film, music television, and popular music have rejected or at the very least questioned.[10] The salience of this civil rights subject and television's own role in the production, legitimation, and circulation of that subject as a role model citizen is especially inspiring for some and troubling for others.

the failure of civil rights discourse

Return for a moment to the question of media representations of the 1960s—notably the civil rights and black power movements—and, for our present moment, the role of television in the representation of this period. Within the discourse of black cultural politics much of the talk, criticism, and pondering—about the end of the innocent black subject; about the need for a post-civil rights discourse; about the emergence of new black subjects (in representation); and about the new cultural politics of difference—concerns political black subjects produced in the 1960s. This pondering has resulted in a number of productive insights: Stuart Hall's insistence that we have reached the end of the innocent and universal black subject; Angela Davis's cautions about the risks of overlooking gender and sexual politics in the discourse of nationalism, especially in its cultural appropriation by urban black youth; Paul Gilroy's critique of the continuing and uncritical political investments in the trope of family constructed by contemporary nationalism; Kobena Mercer's reflections about the political and cultural significance as well as limitations of 1968 in Europe and the United States; and Manthia Diawara's search for different subjects and new ways of thinking through political possibilities and alliances in the street.[11]

Given the post-Fordist condition of global capital and the emergence of rapidly evolving communication technologies, subaltern social formations and traveling labor forces have all exacerbated the crisis of the modern nation-state. And, of course, in the United States the modern civil rights subject is very much a product of the modern state. Black subjects were—in

354

mainstream media representations anyway—tethered to masculine and religious definitions of black personhood and community which formed the basis for a politics that accepted liberal notions of individual responsibility, moral restraint, and an expanded role of the state in the redress of social inequality. This view of self, family, and nation helped to structure the goals and aspirations of the civil rights movement and was, of course, propelled by the mass-based social participation of working-class women, children, and men. Today this discourse remains the dominant one that organizes our thinking and political practice with respect to the urgent issues—economic inequality, sexism, violence, drugs, and crime—facing hundreds of black communities across America. Yet for all the social gains, politically and culturally the discourse of civil rights—with its investment in the goal of public accommodations and desegregation, its desire for individual equality before the law, and its commitment to colorblindness—still remains hotly contested and troubled to this very day. It remains troubled largely because this discourse, perhaps now more than ever, fails to speak to the persistent conditions of poverty, institutional racism, structural inequality, and the loss of trust in the public sphere for large numbers of the poor and disenfranchised. Dominant institutions and instruments of justice and equality simply do not speak to—or for—large segments of poor and black communities.

Structured by the signifying practices and commercial imperatives of contemporary television, the black subject produced by this powerful social discourse continues to elicit identification, and, within the terms of contemporary debates about race, some public support. In the 1960s, the major struggles for social justice and equality by black radical and reform movements for social change made for compelling television because they heightened drama and focused conflict. Good and evil were easily translated into clearly discernible television stories and characters—Martin Luther King vs. Bull Connor; Freedom Riders vs. white racists; Black Panther Party vs. the FBI. So too in our present. In the Huxtable family—as well as most other post-*Cosby* black television characters—we have the perfect realization and embodiment of the aims and goals of the reform wing of these movements—black characters who are usually set in the private world of the domestic sphere and firmly anchored by a commitment to family, upward social mobility, and individual responsibility.

counter-memory vs. nostalgia

I think it is worth pondering these issues in order to recognize, separate, and where possible, forestall retreats into the kind of nostalgia that constantly works discursively to reorganize and reframe this period, to reconstruct history retrospectively. This recourse to nostalgia is a very powerful seduction, for it signals a retreat into the limited and limiting conceptions of citizen subjects based on nineteenth-century ideas of race and nation.[12] Hence my argument that contemporary television is very much engaged in a kind of recuperative work, a kind of retrospective production of black subjects whose cultural labors—for liberals and conservatives alike—is the social and cultural revitalization of a high moment of American power. There is, in other words, a very complex relationship here between blackness, the racialized American nation and cultural struggles over the meaning and place of the 1960s. Within the American discourse of race, the civil rights subject performs important cultural work since it helps construct the mythic terms through which many Americans can believe that our nation has now transcendended racism. Nostalgia also works to displace and contain the most radical impulses and expressions produced in the 1960s, transforming such challenges into icons, marketing strategies, and lifestyle choices.

This kind of cultural containment through nostalgia is evident, for instance, in advertising campaigns and fashion layouts that use the defiant image of Angela Davis for the thematic focus of retro 1970s fashion (as *Vibe* did a few issues ago, or as *Details* did with Malcolm X in 1993). In television this civil rights subject is framed by celebration (*The Cosby Show*), nostalgia (*I'll Fly Away*), irreverence (*In Living Color*), and historical recuperation/correction (*Eyes on the Prize*).[13]

With its commercial imperatives and signifying practices, television levels and conflates what are often conflicted and distinct takes on our collective past, transforming them into digestible and manageable media events— media versions of history. With the more aggressive aim of constructing diverse representations and more critical interrogations of the past, how do we distinguish politically between these various impulses and the cultural work they perform? How do we distinguish, that is, between media events such as television spectacles and the lived experiences, memories and shared history derived from participation in, and relationships to, the movement as a repository of knowledge about that movement? In other words, it is entirely possible that our collective unwillingness and inability to think outside of this powerful cultural discourse of the civil rights subject is connected to, among other things, television's transformation and commercialization of the past.

These are very complex matters, since not all of the representations, memories, and experience of the 1960s and the civil rights past are so thoroughly mediated by this form of historical reconstruction and representation. My aim is not to belittle some of the first-rate films, television programs, and documentaries that critically construct and represent more inclusive and

356

diverse records of a collective past; rather, I want to situate all of these representations within the context of the increased role of the media in the production and circulation of knowledge and memory about the past. More importantly, since I want to push for a politics of media and culture that helps us to critically read television's representation of the past, I want most of all to avoid uncritical celebrations that treat all representations and interventions—progressive (*Eyes on the Prize*), reactionary (*Mississippi Burning*), nostalgic (*I'll Fly Away*)—as simple equivalents. Politically and culturally, they are not.

I understand these seemingly similar, but vastly different, representations as part of the struggle for the meanings of blackness, for notions of a collective past, and ultimately for visions of a collective democratic future. The meanings, resonances, and attachments activated by these representations, whatever their political possibilities, are uneven, unstable, and therefore available for different forms and points of social and cultural articulation. The critical challenge is to call attention to what it means for all of these representations to operate and circulate within the discursive field of commercial media in general and television in particular. No doubt media representations of the past help construct, shape, and organize our contemporary political desires. Hence, we should constantly work to disarticulate and where possible rearticulate these images so that we might more productively engage the active places of countermemory, opposition, and democratic possibility rather than invest uncritically in nostalgia and the limiting and lingering effects of racism and nationalism that continually carry us into the past disguised as the future.

notes

1. Richard Lentz. *Symbols, The News magazines, and Martin Luther King.* (Baton Rouge: Louisiana State University Press, 1990)
2. For discussions of the role of media and popular culture in constructing public representations of blacks see: Clyde Taylor, "The Rebirth of the Aesthetic in Cinema" *Wide Angle* 13 (3–4): 12–30; Mel Watkins *On the Real Side* (New York: Simon and Schuster, 1994); and Michael Winston "Racial Consciousness and the Evolution of Mass Communication in the United States" *Daedalus* 111 (1982): 171–82.
3. Shows with some explicit attention to the social concerns of blacks like *Eastside/Westside* and *The Outcasts* ran early in the decade and experienced very short runs at that.
4. Marlon Riggs, *Color Adjustment* (San Francisco: California Newsreel, 1991).
5. See Robin D. G. Kelley, "Contested Terrain: Resistance on Public Transportation," 55–77 and "Birmingham's Untouchables: The Black Poor in the Age of Civil Rights," 77–103 in his *Race Rebels: Culture, Politics, and the Black Working Class* (New York: The Free Press) 1994. Mary Helen Washington, "Text as Counter-Memory: Resistance to the Reconstruction of the Civil Rights Movement in 'I'll Fly Away'" (unpublished manuscript, April 1995)
6. See John E. O'Connor, ed., *American History, American Television: Interpreting the Video Past* (New York: Frederick Ungar, 1983).

7. Henry Hampton, "The Camera Lens as Two-Edged Sword," *New York Times* (15 January 1995): H29; Richard Lentz, *Symbols, The News Magazines and Martin Luther King* (Baton Rouge: Louisiana State University Press, 1990); George Lipsitz, *Time Passages: Collective Memory and American Popular Culture.* (Minneapolis: University of Minnesota Press, 1990).

8. I am especially interested in the encounter of young people by way of television with our national past. I deliberately single out young people here because, as the scene from *The Cosby Show* suggests, for them television is increasingly and predominately the key point of access, translation, and interaction with the past.

9. See Herman Gray, *Watching Race: Television and the Struggle for Blackness* (Minneapolis: University of Minnesota Press, 1995).

10. I have in mind here a very specific set of tensions, conflicts, and ambiguities in black cultural and racial politics within black communities with respect to class alliances and political strategies.

11. Stuart Hall, "What Is This 'Black' in Black Popular Culture?" 21–37: Angela Davis, "Black Nationalism: The Sixties and the Nineties," 317–25; Paul Gilroy, "Its a Family Affair," 303–17 all in Gina Dent (ed.) *Black Popular Culture.* (Seattle: Bay Press, 1992); Kobena Mercer, "'1968': Periodizing Postmodern Politics and Identity" in Lawrence Grossberg, Cary Nelson and Paula A. Treichler (eds.), *Cultural Studies* (New York: Routledge, 1992), 424–50; Manthia Diawara, "Homeboy Cosmopolitans," Paper Presented at the Conference on African American Youth (African American Studies Department, University of Pennsylvania, March 1994).

12. Here I refer to nineteenth-century notions of race as biologically and genetically based distinctions, rather than social and cultural constructions and to conceptions of nation as natural (and racialized) units and expressions of collective will rather than political units generated as a product of violent historical encounters, conquests, and struggles over power.

13. Using images of affluent whites fox hunting, playing polo, and lounging, Ralph Lauren's print ad campaigns for clothing, interior decorations, and furnishings do similar kinds of cultural work with respect to the relationships between whiteness, gender, nation, and class.

contributors

Mark Alvey works as an administrative assistant at The Field Museum in Chicago. He recently completed his doctoral dissertation entitled "Series Drama and the 'Semi-Anthology': Sixties Television in Transition" at the University of Texas-Austin.

William Boddy is a professor in the Department of Speech at Baruch college and in the Certificate Program in Film Studies at the Graduate Center of the City University of New York. He is the author of *Fifties Television: The Industry and Its Critics.*

Aniko Bodroghkozy received her doctorate from the University of Wisconsin-Madison department of Communication Studies and has taught at Concordia University in Montreal. She is currently working on a book titled, *Groove Tube: Entertainment Television in the 1960s and the Youth Rebellion.*

Steven Classen teaches in the Communication Studies Department at California State University, San Bernardino. He has recently completed his award-winning dissertation, "Broadcast Law and Segregation," and has published in *Critical Studies in Mass Communication*.

Michael Curtin teaches in the Department of Telecommunications and is director of the Cultural Studies program at Indiana University. He is the author of *Redeeming the Wasteland: Television Documentary and Cold War Politics* and is co-editor of *Making and Selling Culture*.

Julie D'Acci teaches in the Department of Communication Arts and the Women's Studies Program at the University of Wisconsin—Madison. She is the author of *Defining Women: Television and the Case of Cagney & Lacey*.

Herman Gray teaches in the sociology board and is the director of graduate studies in sociology at the University of California, Santa Cruz. He is the author of *Watching Race: Television and the Struggle for Blackness*.

Henry Jenkins, Director of Film and Media Studies at MIT, is the author of *Textual Poachers: Television Fans and Participatory Culture* and the co author of *Science Fiction Audiences: Watching Doctor Who and Star Trek*. He is currently working on a history of children and popular culture in postwar America.

Victoria Johnson is a Ph.D. candidate in the Critical Studies Division of the School of Cinema-Television at the University of Southern California. She is currently finishing her dissertation, "Camelot, Hooterville, or Watts? American Network Television and the Struggle for National Identity."

Moya Luckett teaches Film and Television in the School of Communication at the University of Pittsburgh. Her articles on television and film have appeared in several anthologies and in *The Velvet Light Trap*.

Horace Newcomb teaches in the Radio-Television-Film Department at the University of Texas at Austin. He is also Curator at the Museum of Broadcast Communications in Chicago and for the Museum is currently editing the *Encyclopedia of Television*.

Roberta E. Pearson teaches in the Centre for Journalism Studies at the University of Wales, Cardiff. She is co-author of *Reframing Culture: The Case of the Vitagraph Quality Films* and co-editor of the anthology *Back in the Saddle Again: New Writings on the Western*.

Jeffrey Sconce is an Assistant Professor of Communications at the University of Wisconsin-Oshkosh. He is currently working on a book that examines the cultural history of electronic presence from telegraphy to television.

Lynn Spigel teaches in the School of Cinema-Television, University of Southern California. She is author of *Make Room for TV: Television and the Family Ideal in Postwar America* and coeditor of *Private Screenings: Television and the Female Consumer* and *Feminist Television Criticism: A Reader.*

Thomas Streeter teaches in the Sociology Department of the University of Vermont and is the author of *Selling the Air: A Critique of the Policy of Commercial Broadcasting in the United States.*

Joseph Turow is Professor of Communication at the University of Pennsylvania's Annenberg School For Communication. He is Chair of the International Communication Association's Mass Communication Division and author of the forthcoming *Breaking Up America: Advertisers and the New Media World.*